GLOBALIZATION
for
DEVELOPMENT

GLOBALIZATION *for* DEVELOPMENT

TRADE, FINANCE, AID, MIGRATION, AND POLICY

IAN GOLDIN
KENNETH REINERT

A COPUBLICATION OF THE WORLD BANK
AND PALGRAVE MACMILLAN

1 2 3 4 09 08 07 06

A copublication of The World Bank and Palgrave Macmillan.

Palgrave Macmillan
Houndmills, Basingstoke, Hampshire RG21 6XS and
175 Fifth Avenue, New York, N. Y. 10010
Companies and representatives throughout the world

Palgrave Macmillan is the global academic imprint of the Palgrave Macmillan division of
St. Martin's Press, LLC and of Palgrave Macmillan Ltd.

Macmillan® is a registered trademark in the United States, United Kingdom and other countries. Palgrave is a registered trademark in the European Union and other countries.

ISBN-10: 0-8213-6274-7
ISBN-13: 978-0-8213-6274-7
eISBN-10: 0-8213-6275-5
DOI: 10.1596/978-0-8213-6274-7

Library of Congress Cataloging-in-Publications Data has been applied for.

Contents

Boxes

Figures

Tables

Foreword

Globalization has been taking place for centuries and, with time, has accelerated, from the colonization of the inhabited parts of the world to the appearance of nations, from conquests to independent countries, from sailboats and caravans to steamboats, truck fleet and cargo planes, from trade in a few commodities to global production and distribution networks and to the present explosion of international flows of services, capital, and information. Based on Maddison's recent estimates on the world economy over the past millennium, it is possible to calculate that world merchandise exports amounted to approximately US$40 per capita—at today's purchasing power—in 1870. This figure had tripled to US$120 by 1913. After a slowdown due to the two consecutive world wars it was then multiplied by almost 10 between 1950 and 2000, to reach approximately US$1,000 per capita today. Seventeen percent of world output is being exchanged today against less than 5 percent a century ago, and this figure keeps rising at a rapid pace.

Faced with such a dramatic evolution, the issues that arise are whether it is good or bad for humankind, whether it must be encouraged or, on the contrary, curbed down and, if so, by what means. Globalization may be judged by many criteria, but the most important one is undoubtedly development in all its forms and, in particular, poverty reduction. This is the theme of the fascinating book written by Ian Goldin and Kenneth Reinert.

We are today at a crucial point in the history of our fight against poverty in its various dimensions. Probably for the first time in history, the absolute number of people living on less than $1 a day in the world has dropped, from 1.5 billion in 1981 to 1.1 billion in 2001. It is true that the proportion of people living in extreme poverty in the world has been falling more or less continuously since the beginning of the Industrial Revolution. But the pace accelerated considerably over the last 20 years. During that period, the global income poverty rate dropped by almost half. Much of this progress on the global front was concentrated in Asia. By contrast, income poverty rose in Sub-Saharan Africa, both in relative and absolute terms, a region somehow left at the margin of several crucial aspects of globalization. Health gains in the world have also been impressive and more widespread. Infant mortality rates in poor countries are far lower than those of countries at the same income level 25 years or 50 years ago, and life expectancy at birth increased to 64 years in 2002. Unfortunately, there have also been major reversals of progress, in particular the tragedy of HIV/AIDS in Africa. The developing world has also made major strides in education—with the average number of years of education completed among adults steadily increasing (though it is still a meager five years on average) and the number of adults with no schooling falling from half of the developing world's population to just over one-third.

Although progress has been steady and in some instances rather dramatic, global imbalances in the distribution of income and wealth are huge, and the awareness of these imbalances grows as information flows ever more quickly in tandem with globalization. People everywhere can compare themselves to the richest developed societies and are anxious to reduce the yawning gaps in income and consumption. Failing to address these imbalances is bound to produce mounting dissatisfaction. We face a window of opportunity, one that may not stay open for long. The opportunity is to put into practice what we have learned about increasing development potential and reducing poverty, at a time when technology, economics, demographics, and even geopolitics should make that possible. Not doing this will sow discouragement about development and progress in poor and wealthy nations alike—creating barriers to future development efforts and casting increasing doubts about the potential benefit from globalization.

What would it take to increase the benefits of globalization for development? There are tasks that need to be tackled with urgency. In trade, developed countries must follow through on their commitments to give developing countries greater market access. In aid, donor countries must scale up their assistance in ways commensurate with the Millennium Development Goals, reinforcing and accelerating the mild progress of the past few years. In governance, developing countries must continue to move toward greater accountability, transparency, and efficiency. And all countries need to work together to address such disasters as HIV/AIDS and climate change.

In this impressive volume, Ian Goldin and Kenneth Reinert provide a comprehensive introduction to key aspects of globalization—trade, finance, aid, and migration—and their complex linkages with poverty and development.

To prepare a volume accessible to a large audience requires clarity and synthesis. Too often, however, clarity and synthesis invite naive truisms and open the door to ideological statements. Goldin and Reinert have successfully avoided both. Indeed, they provide readers with an understanding of globalization that is rich in its complexity. Beginning with an overview of the dimensions of poverty, Goldin and Reinert explain how trade can reduce poverty by increasing labor-intensive production, human capital accumulation, and technological learning; they examine how foreign direct investment and debt and equity instruments can help finance development; and they consider how migration can allow workers and their families back home to escape poverty through remittances.

At the same time, Goldin and Reinert observe that each of these aspects of globalization can fail to reduce poverty or even harm development. Trade without public investment, without safety nets, and without access to developed-country markets diminishes or even negates the gains for the poor. Volatile capital flows can cause financial crises. Aid can be ineffective when governance is poor or when donors have geopolitical motives. Migration can also involve brain drain, which can harm developing countries and can even harm global efficiency if the positive externalities created by skilled workers are large and are higher in poor countries than in rich ones.

This book also helps to shatter a false dichotomy that holds that policies that favor the poor cannot be pro-market. There is an enormous set of pro-poor *and* pro-market policies that allow for more equal market competition among and within countries, and that ask that policy take account of externalities as much as possible.

Having a nuanced view of development is humbling and sometimes disappointing. There is so much we do not know, and we must acknowledge our knowledge gaps. Yet, Goldin and Reinert show that our understanding of development has substantially improved. And they strongly encourage us to use that new knowledge to get the best out of globalization for development and poverty reduction.

François Bourguignon
Senior Vice President and Chief Economist
The World Bank

Acronyms and Abbreviations

ADB	Asian Development Bank
AERC	African Economic Research Consortium
AFDB	African Development Bank
AIDS	Acquired Immune Deficiency Syndrome
ATC	Agreement on Textiles and Clothing
BIS	Bank for International Settlements
CAF	Corporación Andina de Fomento
CGE	Computable General Equilibrium
CGIAR	Consultative Group for International Agricultural Research
CSO	Civil Society Organization
c.i.f.	cost insurance freight
DAC	Development Assistance Committee (of OECD)
EBRD	European Bank for Reconstruction and Development
EHK	Euler Hermes Kreditversicherungs
EIB	European Investment Bank
EPZ	Export Processing Zone
EU	European Union
FAO	Food and Agriculture Organization (of the United Nations)
FDI	Foreign Direct Investment
FMO	Netherlands Development Finance Company
f.o.b.	free on board
G-8	Group of Eight
GATS	General Agreement on Trade and Services
GATT	General Agreement on Trade and Tariffs
GAVI	Global Alliance for Vaccines and Immunizations
GDP	Gross Domestic Product

GNI	Gross National Income
GNP	Gross National Product
GSP	General System of Preferences
HIPC	Heavily Indebted Poor Country
HIV/AIDS	Human Immunodeficiency Virus/Acquired Immune Deficiency Syndrome
HTME	High Technology Manufactured Exports
IBRD	International Bank for Reconstruction and Development (of the World Bank Group)
ICSID	International Centre for Settlement of Investment Disputes
ICT	Information and Communication Technologies
IDA	International Development Association (of the World Bank Group)
IDB	Inter-American Development Bank
IF	Integrated Framework
IFC	International Finance Corporation (of the World Bank Group)
IMF	International Monetary Fund
IP	intellectual property
IsDB	Islamic Development Bank
ITC	International Trade Centre
LDC	Least-Developed Countries
KAM	Knowledge Assessment Methodology
LIFE	Legal Immigration Family Equity Act
LTME	Low Technology Manufactured Exports
MDG	Millennium Development Goals
MFA	Multifiber Arrangement
MFI	Micro Finance Institution
MIGA	Multilateral Investment Guarantee Association (of the World Bank Group)
MNE	Multinational Enterprise
NAFTA	North American Free Trade Agreement
NGO	Nongovernmental Organization
OCP	Onchocerciasis Control Programme
ODA	Official Development Assistance
OECD	Organisation for Economic Co-operation and Development
OEM	Original Equipment Manufacturer
OPEC	Organization of the Petroleum Exporting Countries

OPIC	Overseas Private Investment Corporation
POEA	Philippine Overseas Employment Agency
POLO	Philippine Overseas Labor Office
PPP	Purchasing Power Parity
PRS	Poverty Reduction Strategy
R&D	Research and Development
SITC	Standard Industrial Trade Classification
SSA	Sub-Saharan Africa
TCBDB	Trade Capacity Building Database
TDG	TeleCommons Development Group
TRIM	Trade-Related Investment Measures
TRIPS	Trade-Related aspects of Individual Property Rights
UAE	United Arab Emirates
UK	United Kingdom
UN	United Nations
UNAIDS	United Nations Programme on HIV/AIDS
UNCTAD	United Nations Conference on Trade and Development
UNDP	United Nations Development Programme
UNHCR	United Nations High Commissioner for Refugees
UNICEF	United Nations Children's Fund
USA	United States of America
USAID	United States Agency for International Development
WHO	World Health Organization
WIPO	World Intellectual Property Organization
WTO	World Trade Organization

Acknowledgments

Many people have supported us in writing this book, and to all our deep thanks are due. Most important, Andrew Beath provided outstanding research assistance. In addition to literature reviews and data collection and analysis, he contributed to writing chapter 6 on Migration. It was Dominique van der Mensbrugghe who introduced us, so we owe this happy collaboration to his matchmaking. Sir Nicholas Stern's encouragement and contributions to Ian's initial ideas for this book provided a vital springboard for our work. Kermal Dervis, Minister Trevor Manuel, Professor Amartya Sen, Sir Nicholas Stern, and Professor Joseph Stiglitz generously gave their time and thoughts to provide comments on this book. François Bourguignon authored the insightful Foreword. We also are indebted to many other colleagues who also have provided very helpful material, comments, and support. They include Amar Bhattacharya, Gerard Caprio, Jean-Jacques Dethier, Desmond Dinan, Amy Heyman, Bernard Hoekman, Michael Klein, Danny Leipziger, David McKenzie, Çaḡlař Özden, John Page, Lant Pritchett, Dilip Ratha, Martin Ravallion, William Rex, David Rivero, F. Halsey Rogers, Eric Swanson, Zhen Kun Wang, L. Alan Winters, Xiao Ye, and Shengman Zhang. Sophia Cox and Ginette Francois provided invaluable assistance with the formatting and organization of this text. The great professionalism of Santiago Pombo-Bejarano, Nancy Lammers, and Andres Meneses, of the Office of the Publisher at the World Bank, and Amanda Hamilton at Palgrave Macmillan, turned the manuscript into a widely accessible product. Mary Fisk skillfully managed the editorial and production processes. Joy le Blanc-Alston and Kris Zedler, through their overall expertise and time management skills, ensured that this project did not interfere with other activities. As this project fell on top of our normal work responsibilities, it is to our families that we are most grateful. Ian's wife Tessa, daughter Olivia, and son Alex, and Ken's wife Gelaye and son Oda Telila once again demonstrated their unstinting support and patience during the many evenings and weekends that this project invaded.

The authors alone take responsibility for the contents of the book, which does not necessarily reflect the views of our colleagues, the World Bank Group, its management, executive directors, or member governments.

Ian Goldin
Ken Reinert
April 2005

About the Authors

Ian Goldin, PH.D. (OXFORD UNIVERSITY), became a Vice President at the World Bank in May 2003. Previously, he was the Director of Development Policy at the World Bank. Prior to rejoining the Bank in February 2001, Dr. Goldin spent five years as the Chief Executive and Managing Director of the Development Bank of Southern Africa (DBSA) where he led the Bank to become a principal financier of infrastructure and small business development in Southern Africa. Before this, he worked as a Principal Economist at the European Bank for Reconstruction and Development (EBRD) in London and as Head of the Trade, Agriculture and Environment Program at the OECD Development Center in Paris. Dr. Goldin has published 11 books and numerous articles. His research and publications have focused on economic policy, development, natural resources and the environment, and trade. His better known books include: *The Economics of Sustainable Development, Open Economies, Economic Reform and Agricultural Development,* and *Trade Liberalization—Global Economic Implications.*

Kenneth A. Reinert, PH.D. (UNIVERSITY OF MARYLAND), is Associate Professor of Public Policy at George Mason University, where he received a Distinguished Teaching Award in 2003. He has held the positions of Senior International Economist at the U.S. International Trade Commission and Associate Professor of Economics at Kalamazoo College. Professor Reinert has published widely in the areas of international trade, economic development, and environmental policy. He co-edited *Applied Methods for Trade Policy Analysis: A Handbook* (Cambridge University Press, 1997), authored *Windows on the World Economy: An Introduction to International Economics* (South-Western Thomson, 2005), and is currently co-editing the *Princeton Encyclopedia of the World Economy.*

Background and Context

The relationship between globalization and poverty is not well understood. For many, globalization is held out as the only means by which global poverty can be reduced. For others, globalization is seen as an important cause of global poverty. Consider the following two quotations:

A world integrated through the market should be highly beneficial to the vast majority of the world's inhabitants.

—Martin Wolf (2004)

While promoters of globalization proclaim that this model is the rising tide that will lift all boats, citizen movements find that it is instead lifting only yachts.

—International Forum on Globalization

To the knowledgeable global citizen, such disparate views are a cause of some confusion and concern. In this book, we aim to resolve this confusion. We want to provide an understanding of the main dimensions of economic globalization and their impact on poverty and development. Although rooted in rigorous inquiry, this is not narrowly an academic book. Our objective is to inform the wider public and to provide a broad foundation for policy discussions on globalization and poverty.

Many claims about the relationship between globalization and poverty are not well founded. By examining both the processes through which globalization takes place and the effects that each of these processes can have on global poverty alleviation, current discussions can be better informed. The processes we examine in this book constitute the main global economic channels affecting poverty: trade, finance, aid, migration, and ideas.[1] By considering each of these processes, confusion about globalization can, to some extent at least, be resolved. To that end, this chapter introduces the five dimensions of globalization and considers the problem of global poverty, placing both globalization and poverty in historical context. Our central message is that, with appropriate national and global policies, globalization can be an important catalyst for alleviating global poverty. In the absence of these policies, however, this catalyst role is diminished. In a few particular instances, globalization without corrective policies can actually exacerbate certain dimensions of poverty. We identify what actions are needed to produce positive global outcomes.

Globalization and Global Poverty

Globalization is an often-discussed but seldom-defined phenomenon. At a broad level, globalization is an increase in the impact on human activities of forces that span national boundaries. These activities can be economic, social, cultural, political, technological, or even biological, as in the case of disease. Additionally, all of these realms can interact. For example, HIV/AIDS is a biological phenomenon, but it affects and is affected by economic, social, cultural, political, and technological forces at global, regional, national, and community levels. In this book, we focus primarily on economic activities, referring to the other realms of globalization only tangentially.[2] This no doubt reflects our bias as economists, but also our observation that global poverty is very much (but certainly not exclusively) an economic phenomenon. In adopting this economic focus, we in no way wish to imply that social, cultural, political, technological, and biological aspects of globalization are unimportant. They are important. But having cast our net widely already to include multiple dimensions of economic globalization, we consider it unwise to cast it even more broadly.

The changing natures and qualities of the five economic dimensions of globalization characterize its process. These dimensions are

- trade
- finance
- aid
- migration
- ideas.

Trade is the exchange of goods and services among countries. *Finance* involves the exchange of assets or financial instruments among countries. *Aid* involves the transfer of loans and grants among countries, as well as technical assistance for *capacity building*. *Migration* takes place when persons move between countries either temporarily or permanently, to seek education and

KEY TERMS AND CONCEPTS

autarky	foreign direct investment (FDI)
bond finance	global public good
capacity building	gross domestic product (GDP)
capital flows	migration
commercial bank lending	poverty
comparative advantage	purchasing power parity dollars
equity portfolio investment	

employment or to escape adverse political environments. *Ideas* are the broadest globalization phenomenon. They involve the generation and cross-border transmission of intellectual constructs in areas such as technology, management, or governance.

Dimensions of Poverty

For each of these five economic dimensions of globalization, the field of investigation is very wide. We will narrow it significantly by considering only those aspects that are most closely tied to issues of poverty alleviation. This process of narrowing our scope requires a large element of judgment. In choosing what to emphasize, we have reflected the issues and concerns of development policy communities as well as our disciplinary backgrounds in economics.

What do we mean by *global poverty*? Although we all have some concept of what it is to be "poor," the notion of **poverty** is not as straightforward as it might first appear. The reason is that poverty is not a *one*-dimensional phenomenon. It is *multi*-dimensional. A number of different concepts and measures of poverty relate to its various dimensions. Each of these dimensions has the common characteristic of representing deprivation of an important kind. The variety of poverty concepts in use in development policy communities reflects the variety of relevant deprivations.[3] The major measures of poverty we consider here are those that encompass:

- income
- health
- education
- empowerment
- working conditions.

Income

The most common measure of poverty is known as *income poverty*, and it derives from a conception of human well-being defined in terms of the consumption of goods and services. In this approach, poverty is viewed as a lack of goods consumption due to a lack of necessary income. At present, the most widely accepted measure of income poverty is in terms of one or two U.S. dollars per day, measured in constant (price adjusted), *"purchasing power parity" dollars*.[4] Individuals who exist on less than one dollar a day are known as the "dollar poor" or the "extremely poor"; individuals who exist on less than two dollars a day are known as the "poor."[5] In this book, we use this concept as one important indicator of global poverty.

Health

There is growing recognition that income poverty is not the only important measure of deprivation.[6] For example, poor health is now recognized as perhaps the most central aspect of poverty. The fact that 6 million persons die annually from AIDS, tuberculosis, and malaria illustrates this point, as do the annual deaths of a roughly equal number of infants from largely preventable causes such as diarrheal disease. Health deprivation characterizing poverty can be assessed in terms of life expectances, infant and child mortality, and a number of other health-related measures.

Education

Lack of education that results in limited literacy and numeracy is another important deprivation. Indeed, lack of education is often an important cause of deprivations in income and health. This dimension of poverty can be assessed in terms of literacy rates, average years of schooling, or enrollment rates. Gender disparities in education are an important and too-often-observed component of educational deprivation and represent a key obstacle to development.

Empowerment

Lack of what is sometimes called "empowerment" is a fourth important dimension of poverty. This includes limits on individuals' abilities to enter into and participate in social realms such as work and political processes because of discrimination of various kinds. Gender disparities are an important kind of empowerment deprivation and interact in detrimental ways with consequences in health and educational deprivations. In many countries, for example, women are socially restricted from entering the workforce or from political participation. In some instances, they do not have the same legal rights as men.[7]

Working Conditions

One important issue that does not always arise in discussions of poverty concepts is working conditions. As emphasized by Bruton and Fairris (1999), "Because a person fortunate enough to have a full-time job will spend at least one half of his/her waking hours at work, it is incumbent on social scientists to investigate the conditions necessary for the maintenance of working conditions that are safe and pleasant and for the creation of jobs that contribute to individual and social well-being" (p. 6). We will turn to these working-condition issues at various junctures in this book, especially to considerations of forced labor, health, and safety.[8]

Assessment of Dimensions of Poverty

Each of these dimensions of poverty can be assessed in *absolute* or in *relative* terms.[9] For example, income poverty can be assessed in terms of the numbers of individuals living below an income level (absolute) or in terms of the lowest 20 percent of households ranked according to income (relative). Both absolute and relative poverty are important for social outcomes. In this book, however, we will place a greater emphasis on absolute poverty. With regard to income poverty, we will emphasize the "dollar a day" or "extreme" poor measure. With regard to other dimensions of poverty, we will emphasize illiteracy (including gender disparities) and infant mortality. The ways in which globalization as described above plays a positive or negative role in such poverty alleviation is our central concern here.

A Historical View

Both globalization and poverty have deep historical roots. Although in popular accounts globalization is a recent phenomenon, historians recognize that, in some important respects, it is not new. The ever-increasing integration of people and societies around the world has been both a cause and an effect of human evolution, proceeding more in fits and starts than in any simple, linear progression. Technological innovations, whether in the form of the marine chronometer or modern fiber optics, have propelled surges in globalization; changes in policy, institutions, or cultural preferences have restrained or even reversed it. In the 15th century, for instance, the Chinese emperor Hung-hsi banned maritime expeditions, slowing down Asian globalization considerably.[10] Similarly, the proliferation of nation states and the imposition of border controls in the early 20th century generated new obstacles to the movement of goods, capital, persons, and ideas among the countries of the world.

Stages of the Modern Era of Globalization

Economic historians date the modern era of globalization to approximately 1870. The period from 1870 to 1914 is often considered to be the birth of the modern world economy, which, by some measures, was as integrated as it is today. A description of this world by John Maynard Keynes can be found in box 1.1. What historians have observed is that, from the point of view of capital flows (the predominately British foreign direct investment and portfolio investment of the era), the late 1800s were an extraordinary time.[11] The global integration of capital markets was facilitated by advances in rail and ship transportation and in telegraph communication. European colonial systems were at their highest stages of development, and migration was at a historical high point in relation to the global population of the time.

This first modern stage of globalization was followed by two additional stages, one from the late 1940s to the mid-1970s and another from the mid-1970s to the present. These, however, were preceded by World War I, the Great Depression, and World War II. During this time, many aspects of globalization were reversed as the world experienced increased conflict, nationalism, and patterns of economic *autarky*. To some extent, then, the second and third modern stages of globalization involved regaining lost levels of international integration.

The second modern stage of globalization began at the end of World War II. It was accompanied by a global, economic regime developed by the Bretton Woods Conference of 1944 establishing the International Monetary Fund (IMF), what was to become the World Bank, and the General Agreement on Tariffs and Trade (GATT) (see box 1.2). This stage of globalization involved an increase in capital flows from the United States, as well as a U.S.-founded production system that relied on exploiting economies of scale in manufacturing and the advance of U.S.-based multinational enterprises.[12] This second stage also involved some reduction of trade barriers under the auspices of GATT. Developing countries were not highly involved in this liberalization, however. In export products of interest to developing countries (agriculture, textiles, and clothing), a system of nontariff barriers in rich countries evolved. Also, a set of key developing countries, especially those in Latin America, pursued import substitution industrialization with their own trade barriers.[13] These developments, along with the Cold War, suppressed the integration of many developing countries into the world trading system.

BOX 1.1 John Maynard Keynes on Globalization

Looking back on the end of the 19th century, and writing in 1919, John Maynard Keynes described the vanishing world of the British economic empire as follows:

The inhabitant of London could order by telephone, sipping his morning tea in bed, the various products of the whole earth, in such quantity as he might see fit, and reasonably expect their early delivery upon his doorstep; he could at the same moment and by the same means adventure his wealth in the natural resources and new enterprises of any quarter of the world, and share, without exertion or even trouble, in their prospective fruits and advantages; or he could decide to couple the security of his fortunes with the good faith of the townspeople of any substantial municipality in any continent that fancy or information might recommend. He could secure forthwith, if he wished it, cheap and comfortable means of transit to any country or climate without passport or other formality, could despatch his servant to the neighbouring office of a bank for such supply of the precious metals as might seem convenient, and could then proceed abroad to foreign quarters, without knowledge of their religion, language, or customs, bearing coined wealth upon his person, and would consider himself greatly aggrieved and much surprised at the least interference. But, most important of all, he regarded this state of affairs as normal, certain, and permanent, except in the direction of further improvement, and any deviation from it as aberrant, scandalous, and avoidable.

Source: Keynes 1920, pp. 11–12.

The third modern stage of globalization began in the late 1970s. This stage followed the demise of monetary relationships developed at the Bretton Woods Conference and involved the emergence of the newly industrialized countries of East Asia, especially Japan, Taiwan (China), and the Republic of Korea. Rapid technological progress, particularly in transportation, communication, and information technology, began to dramatically lower the costs of moving goods, capital, people, and ideas across the globe. For example, as noted by Frankel (2000), "Now fresh-cut flowers, perishable broccoli and strawberries, live lobsters and even ice cream are sent between continents" (pp. 2–3).[14]

Assembly systems in this latest stage of globalization were also significantly modified into a new arrangement characterized by flexible manufacturing. In flexible manufacturing systems, information technology supports computer-aided production and relies less on economies of scale. In this stage, Japan emerged as an important, new source of foreign direct investment (FDI): between 1960 and 1995, Japan's share of global FDI increased from less than

BOX 1.2 International Agreements, Institutions, and Key Players

The **Bretton Woods Conference** was a gathering of world leaders that took place in 1944 in Bretton Woods, New Hampshire, United States, with the aim of placing the international economy on a sound footing after World War II. The conference resulted in the establishment of the World Bank and the International Monetary Fund.

Institutions

The World Bank Group and the International Monetary Fund are sometimes referred to as the *Bretton Woods Institutions*.

The five World Bank Group institutions are as follows:

- **The International Bank for Reconstruction and Development (IBRD)** lends to governments of middle-income and creditworthy low-income countries.
- **The International Development Association (IDA)** provides interest-free loans, called credits, to governments of the poorest countries.
- **The International Finance Corporation (IFC)** lends directly to the private sector in developing countries.
- **The Multilateral Investment Guarantee Agency (MIGA)** provides guarantees to investors in developing countries against losses caused by noncommercial risks.
- **The International Centre for Settlement of Investment Disputes (ICSID)** provides international facilities for conciliation and arbitration of investment disputes.

The International Monetary Fund is a subscription-based, global financial organization whose purpose is to promote international monetary cooperation and the multilateral system of payments. It engages in four areas of activity: surveillance or monitoring, the dispensing of policy advice, lending, and providing technical assistance.

Other international economic institutions include the following:

- Nongovernmental Organizations (NGOs): Private, nonprofit organizations that pursue activities to relieve suffering, promote the interests of the poor, protect the environment, provide basic social services, or undertake community development. NGOs often differ from other organizations in the sense that they tend to operate independently from government, are values-based, and are guided by the principles of altruism and voluntarism.
- Organisation for Economic Co-operation and Development (OECD): An international organization, primarily of high-income countries, helping governments tackle the economic, social, and governance challenges of a globalized society.
- United Nations Development Programme (UNDP): Manages a "network" of development activities undertaken by the United Nations in the areas of democratic governance, poverty alleviation, crisis prevention and recovery, energy and the environment, and HIV/AIDS.
- World Trade Organization (WTO): An international organization governing the system of rules for global trade among its member nations. It is also involved in dispute settlement and compliance monitoring related to international trade.

Sources: World Bank Group institutions: adapted from The International Bank for Reconstruction and Development 2003: box 1.1; other institutions: World Health Organization 2001b.

1 percent to over 10 percent.[15] The thawing of the Cold War, the entry of China into the world economy, and a general reduction of trade barriers in most developing countries beginning in the late 1980s, helped to accelerate global integration during this phase.

Modern Globalization and Global Poverty

What has been the historical relationship between globalization and poverty during these three stages? A partial view is found in figure 1.1. This figure combines a single measure of globalization—exports as a percentage of world *gross domestic product* (GDP), with a single measure of poverty—the number of dollar (extreme) poor people, in a time series from 1870 to 1998. What is clear from this schematic is that, historically, globalization and global poverty can be *either* positively related *or* negatively related to each other. From 1870 though 1929 and the beginning of the Great Depression, globalization (trade) and global poverty increased together. However, the retreat from globalization during the Great Depression and World War II was accompanied by a *continued* increase in global poverty. This can be seen from the 1950 data in figure 1.1 showing that, when exports as a percentage of GDP had declined nearly back to the 1870 level, extreme poverty reached a peak of approximately 1.4 billion persons (a billion is 1,000 million).

As seen in figure 1.1, the increase in globalization as measured by trade in the second and third stages of modern globalization has been associated with a gradual decline in extreme poverty to approximately 1.1 billion people. During these stages, globalization and poverty have been negatively associated with each other, albeit mildly so. A key public policy challenge facing humankind is to *eliminate* this still-prominent level of extreme poverty. Understanding how to do this requires a deeper understanding of the links between globalization and poverty.

The Globalization-Poverty Relationship

As mentioned above, globalization has the five primary economic dimensions trade, finance, aid, migration, and ideas. Increases in these dimensions of globalization, if managed in a way that supports development in all countries, can help to alleviate global poverty under certain conditions. We investigate these pathways and conditions in some detail later in this book. We also consider some particular circumstances where dimensions of globalization can aggravate some dimensions of poverty. Here we define and summarize the five economic dimensions of the relationship between globalization and poverty.

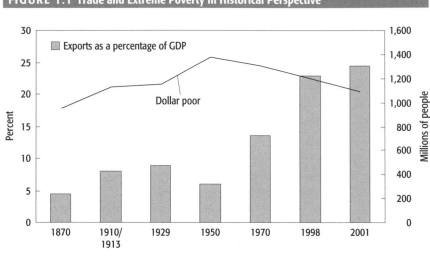

FIGURE 1.1 Trade and Extreme Poverty in Historical Perspective

Sources: Exports as a percentage of GDP from Ocampo and Martin (2003) based on Maddison (2001) and from World Bank (2004d). Dollar poor data from Bourguignon and Morrisson (2002), and Chen and Ravallion (2004).

Trade

Trade is the exchange of both goods and services among the countries of the world economy.[16] The involvement of developing countries as exporters in global trade has increased significantly since the mid-1980s, even in services where their ***comparative advantage*** is typically seen as weak. For a variety of reasons (not least the trade barriers placed by rich countries), the agricultural exports of the developing world have been stagnant. The regional involvement of developing countries in trade varies widely, with Africa's share of world exports declining over time.

Increased international trade can help to alleviate poverty through job creation, increased competition, improvements in education and in health, and technological learning. The impact of increasing trade openness depends critically on the relationship between trade reforms and other reforms and complementary actions at the national and international levels. Increased exports of petroleum and minerals often (but not always or necessarily) fail to support these activities, as many developing countries have found. Many kinds of manu-facturing, agricultural, and service exports, accompanied by complementary infrastructure and training policies, can support these activities, however. In addition, imports of many types—especially health-related imports and imports embodying new technologies—are crucial for alleviating poverty.

The exports of developing countries face many kinds of protective barriers, including tariffs, subsidies, quotas, standards and regulations, and increasing security checks. Rich-world agricultural subsidies, for example, are twice as large as the entire agricultural exports of all developing-country exports combined and six times the value of foreign aid. These subsidies have exceeded the entire GDP of Sub-Saharan Africa in recent years and reducing protection is vital for more inclusive globalization. Conservative estimates suggest that limited trade liberalization could reduce the number of poor people (those who live on US$2 per day) by a minimum of 100 million.[17]

For any increase in market access for developing country exports to positively affect poor people, trade-related capacity building is necessary, particularly to support the diversification of exports away from standard primary products. This is an important area where the trade and foreign aid dimensions of globalization can complement each other. To protect the most vulnerable who can sometimes lose as a result of trade liberalization, social safety nets and complementary antipoverty programs are crucial.[18]

Finance

Global finance in the form of **capital flows** involves the exchange of assets or financial instruments among the countries of the world, either by private or public agents. In this book, we distinguish among four types of capital flows:

- foreign direct investment or FDI
- equity portfolio investment
- bond finance
- commercial bank lending.

Foreign direct investment (FDI) is defined here as the acquisition of part of a foreign-based enterprise that exceeds a threshold of 10 percent, implying managerial participation in the foreign enterprise. **Equity portfolio investment** is similar to FDI in that it involves the ownership of shares in foreign enterprises. It differs from FDI, however, in that the share holdings are too small to imply managerial participation in the foreign enterprise. It is thus *indirect* rather than direct investment, undertaken for portfolio reasons rather than for managerial reasons. Its behavior can consequently differ substantially from that of FDI.

Bond finance (also called *debt issuance*) is a second kind of portfolio activity. It involves governments or firms issuing bonds to foreign investors. These bonds can be issued in either the domestic currency or in foreign currencies, and they carry a number of types of default risk. Both bond finance and equity portfolio investments are held by domestic and international investors as a way to manage wealth, and the entire range of portfolio behaviors apply to both. ***Commercial bank lending*** is another form of debt, but it does not involve a tradable asset as bond finance does.[19]

Private capital flows to developing countries have increased significantly since the early 1990s, particularly in the case of FDI, which has displaced the previously dominant commercial bank lending in importance. Equity portfolio investment and bond finance flows to developing countries, however, have been volatile since the 1997 Asian crisis, although both have recovered somewhat in recent years. Official capital flows, reflecting the activities of central banks, are a different story. Since 2000, the government and trade deficits of the United States have involved that country importing over US$500 billion in recent years, structurally claiming the bulk of world savings, which is provided in part by Asian central banks buying U.S. government debt. As a result of these official transactions, the developing world has recently become a net exporter of capital.

From the point of view of alleviating poverty, capital flows have both significant promise and some particular dangers. Capital flows can help to mobilize and deploy savings, develop the financial sector, and transfer technology. They can also manage various types of risk and channel funds in line with the performance of firms' managers. The financial markets involved in some kinds of capital flows, however, are characterized by a number of imperfections that economists refer to as "market failures." In particular, information is less than perfect in these markets, and this can cause significant volatility in flow levels. Consequently, deepening and regulating these flows poses considerable policy challenges.

Foreign direct investment can contribute to poverty alleviation when it supports the generation of new employment, promotes competition, improves the education and training of host-country workers, and transfers new technology. These benefits are evident in a host of developing countries. Unfortunately, FDI is highly concentrated, and many developing countries receive little or no FDI inflows. FDI that establishes backward links to local suppliers and advances best practices in terms of technology, employment, and social conditions is more beneficial than FDI that remains a low-wage enclave within the host country.

Equity portfolio investment, bond finance, and commercial bank lending can help to alleviate poverty under effective exchange rate regimes and properly regulated and developed financial systems. Equity portfolio investment, in particular, has been positively associated with growth through its support of entrepreneurial activity.[20] Bond finance and commercial bank lending can leave developing countries vulnerable to crises that arise from the volatile nature of portfolio investment. Such crises can increase poverty substantially, as happened in Asia during the late 1990s.[21] Properly managed, however, bond finance and commercial bank lending can be an important part of financial sector development. This aspect of economic globalization, then, must be handled with care.

Aid

Aid is the transfer of funds in the form of some combination of loans or grants and the provision of technical assistance or capacity building. The transfer of funds can be in the form of bilateral aid between two countries or in the form of multilateral aid that is channeled through organizations such as the World Bank. Foreign aid remains a vital resource flow for many developing countries. It can finance investment in infrastructure and services, supplement capabilities in health and education, and provide access to new ideas in the realm of policy. These characteristics make it possible for aid to have a significant impact on global poverty alleviation. The motivations of foreign aid donors have varied widely and include advancing geopolitical objectives, stimulating economic development, ameliorating poverty and suffering, promoting political outcomes, and ensuring civil stability and equitable governance. Given both these mixed objectives and the low quality of some developing country governance systems, aid has not always been effective.

That said, with the end of the Cold War calculus of donors and a greater emphasis on governance in the developing world, evidence that aid is more effective now than ever before is continuing to emerge.[22] Sustaining the positive impact of aid requires both increasing aid flows *and* using them better. Despite the progress made in aid effectiveness, the share of their budgets that rich countries have devoted to aid has declined during the last few decades, going from slightly over 0.35 percent to approximately 0.25 percent of high-income countries' GDP. Only 5 of the 22 high-income countries of the OECD's Development Assistance Committee that have pledged 0.7 percent of their GDP to foreign aid have actually met this goal as of 2004.[23] Indeed, foreign aid has steadily remained at approximately one-sixth of rich-world agricultural subsidies—subsidies that have been shown to significantly worsen global poverty. Recent evidence of a pick-up in aid volumes must be sustained if aid is to fulfill its potential in global poverty reduction.

Compared with private investment, and even with remittances, the value of aid flows is and will remain small. Domestic investment in developing countries is around US$1.5 trillion, much larger than aid levels that over the past decade hovered around US$55 billion per year and foreign investment of around US$200 billion. Recently, a renewed commitment to aid is evident in sharp increases in aid levels and promises. As we show, what matters most in foreign aid are the accompanying ideas, policies, and capacity building. These can increase the overall domestic and foreign investment flows that create jobs and drive sustainable growth and poverty alleviation. A persistent and important challenge for foreign aid is assisting weak or even failed states. These countries often vary widely in their problems, and approaches that work in a "typical" low-income country might not be effective. Large-scale financial transfers are unlikely to work well, and emphasis should be placed on capacity building to facilitate change, as well as on a limited reform agenda, stressing governance, basic health, educational services, and infrastructure.

Migration

We define *migration* as the temporary or permanent movement of persons between countries to pursue employment or education (or both) or to escape adverse political climates. In this book, we do not consider rural-urban and other sorts of migration *within* countries. Migrants can be categorized into permanent settlers, high- and low-skill expatriates, asylum seekers, refugees, undocumented workers, visa-free migrants, and students. Migration has historically been the most important means for poor people to escape poverty. Indeed, by some estimates, 10 percent of the world's population permanently relocated between 1870 and 1910 during the first phase of modern globalization described above.[24] This historical pattern has been greatly reduced by the development of nation states; more recently, at the beginning of the 20th century, it has been further reduced by the use of passports and a growing range of mechanisms to identify and control individual movement. Consequently, migration is much less free but is no less important for poverty alleviation.

In addition to the direct "escape from poverty" function, migrants also provide significant remittance flows to their families in their home countries. These remittance inflows, now measuring over US$150 billion annually, exceed inflows of FDI in some regions by substantial amounts. On the other hand, migration also causes what is known as "brain drain"—the loss of educated and high-skilled citizens to other countries. The effective management of global migration flows is a difficult and controversial, but very important, challenge for the world community.

Current migration restrictions give rise to criminal activity and the exploitation of unsuspecting illegal migrants, often with tragic consequences. Skill poaching by wealthy countries can also have detrimental effects, not least in the health service area. As in the case of capital flows, migration must be managed carefully—preferably through multilateral frameworks.

The dearth of empirical research on key dimensions of migration makes forming policy on this subject particularly hazardous. However, there is one largely unexploited way for migration to positively affect global poverty. This is through the further development of the temporary movement of workers in services trade.[25] These labor-intensive exports of services through the temporary movement of persons have the potential to allow developing countries to benefit from global services trade in a manner similar to the developed countries in other modes of service delivery, namely FDI in financial services and the temporary movement of corporate personnel. Significant further progress is necessary in this area.[26]

Ideas

Ideas are the most powerful influence on development. Ideas are the generation and transmission of distinctive intellectual constructs in any field that can have an impact on production systems, organizational and management practices, governance practices, legal norms, and technological trends. One well-known category of ideas is intellectual property, which can be thought of as an asset defined by legal rights conferred on a product of invention or creation.[27] Ideas are not just commercial, however. For example, the notion of human rights that need to be respected and protected by governments is an idea of paramount importance. Additionally, flows of ideas across borders play an important role in shaping policies, as well as the perceptions and reality of poverty. In this book, we concentrate on ideas that shape economic activities rather than on those that have primarily cultural or political content, although we are mindful that these are distinctions mostly of convenience and need to be treated with care.

The evaluation and adaptation of ideas requires local capacity in the form of both skills and institutions, as well as a culture of learning. Developing countries can bridge existing gaps in knowledge by acquiring, absorbing, and communicating knowledge.[28] Openness to ideas has historically been and continues to be an important way to alleviate poverty.[29] Ideas can affect poverty through a variety of mechanisms and can interact in important ways with all of the other dimensions of economic globalization. More effective policy regimes, better technological innovations, greater respect for human rights, and the improved social status of women can all help the lives of poor people. The challenge in harnessing ideas to alleviate poverty lies in adapting them to the many local sociocultural contexts of the developing world. A full understanding of this challenge is still in progress, but it is clear that supporting the exchange of ideas and learning is vital to accelerating the beneficial impact of globalization.

The development community's understanding of the most effective way to achieve development objectives has evolved over time with the accumulation of evidence and experience. Approaches that appeared at the time to be both correct and obvious have been undermined by experience and closer analysis. This has seen the broadening and deepening of what is meant by "development," from income to include health, opportunity, and rights. Recent years have seen a greater recognition in the policy debate of the *complementarities* between markets and governments. Clearly, experience shows that the private market economy must be the engine of growth, but it shows also that a vibrant private sector depends on well-functioning state institutions to build a good investment climate and deliver basic services competently. Indeed, in many crucial areas—such as health, education, and infrastructure—public-private partnership is essential.

Areas for Action

History and the recent experiences of many countries have taught us that global integration can indeed be a powerful force for reducing poverty and empowering poor people. Poor people are less likely to remain poor in a country that is exchanging its goods, services, and ideas with the rest of the world. Yet, although participation in the global economy has generally been a powerful force for reducing poverty, the reach and impact of globalization remains uneven. In addition, the accelerated pace of globalization has been associated with a rapid rise in global risks, which have outpaced the capacity of global and national institutions to respond. The increasing global impact of national policies, ranging from armaments and contributions to climate change, points to the need for more effective global governance. If the globalization train is to pull all citizens behind it, policies that ensure that the poor people of the world share in its benefits are required.

In our concluding chapter, we draw together the many issues considered in this book and provide a policy agenda designed to ensure that increased globalization assists in alleviating poverty. Here we anticipate that more detailed discussion by briefly distilling four basic areas for action to support positive global outcomes. These are areas designed to accomplish the following:

- to ensure that global trade negotiations allow more equitable access to products of developing countries to the world market
- to increase aid, assistance, and debt relief to countries that demonstrate commitment to its effective use
- to enhance the benefits of migration and mitigate its harmful effects
- to support and encourage the development of global public goods to benefit poor people.

Balanced Outcomes to Global Trade Negotiations

The first area for action is *ensuring that global trade negotiations yield more balanced outcomes*. Rich countries must stop impeding the ability of poor countries to produce and trade a wide range of goods and services. Goods produced by poor people face, on average, double the tariff barriers of those produced in the most advanced countries. The practice of generously subsidizing agricultural production, a practice that is widespread in many high-income countries, has had a devastating impact on many poor producers, denying them not just export markets but also hindering their capacity to sell their produce in their own country. With around US$300 billion per year devoted to agricultural protection alone, the rich countries' policies have created a fundamentally unbalanced playing field. Current policies compound the downward trend in commodity prices, increase instability, and undermine the potential for diversification into higher value added manufactured products. Reforming the world trade system and ensuring more equitable access for the products of poor countries is an essential step toward allowing more of the world's people to enjoy the benefits of globalization.

Increase Aid, Assistance, and Debt Relief

The second area for action is the *increased provision of aid, assistance, and debt relief* to countries that demonstrate a commitment to the effective and equitable use of the additional resources. As mentioned above, aid volumes have declined during recent decades to approximately 0.25 percent of high-income countries' GDP, despite the fact that donor countries are richer now than ever before and that aid has never been more effectively used. With the ending of the Cold War, aid has been increasingly allocated to countries able to use it most effectively. Not surprisingly, the impact of aid on growth and poverty reduction has more than doubled over recent years.[30] Providing increased foreign assistance and implementing more rigorous schemes that monitor and evaluate the effective use of that aid are thus critical to ensuring that the gains provided by globalization are not erased by bad governance and ineffective use of aid.

Foreign aid resource transfers are particularly important in the poorest countries, and much higher levels of aid are urgently required for investments in health, education, infrastructure, and for combating HIV/AIDS and other diseases. These investments *cannot* be financed by domestic savings alone, especially in countries that are currently crushed under burdens of debt and escaping the ravages of past corruption and mismanagement.

Enhance the Benefits and Mitigate the Negative Effects of Migration

The third area for action is *enhancing the benefits and mitigating the negative effects of migration*. Migration remains for many poor people the most effective way to escape poverty. Recorded remittances of over US$150 billion are more than twicce the amount of annual foreign assistance. Whereas barely 20 percent (averaging around US$10 billion over the past decade) of aid is transferred to developing countries in the form of resource transfers, the entirety of remittance flows represents real transfers. These flows could be increased if the transactions costs were reduced from their current average of up to 15 percent of the flows to around 1 percent, which is closer to the cost of transfers between rich countries. While foreign aid goes to governments and FDI flows to a small number of firms, remittances tend to flow directly to a large number of individuals and communities. The loss of skills associated with migration is a severe problem, not least for poor regions such as Africa or the Caribbean, where it is estimated that up to two-thirds of the educated doctors and teachers have left. Positive flows include the ideas and investments that originate with these diasporas, as is evident in the pivotal role of Indian emigrants in the Bangalore information technology boom. Addressing the problems of the current migration system and increasing its ability to provide real gains to poor people will require a multilateral as well as bilateral commitment to effective migration reform and management.

Support of Global Public Goods

The fourth area for action is *support for what is commonly referred to as* **global public goods**.[31] Foremost among these global public goods is the need for global peace and stability. Conflicts lead to reverse development. Wars, big and small, destroy the foundation of growth and development and have a particularly devastating effect on poor people, especially poor children. Although many wars have local origins, they feed off global flows—from the sale of commodities such as diamonds and oil to the trade in arms and ammunition. Managing the wide range of environmental side effects associated with domestic policies is also vital. Chief among these environmental concerns are climate change and the looming water and energy crises, which will have increasing international dimensions. How these crises are managed are among the biggest development challenges facing our planet.

Another crucial global public good involves the management of science and technology in favor of development. Combating diseases, not least HIV/AIDS and malaria, as well as developing higher yield and stress-resistant crops can be addressed only at the global level, and requires a pooling of resources and the management of intellectual property and technology to overcome the widening scientific and digital divides.

The Purpose of this Book

The purpose of this book is to provide an understanding of the main aspects of economic globalization and their impact on poverty and development. By examining these dimensions in some detail, we hope to resolve to some extent the confusion about globalization represented in the quotations at the beginning of this chapter. In our view, globalization can be managed so that its benefits are more widely shared than they are today and so that its negative impacts are identified and mitigated. Achieving these outcomes is a global, national, and local responsibility. In the following chapters, we analyze the dimensions of this responsibility.

Notes

1. Clearly, our coverage is not comprehensive. We do not examine questions of culture, peace, politics, natural disasters, and security, nor global environmental and health issues, except where they are related to one of our primary areas of focus.
2. We are mindful of Gilpin's (2000) statement that "No . . . book . . . can do justice to either the scope or the rapidity of the economic, political, and technological developments transforming human affairs" (p. ix). For an effort complementary to ours, see World Commission on the Social Dimension of Globalization (2004).
3. For a discussion of this variety, see chapter 4 of Sen (1999).
4. *Purchasing power parity dollars* adjust for differences in the cost of living among the countries of the world. This adjustment is especially important because nontraded services tend to be less expensive at low levels of income.
5. See Bourguignon and Morrisson (2002), Chen and Ravallion (2001), and Chen and Ravallion (2004) on the extent of poverty.
6. Again, see chapter 4 of Sen (1999).
7. See Nussbaum (2000) for a powerful, book-length discussion of the lack of empowerment of women in developing countries. Nussbaum notes the often-mentioned fact that "gender inequality is strongly correlated with poverty" (p. 3). See also World Bank (2005d) *World Development Report on Equity and Development,* which stresses the importance of equity and opportunity.
8. To mention just one example, the International Institute of Tropical Agriculture has estimated that well over 150,000 children are involved in hazardous labor in the cacao farms of West Africa, including clearing brush with machetes and applying pesticides, as part of the region's export agriculture. See IITA (2002).
9. See, for example, Fields (2001).
10. Indeed, by 1500 in China, building ships with more than two masts was punishable by death.
11. See, for example, chapter 1 of James (1996), O'Rourke and Williamson (1999), and World Bank (2002c).
12. This production system is known as "Fordism" or "managerial capitalism." To quote John and others (1997), "American corporations consolidated into the position of world leaders across almost the entire range of the advanced industries during the 1950s" (p. 40).
13. See Bruton (1998) for a review of import substitution industrialization.
14. With regard to declines in transportation costs, Frankel (2000) takes up the case of shipping costs. He notes that "The margin for US trade fell from about 9½ percent in the 1950s to about 6 percent in the 1990s" (p. 10). Here Frankel measures shipping cost margins as the ratio of c.i.f. (cost insurance freight) trade value to f.o.b. (free on board) trade value.
15. See Dicken (1998). This new production system is known as "Toyotism."
16. Goods (or merchandise) are tangible and can be stored over time in inventories, while services are less tangible and cannot be stored. As is often remarked jokingly, you cannot drop a service on your toe. Consequently, the production and consumption of a service happens more or less simultaneously.
17. See World Bank (2003a).

18. This point is made by Winters, McCulloch, and McKay (2004).
19. Commercial bank loans, including interbank loans, can be short term or long term and can be made with fixed or flexible interest rates. A single bank or a syndicate of banks can be involved in any particular loan package.
20. See Rousseau and Wachtel (2000) for a discussion of how equity portfolio investment supports entrepreneurial activity.
21. Eichengreen (2004) notes that an "average" or "typical" financial crisis can claim up to 9 percent of GDP. Some of the worst crises, such as those in Argentina and Indonesia, reduced GDP by over 20 percent, declines greater than occurred in the United States during the Great Depression. Suryahadi, Sumarto, and Pritchett (2003) estimate that, in Indonesia alone and at the peak of the increase in poverty following the 1997 crisis, approximately 35 million persons were pushed into absolute poverty.
22. See, in particular, Goldin, Rogers, and Stern (2002). The overall debate on aid effectiveness is reviewed in Clemens, Radelet, and Bhavani (2004).
23. These countries are Denmark, Luxembourg, the Netherlands, Norway, and Sweden. See www.oecd.org/dac/stats.
24. See World Bank (2002c).
25. In the parlance of trade policy, this is known as "Mode 4" service trade.
26. See Winters and others (2003).
27. See Maskus (2000). As defined by the World Trade Organization, *intellectual property* includes copyrights, trademarks, geographical indications, industrial designs, patents, and layout designs of integrated circuits.
28. The terms "acquiring," "absorbing," and "communicating" knowledge are from World Bank (1999).
29. This is the main argument of Landes (1998). Landes' work, however, has come under some criticism for overemphasizing the role of European ideas at the expense of ideas from other part of the world.
30. Goldin, Rogers, and Stern (2002, p. 42). See also chapter 5, this volume.
31. See Kaul, Grunberg, and Stern (1999).

Globalization
and Poverty

The relationship between globalization and global poverty is complex. In chapter 1, we distinguished among three stages of modern globalization:

- the first stage between 1870 and 1914, ending with World War I
- the second stage following the end of World War II and continuing to the mid-1970s
- the third stage from the mid-1970s to the present.

Global poverty rose during the first stage of globalization, but it continued to rise during the retreat from globalization during World Wars I and II. During the third stage of globalization, there is some evidence that global poverty finally leveled off somewhat and that extreme global poverty is now slowly falling. Given these historical facts, it is difficult to make simple statements about globalization and poverty: accurate statements about this relationship are necessarily complex. In this chapter, we begin to unravel some of these complexities, setting the stage for our investigation of the relationship between globalization and poverty in the remainder of this book.

We begin by considering the developing world, where global poverty is concentrated. We then take on particular aspects of global poverty itself. Finally, we consider the five dimensions of globalization: trade, finance, aid, migration, and ideas. Since we take up each of these topics separately in chapters 3 through 6, we concentrate here on comparisons among them.

The Developing World

Global poverty is concentrated in what is commonly referred to as the *developing world*. The countries of the developing world became distinct by the 19th century as their per capita incomes began to lag significantly behind those of other parts of the world (figure 2.1). Although by 1820 per capita

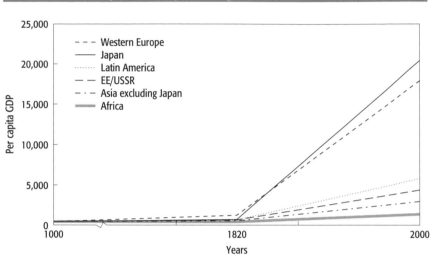

FIGURE 2.1 Per Capita Income by World Region (1990 international dollars)

Source: Maddison 2001, table 1-2.
Note: EE/USSR refers to Eastern Europe and the former USSR.

income in Western Europe was approximately double that of the rest of the world, subsequently the increases in incomes in Western Europe and Japan were far more rapid than they were in Latin American, Eastern Europe, and the former USSR, Asia (excluding Japan), or in Africa. The exact causes of these changes are still being debated and discussed by economic historians. Indeed, in considering the nexus of change in Western Europe—Great Britain in the late 18th century—Crafts (2001) notes

> *This was still an economy which . . . had many limitations, including weak science and technology, small markets, and many attractive rent-seeking opportunities for the talented. Indeed, a World Bank economist, given a basic description of the late 18th century British economy without knowing to which country it applied, might well conclude that here was a case of very poor development prospects.* (p. 313)

Maddison (2001) provides a contrasting perspective, noting Britain's improvements in "banking, financial and fiscal institutions and agriculture" as well as a "surge in industrial productivity" (p. 21). Such varying interpretations of how Great Britain, the other countries of Western Europe, and Japan began their revolutionary economic changes leave the processes not fully explained. That the changes were indeed revolutionary, however, is not

KEY TERMS AND CONCEPTS

extremely poor	overseas development assistance (ODA)
headcount index	poor
gross national income (GNI)	purchasing power parity dollars
low-income countries	Standard International Trade
middle-income countries	Classification (SITC)

in doubt. The absence of these changes in the developing world became one of the main characteristics defining it.[1]

The early 19th century (the midpoint in figure 2.1) featured as a transition between two waves of colonial expansion, the first beginning in 1400 and the second ending with World War I in 1914. The concurrent second phase of colonial expansion and the first phase of modern globalization has been described as "the apex of . . . Western political, economic, military and cultural dominance"[2] in which 80 percent of the surface of the earth came under various European powers. This colonial history, too, began to define the developing world.

The Impact of an Expanding Population

The movement of the world economy through these historic changes was also reflected in dramatic increases in population levels (figure 2.2). This involved an increase in the absolute size of the developing world's population. From 1000 to 2000, the developing world added nearly 4.5 billion persons, while the rest of the world added slightly over 1 billion. What is most apparent here is the rapid expansion of the Asian region in total population. This took place even with Asia's total *share* of world population declining from approximately 65 percent in the year 1000 to 57 percent in 2000. These large increases in the absolute numbers of people in the developing world are part of its long-term history and became apparent in the age structure of its population (figure 2.3). While populations of rich countries become older, those of the developing world become younger. Meeting the development and employment needs of these young people remains a great challenge.

GDP Figures of the Developing World

The increase in the size of the developing world is not confined to population. Large parts of the developing world are emerging in terms of gross domestic product (GDP) as well. Consider figure 2.4.[3] This figure plots GDP for four regions as a percentage of total world GDP, both historically back to 1975 and projected forward to 2015. The developing region, consisting of the 12 largest

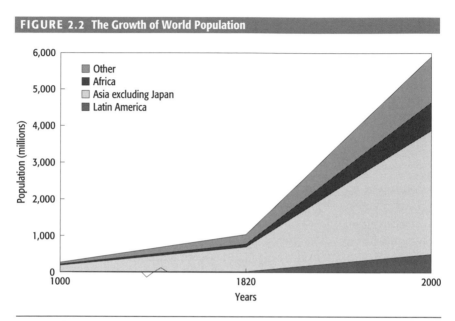

FIGURE 2.2 The Growth of World Population

Source: Maddison 2001, table 1-1.

developing countries, accounted for only one-tenth of world GDP in 1975. It is projected to account for one-fifth of world GDP in 2015, surpassing both Japan and the largest four countries of the European Union. Thus it is evident that at least some parts of the developing world are emerging as relatively economically significant.

Low- and Middle-Income Countries

Today the developing world is divided into two sets of countries for analytical and statistical convenience. These are the low-income countries and the middle-income countries. At the time of this writing and for data through 2002, **low-income countries** are those with a per capita income of less than US$735, and **middle-income countries** are those with a per capita income more than US$735 but less than US$9,076. The list of these two sets of countries is presented in the annex to this chapter.

Poverty

The goal of this book is to relate the globalization activities of trade, finance, aid, migration, and ideas to global poverty and its alleviation. Recall from chapter 1 that we can associate poverty with deprivations of income, health, education, and empowerment. Recall also that, although *relative* deprivations

FIGURE 2.3 Population Age Distributions

Population by age and sex: 1950, 1990, and 2030

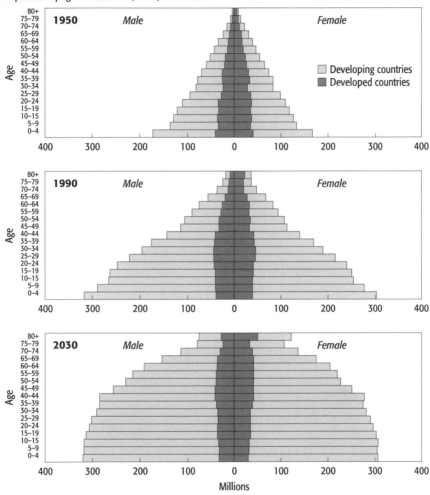

Source: United States Department of Commerce 2001.

are important, we have chosen to focus in this book on the more crucial issue of *absolute* deprivations.[4]

Definition of "Poor"

The longest tracking of world poverty is provided by Bourguinon and Morrisson (2002). These estimates cover the 1820 to 1992 period and include both

FIGURE 2.4 Relative Economic Strength of Developing Countries, Historical and Projected (percent of world GDP in constant US dollars)

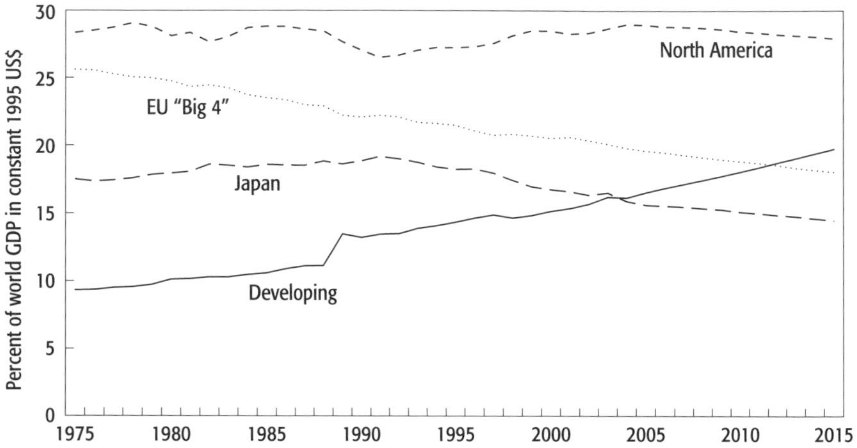

Source: World Bank analysis.
Note: *Developing* refers to the top 12 largest developing economies: Argentina, Brazil, China, India, Indonesia, Mexico, Republic of Korea, Russian Federation, South Africa, Taiwan, Thailand, and Turkey; EU *"Big 4"* refers to France, Germany, Italy, and the United Kingdom.

the "poor" and the "extremely poor" (figure 2.5). The ***poor*** are defined as those living on less than US$2 per day (in 1985 ***purchasing power parity dollars***), and their numbers increase steadily from just under 1 billion persons in 1820 to 2.8 billion persons in 1992. The ***extremely poor*** are defined as those living on less than US$1 per day (in 1985 purchasing power parity dollars), and their numbers have increased and decreased over time, hovering over 1 billion persons for the entire 20th century up to 1992.[5] An example of what poverty entails is given in box 2.1.

Poverty and Global Inequality

According to Bourguinon and Morrisson, the persistence of world poverty over the long term has been associated with an increase in global inequality, both within and among countries. They note

> World economic growth since 1980 could have caused poverty to decline dramatically, despite population growth, had the world distribution of income remained unchanged. Had that been the case, the number of poor people would have been 650 million in 1992 rather than 2.8 billion and the number of extremely poor people 150 million instead of 1.3 billion.

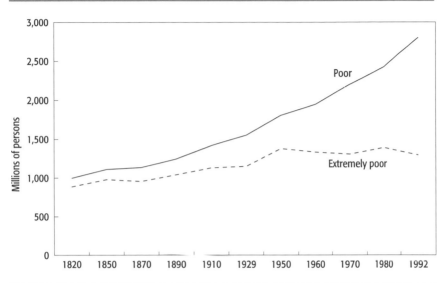

FIGURE 2.5 The Historical Evolution of World Poverty (millions of persons)

Source: Bourguignon and Morrisson 2002.

BOX 2.1 The Experience of Being Poor

For approximately 45 years, until her recent retirement, Jayamma went every day to the brick kiln and spent eight hours a day carrying bricks on her head, 500 to 700 bricks a day. . . . Jayamma balanced a plank on her head, stacked twenty bricks at a time on the plank, and then walked rapidly, balancing the bricks by the strength of her neck, to the kiln, where she then had to unload the bricks without twisting her neck, handing them two by two to the man who loads the kiln. Men in the brick industry typically do this sort of heavy labor for a while, and then graduate to the skilled (but less arduous) tasks of brick molding and kiln loading, which they can continue into middle and advanced ages. Those jobs pay up to twice as much, though they are less dangerous and lighter. Women are never considered for these promotions and are never permitted to learn the skills involved. . . . Nonetheless, they cling to the work because it offers regular employment, unlike construction and agriculture; kilns also typically employ children workers, so Jayamma could take her children to work with her. She feels she has a bad deal, but she doesn't see any way of changing it.

Source: Nussbaum 2000, pp. 18–19.

> *Likewise, the leveling off in the number of extremely poor people since 1970 can be attributed to the stabilization of their relative position since then.* (p. 733)

More recent data on world poverty are provided by Chen and Ravallion (2004).[6] These estimates cover the 1981 to 2001 period and again include both the poor and the extremely poor in terms of 1985 purchasing power parity dollars (figure 2.6). These data provide two pieces of good news. With regard to the number of poor, there has been a recent leveling off for the first time since the early 19th century at approximately 2.7 billion persons, a figure that nevertheless represents a policy challenge of enormous proportions. With regard to the number of extremely poor, there has finally been some downward movement to approximately 1.1 billion. As these authors note, most of this decline occurred in the early 1980s and can be primarily attributed to developments in China and, to a lesser extent, in India.[7]

The Composition of Poverty

The picture of poverty painted by figure 2.7 is improved somewhat when it is considered in terms of what development economists term the ***headcount index*** rather than the number of poor people. This is poverty as a percentage

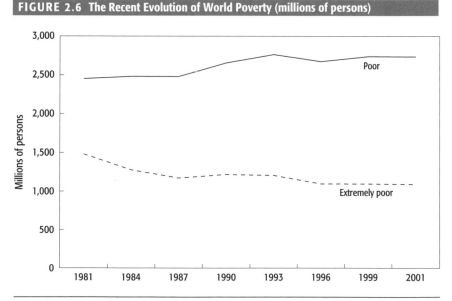

FIGURE 2.6 The Recent Evolution of World Poverty (millions of persons)

Source: Chen and Ravallion 2004.

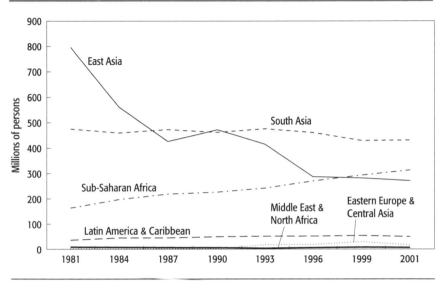

FIGURE 2.7 Regional Incidence of Extreme Poverty (millions of persons)

Source: Chen and Ravallion 2004.

of population. For the poor, the headcount index has fallen from approximately two-thirds of the developing world population in 1981 to approximately half in 2001. For the extremely poor, it has fallen from approximately 40 percent to approximately 20 percent. Thus, relative to significantly expanding populations, poverty incidence as measured by the headcount index has been steadily falling. This does not imply, however, that the absolute numbers of poor and extremely poor people have fallen.

As the case of China illustrates, the *regional* composition of extreme poverty matters. An examination of figure 2.7 reveals that extreme poverty is primarily a South Asian and African phenomenon. In East Asia, the number of extreme poor has been declining steadily and significantly since the early 1980s, primarily due to changes in China. In South Asia, the number of extreme poor has declined somewhat, with almost all of this smaller change being accounted for by India. In Africa, extreme poverty has been *steadily increasing,* with the number of people in this group increasing by over 100 million since the early 1980s.

Poverty Indicators: Life Expectancy

As the various regions of the world diverged in per capita incomes, so they diverged in life expectancy, low levels of which reflect deprivations in health (figure 2.8). It is important to note that the historical evidence suggests that

FIGURE 2.8   Life Expectancy by World Region (years)

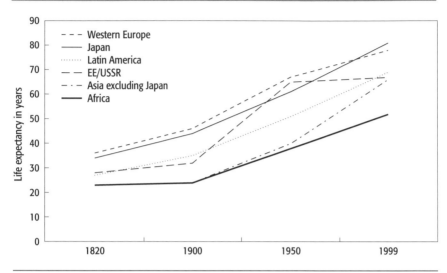

Source: Maddison 2001, table 1-5a.
Note: EE/USSR refers to Eastern Europe and the former USSR.

these changes in life expectancies were not driven entirely by the changes in per capita incomes. Changes in science and public health had significant impacts in their own right.[8] As with the gains in per capita incomes, the gains in life expectancies beginning in the early 19th century were historically unprecedented. For example, Maddison's (2001) estimate of life expectancy in both Roman Egypt at the dawn of the Common Era and 14th century Great Britain are exactly the same: only 24 years.[9] Even the slowest increases in life expectancy in Africa since 1820 have more than doubled that millennial norm. However, the substantial gap remaining between Africa and even the other developing regions is a cause for great concern, especially because it reflects high levels of infant and child mortality. Another major cause for concern is the recent reversal in African life expectancy caused by HIV/AIDS.

Poverty Indicators: Health

Perhaps the most important indicator of health poverty is infant mortality, a sad testament to the global failure to meet the most basic of needs.

Health Deprivation: Infant Mortality

Total infant mortality in 2002 was approximately 7 million, representing an enormous annual tragedy. Examining recent trends in infant mortality (fig-

FIGURE 2.9 Infant Mortality

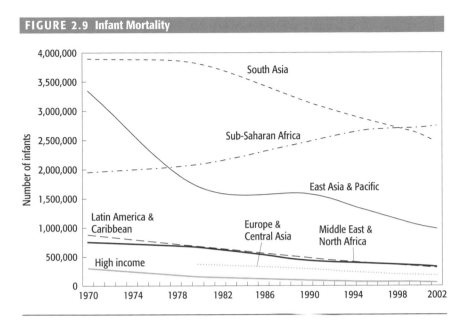

Source: World Bank 2004b.

ure 2.9) leads to some important conclusions. First, as is evidenced by the case of South Asia where annual infant mortality has declined by a million since 1970, it is possible to reduce infant mortality significantly even *without* significantly reducing extreme income poverty. Second, as is evidenced by the case of Sub-Saharan Africa, where annual infant mortality has increased by nearly a million since 1970, increases in extreme income poverty can exacerbate infant mortality.[10] Third, as is evidenced by the Middle East and North Africa, it is possible to have significant infant mortality in the near absence of extreme income poverty. Taken together, these cases indicate that the relationship between income poverty and health poverty is not as direct as one might first assume.

Health Deprivation: Malnutrition

Health deprivation is not by any means limited to infant mortality. For example, approximately 1 billion persons are malnourished; over 150 million of these people are children. Annually, approximately 12 million infants are born underweight, a condition that can have lifetime, deleterious consequences such as lower IQ, cognitive disabilities, and reduced immune function.[11] As noted by Streeten (1995), "Prolonged malnutrition among babies and young children leads to decreased brain size and cell number, as well as altered brain chemistry. . . . Children who suffer from severe malnutrition show lags in motor activity, hearing, speech, social and personal behavior, problem-solving ability, eye-hand coordination and categorization behavior, even after rehabilitation" (p. 57). Health poverty, then, is both serious and pervasive.

Health Deprivation: Implications of Female Education

Substantial evidence suggests that female education is positively associated with infants' and children's abilities to escape mortality and malnourishment. The mediating factors include hygiene, nutrition, and child-care practices. This is a key reason for focusing attention and policy measures on female education in developing countries.[12] Consider the data shown in figure 2.10. This figure plots female youth literacy as a percentage of male literacy using the dark bars. These range from slightly over 40 percent in the case of Niger to slightly over 100 percent in the case of Uruguay. There is thus a wide range of outcomes in the poorer countries with regard to female youth literacy. This is important in its own right but also has implications for infant and child health poverty. The chart also plots infant mortality for these seven countries using lighter bars, and we can see that infant mortality increases significantly

FIGURE 2.10 Female Youth Literacy Relative to Male Youth Literacy and Infant Mortality, 2001

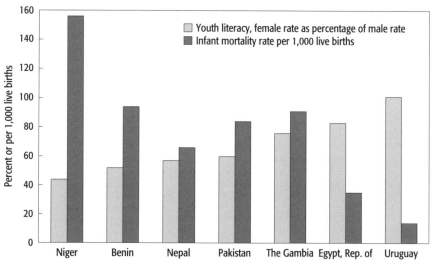

Source: United Nations Development Programme 2004.

as female youth literacy decreases. For reasons such as these, the gender aspects of health poverty matter a great deal.

A Global Imperative

Reducing extreme income poverty and extreme health poverty in the form of infant mortality is a global imperative. It is also an economic imperative, because, according to the research of the World Health Organization (2001b), lower rates of infant mortality are associated with higher rates of economic growth. Although the elements of globalization we consider in this book can have significant effects in reducing infant mortality, we do not want to claim too much for them, except perhaps to emphasize that ideas concerning the social roles of girls and women can be powerful in their effects in this area. Since the processes of globalization are both powerful and longstanding, it is important to explore the wide-ranging ways they can be better harnessed in the battle to improve poor people's lives, at least in this area of infant mortality.

Trade and Foreign Direct Investment

Increases in international trade and foreign direct investment (FDI) are potentially vital means to alleviate global poverty.[13] Examining this possibility requires an appreciation both of the kinds of trade and FDI the developing world engages in and of the way these activities have changed over time. FDI is distinct from other capital flows (portfolio equity investment, bond finance, and commercial bank lending, as well as aid and remittances) in that it primarily reflects managerial rather than portfolio behavior. Trade and FDI can be related to one another through what international economists and business strategists call *intra-firm trade.* This is trade that takes place *within* multinational enterprises (MNEs), and it accounts for approximately one-third of world trade.[14] As developing countries integrate into the world economy, they typically become increasingly involved with global patterns of intra-firm trade. In addition, some FDI can generate exports when the MNEs engage in foreign investment to build export capacity abroad.

The Magnitude of Trade and FDI

For a sense of the magnitudes of trade and FDI consider figure 2.11, which points out a number of important features of both exports and FDI inflows for the developing world:

- First, the exports and FDI inflows of the middle-income countries are much larger than those of the low-income countries.

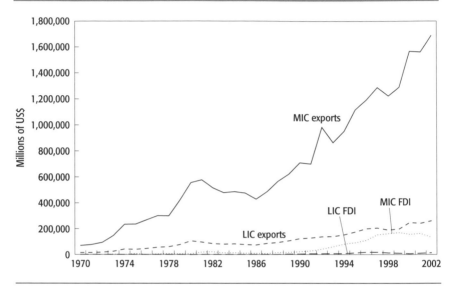

FIGURE 2.11 Trade and FDI for Low- and Middle-Income Countries (millions of current US dollars)

Source: World Bank 2004d.
Note: LIC = low-income country; MIC = middle-income country.

- Second, exports are substantially higher than FDI inflows for *both* the middle-income countries *and* the low-income countries.
- Third, with the exception of investments in extractive industries, low-income countries as a group receive practically no FDI inflows at all.
- Fourth, the exports of the middle-income countries have increased substantially faster than those of the low-income countries

Indeed, the increase of exports from the middle-income countries is one of the recent success stories of the developing world and is not unrelated to the recent improvements in poverty measures discussed above. Because nearly all of Sub-Saharan Africa is composed of low-income countries, there is a regional dimension to some of these trends: aside from petroleum and minerals, Africa is largely left out of global export growth and FDI inflows, although a few African countries have been able to break this mold and have benefited from rapid growth in both investment and trade.[15]

Sectoral Structure of Exports

Examining the sectoral structure of developing-world exports, we learn three things (figure 2.12).

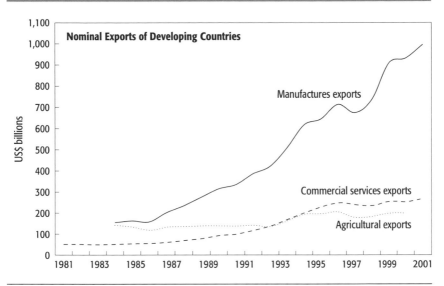

FIGURE 2.12 Sectoral Composition of Developing Country Exports

Source: World Bank 2004d.

- First, increases in exports from the developing world have occurred primarily in manufactured goods. Indeed, despite a few temporary downturns, developing-country manufactured exports have been steadily increasing since the mid-1980s.
- Second, only relatively minor increases in agricultural exports have occurred since the mid-1980s.
- Third, despite a common perception of developing countries as being in "pre-service" stages of development, exports of commercial services have increased faster than—and already exceed—exports of agricultural goods.[16]

Manufacturing Exports

The increases in developing country manufacturing exports and FDI inflows reflect to some degree the increased integration of developing countries into the flexible manufacturing systems of the third stage of modern globalization. As described by Ocampo and and Martin (2003),

This was the first step toward the development of internationally inte-grated production systems, in which production can be divided into vari-

*ous stages (a process known as "the dismemberment of the value chain").
In such systems, the outsourcers in different countries can then specialize
in the production of certain components, in particular phases of the production process, or in the assembly of specific models.* (p. 4)

An increasing number of developing countries took this first step, despite
continued protectionism in areas such as textiles, clothing, and food products. Indeed, the increased involvement of some developing countries in the
global manufacturing system is perhaps the most important characteristic of
the third stage of globalization. It increasingly involved trade within narrowly
defined sectors (intra-industry trade) and, as mentioned above, even trade
within multinational firms themselves (intra-firm trade).

Agricultural Exports

The stagnation of developing countries' agricultural exports has had a number
of causes. Among these causes are the bias against agriculture in most developing countries; the protection against developing-country agricultural exports
in both developed and other developing countries; and the extensive subsi-
dization of agriculture in the developed countries, which undercuts successful
agricultural production in the developing world.[17] This stagnation is an important explanation of the continued stubbornness of rural poverty and of the limitations to developing country participation in the world trading system.

Commercial Services Exports

Finally, the slow increase in commercial services represents the increased
involvement of developing countries in transportation, tourism, and business
services. Because the data on provision of these services are imperfectly col-
lected, the actual increase in commercial services over time might be even
larger than that illustrated in figure 2.12.

There is a tradition in development economics that emphasizes the role of
manufacturing in successful development trajectories. From this perspective,
the upward trajectory in the manufacturing exports of developing economies
is encouraging. However, there is a less well known concern with the potential of agriculture to contribute positively to development trajectories, and
there is some evidence to support this view in the case of East Asia.[18] From this
perspective, as well as from the perspective of the numerous rural poor, the
stagnation of agricultural exports is less than encouraging. Rarely appreciated
is the potential role for service exports to transform economies, a potential
that can be significant.[19] In light of this, it is important to recognize the fact
that even the low-income countries are active in this area.

Capital, Aid, and Remittance Flows

Capital flows, aid, and remittances are important channels through which poorer countries can gain access to resources from abroad. Each of these activities is identified by international and development economists as an additional way to reduce global poverty, albeit with some disagreement.[20] We consider each of these globalization dimensions to gain a sense of their relative magnitudes.

The Role of FDI

If we consider recent trends in capital flows, aid, and remittances for developing countries, a number of important characteristics become visible (figure 2.13). Since the early 1990s, FDI has emerged as the most important foreign resource flow for the developing world as a whole, surpassing foreign aid or *official development assistance (ODA)* by increasing amounts. While a downward trend in FDI has recently appeared, the long-term growth and volume of these flows has been remarkable, inspiring much comment on the possibility of private capital replacing aid. Recent data suggest a recovery of FDI inflows in 2003 and 2004.[21] In part, these new flows are related to the increased manufacturing exports of the developing world, because FDI has been a vehicle for these countries to integrate into the global manufacturing system.[22]

FIGURE 2.13 **Nominal Flows of Aid, FDI, Portfolio Investment, and Remittances to Developing Countries**

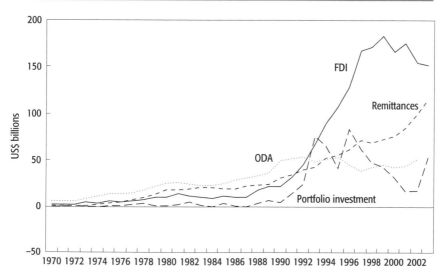

Sources: World Bank 2004b, 2004d.

The Role of Portfolio Flows

Along with FDI, portfolio flows such as equities and bonds began to increase significantly in the 1990s. In contrast to FDI, however, these flows have proved to be volatile, dropping precipitously between 1997 and 2003. They recovered in 2003, and recent data[23] suggest that portfolio flows will hold up well at least through 2005. The volatile nature of portfolio flows gives rise to the cautionary approach we take toward portfolio capital in chapter 4 and is reflected in box 2.2 on "volatile widgets."[24]

The Role of Foreign Aid

In contrast to both FDI and portfolio flows, foreign aid or ODA is a historically recent flow. Aid increased slowly from the 1960s until around 1990. Between 1990 and 2001, aid flows have stagnated, and as a share of rich countries incomes, or per capita requirements of poor people, declined precipitously: from around 0.32 percent of **gross national income (GNI)** or US$35 per African in 1990, to 0.22 percent of GNI or US$17 per African in 2000. More recently, the downward trend in aid has been reversed with a growing number of countries committing to double their aid budgets by 2010. Like other capital flows, aid has been concentrated in a relatively small number of

---

BOX 2.2 Volatile Widgets in the 1990s

Imagine landing on a planet that runs on widgets. You are told that international trade in widgets is highly unpredictable and volatile on this planet, for reasons that are poorly understood. A small number of nations have access to imported widgets, while many others are completely shut out even when they impose no apparent obstacles to trade. With some regularity, those countries that have access to widgets get too much of a good thing, and their markets are flooded with imported widgets. This allows them to go on a widget binge, which makes everyone pretty happy for while. However, such binges are often interrupted by a sudden cutoff in supply, unrelated to any change in circumstances. The turnaround causes the affected economies to experience painful economic adjustments. For reasons equally poorly understood, when one country is hit by a supply cutback in this fashion, many other countries experience similar shocks in quick succession. Some years thereafter, a widget boom starts anew.

Substitute "international capital flows" for "widgets" above and the description fits today's economy quite well. We have just gone through a lending boom-and-bust cycle in Asia that is astounding in its magnitude. In 1996, five Asian countries (Indonesia, Malaysia, the Philippines, the Republic of Korea, and Thailand) received net private capital inflows amounting to US$93 billion. One year later (in 1997), they experienced an estimated *outflow* of US$12.1 billion, a turnaround in a single year of US$105 billion, amounting to more than 10 percent of the combined GDP of these economies.

Source: Rodrik 1998a.

countries, although since the end of the Cold War donors increasingly have directed their aid to countries that are more effective at using the aid and those where most poor people live. The UN Millennium Declaration in 2000 marked the beginning of a renewed push for increased aid and for greater aid effectiveness. Recent years have seen considerable progress toward increasing the impact of aid on the part of both the recipients and donors. As we emphasize in chapter 5, both the quality and the quantity of aid matter enormously for poor people, and the impact of aid is not limited to its monetary value— the associated flow of ideas and capacity building can also play a vital role.

The Role of Remittances

The remittance flows of global migrants have been characterized by a long-term upward trajectory almost as significant as that of FDI, and the rate of increase in remittances shifted upward even as FDI fell in recent years. Remittance flows to developing countries now exceed US$160 billion and are more important than both aid and portfolio investments to the alleviation of poverty. They are the financial manifestation of the international movement of persons. Their increase reflects the fact that the world's foreign-born population has more than doubled since 1965 and currently stands at well over 175 million persons.[25] Increased remittance flows have also responded to declines in money transfer costs that accompany globalization.[26] The rapid increase in recorded remittances since 2001 may also be due to increased scrutiny and recording of these flows and the inclusion of previously unrecorded flows in the official data.

The country-specific nature of remittances can be appreciated from figure 2.14. This figure plots two measures of remittances. It plots data on 2001 per capita remittances in US dollars measured on the upper axis and indicated with vertical bars. The countries are ranked by per capita remittances as a percentage of per capita GDP, which is measured on the lower axis and indicated with a line. Remittances can be significant from both perspectives. For example, per capita remittances are over US$300 for El Salvador, Jamaica, Jordan, Lebanon, and Tonga. Per capita remittances as a percentage of per capita GDP range from approximately 40 percent to 10 percent. For the countries toward the left end of the figure, remittances are a significant fraction of per capita GDP. This indicates that the money sent home by migrants from these countries is a significant source of income compared with domestic production, so it can have a significant impact on poverty.

The Role of Trade

Finally, each of the above flows (FDI, portfolio investment, foreign aid or ODA, and remittances) is of a lesser order of magnitude than trade (see also

FIGURE 2.14 Foreign Remittances Per Capita and as a Percentage of Per Capita GDP, 2003

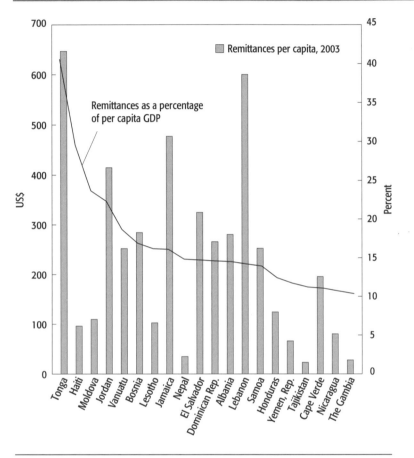

Source: World Bank 2005b.

figure 2.11). That does not make these flows unimportant; it makes the trade aspect of globalization especially important. Additionally, leveraging capital and aid flows in creative ways for effective poverty alleviation becomes crucial given their lower orders of magnitude.

Ideas

Ideas are the generation and transmission of distinctive intellectual constructs in any field that can affect production systems, organizational and management practices, governance practices, legal norms, and technological trends.

By their very nature, it is difficult to accurately compare idea flows to the other kinds of flows considered here.

Ideas for Development

Given our concern with poverty, perhaps the most important set of ideas connected to globalization is what Meier (2001) calls "ideas for development." Meier notes that "ideas are fundamental to the future progress of development" (p. 1). Ideas for development are always emerging, but if one looks hard enough, there is an apparent middle ground among past ideological divisions in development thinking.

Emerging Middle Ground

For example, there is now a better appreciation than in the past of the roles of institutions, history, the public sector, and human welfare in development processes. One recent idea in this realm is that of global public goods, described in box 2.3. This emerging middle ground does not offer any sim-

---

BOX 2.3 The Idea of Global Public Goods

One recent idea in international economic policy that is relevant to our investigation of globalization is that of *global public goods.* A public good is a desired object that has some particular features setting it apart from private goods. First, its consumption is "nonrival" in that more than one person can consume it at the same time. Second, its benefits are "nonexcludable" in that people cannot be easily prevented from claiming them. For example, road safety is a well-known local public good, evident from the fact that we do not privately purchase traffic lights.

A global public good is a public good the benefits of which accrue more or less globally, benefiting persons in most countries. Examples include the multilateral trading system, international peacekeeping, disarmament agreements, disease eradication, and measures to prevent global warming. As noted by Kaul, Grunberg, and Stern (1999), the "concept of global public goods is crucial to effective public policy under conditions of increasing economic openness and interdependence among countries" (p. 9).

Because the benefits of global public goods are spread around the world, no single nation has the incentive to provide them. Unlike local public goods, the absence of a global government leads to their underprovision. Consequently, international cooperation is crucial. As these authors remark, "In today's rapidly globalizing world, peoples' well-being depends on striking a careful balance not only between private and public goods but also between domestic, regional and global public goods" (p. 16). Achieving the cooperation among countries to provide global public goods is a significant and ongoing challenge.

Source: Kaul, Grunberg, and Stern 1999.

ple, one-size-fits-all prescriptions. In some ways, we have arrived at a stage in which "we know that we do not know" (Hoff and Stiglitz 2001), but there is no small measure of ironic comfort in this. There is now intellectual room for multiple, successful routes to development that involve large measures of local learning and experimentation.

Human Rights

Another important idea relevant to reducing deprivation is that of human rights, which has influenced governance practices and legal norms in significant ways. This idea, which is coincident with the second and third stages of modern globalization, is a positive example of what Ocampo and Martin (2003) call the "globalization of values."[27] With its roots in the Universal Declaration of Human Rights (adopted 1948), it is perhaps the International Covenant on Civil and Political Rights (adopted 1966) that has been the most influential. This covenant prohibited torture, slavery, forced labor, and arbitrary arrest. The notion of human rights has been essential in promoting the place of human security (as opposed to national security) as a modern concept.[28] It is also relevant to issues of global poverty in its focus on shortfalls in basic needs.[29]

Role of Ideas in Globalization

The flow of ideas can be closely related to other dimensions of globalization. For example, behind trade, finance, aid, and migration there can be important relationships that assist in learning, and in transmitting and adapting ideas. As will be discussed at various junctures in the chapters that follow, long-term poverty alleviation involves learning of various kinds. For example, learning is involved in the positive transmission of technological change from exporting and FDI inflows. Without the learning relationships for transmitting ideas, these technological changes cannot easily take place. In the case of aid, Pomerantz (2004) emphasizes that "the quality of the relationship may, in fact, be more important in influencing policy directions and ensuring successful outcomes, than the money itself" (p. 8).

Ways to Measure the Flow of Ideas

Ideas can be imagined as a current flowing through channels created by trade, capital flows, aid, and migration. However, it is not easy to accurately measure idea flows as we do the other globalization flows considered here. Instead, we can assess the *capacity* for global idea flows. One measure of capacity is telecommunications connectedness, depicted in figure 2.15. Whether measured in terms of telephone mainlines, mobile phones, or Internet usage, the

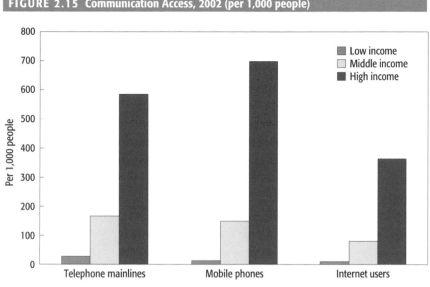

FIGURE 2.15 Communication Access, 2002 (per 1,000 people)

Source: World Bank 2004d.

low-income countries of the world are at a significant disadvantage compared with the middle-income countries, and at even more of a disadvantage compared with the high-income countries. For example, mobile phone usage in the low-income countries is less than 10 percent that of the middle-income countries. This lack of connectedness reflects a lack of infrastructure available to poor people that would enable them to share in the global exchange of ideas, methods, and technology.[30]

Summary

What do we learn from the information presented in this chapter?

- First, and most important, global poverty is a widespread phenomenon (even in its extreme form) that has finally shown some recent trend toward leveling off and even declining somewhat.
- Second, a ranking of the various dimensions of globalization in terms of US dollar value flow volumes appears to be trade, foreign direct investment, remittances (reflecting migration), other capital flows, and aid.
- Third, the impact of globalization as measured through our econom' dimensions are highly uneven—the low-income countries are muc'

less involved in trade and FDI activities, for example, than middle-income countries.

- Fourth, ideas permeate all the other globalization activities, supporting to greater and lesser degrees crucial learning processes that are important to long-run poverty reduction. In fact, poverty is, to an important extent, a poverty of learning, and any improvement in the way globalization benefits poor people will involve supporting poor peoples' learning in multiple realms.

We will begin to examine in detail each of our globalization dimensions and their links to global poverty in chapters 3 through 7. These examinations, along with that of this and the previous chapter, will lead us to a set of policy recommendations we present in chapter 8. This last chapter recognizes that global poverty in all its dimensions requires adequate policy responses from national and world communities.

Annex: Low- and Middle-Income Countries, 2002

Low-Income Countries

Angola, Azerbaijan, Bangladesh, Benin, Bhutan, Burkina Faso, Burundi, Cambodia, Cameroon, Central African Republic, Chad, Comoros, Democratic Republic of Congo, Republic of Congo, Côte d'Ivoire, Equatorial Guinea, Eritrea, Ethiopia, The Gambia, Georgia, Ghana, Guinea, Guinea-Bissau, Haiti, India, Indonesia, Kenya, Kyrgyz Republic, the Lao People's Democratic Republic, Lesotho, Liberia, Madagascar, Malawi, Mali, Mauritania, Moldova, Mongolia, Mozambique, Myanmar, Nepal, Nicaragua, Niger, Nigeria, Pakistan, Papua New Guinea, Rwanda, São Tomé and Principe, Senegal, Sierra Leone, Solomon Islands, Somalia, Sudan, Tajikistan, Tanzania, Togo, Uganda, Uzbekistan, Vietnam, the Republic of Yemen, Zambia, Zimbabwe

Middle-Income Countries

Albania, Algeria, Argentina, Armenia, Belarus, Belize, Bolivia, Bosnia and Herzegovina, Botswana, Brazil, Bulgaria, Cape Verde, Chile, China, Colombia, Costa Rica, Croatia, Czech Republic, Djibouti, Dominica, Dominican Republic, Ecuador, Arab Republic of Egypt, El Salvador, Estonia, Fiji, Gabon, Grenada, Guatemala, Guyana, Honduras, Hungary, Islamic Republic of Iran, Jamaica, Jordan, Kazakhstan, Latvia, Lebanon, Lithuania, FYR Macedonia, Malaysia, Maldives, Mauritius, Mexico, Morocco, Oman, Panama, Paraguay, Peru, Philippines, Poland, Romania, Russian Federation, Samoa, Serbia and Montenegro, Seychelles, Slovak Republic, South Africa, Sri Lanka, St. Kitts and Nevis, St. Lucia, St. Vincent and the Grenadines, Swaziland, Syrian Arab Republic, Thailand, Tonga, Trinidad and Tobago, Tunisia, Turkey, Turkmenistan, Ukraine, Uruguay, Vanuatu, Républica Bolivariana de Venezuela

Notes

1. These revolutionary changes in economic development eventually gave rise to significant "reversals of fortune" over time. For example, in the mid-1950s, Southeast Asia and Africa had the same levels of per capita income. By the late 1990s, Southeast Asia's per capita income was approximately five times that of Africa. See Francois (2000).
2. See Szirmai (2005, p. 51).
3. We are grateful to William Rex, Lead Corporate Strategy Officer, World Bank, Washington, DC, for assistance with the data in figure 2.4.
4. As Streeten (1995) notes, "Some authors regard all poverty as relative, but this is surely confusing inequality—an evil, but a different evil—with poverty. Everyone in a society can be equally starving, and we would not want to say that they are not poor" (pp. 32–33). Various measures of inequality or relative income deprivation are expertly reviewed by Ravallion (2004b). A historical view is given by O'Rourke (2002).
5. Recall from chapter 1 that purchasing power parity dollars adjust for differences in the cost of living among the countries of the world, and that this adjustment is especially important because nontraded services tend to be less expensive at low levels of income.
6. See also Chen and Ravallion (2001) for an earlier set of estimates.
7. Ravallion (2004b) notes that the sharp drop in poverty in China in the early 1980s was due to the de-collectivization of agriculture after Premier Deng's reforms started in 1978 (p. 7).
8. As Crafts (2001) notes, "any index of living standards that gives substantial weight to life expectancy will make the developing countries of the recent past look much better in welfare comparisons with the leading countries of 1870 than does a judgment based simply on real GDP per capita" (p. 325). See also Preston (1975).
9. See table 1-4 of Maddison (2001).
10. As noted by Sen (1999), "the problem of premature mortality is enormously sharper in Africa than in India" (p. 102).
11. See Behrman, Alderman, and Hoddinott (2004).
12. For example, in their study of parental education and health in Brazil, Kassouf and Senauer (1996) concluded, "Some 25% of preschool children with mothers who had less than 4 years of schooling suffered from severe or moderate stunting (of growth). This figure would fall to only 15% if these mothers had a primary education of at least 4 but less than 8 years, and only 3% if these mothers had a secondary education of at least 11 years of schooling. Although not as strong as the effect of maternal education, . . . improved paternal education would also lead to substantial reductions in child malnutrition" (p. 832). See also Schultz (2002).
13. See Dollar and Kraay (2004), for example. An alternative view is given in Rodríguez and Rodrik (2001).
14. An introduction to intra-firm trade is provided in chapter 10 of Reinert (2005).
15. A notable exception to this is South Africa.
16. *Manufactured exports* are defined as commodities in **Standard International Trade Classification (SITC)** sections 5 (chemicals), 6 (basic manufactures), 7 (machinery and transport equipment), and 8 (miscellaneous manufactured goods) excluding division 68 (non-ferrous metals). *Agricultural exports* are defined as commodities in SITC sections 0 (food and live animals), 1 (beverages and tobacco), 2 (crude materials except fuels) excluding division 27 (crude fertilizers and minerals excluding coal, petroleum, and precious stones) and division 28 (metalliferous ores and scrap), 4 (animal and vegetable oils and fats). *Commercial service exports* are total service exports

minus exports of government services not included elsewhere. *International transactions in services* are defined by the IMF's *Balance of Payments Manual* (1993) as the economic output of intangible commodities that may be produced, transferred, and consumed at the same time.

17. See, for example, Krueger, Schiff, and Valdes (1988) and Schiff and Valdes (1995).
18. See Brown and Goldin (1992), Park and Johnston (1995), Reinert (1998), and Martin and Mitra (2001). From different perspectives, each of these sources treats the agricultural sector as *potentially dynamic,* something that has not always been well appreciated.
19. See Francois and Reinert (1996).
20. See, for example, World Bank (2002a and 2002b).
21. See, for example, Institute of International Finance (2005).
22. See Feenstra (1998), who referred to the integration of trade and disintegration of production in the global economy in an early article on out-sourcing. Less emphasized in this and other articles is the process of "in-sourcing."
23. See, for example, Institute of International Finance (2005).
24. On the volatility of portfolio capital, see Obstfeld (1998) and Eichengreen (1999, 2004).
25. See International Organization for Migration (2003b).
26. For the case of migrants from Latin America, see Lapper (2004).
27. Negative or deleterious examples of the globalization of values certainly do exist as well, such as the undermining of diversity through blind, cultural homogenization.
28. See, for example, Axworthy (2001). He notes, "The international discourse on human security is beginning to effect change on the institutions and practice of global governance. . . . Globalization has made individual human suffering an irrevocable universal concern" (p. 20). The contention that the human rights idea is merely "Western" has been shown to be false. See, for example, chapter 10 of Sen (1999) and chapter 1 of Nussbaum (2000).
29. See, for example, Pogge (1999).
30. The World Bank's *World Development Indicators* estimate a 2002 waiting list for telephone mainlines of over 4.5 million persons in the low-income countries, reflecting an unfilled demand for these services. Tom Friedman (2005) illustrates how communication, transport, and other technological advances have produced new opportunities for those countries or firms that are able to capture the benefits of these developments.

3

Trade

International trade is potentially a powerful force for poverty reduction. Trade can contribute to poverty alleviation by expanding markets, creating jobs, promoting competition, raising productivity, and providing new ideas and technologies, each of which has the *potential* for increasing the real incomes of poor people. We emphasize the word "potential" because the link between trade and poverty alleviation is not automatic.[1] Indeed, as the recent histories of a number of countries demonstrate, it would be a mistake to rely on **trade liberalization** alone to reduce poverty. A more comprehensive approach is needed—one that addresses multiple economic and social challenges simultaneously and that emphasizes the expansion of poor people's capabilities, especially in the areas of health and education.[2] Such an approach also needs to address the business climate, infrastructure, and other barriers that prevent potential importers and exporters from benefiting from the opportunities afforded by more open markets. Trade has a vital role to play, and we explore this in the present chapter.

As we emphasize below, improving market access for developing countries is a priority. This would yield benefits that far exceed those of additional aid or debt relief. Additional aid to enhance trade is, however, a vital complement to ensure that low-income countries take advantage of increased access to markets.

International Trade and Its Impact on Poverty

As has been long recognized by international economists, international trade is a means of *expanding markets,* and **market expansion** can generate employment and incomes for poor people. In many discussions of globalization, comparisons have been made between the wages of workers in poor-country export industries and the wages of workers in developed countries. In these comparisons, the wages of workers in developing countries' export industries often appear to be very low. Consequently, globalization has often been identified as worsening poverty. However, comparison between what people may have earned before and after trade opportunities became available is perhaps more relevant. From a poverty perspective, this comparison could be between the wages of export sector workers and agricultural day laborers, both in the same developing country. Often the alternative of work as an agricultural day laborer is much worse than the work of an export sector worker. It is precisely this type of income comparison that draws workers into export industries.[3]

Export Activity

It must also be kept in mind that not all export activity is equal from the point of view of raising the incomes of poor people. The export sector can best help to alleviate poverty when it supports labor-intensive production, human capital accumulation (both education and health), or technological learning. These characteristics were often present in the successful East Asian export expansion of recent decades. Their weakness in other countries' export expansions helps to explain why export expansions have not always done as much as could be done to help poor people. In addition, the incomes of poor individuals depend on buoyant and sustainable export incomes, which in turn depend on export prices. Export activity with declining export prices, a characteristic of many primary commodities, does not lend itself to sustain poverty alleviation.

Competition

International trade is also a means of *promoting competition,* and in many instances, this can help poor people. Increased competition lowers the real costs of both consumption and production. For example, domestic monopolies charge monopoly prices that can be significantly higher than competitive prices. The competition introduced by imports erodes the market power of firms that at times dominate markets and undermine consumer choice. These "procompetitive effects" of trade can make tight household budgets go farther and lower costs of production, for example, through lowering the costs of fertilizer or fuel. Consumers also suffer when they have to pay artificially high prices for food or clothing products. It is estimated that in the European Union, Japan, and the United States, consumers pay over US$1,000 more for their food than would be the case if trade barriers were reduced. This harms poor people in rich and poor countries alike. Lower production costs can have knock-on employment effects advantageous to poor individuals by lowering nonwage costs in labor-intensive production activities. Procompetitive effects can also arise in the case of **monopsony** (single-buyer) power.[4] In this case, sellers (small farmers, for example) to the previously monopsonistic buyer are able to obtain higher prices for their goods as the buying power of the single-buyer is eroded.

KEY TERMS AND CONCEPTS

Export Processing Zones (EPZs)	primary commodities
high-technology manufactured	real (price adjusted) wages
exports (HTME)	tariffs
maquiladora export sector	tariff escalation
market expansion	tariff protection
monopsony	trade liberalization
multinational enterprises (MNEs)	value chains
openness ratio	

Productivity Increases: Exports

For export activities to support poverty alleviation in a sustained manner, it helps if those activities lend themselves to technological upgrading and associated learning processes. There is some evidence that international trade can *promote productivity* in a country, and it is possible that productivity increases can in turn support the incomes of poor people. Neither of these processes is automatic, however. It is not the case that exports *of all types* or *in all countries* generate positive productivity effects, but there is evidence that this is the case in certain instances. The export process can place the exporting firms in direct contact with discerning international customers, thus facilitating upgrading processes. There is no consensus among international economists on the extent of these upgrading effects, but they nonetheless remain an important possibility that has been active in sectors such as the Indian software industry.[5]

Productivity Increases: Imports

Productivity increases can occur because of imports as well as exports. In this case, the process is typically related to the imports of new machinery that embody more advanced technologies than the machinery they replace in the importing country. Again the issue arises as to the extent to which this upgrading supports the incomes of poor people. For example, as Chile and Costa Rica liberalized their trading regimes, firms imported more physical capital (machines) to remain competitive. Embodied in these machines was a newer technology level that demanded relatively more skilled workers than the old technology that had been in use. Consequently, as trade was liberalized, the unskilled workers lost in terms of relative wages, while workers who were more highly skilled gained. Because poor people are almost always unskilled, these particular changes worked against them.[6] As discussed by de Ferranti and others (2002) in the context of Latin America, this is one of a number of reasons why upgrading skills is crucial for trade (and for foreign direct investment [FDI], discussed in chapter 4) to have a positive impact on poverty.

Access to Foreign Markets

For positive effects of trade to occur, developing countries need access to foreign markets. Unfortunately, as has been very well documented by both trade economists and development organizations, the high-income countries of the world maintain their greatest protective measures in exactly the same markets that are most important for the developing world: agriculture, food processing, and labor-intensive manufactures. In addition, there is substantial evidence of what trade economists call *tariff escalation,* where high-income countries increase the level of protection along with the degree of processing of a product, resisting diversification up and down *value chains* that are so important to development processes.[7] In many cases, lack of market access hurts poor individuals both directly by reducing employment opportunities and indirectly by contributing to declining export prices, particularly for primary commodities.[8]

Impact on Health and Safety

International trade can have direct health and safety effects on poor individuals, which can be beneficial or detrimental. Perhaps most important, improving the health outcomes of poor people usually involves imports of medicines and medical products. It is simply not possible for small developing countries to produce the entire range of even some of the more basic medical supplies, much less more advanced medical equipment and pharmaceuticals. It is also the case that many developing counties import (legally or illegally) large amounts of weaponry and export sexual services, both of which can have dramatically negative outcomes for the health and safety of poor individuals.[9] In addition, the production processes of some export industries can adversely affect the health of workers in those industries, and a small but important amount of trade involves hazardous waste dumping. We will address both the positive and the negative impacts of trade on health and safety in this chapter.

Characteristics of Developing-Country Trade

Before we begin our analysis of the relationship between trade and poverty alleviation, let's recall a few relevant characteristics of developing-country trade from chapter 2.

- First, total trade flows (for example, total exports) of developing countries are substantially larger than inflows of FDI, portfolio investment, and foreign aid receipts. Even the largest of these (FDI) is only approximately one-fifth the size of exports. Trade is therefore of utmost importance for developing countries as a whole.

- Second, for low-income countries (but not for middle-income countries), we need to modify the first statement somewhat. For these countries, aid sometimes reaches the value of a third of their exports. Relative to exports, aid is more important than FDI for these poorer countries.
- Third, manufactured exports are increasingly important for developing countries, both low- and middle income, although agricultural exports are more important for low-income countries than for middle-income ones.
- Fourth, commercial service exports are important for all developing countries, especially when compared with agricultural exports.

These are a few important characteristics of trade that we will keep in mind as we investigate its role in global poverty alleviation. We begin with the market expansion effects of trade.

Market Expansion

The development NGO Oxfam (2002a) has rightly noted that "History makes a mockery of the claim that trade cannot work for the poor" and that "Export success can play a key role in poverty reduction" (p. 8). Some in the anti-globalization movement would deny such claims, while many pro-globalist observers would claim that these processes are automatic. Here we take an intermediate view, observing that export expansion has the *potential* for increasing the real incomes of poor people.

Role of Trade in Alleviating Poverty

In discussions of the more high-tech aspects of globalization, it is often forgotten that 70 percent of the world's "dollar poor" (those consuming below US$1 per day at 1985 purchasing power parity levels) reside in rural areas.[10] For this reason, poverty alleviation cannot ignore rural development, and the potential role that trade can play in poverty alleviation depends in large measure on the possibility of supporting rural incomes, either through farm or nonfarm activities. One such example can be found in Vietnam's rice sector.

Supporting Rural Incomes: Vietnam's Rice Sector

In the case of Vietnam, this support of rural areas has occurred, at least to some degree. As a result of a package of reforms in the late 1980s that included gradual trade liberalization, Vietnam turned from a rice importer to a rice exporter despite the role of this crop as the country's main staple food. Vietnam is now one of the largest rice exporters in the world.

This trade-based market expansion in Vietnam supported household incomes because of the widespread participation of small farms in Vietnam's rice sector. Indeed, rice is grown by two-thirds of Vietnam's households. Rice exports increased the incomes of these small farms and, because rice production is labor intensive in Vietnam, increased demand for rural labor.[11] Thus, Vietnam's rice exports have indeed supported rural incomes, helped to alleviate poverty, and even improved nutrition and reduced child labor.[12] The key here is the involvement of labor-intensive, smallholder farmers; such success has been noted in other countries such as Uganda, where smallholder agriculture has been supported by export market expansion. Where export expansion supports large-scale, capital-intensive agriculture, and where land ownership is highly concentrated, these poverty alleviation effects are weaker. Finally, it is important to note that Vietnam's trade liberalization has not been orthodox. For example, it has employed an export quota (maximum exports) to ensure that domestic rice prices do not rise too much to the detriment of consumption. This has been important for the rural poor for whom the bulk of caloric intake is from rice.

Supporting Manufacturing Incomes: Bangladesh's Clothing Industry

Although rural incomes are most often central to large-scale poverty alleviation, supporting goals of poverty alleviation is not confined to agriculture. Indeed, labor-intensive manufacturing has been an important part of poverty-alleviating trade expansions in much of the developing world. This was the case in the famed export expansion of East Asian countries, and it has also been seen in more recent cases such as Bangladesh's clothing exports. In Bangladesh's case, poverty reduction during the 1990s was quite dramatic and, although changes in the nontradable sector were a significant factor in this reduction, clothing exports also played an important role. Nearly 2 million Bangladeshis work in the clothing sector's nearly 3,000 factories. Oxfam's (2002a) description of this sector illustrates the point that wage comparisons must be relevant to the workers themselves to be truly useful:

> *Most of the (clothing) workforce consists of young women, many of whom have migrated from desperately poor rural areas. The wages earned by these women are exceptionally low by international standards, and barely above the national poverty line. Yet their daily wage rates are around twice as high as those paid for agricultural labourers, and higher than could be earned on construction sites. Employment conditions in the export zones are scandalously poor, with women denied even the most basic rights. Yet for most women working in the garments sector, their employment offers a higher quality of life than might otherwise be possible. (p. 56)*

Although it is true that the wages in the Bangladesh garment sector are barely US$2 per day, this labor-intensive employment has provided an opportunity to leave worse conditions in rural and urban poverty. To be blunt, it has been a difference between poverty and *extreme* poverty. Indeed, using survey data from 1990 and 1997, Zohir (2001), Kabeer (2004), and Kabeer and Mahmud (2004) provide evidence that work in the garment sector has had a number of beneficial effects on women workers in Bangladesh. These include first-time access to cash income, support of families in rural areas through remittances, support of siblings' education, and increased household status. Zohir's conclusion is that "employment in the garment industry has definitely empowered women, increased their mobility and expanded their individual choice" (p. 67).[13] Similar evidence in five additional countries of the way exports can support women's incomes is provided by Nordas (2003), who concludes that export industries in Mauritius, Mexico, Peru, the Philippines, and Sri Lanka are more likely to employ women than men and that they also tend to increase women's wages relative to men's.

Promise of Technological Upgrading

While labor-intensive manufacturing offers an important way to support the incomes of poor people, its long-run promise lies in the potential for technological upgrading. Without technological upgrading, it is likely that the economy will not contribute to long-term poverty alleviation. We will consider this process in the section on productivity. First, however, we consider the issue of competition.

Competition

International economists have begun to understand the ways that international trade can promote competition in developing countries. In many instances, increased competition can help poor people by lowering the real costs of household consumption and production. As mentioned earlier, a domestic firm with market power can raise prices above competitive levels, and import competition can erode this market power.

What trade economists call the "procompetitive effects" of trade does have the potential to help the poor in some instances.[14] Procompetitive effects can also occur in the case of monopsony (single-buyer) power. Here, sellers (small farmers, for example) to the monopsony buyer are able to obtain higher prices for their goods as the buying power of the monopsonist is eroded. We give examples of each of these possibilities here.

Procompetitive Effects: Grameen Bank's Village Phone Program in Bangladesh

The Grameen Bank's Village Phone Program demonstrates how imported technologies, when introduced in the context of a well-thought-out and targeted policy framework, can make a dramatic difference in the lives of the poorest of the poor. Before this program, Bangladesh had one of the lowest telephone penetration rates in the world: only 1.5 percent of households had access to a telephone. Although the lack of a functioning telecommunications service posed serious frustrations for all Bangladeshis, it was particularly costly for the country's farmers and local producers. For these individuals, the lack of telecommunication service imposed serious costs by denying them critical access to the price information necessary to make efficient production decisions and to negotiate with middlemen and marketers on a fair basis.

In 1997, the Grameen Bank, Bangladesh's renowned village-based microcredit organization, launched the Village Phone Program. The program provided selected female members of Grameen Bank's peer-based microcredit networks with loans of taka 12,000 (US$200) to purchase an imported cellular handset and mobile service subscription. The women were then trained on the use and marketing of mobile phone technology, enabling them to earn money while helping their fellow villagers gain access to information at a fraction of what it had previously cost them.[15]

As of late 2003, Grameen Phone estimated that the Village Phone Program was providing 50 million people living in remote rural areas with access to telecommunications facilities. Critically, the advent of village phones has dramatically improved the profitability of small farmers. Farmers in villages with village phone programs, for instance, receive 70 to 75 percent of the retail price, compared with 65 to 70 percent received by farmers in villages without phones.[16] Participants also reported that village phones have significantly helped facilitate the regular delivery of inputs at low cost, reduced the risk of new diseases infecting poultry or livestock, and have offered immeasurable assistance in averting the adverse effects of natural calamities and crime.[17] Thus, the combination of imported technology with an antipoverty policy framework has improved competition in a manner that has been quite beneficial for poor individuals. By vesting control of this new technology in the hands of poor female villagers, the Grameen Bank program represented a dramatic change in economic tradition for Bangladesh, where local elites had ordinarily introduced new innovations and reaped large profits as a consequence.

Procompetitive Effects: Cotton Farmers in Zimbabwe

Examples of procompetitive effects that support the poor can be found in other areas. For instance, there is some evidence that trade liberalization in

Zimbabwe during the early 1990s eroded the monopsony buying power of the national cotton marketing board and thereby supported the entry, output, and incomes of smaller cotton producers.[18] Following trade liberalization, additional cotton buyers emerged, including one owned by the cotton farmers themselves. This particular buyer became involved in providing extension services to smallholder cotton farmers that previously were not available. Also during this period in Zimbabwe, there was entry of over 3,000 new, small-scale hammer mills in the maize processing sector, employing thousands of new workers and leading to an increase in the consumption of hammer-milled maize meal.[19]

Assessing Effects of Procompetitive Trade

Examples such as these indicate that, under certain circumstances at least, poor people can take advantage of increased competition that can result from international trade. Assessing such effects is an emerging area of inquiry. Nevertheless, we are convinced that such effects matter for poor people. It also must be recognized, however, that there are circumstances where certain kinds of liberalization that accompany trade liberalization episodes can actually be anticompetitive (for example, some kinds of privatization where new monopolies are created) and hurt the poor. It is necessary to keep an eye on competitiveness issues to fully assess the impact of trade on poverty.

Productivity

There is an insight from the field of the microeconomics of labor markets that has important implications for poverty alleviation. This insight is that long-term increases in **real *(price adjusted) wages*** require long-term increases in productivity. As noted by UNCTAD (2004), "sustained poverty reduction occurs through the efficient development and utilization of productive capacities in a manner in which the working age population becomes more and more fully *and productively* employed" (p. 90, emphasis added). There is some evidence that international trade can promote productivity in a country, and that productivity increases can in turn support the incomes of poor people. The link between trade and productivity improvements is a *potential* one and is not automatic. It can be related to both imports and exports.[20]

Trade and Productivity: Import Side

On the import side, trade allows countries to import ideas and capital goods (such as machinery) embodying the new technologies that make productivity increases possible. New technologies, however, require a learning process both to master them and to adapt them to local conditions. As described by Rodrigo (2001), "Learning takes place when unit variable cost in production declines with cumulative output as workers, supervisors and managers build up skills around a specific production process" (p. 88). Without learning, technological improvements are usually impossible.

Trade and Productivity: Export Side

On the export side, foreign market access supports the learning process. Again, as described by Rodrigo (2001), "By opening up a channel to the world market, trade . . . serves to promote specialization and sustain production tempos of goods in which learning effects are embodied; if constrained by domestic market size alone along with associated domestic business cycle uncertainty of demand, firms would be less willing to make the investments needed to capture gains from learning" (p. 90). Thus, openness to trade, both import and export, can support technological upgrading via learning.[21] For this process to occur, trade needs to support human capital accumulation upon which learning depends.[22] It also, as Friedman (2005) vividly highlights, requires openness to ideas, which we discuss in chapter 7.

Trade and Productivity: Importance of Learning

Productivity increases can occur in agriculture, manufacturing, and services. They are not, as often supposed, limited to manufacturing alone.[23] As discussed in chapter 2, trade in agriculture, manufacturing, and services are all important for the low- and middle-income countries of the world, and trade-induced learning processes can operate across all three of these sectors in the developing world. That said, evidence on learning and technological upgrading is more readily available for the manufacturing sector, so it is worth considering this sector as an example of the way that trade-induced learning can support real incomes over the long term.

In the realm of manufacturing, the importance of learning is reflected in the observation of Lall and Teubal (1998) that, for developing countries, mastering existing technologies is more important than innovating new technologies. The learning process in manufacturing is characterized by these authors as "constant, intensive and purposive" and requires the external support of education and training that is technology specific. This indicates that complementary education policies of the public sector are important for trade-supported productivity gains. Trade alone is not sufficient. One example of this is the initiative of the Costa Rican government to supply schools with computer technologies in support of a hoped-for emergence of an export-oriented computer products sector. This effort proved to be successful.

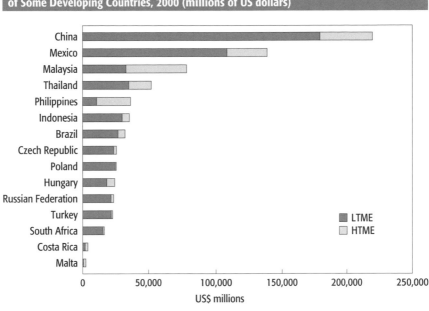

FIGURE 3.1 Low- and High-Technology Manufactured Exports of Some Developing Countries, 2000 (millions of US dollars)

Source: World Bank 2005.
Note: LTME is low-technology manufactured exports; *HTME* is high-technology manufactured exports.

Empirical Evidence of Successful Learning

The empirical evidence on the manufacturing sector suggests that successful learning is not as widespread as one would hope.[24] Note the evidence presented in figure 3.1. This figure considers the sophistication of manufactured exports for a set of low- and middle-income countries for the year 2000. These 15 countries account for 98 percent of reported *high-technology manufactured exports (HTME)* from the low- and middle-income countries. High-technology manufacturing exports are *highly concentrated* in the developing world. Even within the 15 countries reported in this figure, the bulk of high-technology exports are concentrated at the top of the list: in China, Mexico, Malaysia, Thailand, and the Philippines. As emphasized by Lall (1998),

> *The nature of learning varies greatly by country, depending on initial capabilities, the efficacy of markets and institutions, and the policies undertaken to improve them. Some countries lack the skill and technical*

base to engage in modern manufactured exports, except for the simplest ones (low quality garments or toys) where foreign investors bring in the technology and provide the (minimal) training needed; some can tackle the manufacture of complex products (automobiles); and some can manage the design and development of new technologies in advanced products. Their capability differences determine the nature and dynamism of comparative advantage. (p. 66)

Learning and Skill Levels

Indeed, one can distinguish (as Lall [1998] does) between the *basic learning* that is required to export low-technology manufactured exports and the *deep learning* that is required to export high-technology manufactured exports. The required complementary education and training policies differ in these two instances. As Lall points out, "In early stages of industrialization, when skill needs are fairly low and general, the correct policy is functional support for schooling and basic vocational training. In later stages, with more complex activities and functions, skill needs grow more demanding, diverse, and specific to particular technologies" (p. 68). Beginning the process of basic learning, supported by functional educational advances, and then transitioning into deep learning, supported by more specific educational advances, are both important but not easy to achieve, especially when educational resources are scarce. But it is essential, as the long-run support of real incomes depends on countries' abilities to do this.[25]

Learning for High-Technology Manufacture Exports: The Maquiladora Export Sector

The deep learning process that supports high-technology manufacture exports is important because there is some evidence that low-technology manufacturing exports can fail to deliver long-term real wage increases. It is becoming clear that not all manufacturing activity supports productivity increases from technological learning over the long term. The country in figure 3.1 with the third-highest level of high-technology manufacturing exports is Mexico. However, as can be seen in that figure, the bulk of its manufacturing exports are low-technology in nature. In the case of assembly or **maquiladora *export sector*** of Mexico, there are limits to productivity increases despite the generation of over 1 million jobs. For example, figure 3.2 plots imported inputs, value added, and wages as a percentage of gross production value for a quarter of a century in Mexico. As can be seen in this figure, imported intermediate products as a percentage of production value has been on a steady rise, while value added and wages as a percent of production value have been on a steady

FIGURE 3.2 Some Characteristics of the *Maquiladora* Industry in Mexico

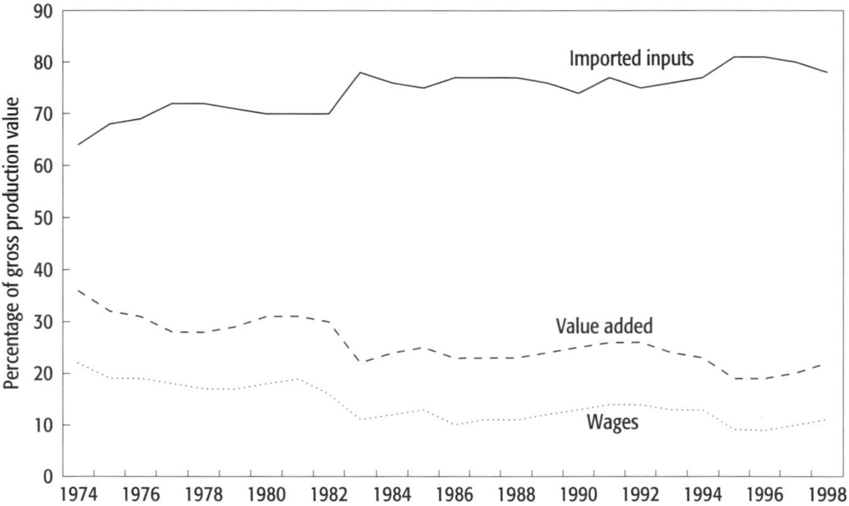

Source: Buitelaar and Padilla Pérez 2000.

decline. Why does this matter? There is a great deal of evidence that long-term productivity in exporting activities in support of long-term increases in real wages relies on manufacturing export activities being integrated into the local economy via sourcing of local inputs and local value added. Just the opposite appears to have occurred in the Mexican *maquila* sector.

Inward FDI

The manufacturing exports of developing countries are often the result of inward FDI. This is an important link between two realms of globalization we examine in this book: trade and FDI. From the point of view of poverty allevi-ation, the question becomes: how can the FDI-export process support domes-tic learning and upgrading, leading to productivity and real wage gains? One way of maximizing the benefits of FDI in the areas of employment and tech-nology is by facilitating the use of local suppliers on the part of the foreign ***multinational enterprises (MNE)*** by developing *backward links.* The increased role of MNEs in an economy without significant backward links results in "enclaves," which have little connection to the rest of the economy and little contribution beyond direct employment effects. Traditionally, the way to avoid enclave FDI was through local content requirements, but with the advent of the WTO in 1995, such requirements for local inputs became illegal.[26]

The key policy question for developing countries is how to foster backward links between foreign MNEs and potential local suppliers. The link promotion process involves many players, including the government, the foreign MNEs, the local suppliers, professional organizations, commercial organizations, and academic institutions. The key role of the government is one of *coordination*, attempting to bridge the "information gaps" among the players. We will address this issue in more detail in chapter 4 on capital flows.

Mauritius: Example of Trade-Supported Productivity Increase

The most well known group of countries that have pursued trade-supported productivity increases for long-term poverty reduction is East Asia.[27] However, another notable example is the African country of Mauritius. As described by Subramanian and Roy (2003), Mauritius pursued a trade strategy that supported productivity and income gains throughout the 1980s and 1990s. Indeed, a very high **openness ratio** (the sum of imports and exports as a percentage of GDP) helps explain the fact that productivity gains of Mauritius in the 1990s nearly reached those of East Asia in the late 1980s to early 1990s. **Export processing zones (EPZ)** helped in this endeavor (box 3.1). However, as these authors note, this process of trade-supported productivity gains "would probably not have been a success, or at least not to the same extent, without the policies of Mauritius's trading partners, which played an important role in ensuring the profitability of the export sector" (p. 223). Indeed,

---

BOX 3.1 Export Processing Zones

One means by which developing countries have tried to promote the upgrading of their exports is through the use of export processing zones (EPZs). EPZs are areas of developing countries in which multinational enterprises (MNEs) can locate and in which they typically enjoy, in return for exporting the whole of their output, favorable treatment in the areas of infrastructure, taxation, tariffs on imported intermediate goods, and labor costs. EPZs have been used in many developing countries around the world. Indeed, some estimates suggest that there are over 500 EPZs in over 70 host countries. In most cases, EPZs involve relatively labor-intensive, "light" manufacturing such as textiles, clothing, footwear, and electronics and involve only basic learning. A number of studies have tried to assess EPZs from a benefit and cost framework. These studies show that in many (but not all) cases, the benefits *do* outweigh the costs. For example, Jayanthakumaran (2003) assessed EPZs in China, Indonesia, Malaysia, the Philippines, the Republic of Korea, and Sri Lanka. He concluded that the EPZs were an important source of employment in all six of these countries. Also, in all but the Philippines, the benefits outweighed the costs. In the case of the Philippines, the infrastructure costs incurred in setting up the EPZ were too high for a net positive benefit. Thus, one cannot make general statements on the success of EPZs. They need to be examined on a case-by-case basis.

Sources: Johansson and Nilsson 1997; Schrank 2001; and Jayanthakumaran 2003.

at least 90 percent of Mauritian exports were accounted for by *preferential market access* for sugar, textiles, and clothing in the European Union and the United States. Unfortunately, most low- and middle-income countries cannot count on such market access. This is the problem we turn to next.

Market Access

Poverty-alleviating trade requires market access for developing-country products, whether in agriculture, manufacturing, or services. Unfortunately, poor people face substantially more trade protection than the nonpoor. Products from developing countries face at least five hurdles in gaining access to foreign markets:

- tariffs
- subsidies
- quotas
- standards and regulations
- security checks.

Tariffs

Tariffs are taxes on imports, imposed to various degrees by all countries of the world. They have the effect of reducing import levels and raising the price of the imported good within the importing country.

Tariff Levels

Poor people face higher tariffs than the nonpoor. For example, for 1998, the World Bank (2002b) compared the effective tariffs faced by poor people and by the nonpoor.[28] The results were that *poor people face effective tariffs that are more than twice as high as those faced by the nonpoor,* an average of 14 percent as opposed to 6 percent. Poor people also face significant tariff peaks in products of export interest to them, where the tariffs are several times the average rate and can range to over 100 percent.[29] There is thus a significant bias in the world trading system against poor people, the more than 2 billion individuals (a billion is 1,000 million) living on less that US$2 per day. These are the people who should be supported, not undermined, by trade policies. As it is, the global tariff system represents a regressive tax on poor people. This is true both for developing countries, where poor people on average face double the barriers, and rich countries, where poor people are most affected by the high cost of food and clothing.

Tariff Escalation

Tariff levels faced by poor people are only one part of **tariff protection.** The rich countries of the world also engage in policies known to trade policy

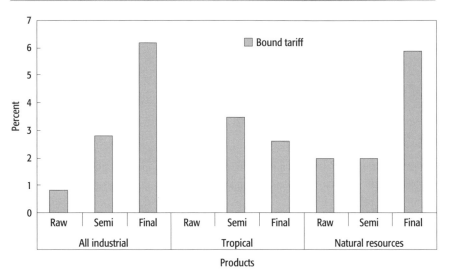

FIGURE 3.3 Tariff Escalation on Developing-Country Exports to Developed Countries (percent)

Source: Laird 2002.

experts as tariff escalation. This means that the rich countries increase their protection with the level of processing or value added in a product. This type of protection, depicted as overall averages in figure 3.3, occurs in food, textiles and clothing, footwear, and wood products—all sectors in which the developing world has the most interest in exporting labor-intensive goods. For example, UNCTAD (2000) has shown that "effective protection doubles in the United States and Canada from the stage of leather industry to that of footwear production" (p. 10). To take another example, the tariff on cocoa beans in the European Union is 1 percent, but the tariff on chocolate is 30 percent.[30] The problem with tariff escalation is that it prevents developing countries from capturing more value added domestically and from vertically diversifying their exports. It also inhibits basic and deep learning processes required for long-term productivity gains, as discussed in the previous section.

Subsidies

Unequal tariff protection is only one component of limited market access for developing countries. Data from the Organisation for Economic Co-operation and Development (OECD) indicate that, since 1986, total support to OECD agriculture has ranged between US$300 billion and US$375 billion, depend-

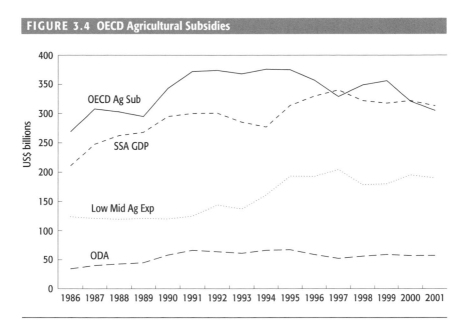

FIGURE 3.4 OECD Agricultural Subsidies

Sources: OECD www.oecd.org/dataoecd; World Bank World Development Indicators.

ing on the year. The bulk of this expenditure has been in the United States, the European Union, and Japan. These data are illustrated in figure 3.4. The solid line at the top of the figure is total OECD agricultural subsidies between 1986 and 2001, the years for which these data are available. The dashed line beneath it is the nominal GDP of Sub-Saharan Africa (SSA). For almost all of the past 20 years, the OECD spent more per year on agricultural subsidies than the entire GDP of Sub-Saharan Africa. The dotted line in the middle of the graph shows the agricultural exports of both low- and middle-income countries. OECD agricultural subsidies are generally approximately twice as large as the entire agricultural exports of developing countries. Finally, the bottom dashed line is official development assistance (ODA). The OECD spends nearly five times the amount spent on ODA on agricultural subsidies.

The information contained in figure 3.4 leads to one important conclusion. In the overall "subsidy war" of global agricultural trade, *developing countries simply do not have anywhere near enough resources to compete.* The notion that one could somehow create a level playing field by equally applying distortions is misguided. The only solution to the subsidy problem is that they be reduced. This is not to suggest that rich OECD countries do not have the right to look after their own rural areas, but when this is done, it should be in a nondistortionary manner. Such policies could be in the form of income subsidies and conservation-specific support. Indeed, from the point of view of either environmental or small-farmer considerations, most agricultural subsidies are harmful. For example, 70 percent of the nitrogen oxide pollution in the European Union is due to agriculture. And although people imagine that EU agricultural subsidies support the goat farmers and other small farmers of Provence, all but a small fraction of the subsidies in the European Union and the United States are captured by large farmers. Protectionism in the European Union, Japan and the United States has a regressive impact because citizens pay on average about US$1000 more per year for their food and textile products than they would if developing countries could have open access to their markets. Protectionism hurts poor people in both rich and poor countries.[31] The detrimental impacts of subsidies and protectionism in developed countries, however, pale in comparison with their effects on the poor in developing countries.

Quotas

Throughout the period following the end of World War II and the liberalization of (some kinds) of trade under the auspices of GATT and WTO, developing countries have faced extensive quota protection in developed-country markets for their agricultural, textile, and clothing exports. These quota systems evolved beginning in the early 1960s and continued in full force through the end of the Uruguay Round in 1994. In the case of agriculture, these quotas were finally replaced by (equally protective) tariffs. In the case of textiles and clothing, the quotas were phased out by 2005, although there have been calls for their extension through 2007. The developing world has suffered through 40 years of extensive quota protection in the very sectors where their comparative advantage tends to be strongest. The case of textiles and clothing is briefly described in box 3.2.

Standards and Regulations

Increasing evidence suggests that developing countries face challenges in gaining market access due to standards and regulations. It is important to recognize that, whereas tariffs and quotas are in almost all cases welfare worsening for the country imposing them, this is not the case with standards and regulations, which have important public goods characteristics. As such, they should not be condemned in general. However, there is growing evidence that, in some cases at least, standards and regulations constitute important nontariff measures.

EU Food Standards

Consider the case of EU food standards. Otsuki, Wilson, and Sewadeh (2001) have examined EU standards for aflatoxin (toxic compounds produced by molds) in food exports from Africa. These authors estimated that these stan-

---

BOX 3.2 Textile and Clothing Protection

Trade protection in the textile and clothing sectors has a long history. It began in the late 1950s when Hong Kong (China), India, Japan, and Pakistan agreed to "voluntary" export restraints for cotton textile products. In 1961, the United States introduced protective quotas in cotton textile trade under the GATT-sponsored Short-Term Arrangement Regarding International Trade in Cotton Textiles (STA). In 1962, the STA was replaced by the Long-Term Arrangement Regarding International Trade in Cotton Textiles (LTA), expanding quota coverage. The LTA was renewed in 1967 and in 1970. In 1974, the Arrangement Regarding International Trade in Textiles or the Multifiber Arrangement (MFA) expanded quota coverage beyond cotton textiles. The MFA was renewed in 1977, in 1981, in 1986, and in 1991. The last extension was through 1994. By some estimates, the MFA cost the developing world about 20 million jobs in lost exports.

In April 1994, the Uruguay Round of multilateral trade negotiations concluded with the signing of the Marrakesh Agreement Establishing the WTO. Developing-country concerns about the textile sector were addressed in the Agreement on Textiles and Clothing (ATC), which composed one component of the Agreement. The ATC was designed to facilitate the re-integration of the textiles and clothing sector into GATT principles for the first time since 1962. This integration was to take place in four stages, concluding with the complete integration of textiles and clothing trade into the GATT at the end of 2004.

Even with the removal of quotas beginning in 2005, textile and clothing protection will remain significant. On average, rich-country tariffs on these products are three times the average tariffs on manufacturing goods, with tariff peaks of up to 40 percent. These tariffs can have perverse effects. For example, as noted by Oxfam (2004b), "In 2001, exports from Bangladesh to the United States generated $331 million in tariff revenue for the U.S. Treasury; in the same year, net U.S. aid to Bangladesh was just $87 million" (p. 1). In addition to these high tariffs, both the United States and the European Union often employ overly restrictive rules of origin in preferential and regional trade agreements, safeguard actions, and unjustified antidumping and antisubsidy duties.

Sources: Reinert 2000; Kim, Reinert, and Rodrigo 2002; and Oxfam 2004b.

---

dards, which would reduce EU health risks by less than 2 deaths per billion per year, would decrease African exports of cereals, dried fruits, and nuts by 64 percent ($US 670 million). EU food standards are currently being tightened to include stringent reporting requirements of developing-country farmers. As reported by Wallace (2004), "new food safety regulations [are] due to come into force in the European Union in 2005. These will make it mandatory for all fruit and vegetable products arriving in the EU to be traceable at all stages of production, processing and distribution" (p. 16). EU assistance to help farmers meet these new, stringent standards that involve tracing production back to the seed is reported to be "inadequate." Consequently, many developing-country farmers risk being closed out of this important market.[32] An additional problem is that the standards are applied in a discriminatory fashion and require specialized skills and equipment beyond the capability of most of the low-income countries.

Facing Rising Standards and Increasing Regulations

If developing countries are to face increases in standards and regulations in rich-country markets, they need to be assisted with capacity building in the areas where standards are applied. We take up capacity building issues below.[33]

Security Checks

Since the attacks in the United States in September 2001, the exports of some developing countries have been subject to increased surveillance and security checks. For some developing countries, such as Pakistan, this has had a negative impact on sustained market access because imports into developed countries have been sourced from other countries seen as more secure. Because countries perceived to be insecure tend to be low-income, there are negative impacts on poverty of these increased security measures.

Trade Protectionism: Costs for Developing Countries

What are the costs of trade protectionism for the developing world? A number of studies have tried to assess this. To take one example, the World Bank (2003a) has considered the impact of a "pro-poor" trade liberalization scenario. This scenario involves *only* tariff reductions and agricultural subsidies reform. The welfare gains to developing countries of this liberalization scenario are estimated to be over US$250 billion in 2003 prices.[34] This is *four times* the value of foreign aid. The number of individuals moved out of poverty (US$2 of income per day) due to this trade liberalization exceeds 100 million. Less rigorous calculations by Oxfam (2002a) also conclude that more than 100 million persons can be moved out of poverty by increased trade. Both studies conclude that a significant part of this poverty reduction would occur in Sub-Saharan Africa. Thus, a *very* conservative estimate of the costs of protectionism to the developing world would be an additional 100 million persons moved out of poverty—a significant number.

The Primary Product Problem

If the exports of developing countries are to support the incomes of their poor residents, the incomes generated by those exports must increase over time. Export incomes can increase in three ways: increases in export quality, increases in export quantities, and increases in export prices. Many developing countries depend on the exports of a small number of natural-resource-based goods known as **primary commodities.** Examples are aluminum, coffee, leather, rubber, and sugar. By their very nature, primary commodities are characterized by low levels of value added and limited room for quality improve-

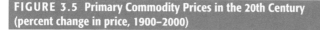

FIGURE 3.5 Primary Commodity Prices in the 20th Century
(percent change in price, 1900–2000)

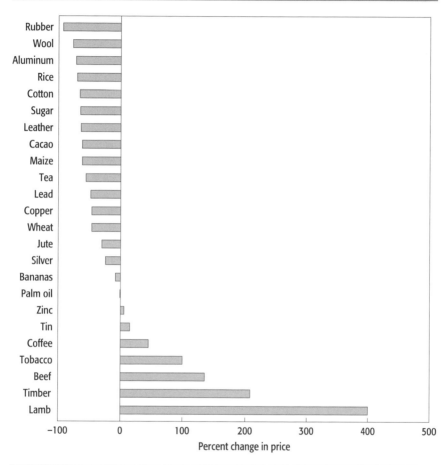

Source: Ocampo and Parra 2003.

ment. Unfortunately, they are also characterized by a century-long downward trend in export prices.

Commodity Prices

Consider figure 3.5, which presents data on primary commodity prices during the 20th century. Seventeen of the 24 primary commodities in this figure experienced declines, most of them of significant magnitude. In addition, and as reported in Ocampo and Parra (2003), an overall index of food products fell by 50 percent, an index of nonfood products fell by 15 percent, an index of metals fell by 7 percent, and the well-known *Economist* commodity price index fell by 60 percent.[35] Evidence suggests that the period since 1980 has been characterized by particularly steep price declines.

Commodity Price Declines

Declines in commodity prices can be disastrous for the very poor. As noted by UNCTAD (2004), "the major sin of omission in the current international approach to poverty reduction is the failure to tackle the link between commodity dependence and extreme poverty" (p. xii). For example, recent declines in coffee prices to a 30-year low (not recorded in figure 3.5) have caused death from malnutrition in Guatemala where such tragedies had been thought to have been a thing of the past. In Ethiopia, where coffee accounts for approximately one-half of export revenues, coffee farmers have been forced to shift to the production of *chat,* a stimulant used in the region around the Red Sea. Overall, Oxfam (2002b) estimates that the livelihoods of 25 million coffee farmers are under threat due to these recent declines in coffee prices.

Impact of Protectionist Policies

It is very difficult for developing countries to overcome these secular trends in commodity prices. However, the protectionist policies of the rich world make it more difficult than it needs to be.

- First, the agricultural subsidies discussed above contribute to declines in world prices for these goods.
- Second, tariff escalation makes it difficult for developing counties to escape primary product traps by vertically diversifying their exports along value chains toward greater value added to commodities (for example, from cacao to chocolate).
- Third, manufactures protection of the type described above (for example, in textiles and clothing) tends to concentrate developing countries in primary commodities, limiting horizontal diversification out of primary community exports, thereby exacerbating commodity price declines and contributing to the instability of export revenues.
- Finally, limited market access increases the uncertainty developing countries face with regard to future protection levels as does the unpredictable management of quotas and phyto-sanitary and other non-tariff barriers; this reduces investor confidence in both primary and non-traditional productive sectors.[36]

For these reasons, protection levels are doubly damaging to the world's poor.

Impact of Foreign Aid

It is also necessary for foreign aid to take into account the limited prospects for primary commodities. Hard thinking about realistic alternatives to rural development must yield alternative routes to support incomes of the poor over the long term. This is no easy task. Until such alternatives are found, the promotion of "fair trade" commodities that ensure the maximum value for developing-country producers and help develop niche markets can play a useful role in mitigating the negative effects of price declines in some important cases.[37]

Trade-Related Capacity Building

Market access for developing country exports is an important step in allowing for poverty-reducing international trade. However, market access must be combined with efforts to promote export *capacity* in low- and middle-income countries. These capacity constraints are multidimensional and include infrastructure, market information, skills, and credit. For example, the promotion of capacity can assist "an Algerian diplomat to negotiate his country's WTO accession, and an Indonesian civil servant to prepare a legislative proposal on copyrights, or a Mali exporter to understand business implications of the WTO Agreement on Textiles" (Kostecki 2001, p. 4). In the past, efforts to relax these constraints occurred under what was known as *trade-related technical assistance.* However, more recent appreciation of capacity constraints has motivated a change of focus to what is now known as *trade-related capacity building.* There is also a recognition that trade-related capacity building relies, at least to some significant extent, on outside assistance, making this an issue of foreign aid.

Aid and Trade: A Complementary Relationship

Most discussions of aid and trade view them as substitutes for one another, with trade being the favored of the two. It is indeed true that, from a poverty-alleviation standpoint, trade can play a much larger and sustained role than aid. That said, however, it is important to appreciate the potential complementary relationship between aid and trade, what is sometimes called "aid for trade."[38] Indeed, trade policy experts now recognize that, without such assistance, developing countries will not be able to exploit the market access that is available to them.39

Needs of Developing Countries: Capacity Building

If aid for trade is conceived of as trade-related capacity building that is responsive to developing countries' needs, can we say something about what those needs are, at least in general terms? In international forums of various kinds, the developing countries have requested assistance in the following areas:

- Better representation in international organizations related to trade such as the WTO.
- Improving infrastructure such as roads, ports, and customs to facilitate exports.
- Upgrading negotiating capacities of trade ministries, including training in WTO legal matters and accession processes.
- Efforts to promote diversification of exports to escape the primary product problems described above.
- Upgrading systems to meet the increasing standards and regulations in developed-country exports markets.
- Developing information systems regarding potential export markets.

Efforts to meets some of these needs in the case of the least-developed countries in the form of the Integrated Framework are described in box 3.3.

Promises of the Developed Countries and the WTO

It is fair to say that, while making onerous demand on the developing world to meet strenuous WTO commitments, the developed world has not met its promises to provide trade-related capacity building.[40] Some initiatives have been ongoing, including the Advisory Centre on WTO Law, the Swiss-funded Agency for International Trade Information and Cooperation, and the Canadian-funded Centre for Trade Policy and Law, and the International Trade Centre's World Tr@de Net. Despite these initiatives, evidence suggests that the major players in trade policy formation have a long way to go in providing adequate trade-related capacity building. The review of Kostecki (2001), for example, suggests that greater emphasis must be placed on genuine needs assessment and beneficiary orientation, sufficient funding, escaping bureaucratic restrictions through arm's-length delivery organizations, and a reevaluation of the professional qualifications of capacity-building staff. There has been progress in this area, but much remains to be done if trade-related capacity building is to fulfill its promise.

Health and Safety

We mentioned in the introduction that, to help poor people, trade activities need to support forming human capital in the forms of education, training, and health. There are cases in which trade activities (both imports and exports) can actually undermine human capital by compromising the health and safety of the poor. In the case of imports, a notable example is arms, which can have disas-

BOX 3.3 The Integrated Framework

One example of trade-related capacity building that focuses on the least-developed countries (LDCs) is the Integrated Framework or IF. The roots of the IF lie in the 1996 Singapore Ministerial Meeting of the WTO, which adopted a plan of action for the least-developed countries. This plan of action called for "closer cooperation between the WTO and other multilateral agencies assisting least-developed countries" in trade-related matters. Subsequently, a consensus emerged that the WTO should work with the International Monetary Fund (IMF), the World Bank, the United Nations Conference on Trade and Development (UNCTAD), the International Trade Centre (ITC), and the United Nations Development Programme (UNDP) in the Integrated Framework. The precipitating event in this consensus was a high-level meeting on least-developed countries, convened by the WTO in October 1997.

Originally, the IF planned to address trade-related capacity building needs through a twofold process of needs assessment and round table discussion. Despite early enthusiasm and 40 completed needs assessments, by the end of 1999, only five roundtables had been held (Bangladesh, The Gambia, Haiti, Tanzania, and Uganda), only one of which had been considered to be successful (Uganda).

Representatives of the six IF agencies met in New York in July 2001 and issued a joint communiqué suggesting a redesign of the IF. The "new IF" involved LDCs in "mainstreaming" trade into their development policies through a "trade integration chapter" that was to be included in their Poverty Reduction Strategy Papers (PRSPs) submitted to the World Bank and IMF. Additionally, three of the six IF agencies agreed to take lead roles: the World Bank as lead agency for "mainstreaming," the WTO as secretariat, and the UNDP as manager of an IF Trust Fund (IFTF).

LDCs chosen to participate in the IF engage in a process known as "diagnostic trade integration studies" or DTIS. This process consists of five components: a review and analysis of the country's economic and export performance; an assessment of the country's macroeconomic and investment climate; an assessment of the international policy environment and specific constraints that exports from each country face in world markets; an analysis of key labor-intensive sectors where there is a potential for output and export expansion; and a "propoor trade integration strategy," with proposed policy reforms and action plans.

Support of the IF process by the IFSC was reaffirmed in July 2003. Diagnostic studies have been undertaken in 21 countries with a further 16 in the pipeline. Financial commitments to the process continued to grow to reach US$13 million by 2005. The IF donors have summed up some of the most important goals of trade-related capacity building as follows: "We stand ready to help developing countries and LDCs engage in the multilateral trading system. Removing supply-side constraints to trade is important in generating a response to market access opportunities. We will step up assistance on trade-related infrastructure, private sector development and institution building to help countries to expand their export base." To achieve this end, it has been estimated that a further US$200 to US$400 would be required in IF grants.

Source: The Integrated Framework for Trade-Related Technical Assistance to Least-Developed Countries, http://www. integratedframework.org/.

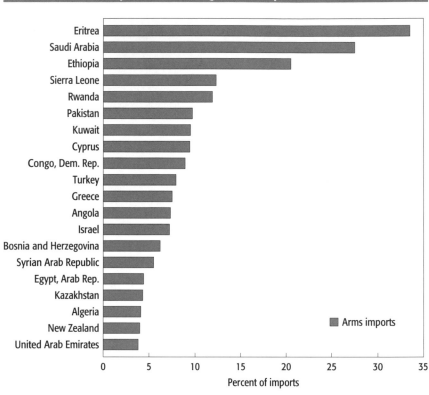

FIGURE 3.6 Arms Imports as a Percentage of Total Imports, 1999

Source: World Bank, *World Development Indicators* CD-ROM.

trous impacts on the safety of citizens in the importing country. Another example is imports of toxic waste. In the case of exports, some production processes can compromise the health of the workers producing the exported products.

Trade in Arms

Despite the pressing human-development needs of poor countries, arms can compose a large part of low- and middle-income country imports. It is not unusual for arms to constitute 10 percent of developing country imports, and these can exceed even 20 percent in some cases (see figure 3.6). Civil conflicts and other forms of violence in poor countries have been estimated to result in an annual loss of at least a half million lives; conflict tends to result in development in reverse.[41] Approaches to regulate the global arms trade to conflict zones therefore require serious consideration.[42]

Trade in Hazardous Waste

Similar health and safety issues can arise through the imports of hazardous waste, which can cause serious environmental effects as well.[43] These harmful effects can be long term as well as immediate and can impose economic costs. Importing hazardous waste into poor countries is motivated by lower disposal costs in those countries, as well as by growing opposition to disposal in rich countries. In contrast to the case of arms trade, however, there is already a multilateral agreement governing hazardous waste trade—the Basel Convention on the Control of Trans-boundary Movements in Hazardous Wastes and their Disposal. This was signed in 1989 and entered into force in 1992. Although the Basel Convention has not been without controversies and disagreements, it has nevertheless been important in controlling hazardous waste trade, and it is in the process of improving compliance efforts with a central office and staff.[44] Similar efforts need to be made in the area of arms trade.

Export Production Processes and Health

There are cases in which the export production processes compromise the health of workers.

The export of Nemagon, an insecticide used in banana production, is a case in point.[45] This insecticide was banned in 1979 in the United States because it causes skin diseases, sterility, and birth defects. Despite this, it was used in Central American banana production through the 1980s and, in some cases, through the mid-1990s. Banana workers in Central America began to report many severe symptoms, including anencephaly, a malformation in which conceived fetuses fail to develop brains. This issue is still current. In 2004, over 1,000 affected Nicaraguan workers marched to their capital city, Managua, to demand compensation, and similar concerns were voiced in Honduras and in some cut flower export industries of Colombia and Ecuador, again involving the use of insecticides. In Ecuador, for example, Thomson (2003) reports that "studies that the International Labour Organization published in 1999 and the Catholic University issued here last year showed that women in the industry had more miscarriages than average and that more than 60 percent of all workers suffered headaches, nausea, blurred vision or fatigue."

The health threat of pesticides that do not meet international standards in both export and domestic industries is an issue that has gained the attention of the World Health Organization (WHO). According to its estimates (2001a), nearly one-third of the pesticides marketed in developing countries do not meet international standards. These "frequently contain hazardous substances and impurities that have already been banned or severely restricted elsewhere" or "the active ingredient concentrations are outside internationally accepted tolerance limits." The WHO calls upon all governments and international and regional organizations to adopt the World Health Organization/Food and Agricultural Organization pesticide specifications to help alleviate these health threats. Again, greater multilateral efforts are needed.

Cost of Generating Income: Health and Safety Compromised

In all these cases, a similar issue arises. Although trade activities typically generate incomes and other potential benefits for poor people, health and safety may be compromised, sometimes seriously. From a development perspective, this is a trade-off to be avoided if at all possible. The alleviation of income deprivation by increasing health deprivation is not an escape from income poverty but an exacerbation of health deprivation. In these instances, trade cannot be claimed to be fully alleviating poverty.

Illegal Trade

As Moisés Naim (2005) has highlighted, increased globalization has been associated with an escalation of illicit trade. Increased trade and movement of people, together with technological advances in financial markets, communication and transport, have been exploited by criminals to what Naim warns are unprecedented levels. He estimates that money laundering exceeds US$1 billion per year; the illegal drug trade US$800 billion; counterfeiting US$400 billion; illegal arms sales US$10 billion; cross-border human trafficking US$10 billion; and cross-border sales of art US$3 billion. These figures suggest that illegal flows account for as much as 20 percent of trade. Naim emphasizes the interconnected nature of illegal flows (for example, the money laundering of drug sales), and of legal and illegal flows (for example, drugs concealed in shipping containers). The challenge is to control illicit flows while preserving the underlying benefits of increased trade and globalization. The need for enhanced security and regulation carries the risk of adding considerable friction to the movement, not only of goods and services, but also of financial flows and migration.

Conclusions

The link between trade and poverty alleviation is not automatic. However, trade has been a powerful force for poverty alleviation in a number of ways. Exports can expand markets, helping to generate incomes for the poor. Both imports and exports can promote competition, lowering consumption and production costs in the face of monopoly (single seller) power, and raising prices for suppliers in the case of monopsony (single buyer) power. Both imports and exports can support productivity improvements through access to new machinery and contact with discerning international customers. Imports are also important for health aspects of human development, because many medical supplies need to be imported to combat deprivations of health.

Trade Protectionism: A Barrier to Alleviating Poverty

The possibility of exports helping to alleviate poverty is significantly curtailed by trade protectionism in rich countries. This occurs in the form of tariffs, subsidies, quotas, standards, and regulations. Even conservative estimates of the potential gains from reducing protectionism in rich countries are many times the size of annual foreign aid flows. Rich-country protectionism poses a significant barrier to poverty alleviation, not to mention the overall participation of the developing world in the global economy.

Commodity Price Declines

Developing countries relying on the export of primary commodities have suffered from a century-long decline in primary commodity prices that continues to this day. Although export diversification is one way to lessen the effects of such commodity price declines, the impact of these secular trends is exacerbated by rich-country protectionism. Agricultural subsidies and tariff escalation are particularly pernicious in this regard.

Capacity Building

For trade to benefit poor people, increases in market access for developing countries must be combined with trade-related capacity building. These capacity-building efforts are often *prerequisites* for developing countries to overcome supply constraints, and this is an area where trade and aid act as positive complements. As new thinking in development policy stresses, capacity building should be beneficiary-driven and partnership-based, strive to develop local capacities and skills, and place trade issues in a broader development perspective.[46] These include considerations of the broader business and investment environment (the "software"—including questions of health, education, governance, and corruption) as well as the physical infrastructure (the "hardware"—including roads, power, water, and ports). Both these broad areas of action are vital for governments and aid agencies alike.

Trade: Impact on Health and Safety of the Poor

In some cases, trade can have a very direct and negative impact on the health and safety of the poor. This occurs with imports of arms and toxic waste and also with production processes of exports that compromise the health of workers. In each of these cases, concrete, multilateral steps need to be taken to ensure that trade does not compromise poverty reduction and human development but supports it.

Trade Liberalization

We have shown in this chapter that trade reform in both rich and developing countries has a vital role to play in ensuring that globalization benefits the poor. The movement of economies toward more trade-oriented profiles typically involves processes of trade liberalization, often under the auspices of the WTO, the World Bank, the IMF, or regional trade agreements. As emphasized by Harrison, Rutherford, and Tarr (2003); Winters, McCulloch, and McKay (2004); and UNCTAD (2004), the transition costs associated with these reforms can be significant and may actually worsen poverty for some classes of households. For this reason, as developing countries consider the role that increased trade can play in poverty alleviation, they need to guard against the real possibility of increasing the poverty of some groups. Safety nets (social protection), complementary antipoverty programs, and direct compensation might be necessary to achieve poverty-alleviating transitions.[47] Again, trade reform is vital but should be placed within a comprehensive approach to overcoming poverty.

Notes

1. The fact that the trade–poverty alleviation link is not automatic has also been stressed by UNCTAD (2004) in the case of the least-developed countries.
2. In this chapter, we are in broad agreement with the assessment of Oxfam (2002a), that "In itself, trade is not inherently opposed to the interests of poor people. International trade can be a force for good, or for bad. . . . The outcomes are not pre-determined. They are shaped by the way in which international trade relations are managed, and by national policies" (p. 28).
3. To make this observation is not to downplay the exploitation that can often occur in export sectors, such as 14-hour days. Labor standards do matter. But it is decidedly *not* the case that exploitation is absent from agricultural day labor. We will discuss these issues in more detail, especially health and safety concerns.
4. Readers are probably familiar with the notion of a *monopolist*—a single seller in a market that can increase the price of its product above the competitive level to the detriment of buyers in the market. A *monopsonist* is a single buyer in a market that can lower the price of the product it purchases below the competitive level to the detriment of sellers in the market.
5. See Kapur and Ramamurti (2001), for example. These authors show that the large and fast-growing software market within the United States with its sophisticated software buyers has contributed significantly to the competitiveness of the Indian software sector. The remaining issue, however, is the extent to which the expansion of incomes generated by the Indian software industry supports the incomes of poor Indians. In this instance the answer might be "only a little."
6. See Cragg and Epelbaum (1996), chapter 5 of de Ferranti and others (2002), Gindling and Robbins (2001), and Robbins and Gindling (1999). For the case of South Africa, see Edwards (2004). More generally, Winters, McCulloch, and McKay (2004) note that "trade liberalization may be accompanied by skill-biased technical change, which can mean the skilled labor may benefit relative to unskilled labor" (p. 75).
7. A *value chain* is a series of value-added processes involved in the production of a good or service.
8. To be fair, there are also market access issues *between* developing countries that are becoming increasingly important as what international economists call "South-South trade" increases. See, for example, World Bank (2002b) and Laird (2002).
9. See, for example, Reinert (2004).
10. See, for example, Lipton (2005).

11. Minot and Goletti (2000) report that "Rice production in Vietnam is characterized by small irrigated farms, multiple cropping, labor-intensive practices, and growing use of inorganic fertilizer, though there are substantial regional differences" (p. xi). Average farm size is only 0.25 hectares.

12. See Minot and Goletti (1998, and 2000) as well as chapter 2 of Oxfam (2002a). The latter does note that "the advances (in Vietnam) have been unevenly distributed, and many of the poorest producers lack access to the marketing infrastructure and productive resources needed to take advantage of export opportunities" (p. 53). Similar conclusions are provided by Jenkins (2004). On the impact on child labor, see Edmonds and Pavcnik (2002).

13. Zohir (2001) did raise concerns about the effect of garment-sector work on women's health and the increased risk of harassment. We take up health and safety issues in their own right later in the chapter.

14. On the procompetitive effects of trade, see Markusen (1981).

15. A 2000 study by the TeleCommons Development Group (TDG) of Canada found that "the consumer surplus from a single phone call to Dhaka, a call that replaces the physical trip to the city, ranges from 2.64 percent to 9.8 percent of the mean monthly household income. The cost of a trip to the city ranges from 2 to 8 times the cost of a single phone call, meaning real savings for poor rural people of between 132 to 490 Taka (USD 2.70 to USD 10) for individual calls" (Grameen Phone, www.grameenphone.com).

16. See Bayes, von Braun, and Akhter (1999).

17. Again, see Bayes, von Braun, and Akhter (1999).

18. See Winters (2000) and Poulton and others (2004). Recent economic setbacks in Zimbabwe have dramatically erased gains associate with trade liberalization.

19. See Winters (2000) and Jayne and others (1995).

20. For a review of the evidence on trade liberalization and productivity, see Winters, McCulloch, and McKay (2004).

21. As emphasized by Bruton (1998), "For the development objective, the main role of exports is its possible contribution to the acquisition of new technical knowledge and consequent increase in productivity through contact with foreign importers combined with the pressures of strong competition" (p. 924). The same can be said of imports. There is a tradition in international economic policy of claiming a great deal for exports in terms of resulting productivity gains. For a critical review of this tradition, see chapter 2 of Rodrik (1999).

22. As emphasized by Szirmai (2005), "the most important contribution of education is indeed 'learning to learn' " (p. 221).

23. On the presence of productivity increases in agriculture, see Martin and Mitra (2001). On the role of services in supporting productivity increases in manufacturing, see Francois and Reinert (1996).

24. See, for example, Lall (1998).

25. It is important to emphasize that basic education is only a necessary but not a sufficient condition for learning. Indeed, measures of human capital such as average years of schooling explain very little of the variation among developing countries in either low-technology manufacturing exports or high-technology manufacturing exports.

26. The equivalent of local content requirements is still included in government procurement, however. One example is the South African government's agreement for military aircraft with Airbus. See Odell (2004).

27. See, for just one example, Rodrigo (2001).

28. The assumption here is that poor people earn their incomes from labor-intensive merchandise production, while the nonpoor earn their incomes across the full array of economic activities. The "poor" are defined as those living on less than US$2 per day. See chapter 2.

29. This point is made by Laird (2002), among others.

30. See US Foreign Agricultural Service (2003).

31. See Messerlin (2001); Goldin and Winters (1995); and www.oecd.org/statisticsdata.

32. See also Barnes (2004).

33. For a further discussion of standards and regulations issues, see Wilson (2002). This author notes that "relatively little is known about the cost impacts of differing product standards and how they affect exporters in developing countries" (p. 436).

34. This figure includes "static" gains only; "dynamic" gains that reflect growth effects are much higher. These dynamic gains reflect alleged productivity gains that are the result of increased exports. However, the magnitude of these dynamic gains is uncertain.

35. For the century and a half between 1850 and 2003, *The Economist's* commodity price index fell by 80 percent. See *The Economist* (2004a).

36. Francois and Martin (2002) note that foreign market access security "serves to reduce uncertainty for foreign investors about the ability of an economy to link itself with the global economy and hence to generate returns that can ultimately be repatriated" (p. 545).

37. See Raynolds (2000) and references therein. The "fair trade" designation is the responsibility of the Fairtrade Labelling Organizations International (FLO). While we support the goals of this effort with respect to maximizing the incomes of poor people, we do not embrace some of its general, antimarket statements.

38. The subject of aid for trade actually overlaps with two other chapters of this book: chapter 5 on aid and chapter 7 on ideas. Aid for trade and trade-related capacity building are development ideas that are effected through foreign aid.

39. One example is the generalized system of preferences (GSP) granted the least-developed countries (LDCs) by the developed world. As observed by Inama (2002), "Almost 30 years of experience with trade preferences, and particularly with the GSP schemes, have largely demonstrated that the mere granting of duty-free market access to a wide range of LDCs' products does not automatically ensure that the trade preferences will be effectively utilized by beneficiary countries" (p. 114).

40. As noted by Kostecki (2001), "Most of the WTO provisions calling for . . . technical assistance are 'best endeavour' promises which are not binding on donor countries" (pp. 11–12).

41. Former World Bank president James Wolfensohn (2002), for example, highlighted that "the world's leading industrial nations provide nearly 90 percent of the multibillion dollar arms trade—arms that are contributing to the very conflicts that all of us profess to deplore, and that we must spend additional monies to suppress" (p. 12).

42. The Commission for Africa (2005) and the United Kingdom Foreign Secretary have recently highlighted the need for further progress in this area, as have organizations such as Oxfam, Amnesty International, and the International Action Network on Small Arms. See, for example, www.iansa.org.

43. Krueger (2001) writes that "Hazardous waste can range from materials contaminated with dioxins and heavy metals, such as mercury, cadmium, or lead, to organic wastes. The waste may take many forms, from barrels of liquid waste to sludge, old computer parts, used batteries, or incinerator ash" (p. 43).

44. For a concise but detailed review of the Basel Convention, see Krueger (2001).

45. Nemagon is derived from debromochloropropane (DBCP) and kills a nematode that damages banana production.

46. See World Bank (2005d and e), and UNCTAD (2004).

47. As Winters, McCulloch, and McKay (2004) note, "Such polices are likely to be desirable even in the absence of trade reform, but they might become more important if trade reforms do have important adjustment effects on the poor or near poor. . . . (I)t is preferable for there to be a careful analysis of each country's circumstances so that appropriate 'flanking' mechanisms can be derived to accompany the liberalization" (pp. 107–108).

4

Finance

Global financial flows are an important resource for developing countries. These capital flows augment domestic savings and can contribute to investment, growth, financial sector development, *technology transfer,* and poverty reduction. These possibilities are reflected in the long-standing view in international economics that capital flows are beneficial in almost all circumstances. This view is backed by evidence suggesting that the growth gains from capital flows are of the same order of magnitude as the growth gains from trade.[1] However, there is also evidence that capital flows may entail potential costs that are both larger than in the case of trade and tend to be disproportionately carried by poor people.[2] Additionally, it has become clear that not all capital flows are the same in their benefit and cost characteristics. For these reasons, a careful assessment of the impact of capital flows on global poverty does not lend itself to across-the-board statements. Rather, the cost and benefit characteristics of distinct types of capital flows must be considered in some detail.

Capital Flows and Balance of Payments

From a macroeconomic standpoint, capital flows are activities that influence the "capital account" of countries' *balance of payments* involving the exchange of assets, whereas trade activities influence the "current account" of the balance of payments where no assets are exchanged. Both of these components of the balance of payments accounts record transactions between each country and the rest of the world. The assets exchanged on the *capital account* of the balance of payments consist of various financial objects with monetary values that can change over time in the portfolios of both individuals and firms.[3]

Capital Flows: Classifications

There are a number of legitimate ways to classify capital flows and various subcomponents of the capital account. In this chapter, we will distinguish among four types:

- foreign direct investment
- equity portfolio investment
- bond finance
- commercial bank lending.

Foreign Direct Investment

Foreign direct investment (FDI) is the acquisition of shares by a firm in a foreign-based enterprise that exceeds a threshold of 10 percent, implying managerial participation in the foreign enterprise.[4] FDI is one means of effecting services trade, such as when a bank uses a foreign subsidiary to provide financial services abroad, but is also important in the production of merchandise. Under the right conditions, FDI can generate direct and indirect increases in employment, promote competition, improve the training of host-country workers, and transfer technology from developed to developing countries. It may also subject workers to unsafe working conditions, compromise the natural environment, and increase the dominance of foreign culture over host-country cultures.[5]

Equity Portfolio Investment

Equity portfolio investment is similar to FDI in that it involves the ownership of shares in foreign countries. It differs from FDI in that the share holdings are too small to imply managerial participation over the foreign enterprise. It is thus *indirect* investment, rather than direct investment. Because equity portfolio investment is undertaken for portfolio reasons rather than managerial reasons, the behavior of investors can be quite different than with FDI. To generalize, equity portfolio investment tends to be motivated by a shorter time horizon than FDI's horizon and is subject to the portfolio considerations of investors.

Bond Finance

Bond finance or *debt issuance* is a second kind of portfolio activity. In a bond finance transaction, the government or firms in developing countries issue bonds to foreign investors. These bonds can be issued in either the domestic currency or in foreign currencies, and can involve different kinds of default risks. Bond portfolio investment has in common with equity portfolio investment that both are held along with equities in international portfolios. Port-

KEY TERMS AND CONCEPTS

absorptive capacity
backward links
balance of payments
bond finance
capital account
commercial bank lending
contagion

equity portfolio investment
flight capital
foreign direct investment (FDI)
market failure
microfinance institutions (MFIs)
technology transfer

folio considerations and their relatively short-term characteristics are therefore important to both. Indeed, they are often combined in simple balance of payments accounts under the heading of "portfolio investment."

Commercial Bank Lending

Commercial bank lending is another form of debt. Unlike bond finance, it does not involve a tradable asset.[6] Commercial bank loans can be short-term or long-term loans, can be made with fixed or flexible interest rates, and can take the form of inter-bank loans. A single bank or a syndicate of banks can be involved in any particular loan package. As we discuss in this chapter, commercial bank lending can potentially play a role in financial crises.

Impact of Capital Flows

Although FDI can affect poor people directly by generating employment and transferring technology, much of the potential impact of other capital flows on poverty is indirect, taking place through the broad process of financial development. For this reason, before taking up the individual categories of capital flows and their potential impacts on poor people in the rest of this chapter, we consider both the recent trends in capital flows to the developing world and the overall process of financial development.

Recent Trends

To understand the role of capital flows in the economies of developing countries, as well as their implications for poor people, we need to look at their evolution over time. In chapter 2, we noted the volatile nature of debt and equity relative to FDI. Here we distinguish among four types of capital flows: FDI, equity portfolio investment, bond portfolio investment, and commercial bank lending.

Capital Flows to Low-Income Countries

When we consider these flows for the low-income countries (figure 4.1), a number of important observations can be made.

Commercial Bank Lending as Primary Source

First, until the 1990s, commercial bank lending was the primary source of foreign capital for the low-income countries, although it declined significantly after the 1982 debt crisis. On a net basis, bank lending remained positive during the 1990s but then became negative in 1998 after the Asian financial crisis (box 4.1). This reflected the drastic decline in access to commercial bank funds suffered by the low-income countries and their continued payments of old commercial bank debt. This net outflow continued until 2003, when commercial bank lending again became positive.

Increase in Significance of FDI

Second, although FDI comprised a significant portion of total capital inflows to the low-income countries in the 1970s, it became even more significant in the 1990s, far exceeding commercial bank lending. Despite its stagnation after

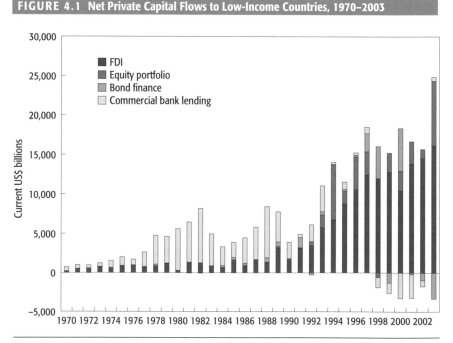

FIGURE 4.1 Net Private Capital Flows to Low-Income Countries, 1970–2003

Source: World Bank 2005b.

Balance of payments, debt, and financial crises have plagued the developing world with detrimental impacts for poor people. One notable crisis of the 1980s was that of Mexico. The decade of the 1980s began with a significant increase in real interest rates and a significant decline in non-oil commodity prices. These increased borrowing costs and reduced export revenues for many developing countries, including Mexico. In August 1982, in the face of capital flight, the Mexican government announced that it would stop servicing its foreign currency debt. Subsequently, both Argentina and Brazil entered into similar debt and balance of payments crises.

Despite the efforts of the International Monetary Fund to effectively address these crises, international commercial banks began to withdraw credit from many of the developing countries of the world, and the debt crisis became global. Within a few years of the outbreak of these crises, the phenomenon of net capital outflows appeared in which the capital account payments of debtor countries exceeded their capital account receipts. Poverty increased substantially, and much of the developing world, particularly Latin America and Africa, entered what came to be known as *the lost decade.*

Mexico underwent a second crisis in late 1994 and early 1995, and this was soon followed by the "Asian crisis." Beginning in July 1997, crises struck Thailand, Indonesia, the Republic of Korea, and Malaysia, and in August 1998, a crisis also hit Russia. In each of these cases, sharp depreciations of the currencies resulted. Subsequent crises hit Brazil in 1999 and Argentina in 2001, bringing the crisis process back to Latin America again.

Eichengreen (1999) makes a distinction between "low-tech" debt and balance of payments crises such as those of the 1980s and "high-tech" financial crises of the 1990s. According to Eichengreen, the following features distinguish the latter, more recent crises: 1. Financial firms have significant exposures in real estate and equities; 2. Capital accounts are liberalized to allow firms (including banks) to take on short-term foreign debt, including debt denominated in foreign currencies; 3. Banks are less than fully regulated and supervised as the countries involved liberalize financial markets and capital accounts; and 4. Firms (including banks) do not adequately hedge their foreign exchange exposures, resulting in vulnerable financial positions. Policy makers need to be aware of each of these potential causes to better mitigate the risks poor people suffer when hit by the effects of crises.

Source: Authors.

the 1997 Asian crisis, FDI remains the most important source of foreign capital flows for the poorest nations of the world, increasing in the 2001 to 2003 period. As we will see in this chapter, however, these FDI flows are both small relative to the total population of the low-income countries and very unevenly distributed among them.

Unreliability of Portfolio Investment

Third, portfolio investment in the form of bonds and equities has been a signigicant although somewhat fickle source of resources for the low-income countries. These investments provided substantial positive net flows for a few years in the 1990s, and took on a negative value after the Asian crisis. As noted by Prasad and others (2003), "FDI flows are the least volatile of the different categories of private capital flows to developing countries. . . . Portfolio flows tend to be far more volatile and prone to abrupt reversals than FDI" (p. 16). This was indeed the case for the low-income countries after the Asian crisis, but their net portfolio equity inflows recovered in 2003.

Capital Flows to Middle-Income Countries

Capital flows to the middle-income countries (figure 4.2) have behaved some-what differently than those to the low-income countries. Again, in the early years, commercial bank lending was the most important source of foreign capital. This type of lending was reduced after the 1982 Mexican crisis, and FDI began to replace it in the late 1980s. As with the low-income countries, despite some stagnation after the 1997 Asian crisis, FDI currently dwarfs all other sources of capital flows to the middle-income countries. Commercial bank lending and portfolio bond and equity flows were important during the 1990s.[7] Portfolio bond flows held up better after the Asian crisis than they did

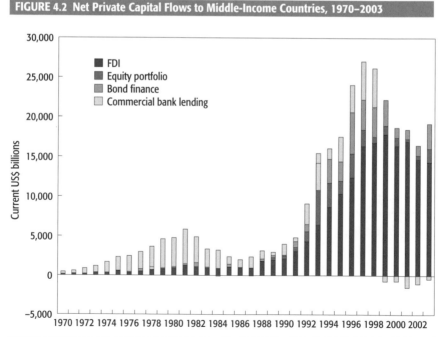

FIGURE 4.2 Net Private Capital Flows to Middle-Income Countries, 1970–2003

Source: World Bank 2005b.

in the low-income countries, and these flows recovered substantially from 2003; in the low-income countries equity investment is currently more important. However, on a net basis for the middle-income countries, currently none of these three, nondirect capital flows is large compared with FDI.[8]

Reasons for Increase in Capital Flows

What explains the significant increase in capital flows to the developing world beginning in the 1990s? Analysts such as Calvo, Leiderman, and Reinhart (1996) and de la Torre and Schmukler (2004) typically divide explanations into internal or "pull" factors and external or "push" factors. Internal factors included improved relationships between developing countries and their creditors, the pursuit of more sound fiscal and monetary policies, capital account liberalization, and the privatization of state-owned assets.[9] External factors included the decline in world interest rates that made assets in developing countries relatively more attractive for portfolio investments, recessions in major developed countries, and a growing integration of world capital markets. This last external factor involved the increased participation of global financial firms in developing-country markets and the increased role of institutional investors. As such, trade in financial services supported expansions in capital flows, with the trade and capital flow dimensions of globalization interacting to support the expansion in private capital flows. All of these factors changed the global capital flow regime in significant ways.

Capital Flows as a Percentage of GDP

It is useful to consider the recent history of total capital flows to the developing countries as a percentage of GDP for both low- and middle-income countries (figure 4.3). Until the 1990s, these ranged between 1 and 2 percent of GDP. During the 1990s, for the reasons just described, these values increased to a maximum of just over 2 percent and 5 percent of GDP for the low- and middle-income countries, respectively. The flows fell precipitously as a percentage of GDP for the middle-income countries after the 1997 Asian crisis, however. Private capital flows are therefore relatively small as a percentage of developing country GDP and somewhat volatile. Over the last three decades, capital flows have increased only slightly as a percentage of GDP for the developing world.

Summary of Evolution of Capital Flows

To summarize, before the late 1980s, commercial bank lending was an important source of foreign capital. Since then, however, FDI has become the most important capital flow for both the low- and middle-income countries. To a

FIGURE 4.3 Net Private Capital Flows to Low- and Middle-Income Countries as a Percentage of GDP, 1970–2003

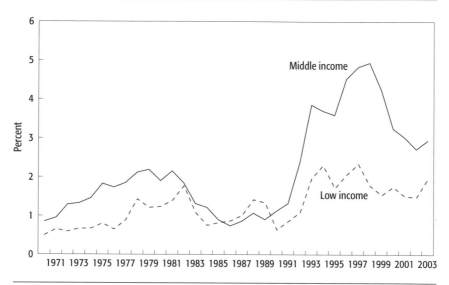

Source: World Bank 2005b.

significant extent, this reflected mergers and acquisitions in response to the privatization that began in the late 1980s. FDI has become somewhat stagnant for both low- and middle-income countries in recent years. However, as noted by Mody (2004), "during a period when portfolio flows boomed and then crashed, FDI remained a resilient form of external finance" (p. 1218). Commercial bank lending and portfolio bond and equity flows experienced something of a renaissance during the early 1990s, but they are not currently significant sources of capital for the developing world. When these flows have been significant, they have been more volatile than FDI flows.[10]

Financial Development

A basic, theoretical insight in the field of international finance suggests that flows of capital from developed to developing countries can improve welfare for the countries' populations.[11] Developing countries can receive net inflows of capital and invest it at relatively high rates of return, the capital being supplied from developed countries where rates of return are relatively low. This reflects the fact that, at early stages of development, the need for capital is high, while domestic saving is low. As development proceeds, the need for capital slowly declines and domestic saving slowly increases. This theoretical frame-work is highly idealized, however, and a number of intervening factors inhibit capital flows from developed to developing countries. These include political risk, default risk, differences in levels of human capital and technology, and differences in institutional quality.[12] In addition, as first pointed out by Hymer (1976), rate of return analysis is wholly insufficient to explain FDI flows.[13]

The Developing World as Exporter of Capital

Since 2000, the idealized flow of funds has been turned on its head. Due in large part to a current account deficit in the United States that has exceeded 5 percent of its GDP, and reflecting the high level of savings of central banks in developing countries, the developing world is now an *exporter* of capital to the developed world rather than an importer. Chinese official reserves alone exceed US$850 billion. For rich countries as a whole, for example, global cap-ital *imports* exceeded US$300 billion in 2004. The United States actually imported approximately US$650 billion in 2004, with capital exports of Japan, the European Union, and other high-income countries making up the $350 billion difference.[14] Most of these developing-country capital exporters are in East Asia and the Middle East. What is worrying about this situation is that U.S. capital imports failed to decline as much as would normally be expected in the 2001–2 recession. This indicates that the United States is *structurally* rather than cyclically claiming the bulk of the world's savings, the opposite of what we would desire from a development or poverty-alleviation standpoint. Estimates and forecasts of the Institute of International Finance (2005) indi-cate that this situation will persist. Addressing fiscal imbalances in the United States is, therefore, of key importance to poverty-alleviating capital flows.

Financial Markets: Global and Domestic Capital Flows

Financial markets, both global and domestic, are an important component of economic development and poverty alleviation. Capital flows can support savings mobilization and deployment, financial sector development, and tech-nology transfer. They also have the potential to manage various types of risk and to monitor the performance of firms' managers. Empirically, there is some evidence that financial sector development helps to explain economic growth.[15] It appears that this growth effect occurs primarily through increasing pro-ductivity and reducing external finance costs rather than through increases in savings. As the World Bank (2001) notes, "Rigorous and diverse economet-ric evidence shows that the contribution of finance to long-term growth is achieved by improving the economy's total factor productivity, rather than on the rate of capital accumulation" (p. 6).[16] The growth effects of financial sector development appear to be important for both banking and equity markets.[17]

Impact of Global Capital Flows

Global capital flows are only one aspect of financial sector development, and the flows themselves are not always taken into account in growth investigations. There is evidence that not all types of capital flows have the same impact on growth. For example, capital inflows in the form of equity portfolio investment appear to be more beneficial than both bond finance and commercial bank lending.[18] More generally, there is widespread agreement that financial globalization via capital flows can make effective financial development more challenging by increasing *both* benefits *and* risks.[19] General, across-the-board statements about the role of capital flows in financial development are thus difficult to support.

The Importance of Domestic Savings

It is also important to view capital flows in the context of domestic capital mobilization. As we saw in figures 4.1 and 4.2, the most important type of capital inflow into developing countries is FDI. However, on average, FDI is but a small portion of total domestic investment (and savings) in low- and middle-income countries. For these countries in 2002, it was less than 6 percent and 11 percent of total domestic investment, respectively. Therefore, increases in the capital flow dimension of economic globalization have in no way lessened the importance of domestic investment, domestic savings, and the domestic environment influencing them.

Flight Capital

Residents of low- and middle-income countries hold a great deal of their wealth in the form of *flight capital,* which are assets held abroad because of poor domestic investment opportunities and high domestic risks. Estimates of the magnitude of flight capital vary and, because such flows are not always officially recorded, must be regarded with some caution. They suggest, however, that approximately 40 percent of the private wealth of Africa and the Middle East is held by its residents outside of these regions, and that the figure for Latin America is approximately 10 percent.[20] Consequently, any significant improvement in the investment and financial climates of these developing regions could result in a substantial repatriation of resources. Not all resources for development and poverty alleviation need to come from foreign sources—it would be possible for repatriated wealth to provide a substantial portion of a country's resources.

Financial Market Failures

The financial markets involved in equity portfolio investment, bond finance, and commercial bank lending are characterized by a number of imperfections, which economists call *market failures.* In normal circumstances, these imperfections contribute to a certain amount of market volatility. Under certain circumstances that are not fully understood, they can lead to full-blown financial crises of the kind experienced in Mexico (1994–5), Asia (1997), Russia (1998), Brazil (1999), and Argentina (2001) (see box 4.1).[21] It is important to understand these market imperfections to appreciate the effects of these three types of capital flows on poor people.

Asymmetry of Information in Financial Markets

Financial markets do not operate with full information. By their very nature (which involves the exchange of assets), financial markets have an important intertemporal component, and no market participant possesses perfect information about the future. Consequently, financial markets inherently involve an intertemporal "leap in the dark" of one sort or another. There is often an *asymmetry* in the information available to borrowers and lenders in which borrowers have more information about their creditworthiness than lenders.[22] Such asymmetries in information can lead to market failure in which changes in expectations cause swift changes in behavior, despite the lack of change in fundamental economic conditions. This can be pernicious because lender confidence consequently tends to be "pro-cyclical," remaining strong in business upturns but suddenly evaporating during downturns of various sorts. Attempts to overcome certain market failures in microfinance to better provide financial services to poor people are described in box 4.2.

Credit Rating Agencies

Credit rating agencies provide information to potential investors in capital markets. Their ratings are closely scrutinized by investors, and achieving "investment-grade" status is an important milestone for governments, public utilities, and corporate entities seeking to raise money in internationsl markets. Extending the reach of credit rating agencies to include a growing number of developing countries has helped to widen information about these markets.

Credit rating agencies play a vital role in overcoming information asymmetries in financial markets, but the fact that they only partially extend across middle-income countries and are virtually absent from low-income countries means that their limitations need to be recognized. Their ratings also are not predictive in nature: countries and companies that have performed well in ratings have succumbed to crises and failure. Credit rating agencies enhance information flows, and this may even at times exacerbate herding in markets. They perform a vital function, but are no panacea for asymmetry of information in the markets.

BOX 4.2   Targeting Poor People: Commercial Microfinance

From the point of view of alleviating poverty, some of the informational imperfections of financial markets make it difficult for commercial financial corporations to assess the credit-worthiness of poor borrowers, including poor entrepreneurs. These imperfections or barriers include physical remoteness, the lack of tangible assets to serve as collateral, the lack of property rights, and the cost of contracting. All of these factors tend to exclude poor people from basic financial services.

What are now called *microfinance institutions (MFIs)* have evolved over the last few decades to fill these gaps in commercial finance. An MFI is an organization that provides financial services of any kind to the poor. At present, they provide such services to poor individuals, including entrepreneurs. MFIs overcome financial market imperfections through group lending practices in which a borrower's associates become co-signers to the loan. Along with group lending, MFIs use a number of other mechanisms to facilitate effective credit provision. These include creative incentives such as progressive lending, tailored repayment schedules, collateral substitutes, and a focus on women who typically have significantly better repayment rates. In addition, MFIs are beginning to offer noncredit financial services such as savings arrangements to poor people.

The question on the minds of many in the MFI community is whether these institutions will be able to move in large numbers in the direction of commercialization. The steps in this process include an increasingly business-oriented approach, achieving operational and financial self-sufficiency, the increased use of commercial funding sources, and operating as for-profit institutions.

The difficult challenge in making the transition to increased commercialization is not losing sight of the central mission of serving poor populations. There is thus a tension between commercialization and "mission drift." This has been a central problem for MFIs pursuing commercial status, such as BURO Tangail (BT) in Bangladesh, and Bank Rakyat's Micro-business Division in Indonesia. Evidence presented in Morduch (1999) suggests that most MFIs will have difficulty in making this transition, but those that do will have contributed significantly to the design of poverty-alleviating finance, no small achievement.

Despite some skepticism, steps have indeed been taken in the direction of commercial microfinance. In 2001, a number of aid organizations and MFIs launched AFRICAP, a commercial MFI facility in Africa. AFRICAP is a for-profit equity investment company incorporated in Mauritius and operating out of Dakar, Senegal. It invests in leading African MFIs and is capitalized at US$13 million. Commercial banks are also beginning to investigate microfinance. For example, in 2004, Deutsche Bank launched a commercial microfinance facility based on its previous experience with MFIs. The facility will serve MFIs in Africa, South Asia, and Latin America using local commercial banks as intermediaries. This lending facility is funded at a level of US$60 million. Time will tell whether these initiatives prove to be successful. Given the importance of the credit constraint for small firms and entrepreneurs, and the central role in job creation and poverty reduction, it is essential that policy makers at the national and global levels focus their attention on developing vibrant microfinance institutions.

Sources: Charitonenko and Campion undated; Morduch 1999; and World Bank 2001.

Role of Government Failure in Financial Market Failure

The market failure of financial markets is compounded by government failure in that necessary attempts to regulate financial markets can at times make matters worse. Like other financial market participants, governments also suffer from imperfect information, and their attempts to offer support in times of crisis can provide an incentive for excessively risky behavior in financial markets, something that economists call "moral hazard." Both market failure and government failure characterize markets in equities, bonds, and bank lending, and they can complicate hoped-for effects of poverty alleviation. For example, market failure and government failure in financial markets combine in certain circumstances to generate a behavior known as *contagion*. This is where problems with regard to one financial instrument or country spread to other financial instruments or countries. The key contributing factor is attempts by market participants to maintain liquidity.

Role of Foreign Short-Term Lending in Financial Market Failure

Imperfections in financial markets appear to be particularly problematic when commercial banks in developing countries are given access to short-term, foreign lending sources.[23] The resulting problems have three causes:

- First, systems of financial intermediation in developing countries tend to rely heavily on the banking sector, because other types of financial intermediation are typically underdeveloped.
- Second, developing countries have been encouraged to liberalize domestic financial markets, sometimes before systems of prudential bank regulation and management are put in place.
- Third, developing countries have sometimes prematurely liberalized their capital accounts, on which most of the private capital flows examined in this chapter take place.[24]

Consequently, and as will be discussed below, care must be taken in managing evolving banking systems and their access to international capital flows.

Impact of Market Failure on Poor People

What is the implication of market failure for poor people? Financial crises are devastating to poor people and should therefore be avoided if at all possible. Poor people are particularly vulnerable to crises because they do not have the savings or safety nets to protect themselves from the income losses that are an inherent part of these events. It is common to consider the costs of crises in terms of the percentage of GDP lost in a particular country or region. For example, Eichengreen (2004) estimates the cost of an average crisis to be approximately 9 percent of GDP for the country in question. In the case of the Asian crisis, Dobson and Hufbauer (2001) estimated the cost to the *region* at up to 1.5 percent of GDP, but World Bank estimates suggest that it involved 20 million persons falling back into poverty and 1 million children being withdrawn from school.[25] Even this estimate may understate the impact. More recent estimates by Suryahadi, Sumarto, and Pritchett (2003), suggest that, in Indonesia alone and at the peak of the increase in poverty, approximately 35 million persons were pushed into absolute poverty. During the Argentine crisis of 2001, close to one-fourth of the population became extremely poor, while one-half of the population fell below the national poverty line.[26] Changes in poverty of these magnitudes matter a great deal.[27] As recognized by Eichengreen (2004),

> *To remind oneself of the immediacy of these effects, it is only necessary to observe that Indonesia and Argentina experienced larger falls in output and real incomes than that suffered by the United States in the Great Depression, an event that produced a revolution in social and economic policy. This is another way of saying that the social impact of financial crises can be enormous.* (pp. 9–10)

Financial Sector Reforms

Given these potentially severe poverty effects, caution is warranted. Although there is not complete agreement among those who have examined these issues, there is some evidence that the sequence and timing of financial sector reforms can mitigate financial turmoil and, thereby, prevent negative effects on poor people. As mentioned above, the liberalization of financial markets can strengthen the development process in the long run. However, financial liberalization without the proper surveillance capability may destabilize local financial sectors, real economies, and domestic political environments.[28] There are many examples where excessive liquidity associated with booms and market overconfidence were followed by excessive pessimism and capital flow reversals. In all of these outcomes, poor people suffer the most. Careful financial sector development should therefore be combined with carefully-targeted safety nets to protect poor people.[29]

Foreign Direct Investment

Foreign direct investment can have positive effects on poverty by creating employment, improving technology and human capital, and promoting competition. While much of FDI contributes in this way, at times it may adversely affect certain dimensions of poverty through unsafe working conditions and

FIGURE 4.4 Global Shares of Population, GDP, and FDI, 2002

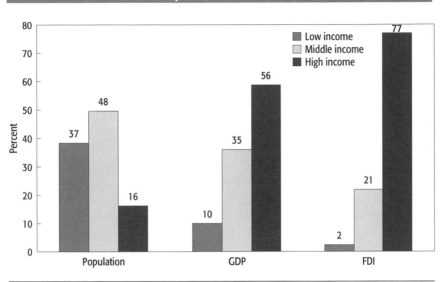

Source: World Bank, *World Development Indicators* 2004 CD-ROM.

environmental destruction. Nevertheless, if we were to identify the most promising category of capital flows from the point of view of poverty alleviation, FDI would be it.

FDI Recipient Countries

Global flows of FDI are highly concentrated, with the low-income countries being dramatically uninvolved as FDI recipients (figure 4.4). In 2002, for example, the low-income countries accounted for 37 percent of global population, only 10 percent of global GDP, and a mere 2 percent of global FDI. The middle-income countries are much more active as FDI recipients. In 2002, these countries accounted for 48 percent of global population, 35 percent of global GDP, and 21 percent of global FDI. The bulk of global FDI (77 percent in 2002) goes to the high-income countries of the world. As Dobson and Hufbauer (2001) put it, "the vast bulk of FDI represents investment made by one rich country in another rich country" (p. 33).

The lack of involvement on the part of low-income countries as FDI hosts is a major impediment to poverty alleviation. Even the fact that the low-income countries received only 2 percent of FDI in 2002 vastly understates the problem, because this 2 percent of the total flows is highly concentrated among these poor countries. Just two countries—India and Vietnam—receive nearly one-half of this 2 percent, for example. For most of the low-income countries, access to FDI has remained elusive. Growth is essentially driven by domestic investment to an even greater extent than when FDI is present. Foreign aid in support of growth is important to these countries, a fact that we will return to in chapter 5.

Multinational Enterprises

Many developing countries lack access to the technologies available in developed countries. Since multinational enterprises (MNEs) account for approximately three-fourths of worldwide civilian research and development, hosting MNEs from developed countries is, potentially, one important way to gain access to that technology. There are two problems with this idealized scenario, however. First, MNEs will employ the technology that most suits *their* strategic needs, not necessarily the development needs of host countries. For example, MNEs can employ processes that are much more capital intensive than host-country employment considerations may want.[30] Second, there is a strong tendency for MNEs to conduct their research and development in their home bases rather than in host countries.[31] Consequently, there are limits to the transfer of new technologies to host countries; as we show below, there is considerable scope for enhancing the benefits of foreign investment.

Potential Benefits of MNEs to Host Country: Technology Transfer

Despite these limitations, there is evidence that, in some important cases, MNEs do transfer technology and establish significant relationships with host-country suppliers by what economists call **backward links.** Moran (2001), for example, reviewed the evidence in the automotive, computer, and electronics sectors. He summarizes his conclusion as follows:[32]

> *Foreign investors whose local operations comprise an integral part of the parent's global or regional sourcing network introduce state-of-the-art technology and business practices into the host economy both via the investment that the parent makes in the performance of its own subsidiary and via the supervision that the parent and subsidiary exercise over the performance of local suppliers. (p. 24)*

Benefits from Local Source Inputs

If the foreign MNE begins to source inputs locally rather than importing them, the host country can gain a number of important benefits:

- Employment can increase because the sourced inputs represent new production.
- Production technologies can be better adapted to local conditions because suppliers are more likely to employ labor-intensive processes.

T he World Trade Organization includes an Agreement on Trade-Related Investment Measures (TRIMs) that prohibits domestic content, trade balancing, foreign exchange balancing, and domestic sales requirements placed on the MNEs hosted by WTO members. Indeed, many international economic policy experts are now calling for policies that would go beyond TRIMs to require the abandonment of all policies that discriminate between domestic and foreign firms. In this changed policy context, how can developing countries use policies to obtain the most benefits from FDI?

New thinking suggests that local content requirements should be replaced by efforts to support local suppliers in their efforts to secure contracts with foreign MNEs. The backward linkage promotion process involves many players, including the government, foreign MNEs, local suppliers, professional organizations, commercial organizations, and academic institutions. The key role of the government is that of *coordinator,* attempting to bridge the "information gaps" among the players. The government can do this in a number of different ways:

- First, in the realm of information, attempts can be made to provide a matching service between MNEs and local suppliers. This can be done by inviting the relevant players to link-promotion forums.
- Second, in the realm of technology, efforts can be made to provide support in standards formation, materials testing, and patent registration. Providing support in these areas has been part of the function of the Singapore Institute of Standards and Industrial Research. In addition, foreign MNEs can be invited to be involved in programs designed to upgrade local suppliers' technological capabilities.
- Third, in human resources development, efforts can be made to provide technical training and managerial training.
- Finally, in the area of finance, obstacles to access on the part of small firms can be removed. This has been one of the functions of the Korean Technology Banking Corporation, for example.

Efforts in these and other areas typically must be coordinated by a lead agency. In the cases of Costa Rica, Ireland, and Singapore, the Costa Rican Investment Board, an Irish National Linkage Program, and the Singapore Economic Development Board have played this role. Other developing countries can learn from these experiences.

Sources: Battat, Frank, and Shen 1996; UNCTAD 2001; and Reinert 2005.

- The MNE can transfer state-of-the-art business practices and technologies to the local suppliers.
- It is possible that the local suppliers can coalesce into a spatial cluster that supports innovation and upgrading.[33]

The policies required to support such links are considered in box 4.3.

Taking Japanese MNEs in Thailand as an example of creating links, Moran (2001) reports

As for the impact of foreign investors on local Thai firms, the Japanese assemblers took an active role in organizing "cooperation clubs" of the kind that were characteristic of supplier relations in the home country to assist with quality control, cost reduction, scheduling and delivery, and product improvement. Within the first 10 years after the turn toward offshore sourcing by the Japanese parents, some 150 local firms qualified for original equipment manufacturer (OEM) status. . . . An additional 200 to 250 Thai firms received replacement equipments manufacturer (REM) certification. These suppliers, like the foreign affiliates themselves, were able to capture economies of scale, and to use different and more sophisticated production techniques, than local firms elsewhere in Asia. (pp. 17–18)

Benefits from Spillover Effects

Another avenue through which MNEs can positively affect host economies is through "spillovers" to other sectors of these economies. For example, FDI in the automotive sector might benefit production in the machine tools sector. Indeed, there is a presumption in much of the literature on FDI that MNEs provide positive spillovers in the form of upgrading technology to domestic firms in the host country. This line of thinking goes back to Caves (1974) who tested this possibility for Canada and Australia. The evidence to date suggests that such spillovers do occur in some circumstances and can be significant.[34] However, in the words of Blomström and Sjöholm (1999), they are not "guaranteed, automatic, or free." For example, Haddad and Harrison (1993) and Kokko, Tansini, and Zejan (1996) failed to find such effects for Morocco and Uruguay, respectively. Aitken and Harrison (1999) also failed to find such positive spillovers for the case of Venezuela. Indeed, their evidence suggests the presence of *negative* spillovers due to market-stealing effects. Blomström and Sjöholm (1999) find positive spillovers in the case of Indonesia, attributing them to the increased competition that FDI brings. Haskel, Pereira, and Slaughter (2002) found positive spillovers in the United Kingdom, but such evidence might not apply to the developing country context.

Factors that Determine Spillover Effects

What determines whether positive technology spillovers will occur? Many factors are involved, and these include host country policies, MNE behavior, and industry characteristics.

Learning and Education

One key factor is the capacity of local firms to absorb foreign technologies. Blomström and Kokko (2003) suggest that *learning* is a key capacity that is responsive to various host country policies, and evidence presented in Tsang, Nguyen, and Erramilli (2004) in the case of Vietnam supports this view. Because learning is so important, a lack of human capital in the form of skills and education tends to prevent the generation of positive spillovers. For example, Kokko (1994) found evidence of these learning barriers in Mexico in that spillovers were negatively related to the productivity gaps between MNEs and domestic firms. Additionally, Kokko and Blomström (1995) found evidence that the technology transfers of U.S. MNEs have been positively affected by levels of education in host countries.

Wages

There is some evidence that MNEs offer higher wages than domestic firms. This is the conclusion of te Velde and Morrissey (2003) based on evidence from five African countries. This effect is more predominant for skilled than unskilled workers. In the long run, wages depend on education and training levels, and there is some evidence that MNEs will engage in important training activities. This appears to be more likely when MNEs are large, operate in competitive environments, and are export oriented.[35] As with the wage effects, however, training is more likely to be directed toward skilled than toward unskilled workers.[36] In a way similar to that of international trade (discussed in chapter 3), then, FDI can have differential effects that are positive for skilled workers but that exclude unskilled workers. This can result in what te Velde (2001) refers to as the "low-income low-skill trap."

Avoiding the Low-Income, Low-Skill Trap

Basic education and skills development have a major role in making the most of FDI for poverty alleviation.[37] Even Singapore, the preeminent example of free market development, has intervened in labor markets to avoid any possible low-income low-skill trap. As described by te Velde (2001),

> *The Skills Development Fund (SDF) in Singapore is an example of how MNEs (and other firms) can be engaged in more training. The Productivity and Standards Board (PSB), responsible for the SDF, imposes a 1 percent levy on the payroll of employers for every worker earning less than a pre-determined amount. This levy is distributed to firms that send their low-paying employees to approved training courses. This has had a significant impact on skill-upgrading in Singapore.* (p. 24)

This is just one example of efforts to make the most of FDI to alleviate poverty. Generalizing such processes throughout the developing world requires new policy efforts along the lines of those outlined in box 4.3 for building a synergistic relationship between skills development and FDI.

Costs of Hosting FDI

Hosting FDI is not without its potential costs.[38] Concern has been raised about the practice of transfer pricing. *Transfer pricing* involves the manipulation of the prices of intrafirm trade by MNEs to reduce their global tax payments. In the case of the United States, with more resources to martial against this practice than any other country, it has been estimated that annual losses in tax revenue are on the order of US$50 billion.[39] The solution to the transfer-pricing problem is multifaceted and not straightforward, but it is clear that a multilateral approach is the preferred solution.[40] Such options include forming international guidelines and codes of conduct, using international standards of invoicing and customs procedures, harmonizing global tax systems, negotiating and concluding international conventions, and establishing international arbitration procedures. However, to make these options work, resources would need to be provided for many developing countries for them to effectively combat transfer-pricing abuses.

FDI and Poverty Alleviation: An Assessment

FDI is perhaps the most important capital flow from the point of view of poverty alleviation. FDI can be a means of employment generation, especially when it takes place in labor-intensive sectors. It can also be a means of technology and management transfer, especially where effective backward links have been established. This gain, and its potential to help poor people, involves learning processes; these, in turn, require that minimal thresholds of human capital be met. Without advances in education, training, and health, few long-term gains from FDI take place. Advances in the investment climate and the environment for doing business, both for foreign and domestic investors, are also vital. Policy makers have a role to play in facilitating investment by combating corruption, steamlining procedures, and investing in the physical and human capacities that are the foundation for not only foreign but more importantly for domestic investment (See World bank 2005e).

For FDI to have a greater role in poverty reduction, it is also neccessary to addree thw following issues. First, it is highly concentrated among developed countries and just a handful of developing countries. Second, for extractive industries (such as mining and petroleum), steps must be taken to ensure that the FDI does indeed contribute to poverty alleviation, especially in the context of weak governance mechanisms. Third, transfer pricing abuses may rob developing countries of the tax revenues they desperately need to make the very investments required for FDI to contribute positively to poverty alleviation. We return to some of these issues in chapter 8.

Equity Portfolio Investment

Evidence suggests that financial development has a positive impact on growth, but not all types of financial activity and capital inflows have the same effects. In particular, capital inflows in the form of equity portfolio investment might be more beneficial than either bond finance or commercial bank lending. Reisen and Soto (2001) have examined the impact of all four capital inflows considered in this chapter on growth for a sample of 44 countries. They found that FDI did indeed have a positive impact on economic growth. The most positive growth impact, however, came from equity portfolio flows. Bond finance, considered below, did not have any impact on growth; commercial bank lending, also considered below, had a negative impact. These results suggest that equity inflows, along with FDI, could play an especially positive role in growth, development, and poverty alleviation.

Reasons for High Equity Portfolio Impact

Why can equity portfolio investment play a positive role in growth and development, at least under some circumstances? Rousseau and Wachtel (2000) summarize research on this question with four possibilities:

- Equity portfolio inflows are an important source of funds for developing countries.
- The development of equity markets helps to provide an exit mechanism for venture capitalists, and this increases entrepreneurial activity.
- Portfolio inflows assist developing countries to move from short-term finance to longer-term finance. They also help to finance investment in projects that have economies of scale.
- The development of equity markets provides an informational mechanism evaluating the performance of domestic firms and can help provide incentives to managers to perform well.

Some evidence suggests that institutional investors managing equity flows are less likely than banks to engage in herd and contagion behavior, thus making volatility less of an issue.[41] However, under some circumstances, these herd and contagion behaviors do indeed appear, especially for nonresident, foreign investors who are at an informational disadvantage.[42] The degree of recent volatility in net inward portfolio equity flows to developing countries can be seen in figure 4.5. The Asian crisis of 1997 had a significant, detrimental effect on these inflows, as did the 2001–2 recession (see box 4.1). Recovery began in 2003, supporting significant gains in emerging-market stock indices, and con-

FIGURE 4.5   Net Inward Portfolio Equity Flows to Developing Countries, 1995–2004

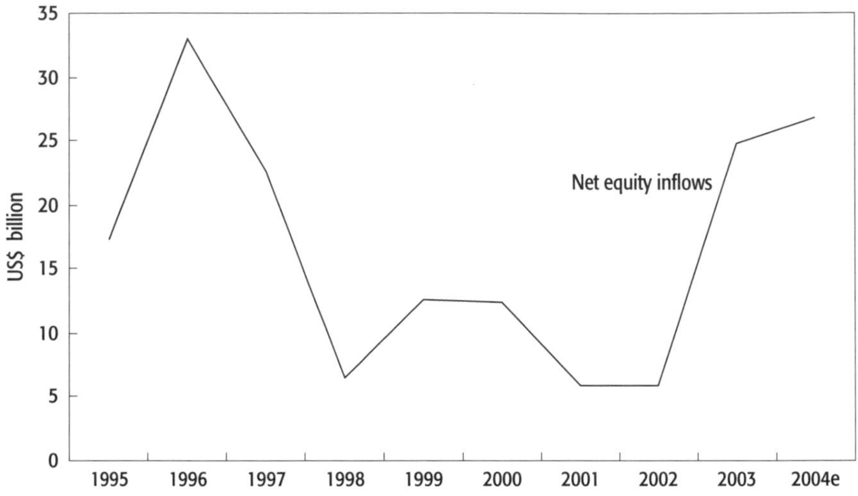

Source: World Bank 2004b, 2005a.
Note: e refers to estimate.

tinued through 2004 despite equity market corrections. Estimates and forecasts from the Institute of International Finance (2005) indicate that portfolio
equity investment will maintain itself at least through 2005. More long term,
according to the World Bank (2004b), prospects for equity finance are positive,
although risks remain. As noted by World Bank (2005a), the increases in equity
flows during 2003 and 2004 were highly concentrated regionally in East Asia,
South Asia, and South Africa. The Latin America and Caribbean region actually
experienced a loss.

Role of Equity Market Prices

The evidence on the role of global integration on equity market prices, as
opposed to flows, is more mixed. For example, Asian equity markets recovered
values fairly quickly after the 1997 crisis. More to the point, as noted by the
World Bank (2001), "There is no clear theoretical presumption as to whether
local stock prices will be more or less volatile after integration into the world
market. Integration should insulate the prices from shocks that affect the non-
market wealth or savings behavior of local investors, but could expose them
more to fluctuations in world asset prices and to shifts in external investor
preferences" (p. 173). There appears to be no clear evidence that one or the
other of these two influences dominates in practice.[43]

Features of Developing-Country Equity Markets

In general, equity markets are underdeveloped in much of the developing world. For example, nearly the entire net portfolio equity inflows into Sub-Saharan Africa are accounted for by one country alone: South Africa. The World Bank (2004b) summarized the features of developing-country equity markets as follows:

> *Market capitalization as a share of GDP in low-income countries is about one-sixth of that in high-income countries. Even in the middle-income countries, the share is only about one-third of that in industrial countries. Stock exchanges in developing countries also tend to lag technologically behind developed markets. Technology plays a major role in the trading, clearance, and settlement processes; problems in those areas can discourage sophisticated investors. Institutions that supervise and support the operation of the stock exchange also tend to be weaker in developing countries.* (p. 95)

The example of the Nairobi Stock Exchange is taken up in box 4.4. Elsewhere in Africa, the Johannesburg stock market has a capitalization that far exceeds that of the rest of Africa. In many respects, it has become a model for emerging markets, but it too has suffered from the migration of some of the most global listings to London and New York.

BOX 4.4 The Nairobi Stock Exchange

Although equity exchange in Kenya has a history going back to the 1920s under British colonial rule, the Nairobi Stock Exchange (NSE) came into being only in 1954. From its inception until 1991, it was a voluntary association registered under the Kenyan Societies Act. At about the same time, the NSE came under the regulation of the Capital Markets Authority (CMA). In 1995, exchange controls that limited foreign participation in the NSE were removed.

As with most other African stock exchanges, the NSE has some characteristics of a frontier market. Its market capitalization peaked at approximately US$2 billion in 1998, and its value traded peaked at only approximately US$100 million in 1997. The number of companies listed in 2002 was only 50, down from 57 a decade earlier. That said, there are institutional changes that have strengthened the exchange, such as the implementation of an electronic central depository system, the adoption of international accounting standards, and the establishment of a Capital Markets Appeals Tribunal. All of these are valuable changes, but the exchange has some distance to travel in fulfilling development promises.

Source: Ngugi, Murinde, and Green 2002; Nairobi Stock Exchange, *Market Intelligence* (Kenya) accessible at http://www.mi.co.ke/economy_and_markets/markets/nse/rise_growth_of_nse.asp.

Development of Equity Markets

The development of equity markets in low- and middle-income countries is more complex than it might first appear. This is because of the recent trends in the globalization of financial services. Observers have pointed to a set of domestic factors as particularly important in equity market development. These factors include sound macroeconomic policies, minimal degrees of technology, legal systems that protect shareholders, and open financial markets. However, as pointed out by Claessens, Klingebiel, and Schmukler (2002), these are precisely the factors that tend to promote the "migration" of equity exchange out of developing countries to the major exchanges in financial capitals of developed countries. This migration process complicates standard notions of equity market development. Steil (2001) has argued that the way forward is to link local markets with global markets. However, medium-size firms with local information needs might still benefit from some kind of domestic equity market. This is an area that urgently requires the development of novel approaches.

The Promise of Portfolio Equity for Poverty Alleviation

Capital flows in the form of portfolio equity hold out some promise for poverty alleviation. Along with FDI, these indirect equity investments appear to have a positive impact on growth through a variety of mechanisms. Contagion and herd behavior are less prevalent than they are with commercial bank lending, and flows are expected to hold relatively steady in the near future. However, the underdeveloped nature of equity markets in most developing countries and some degree of market volatility are two obstacles associated with global equity flows. Developing equity financing to ameliorate these obstacles is a long-term priority for poor people, as these indirect investments can help to offset some of the problems with other sources of flows. This development needs to proceed in an open fashion that does not favor a narrow, investing elite with inside knowledge, but rather offers an open system for all medium-size and large firms.

Debt: Bond Finance and Commercial Bank Lending

In the financial world, there are significant differences between portfolio equity investment and debt. This shows up in the fact that, in bankruptcy, debt is given priority over equity. This tends to support the preference for debt over equity in markets, a preference that might well be misplaced from the perspective of development and poverty alleviation. In this section, we consider two types of debt: bond finance and commercial bank lending. The main difference between these two forms of debt is that bonds are in the form of tradable assets. This provides more flexibility to lenders than bank lending.

FIGURE 4.6 **Net Inward Debt Flows to Developing Countries, 1997–2004**

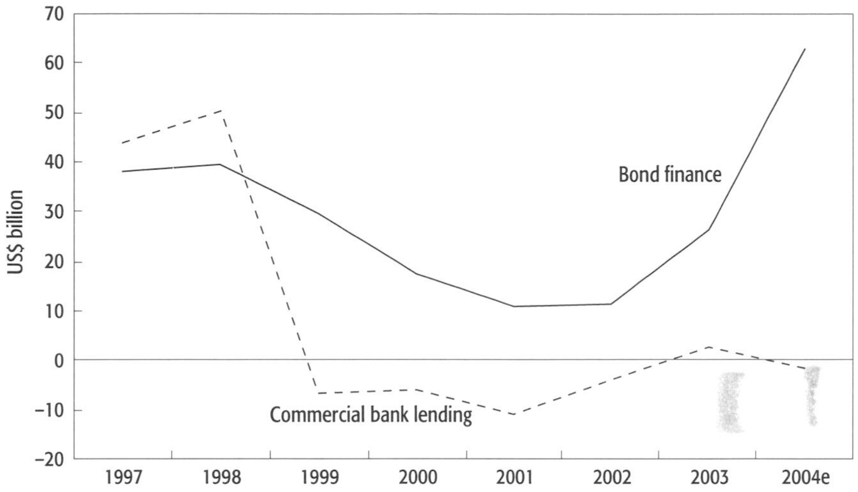

Source: World Bank 2004b, 2005a.
Note: e refers to estimate.

Bond Finance

Net debt flows to the developing world have evolved markedly in recent years (figure 4.6). Bond finance fell gradually between 1998 and 2001, and the 2003 to 2004 period showed substantial recovery in net flows to a level above the 1997 to 1998 period. That said, the World Bank (2004b, 2005a) identifies a number of risks with regard to bond investment. These include interest rate increases in high-income countries, which are already beginning at the time of this writing and continued fiscal imbalances in some developed countries such as the United States.[44] The World Bank (2005a) warns that "The risk of an abrupt increase in U.S. interest rates remains a serious concern. Large, sudden movements in long-term rates, in particular, could provoke a sharp widening of emerging market bond spreads" (p. 21). This potential increase in bond spreads could raise the cost of capital via bond finance for the developing world. At the time of writing, however, these spreads are at a historical low, reflecting the strength of emerging markets' macroeconomic performance, as well as the low yeilds offered by alternative investment classes. The heightened appetite for emerging markets has seen a growing number of developing countries accessing significant volumes of finance from the bond markets. Traditional issuers, such as Mexico, have been able to extend the term of their bond issuance up to 30 years. At the same time, corporate borrowing has grown significantly and in 2004 accounted for about half of total emerging market bond issuance. The long-dated sovereign bonds better match the assets and liabilities of governments and build the benchmark yield curve (which plot the yields of different maturities) Increased issuance in local currencies–such as Panda (Chinese Renminbi), Peso (Mexico), Real (Brazil), and Rand (South Africa) bonds–reduces the currency mismatch, which has been a major cause of past financial instability. Meanwhile, greater corporate access has provided a new and often lower cost of finance for emerging businesses. As the need for sovereign borrowing by middle-income countries has declined—not least in those Asian economies with large foreign exchange surpluses, corporate borrowing has provided a welcome alternative for investors seeking relatively high yields. Longer-dated offerings by their governments have enabled corporate issues in certain emerging markets to price their own longer-dated offerings by reference to these government benchmarks. The challenge for policy makers is to sustain and deepen this access and to broaden this access from the handful of countries with investment-grade that has been able to benefit from this widening access to capital markets. Enthusiasm for this asset class, however, has in the past proved short-lived. Prudence and a balanced portfolio approach thus remain necessary.

Commercial Bank Lending

Commercial bank lending fell precipitously in 1999 on a net basis and did not recover through 2004 (figure 4.6). Commercial bank lending on a gross basis is a different story (figure 4.7). As noted by the World Bank (2005a), despite declines in net lending, commercial bank lending is still used by a wide variety of developing countries: "Twice as many countries tapped this segment of the debt markets in 2004 than the bond financing segment" (p. 20). The private or corporate sector is emerging as an increasingly important borrower in this regard.

Above, we briefly analyzed some features of financial markets that give them some important, "imperfect" characteristics. As mentioned, commercial bank lending appears to be particularly prone to these imperfections. For example, Dobson and Hufbauer (2001) note that "Bank lending may be more prone to run than portfolio capital, because banks themselves are highly leveraged, and they are relying on the borrower's balance sheet to ensure repayment" (p. 47). The World Bank (2001) also notes that "Incentives are key to limiting undue risk-taking and fraudulent behavior in the management and supervision of financial intermediaries—especially banks that are prone to costly failure" (p. 3).

Before the Asian crisis, such an assessment might have been seen as exaggerated. Indeed, the precrisis data examined by Sarno and Taylor (1999) provided a relatively sanguine conclusion about commercial bank lending. Subsequent

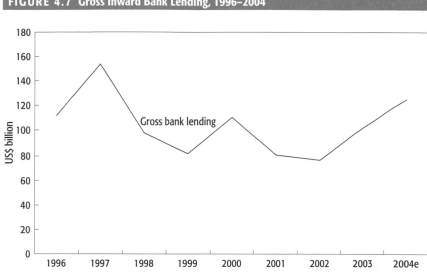

FIGURE 4.7 Gross Inward Bank Lending, 1996–2004

Source: World Bank 2004b, 2005a.
Note: e refers to estimate.

events, however, showed otherwise. Much of the debt involved in the Asian crisis was composed of short-term, interbank loans, and, as we saw in figures 4.1 and 4.2, net commercial bank lending flows quickly became negative for both the low- and middle-income countries after 1997. Indeed, Goldstein, Kaminsky, and Reinhart (2000) include short-term capital flows (most of which are interbank commercial lending) as a significant predictor of future financial crises based on a broad sample of countries.

Supporting the Development of Banking Sectors

What can be done to support the safe development of banking sectors in developing countries? Some of the necessary steps can be thought of in terms of information, institutions, and incentives. For information, it is important for banks to embrace internationally sanctioned accounting and auditing procedures and to make the results of these assessments available to the public. For institutions or the rules of the "banking game," risk management practices (both credit and currency) must be sufficiently stringent and prudential regulation systems must be well developed. For currency risk, the World Bank (2004b) notes that "particular care should be taken to ensure that foreign-currency liabilities are appropriately hedged" (p. 30).[45] These information and institutional safeguards are no small task, and they inevitably cannot be achieved in the short term.[46] Consequently, these safeguards should be buttressed with incentive measures in the form of market-friendly taxes on banking capital inflows. For example, Eichengreen (1999) argues that "banks borrowing abroad should be required to put up additional noninterest-bearing reserves with the central bank" (p. 117). Such taxes on short-term capital inflows have been applied by Chile and others to prevent destabilizing episodes of overborrowing.[47]

Debt Flows Compared with Equity Flows

Debt flows in the form of bond finance and commercial bank lending appear to have different properties than equity flows in the form of FDI and portfolio equity investment. They are more prone to the imperfect behaviors that characterize financial markets and their positive growth effects do not seem to be as large as those associated with equity flows. Consequently, debt finance must be used cautiously and should be hedged against exchange rate risks.[48]

Summary

The different forms of capital flows are best seen as complements, not substitutes. The capital flows with the greatest potential contribution to poverty alleviation are both FDI and equity investment. Equity-related finance brings with it the natural benefits of risk-sharing, and is far less subject to the sudden stops and reversals of debt flows. In the case of FDI, this is because investors have a tendency to reinvest a portion of retained earnings. Also, FDI capital stock depreciates, and new inflows are needed to sustain the existing capital stock. Finally, the benefits of FDI go beyond those relating to narrow financial issues: new ideas, technologies, and improvements in skills and training are all potential and important spillovers.[49]

Long-Term Trend of Financial Development

The *long-term* trend of financial development is probably toward a mix of all four capital flows described in this chapter. The positions of developing countries with regard to capital flows can be generalized as in figure 4.8. Here, for simplicity, our four types of capital flows are represented as the four corners of a diamond, with the relative strength of any particular flow indicated by proximity to a corner of the diamond. In the short term, most developing countries have no choice about their position in the diamond because they are constrained by the availability and cost of different capital flows. In the medium term, however, their actions can yield some influence over the availability and cost of capital flows: their choices can expand.

For example, there is a group of low-income countries who find themselves at approximately point "1" in the diagram, relying primarily on the

FIGURE 4.8 Composition of Financial Development

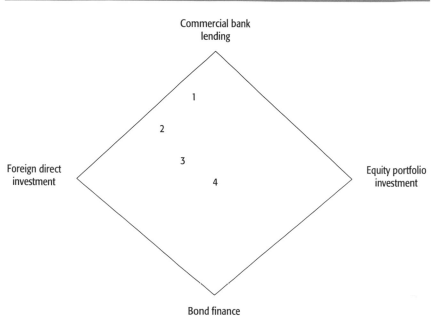

commercial bank lending form of capital flows.[50] Another set of low-income countries find themselves at approximately point "2," with a mix of commercial bank lending and FDI, the latter probably concentrated in petroleum or minerals. Many middle-income countries find themselves at approximately point "3," with the addition of some bond finance and equity portfolio investment. As financial development proceeds, there will be a move to somewhere in the vicinity of point "4" in which there is a broad mix of all four capital flows. Maintaining this position in a stable way would require that the financial development of the country be designed to mitigate the imperfections discussed in this chapter. Capital inflows have a vital role to play. As noted by Fernandez-Arias and Montiel (1996), "the possibility that capital inflows may be welfare reducing does not mean that they are *invariably* harmful" (p. 57, emphasis added).

Absorptive Capacity Requirements

If there is any convergence in the emerging literature on capital flows in the developing world, it concerns ***absorptive capacity,*** which acts as a set of necessary conditions for potential poverty-alleviating effects. That is, for capital flows to positively help poor people, a number of things must be true:

- First, human capital must be developed. Without it, the hoped-for positive spillovers from FDI will not emerge.
- Second, the domestic financial markets must be "deep" enough to support liquidity. Without liquidity, volatility will be a problem.
- Third, systems of oversight and regulation of domestic financial markets must be developed enough to prevent excessive volatility and crises.
- Fourth, levels of corruption should be low and strenuously combatted.[51]

Each of these conditions takes some time to fulfill. Until they are achieved, caution is warranted. Thus, we sound a note of warning in providing an overall assessment of global capital flows and their relationship to poverty. As Hanson, Honohan, and Majnoni (2003) concluded, "the globalization of finance is not an unmixed blessing, but it appears to be inexorable" (p. 25). Capital flows are an "inexorable" aspect of financial globalization, which have potential benefits *and* costs that are significant. Because poor people are particularly vulnerable to the potential costs, any errors in managing capital flows should be on the side of caution.

Impact of Fiscal Imbalance in the United States on Poverty Alleviation

Finally, as discussed in the beginning of this chapter, in significant measure because of unaddressed fiscal imbalances in the United States, aggregate capital flows are currently from developing to developed regions of the world. The United States continues to claim the bulk of world savings, the opposite of what is optimal from a poverty-alleviation perspective. Given the globalization of finance—particularly in the market for government bonds— addressing fiscal imbalances in the United States is of key importance to freeing up capital flows that alleviate poverty.

Notes

1. Dobson and Hufbauer (2001) estimate that developing country GDPs are, on average, approximately 5 percent higher due to *both* trade and capital flows. They themselves call this a "cautious assertion" to be taken as a first approximation. Prasad and others (2003) are even more cautious, noting that "if financial integration has a positive effect on growth, there is as yet no clear and robust empirical proof that the effect is quantitatively significant" (p. 5). For a general review, see chapter 4 of Hossain and Chowdhury (1998).
2. The latter point regarding cost and poor people is emphasized by Stiglitz and Bhattacharya (2000).
3. In the case of firms, it is not only financial portfolios that are involved, but also productive portfolios such as plant and equipment in the form of foreign direct investment.

4. The precise definition in the World Bank's *World Development Indicators,* for example, is "lasting interest in or effective managerial control over an enterprise in another country" (World Bank, various years).
5. Szirmai (2005), for example, notes the "overwhelming impact of Western culture, which is frequently transferred only in the rudimentary form of consumption-oriented behavior and technology" (p. 509).
6. We discuss noncommercial lending, such as that of the World Bank, in chapter 5 on foreign aid.
7. Chuhan, Claessens, and Mamingi (1998) examine some factors behind bond and equity flows to Latin America and Asia during the late 1980s and early 1990s. They suggest that equity flows tend to respond to price-earnings ratios and relative rates of return, while bond flows tend to respond to credit ratings and debt prices in secondary markets.
8. One potential point of confusion can arise in interpreting figures 4.1 and 4.2. As we will see in the next section on financial development, beginning in 2000, the developing world became an *exporter* of capital to the developed world rather than an importer. How then can the positive inflows of capital into the low- and middle-income countries take place? The answer is that the *private* capital inflows of figures 4.1 and 4.2 are offset by *official* capital outflows that take place through the actions of central banks, especially in the case of the middle-income countries.
9. de la Torre and Schmukler (2004) note that privatization proceeds in developing countries increased from US$ 2.6 billion in 1988 to US$ 25.4 billion in 1996.
10. On this last point, see also Osei, Morrissey, and Lensink (2002).
11. See, for example, Taylor and Williamson (1994).
12. See, for example, Lucas (1990).
13. This insight is reviewed at some length in chapters 1 and 2 of Caves (1996).
14. See World Bank (2004b, 2005a). The World Bank (2005a) notes that "The buildup of foreign exchange reserves in the hands of developing countries' central banks and monetary authorities—and its use in financing global payment imbalances—marks a new phase in the postwar system for financing international payments" (p. 59).
15. This possibility is discussed in Pagano (1993). Evidence is provided by King and Levine (1993).
16. On productivity effects, see Beck, Levine, and Loayza (2000). This research supports what is known as the "Schumpetarian view" of the role of finance in development (after Schumpeter, 1934) in which the primary effects of financial development are on the productivity of firms. On external finance effects, see Rajan and Zingales (1998).
17. See Levine and Zervos (1998).
18. See Reisen and Soto (2001). The overall growth effects of FDI had been called into question by Caves (1996), who wrote: "Some researchers have tried to identify the overall effects of MNEs' presence in developing countries on . . . subsequent rates of economic growth. The possible causal connections are numerous but speculative and ill-defined in terms of economic models. Empirical investigations, whether by those disposed to think good or ill of the MNEs, have employed inadequate research procedures and have yielded no trustworthy conclusions" (p. 242). This ambiguity is reiterated in the case of Africa by Bhinda and others (1999).
19. For example, the World Bank (2001) notes that "Globalization . . . challenges the whole design of the financial sector, potentially replacing domestic with international providers of some of these services, and limiting the role that government can play—while making their remaining tasks that much more difficult" (p. 1). See also Calvo, Leiderman, and Reinhart (1996).
20. These estimates are from Collier, Hoeffler, and Pattillo (2001).
21. Reviews of the economic literature on crises can be found in more- and less-technical terms, respectively, in Appendix B of Eichengreen (1999) and chapter 17 of Reinert (2005). For a specific focus on the role of exchange rate regimes in crises, see Cordon (2002).
22. See, for example, Stiglitz and Weiss (1981) and Williamson (1987). For the role of asymmetric information in influencing institutional investors, see Frenkel and Menkhoff (2004).
23. International Monetary Fund statistics record 64 banking crises between 1970 and 1999 (Crook 2003). Crook writes that "breakdowns in banking lie at the center of most financial crises. And

banks are unusually effective at spreading financial distress, once it starts, from one place to another" (p. 11). The World Bank (2001) notes that "If finance is fragile, banking is the most fragile part" (p. 11).

24. For a critique of premature capital account liberalization, see Stiglitz (2000). As the World Bank (2001) notes, "Poor sequencing of financial liberalization in a poor country environment has undoubtedly contributed to bank insolvency" (p. 89). Hanson, Honohan, and Majnoni (2003) also note that "the riskiness of capital account liberalization without fiscal adjustment . . . , and without reasonably strong financial regulation and supervision and a sound domestic financial system, is well recognized" (p. 10). See also Bhattacharya and Miller (1999).

25. See Wolfensohn (1998).

26. See Fiszbein, Giovagnoli, and Thurston (2003).

27. Even short of actual crises, there is some reason for concern about the potentially negative impact of capital flows on poor people. For people at or near poverty lines, any volatility in consumption can be quite detrimental or even disastrous. From a theoretical point of view, capital flows can reduce the volatility of consumption by de-linking it from national output volatility. Unfortunately, there is empirical evidence that increased financial integration through expanding capital flows can increase rather than decrease consumption volatility in developing countries. See Prasad and others (2003) and Kose, Prasad, and Terrones (2003).

28. These risks are all the more significant when countries are characterized by "currency mismatches" in which assets are denominated in the local currency and liabilities in foreign currencies. Consequently, net worth is directly tied to the value of the local currency. On this issue, see Jeanne (2000), Eichengreen, Hausmann, and Panizza (2003), and Goldstein and Turner (2004). As noted by Eichengreen (2004), "Currency mismatches are widely implicated in financial crises in developing countries" (p. 27).

29. Stiglitz and Bhattacharya (2000) discuss the role of food subsidies, education subsidies, rural infrastructure, and microfinance in this regard.

30. There is a long-standing inquiry into this issue, the results of which are summarized by Caves (1996): "Survey evidence indicates that MNEs do some adapting (of technologies to labor-abundant conditions), but not a great deal, and it appears that the costs of adaptation commonly are high relative to the benefits expected by individual companies" (p. 241).

31. "With the exception of some European-based companies, the proportion of R&D activity by MNEs undertaken outside their home countries is generally quite small and, in the case of Japanese firms, negligible" (Dunning, 1993, p. 301).

32. See also Moran (1998).

33. For an introduction to the role of clusters in technological upgrading, see chapter 11 of Reinert (2005) and the references therein. For the role of clusters in natural resource–based development, see Ramos (1998).

34. Evidence presented by Hejazi and Safarian (1999) indicate that spillovers for research and development are more important for FDI than they are for international trade.

35. See te Velde (2001) and references therein.

36. See Tan and Batra (1995), for example.

37. For readers familiar with "growth and poverty" research, we note that Borensztein, De Gregorio, and Lee (1998) find that it is the *combination* of FDI and education that has a statistically significant impact on growth.

38. For a review of both benefits and costs of hosting FDI, see chapter 21 of Reinert (2005).

39. See Plender (2004).

40. Unilateral policy options exist, but "because there is competition for MNE activity between home and host countries, and between different host countries, the opportunities for MNEs to play one nation against another are enhanced without the establishment of supra-national institutions and harmonized inter-governmental action towards (transfer pricing)" (Dunning, 1993, p. 523).

41. This evidence is reviewed in chapter 1 of Dobson and Hufbauer (2001).

42. For the case of Korea, see Choe, Kho, and Stulz (1999) and Kim and Wei (2002).

43. See also Hanson, Honohan, and Majnoni (2003).
44. As of January 2005, the Argentine government had made a "final offer" to its bondholders. By the end of February 2005, the country had negotiated a debt swap, which replaced a portion of this debt with lower-value bonds. The Argentine government hopes that this restructuring will begin to bring home the approximately US$150 billion its citizens hold abroad in the form of flight capital. See *The Economist* (2005a, b).
45. Mistakes made in these areas have proved to be too costly to poor people for countries to relax their vigilance. Prasad and others (2003) conclude that "The relative importance of different sources of financing for domestic investment, as proxied by the following three variables, has been shown to be positively associated with the incidence and the severity of currency and financial crises: the ratio of bank borrowing or other debt relative to foreign direct investment; the shortness of the term structure of external debt; and the share of external debt denominated in foreign currencies" (p. 49).
46. Eichengreen (1999) notes that "the sad truth in all too many countries is that banks have a limited capacity to manage risk and that regulators have limited capacity to supervise their actions" (pp. 11–12).
47. This overborrowing is described by McKinnon and Pill (1997).
48. We take up the accumulated debt burdens of developing countries, as well as the issue of debt relief, in chapter 5.
49. China, for example, has focused on equity rather than debt, and inroads into poverty reduction have been significant.
50. This group of countries, as well as those at point "2," would no doubt also be relying on foreign aid, but we leave this discussion to chapter 5.
51. According to the results of Wei (2000), corruption has a tendency to bias capital flows away from FDI and toward commercial bank lending.

5

Aid

T his chapter examines foreign aid flows, historically the most recent of the global flows we consider in this book.[1] Although ideas, goods, investments, and people have crossed great distances for millennia in response to a host of economic opportunities, it is only relatively recently that governments began to provide financial and ***technical assistance*** to foreign countries. The purpose of this assistance has varied and has included geopolitical purposes as well as stimulating economic development, ameliorating poverty and suffering, promoting political outcomes, and ensuring civil stability and equitable governance. Although foreign aid is often visualized by citizens in rich countries in terms of financial "handouts" by rich countries to the world's poorest inhabitants, the truth is much more complex. Indeed, contrary to popular perception, low-income countries generally receive less than half of total aid. Much of the remainder is made up by flows to middle-income countries such as Colombia and the Arab Republic of Egypt, and some countries of particular interest—Israel, and most recently, Afghanistan—have received significant amounts of assistance.[2] The good news is that recent years have seen sharp improvements in both the quality and quantity of aid.

Aid, or ***official development assistance (ODA)*** as it is technically known, covers a wide range of both financial and nonfinancial components.[3] Cash transfers to developing countries can be vital, but currently they account for less than half of the aid that goes to those countries. Nonfinancial forms of assistance include grants of machinery or equipment as well as less tangible contributions such as providing technical analysis, advice, and capacity-building. Many donors also count their own administrative costs in their aid budgets as well as contributions to debt reduction and other financial allocations that never reach developing countries.[4] Just as there is considerable heterogeneity in the types of aid disbursed, there is also a surprising amount of diversity in the countries that receive ODA. For some countries—such as those in early post-conflict situations or where institutions are particularly weak and corruption is prevalent—technical assistance may have a more positive impact than cash transfers, but in the majority of countries, cash transfers in support of government programs are most effective in contributing to growth and reducing poverty.

An analysis of *aid flows* cannot be separated from an analysis of the development of the international development finance system and the role of institutions such as the World Bank as conduits for financial and other flows. This chapter therefore focuses on both bilateral and multilateral flows as well as on related issues such as the role of official debt and its cancellation.

A Brief History of Aid Flows

In many ways, the histories of modern aid and colonialism are intertwined. In so far as colonialism was an exercise driven by a desire to stimulate and then exploit economic activity abroad, providing investment capital, technology, and technical assistance to colonies was integral to the process. This included constructing a railroad network in the Congo by Belgium to facilitate the extraction of ore deposits, establishing foreign legions of civil service employees, and constructing the Suez and Panama Canals.

Colonial Nature of Early Foreign Aid

It was not until the early 20th century, however, that colonial powers considered providing assistance to support general aspects of economic development that were not exclusively tied to extraction and exploitation. Even here, as noted by Little and Clifford (1965), in the case of the United Kingdom's 1929 Colonial Development Act, infrastructure rather than, say, education, played a central role. As stressed by Kanbur (forthcoming), it was not until the 1940 and 1945 Colonial Development and Welfare Acts that the United Kingdom began to support education in its nascent foreign aid efforts, although its 1948 Overseas Development Act established the Colonial Development Corporation.

Even after countries gained independence, the colonial nature of foreign aid persisted. Szirmai (2005, chapter 14) stresses the role of aid in decolonization processes, as well as in post-independence assimilation policies, particularly in the cases of the United Kingdom and France. The Netherlands was not exempt in this process either. As Szirmai states, in an example not atypical of the early years of other aid programs,

> *In the case of the Netherlands, there was a sudden rift with Indonesia in 1949 after the so-called police actions of 1947–49. The Netherlands attempted to restore its damaged international prestige by participating*

KEY TERMS AND CONCEPTS

adjustment programs	capacity building
aid flows	Green Revolution
Cold War	technical assistance
debt overhang	tied assistance
debt-service-to-export ratios	Washington Consensus
official development assistance (ODA)	

on a large scale in multilateral technical assistance which was beginning at that time. The Netherlands had a reservoir of experience in the form of colonial training programmes, unemployed colonial civil servants and technical experts. It was quite successful in finding employment for its experts in multilateral aid programmes. (p. 586)

Tied Nature of Early Foreign Aid

A key feature of these early forms of development assistance was its "tied" nature, in which aid was restricted to importing from the donor country.[5] This was true of the Colonial Development Act in the United Kingdom and the "Good Neighbor Policy" of the United States toward Latin America. The practice of *tied assistance* dominated bilateral aid flows during much of the **Cold War** and, although there has been considerable progress in untying aid, it remains a feature of a number of aid programs today. To the extent that aid is tied, receiving countries have struggled to extract the full potential benefit, as the assistance provided does not necessarily fit with local choices and priorities. At times, ostensibly magnanimous donations of assistance have in fact had a discernibly detrimental impact on local producers, to the advantage of exporters in the donating country. Concerns are often raised about the efficacy of foreign food aid, for instance, which may ultimately serve to undermine the markets of domestic growers while at the same time providing a captive source of demand for producers in the donor country.[6]

Modern Foreign Aid in the Wake of World War II

The advent of modern foreign aid may be traced back to the Marshall Plan for bilateral assistance between the United States and Europe in the wake of World War II, as well as to the Bretton Woods Conference and the creation of durable multilateral institutions to facilitate increased international assistance and cooperation, such as the United Nations, the World Bank, and the International Monetary Fund (see box 1.2 in chapter 1).[7] These efforts were informed by the adverse experiences of past conflicts, whereby the vanquished often had been compelled to pay reparations to the victors. As had been the case with Germany after World War I, such reparations often exacerbated and prolonged the impact of the conflict, leading to financial crises and a lasting sense of resentment. The succession of European wars and failed armistices that resulted had, by 1945, provided a compelling lesson in the need to invest in peace and economic integration. Thus, it was in the shadow of World War II that the international aid architecture was first articulated. Together with much smaller but increasingly significant assistance from private foundations, the combination of bilateral assistance and multilateral institutions has remained the dominant paradigm of international aid flows to the present day. The amount of aid provided and the evolution of aid programs are traced in table 5.1 and figure 5.1.[8]

Figure 5.1 and table 5.2 highlight the changing nature of the aid agencies over time, from agencies that focused almost exclusively on promoting exports to a broader multilateral agenda and then, more recently, to underpinning private sector investment. The European Bank for Reconstruction and Development (EBRD), established in 1991 after the collapse of the Berlin Wall to support the transition to a market economy in Eastern Europe, is the most modern of the multilateral development banks, and combines lending to both public and private sectors with and without government guarantees.

From 1944, upon their incorporation in Bretton Woods, New Hampshire, the initial focus of the World Bank and the International Monetary Fund (IMF) was on helping to rebuild and reinvigorate war-torn Europe and on ensuring the stability of the world financial system.[9] Of the World Bank's first six loans, five went to countries in Western Europe; the first four were explicitly for postwar reconstruction. The poor countries of the world were not the first priority, and the focus was on raising production and income rather than on broader notions of development. However, with rapid reconstruction progress and the

TABLE 5.1   Average Annual Aid Flows per Person in Real 2000 US Dollars, 1960–2003

Categories of recipients	1960–9	1970–9	1980–9	1990–9	2000–3
Low-income countries	$14.72	$16.85	$16.23	$13.82	$11.41
Middle-income countries	$6.86	$9.43	$8.52	$10.78	$8.34
High-income countries	$3.38	$4.16	$3.94	$2.94	$1.50

Source: Authors' calculations based on World Bank 2005b.

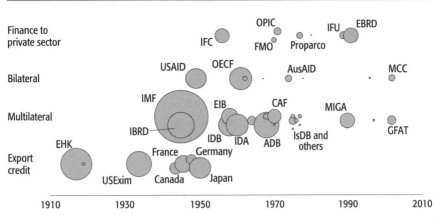

FIGURE 5.1 Magnitude and Vintage of Major Aid Organizations

Source: World Bank 2004a.
Note: Agencies are shown in year of creation, with the area of the circles proportional to their most recent annual aid commitments in US dollars. ADB is Asian Development Bank; AusAID, Austrailian Agency for International Development; CAF, Corporación Andina de Fomento; EHK, Euler Hermes Kreditversicherungs; EIB, European Investment Bank; FMO, Netherlands Development Finance Company; GFAT, Global Fund to Fight Aids, Tuberculosis, and Malaria; IBRD, International Bank for Reconstruction and Development; IDA, International Development Association; IDB, Inter-American Development Bank; IFC, International Finance Corporation; IFU, Industrialisation Fund for Developing Countries; IMF, International Monetary Fund; MCC, Millenium Challenge Corporation; MIGA, Multilateral Investment Guarantee Agency; OECF, Overseas Economic Corporation Fund; OPIC, Overseas Private Investment Corporation; and USEx/Im, Export-Import Bank of the United States. "IsDB and others" includes the Islamic Development Bank, the OPEC Fund, and the Arab Monetary Fund. Some organizations with annual commitments of less than US$1.75 million are not labeled.

increasing demands of the Cold War, this slowly began to change, and many low- and middle-income countries received increasing flows of international assistance. In 1949, U.S. President Harry Truman set in motion the "Point Four" program for technical assistance in developing countries.[10] In 1961, the United States established the Agency for International Development (USAID), and this was followed by similar actions by Sweden in 1962 and Britain in 1964.[11] These agencies, along with the African, Asian, and Latin American regional development banks that were established around the same time, complemented the work of the World Bank and provided channels for increased aid flows to the world's poorest countries. The resulting flows of aid are plotted in figure 5.2. They are given in per capita terms in table 5.1.

For many European countries, the national aid agencies at first mainly concentrated on supporting their former colonies, leaving the broader global challenges of reconstruction and development to global and regional institutions such as the World Bank and the African Development Bank. Increasingly over time, however, there has been a convergence of objectives and strategy, and a global professional cadre of development specialists has been built up. With rapid progress in post-war reconstruction, development assistance began to

TABLE 5.2	Developments in the History of Foreign Aid			
Decade	**Dominant or rising institutions**	**Donor ideology**	**Donor focus**	**Types of aid**
1940s	Marshall Plan, Bretton Woods, and UN system	Planning	Reconstruction	Program assistance
1950s	United States, with USSR	Anti- or pro-Communist, building regime capacity	Community development	Food aid and project-based financing
1960s	Bilateral programs	Anti- or pro-Communist, building regime capacity	Productive sectors (e.g., Green Revolution), infrastructure	Technical assistance, budgetary support
1970s	Expansion of multilaterals (World Bank and IMF)	Building state capacity, fulfilling basic needs	Poverty and basic needs	Import support
1980s	Nongovernmental organizations	Structural adjustment	Macroeconomic reform	Program-based, debt relief
1990s	Eastern Europe and Ex-USSR as recipients	Structural adjustment, then state capacity	Macroeconomic reform and institutions	Human development and sector-focused assistance
2000s	Security and G-8 agenda MDGs	Aid effectiveness, partnership, coherence	Results measurement, governance, post conflict	Budget support, global programs (e.g., HIV/AIDS)

Source: Adapted from Hjertholm and White 2000.
Note: MDGs are Millennium Development Goals.

focus on raising incomes in what came to be called the developing world. At first, the goal was largely confined to raising *aggregate* national incomes. Then, with the growing recognition that population growth rates vary sharply (so aggregate income did not necessarily give a clear picture of changes in living standards), attention turned to *per capita* incomes. Soon, with increased understanding of the importance of income distribution, simply raising average per capita incomes also was recognized to be too limited a goal.

By the 1970s, the attention of international aid agencies focused on the twin problems of growth and income distribution and also, increasingly, on the basic

FIGURE 5.2 Inflows of Official Development Assistance by Region, 1960–2003

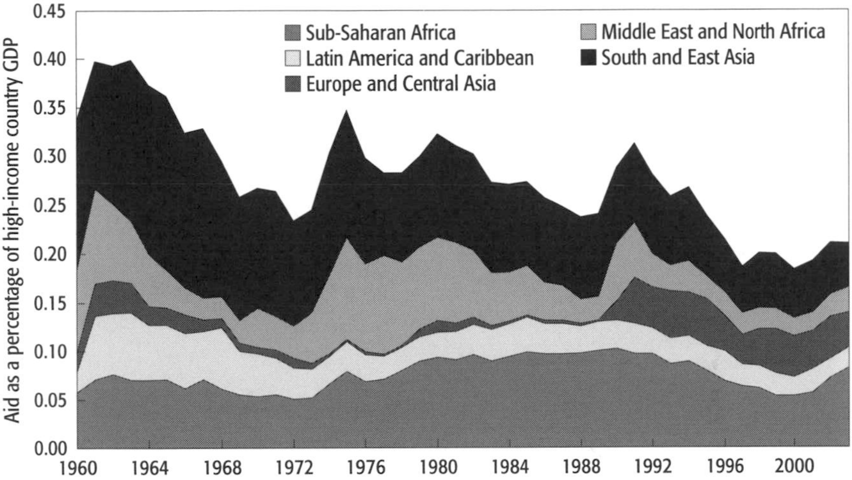

Source: World Bank 2004d.

needs of poor people.[12] Reducing income poverty became a greater priority for the international financial institutions as well as for governments. Some of the major deployments of aid relative to the size of the recipients' economies are summarized in table 5.3. The table illustrates that, for very small economies, aid can even exceed the size of the national domestic economy. On average, for developing countries, aid contributes around 3 percent of national income, and in Africa the average contribution is around 5 percent. However, as the table shows, some countries—such as Mozambique and Zambia in recent years— have seen aid levels well in excess of half of their domestic economy. Very small economies, with total national incomes of less than US$250 million and populations of fewer than 1 million people, and those emerging from conflict are most prone to very high levels of aid dependence, as table 5.3 illustrates.

Foreign Aid and the Cold War

Although the motivation for providing aid in the immediate post-World War II period was driven at the Bretton Woods Conference by reconstruction and broader considerations, this soon was coupled by a growing preoccupation with the politics of the Cold War. From the mid 1950s to the fall of the Berlin Wall in 1990, aid was increasingly used as a means to support friendly states. Also, originating in the foreign policy of the United States during the early years of

TABLE 5.3	Major Deployments of Foreign Assistance					
Country	Year	ODA/GDP (percent)	Country	Year	ODA/GDP (percent)
Palau	1994	242	Micronesia	2001	60
São Tomé & Principe	1995	185	Zambia	1995	58
Liberia	1996	108	Albania	1992	57
Rwanda	1994	95	Nicaragua	1991	56
Mozambique	1992	79	The Gambia	1986	55
Kiribati	1992	79	Tonga	1979	53
Marshall Islands	2001	75	Cambodia	1974	52
Guinea-Bissau	1994	74	Cape Verde	1986	51
Timor-Leste	2000	73	Samoa	1991	51
Somalia	1980	72	Equatorial Guinea	1989	51

Source: Authors' calculations based on World Bank 2004c.

the Cold War, economic and military aid were closely interconnected, and aid's strategic purpose was seen to be at least as much geopolitical as it was humanitarian. It was in this context that Hawkins (1970) in *The Principles of Development Aid,* suggested that foreign aid belonged to the field of political economy rather than economic analysis. Hayter's (1971) title, *Aid as Imperialism,* was even more direct. And Milton Friedman (1958, cited in Kanbur [2003]) from the other end of the ideological spectrum similarly observed, "Foreign economic aid is widely recognized as a weapon in the ideological war in which the United States is now engaged. Its assigned role is to help win over to our side those uncommitted nations that are also underdeveloped and poor" (p. 63).

Foreign Aid after the Cold War: Poverty Reduction Efforts

When aid is disbursed for political or military reasons, with an eye to supporting donor-country exports, or for transition or disaster relief in post-conflict stabilization, any positive effects for poor people generally occur with a long lag time. The end of the Cold War and progress in transition countries have made possible a more direct targeting of aid to poverty reduction efforts. As stated by Goldin, Rogers, and Stern (2002),

> *Donor financial assistance is targeted far more effectively at poverty reduction than it was a decade ago. At that time, Cold War geopolitics*

*was still exercising a heavy influence on aid allocation, and too many
recipient economies were poorly run, often suffering from excessive state
intervention in economic activity and poor governance. . . . As a result,
the poverty-reduction effectiveness per dollar of overall ODA has grown
rapidly.* (pp. 42–43)

Unfortunately, the increase in the effectiveness of aid until 2001 was not accompanied by an increase in its availability. After rising rapidly from 1945 to the early 1960s, flows of aid declined in subsequent decades. Expressed as a percentage of high-income country income (figure 5.2), aid has trended down from slightly over 0.35 percent to approximately 0.25 percent of the GDP of high-income countries in 2001. The good news, however, is that this decline finally appears to have been reversed and the last couple of years have seen a renewed commitment to increasing aid flows. Table 5.4 presents the latest data as well as a simulation of prospects for ODA for 2006.

On the recipient side, when expressed as a percentage of the recipient country's GDP, (or GNI) aid has been relatively constant over the entire period since 1967 (figure 5.3). The average amount of aid received by low-income and middle-income countries over this period was 2.7 and 0.5 percent of GDP, respectively. That said, however, there have been significant declines since the early 1990s, especially for low-income countries. Thus, from the point of view of helping poor people, foreign aid as an aspect of economic globalization can be characterized as a significant, missed opportunity.

These numbers reflect the upper limit of what countries actually receive, because we know that most bilateral aid does not in fact end up as a cash transfer in the hands of the recipient country. Figure 5.4 illustrates that a great deal of aid is not provided in the form of transfers of financial resources, but rather as food aid, emergency relief, technical cooperation, and debt relief. Although these nondiscretionary forms of aid may make an important contribution, they too often are driven by the priorities of the donors rather than the recipients. They are no substitute for predictable, multiyear flows of aid that are mobilized behind government budgets in national programs that are agreed to across the donor community. Improvements in the quality of aid are necessary as are increases in the volume of aid. For many countries, only a small part—on average around 20 percent—of the aid is provided in the form of direct support to budgeted government programs. This is one of the reasons that the transaction costs of aid are very high and in many cases divert scarce personnel from their ordinary activities of managing public resources.

Harmonization and coordination is vital to reduce the transaction costs of aid and to ensure that the national priorities of recipient countries are sup-

TABLE 5.4 ODA as a Share of GNI, 2004 and Projected for 2006			
Country	Net ODA 2004 (US$ millions)	ODA as % of GNI 2004	ODA as % of GNI Projected 2006
Austria	691	0.24	0.33
Belgium	1,452	0.41	0.64
Denmark	2,025	0.84	0.83
Finland	655	0.35	0.41
France	8,475	0.42	0.47
Germany	7,497	0.28	0.33
Greece	464	0.23	0.33
Ireland	586	0.39	0.61
Italy	2,484	0.15	0.33
Luxembourg	241	0.85	0.87
Netherlands	4,235	0.74	0.80
Portugal	1,028	0.63	0.33
Spain	2,547	0.26	0.33
Sweden	2,704	0.77	1.00
United Kingdom	7,836	0.36	0.42
EU members, total	42,920	0.36	0.44
Australia	1,465	0.25	0.26
Canada	2,537	0.26	0.27
Japan	8,859	0.19	0.22
New Zealand	210	0.23	0.26
Norway	2,200	0.87	1.00
Switzerland	1,379	0.37	0.38
United States	18,999	0.16	0.19
DAC members, total	78,569	0.25	0.30

Source: OECD-DAC 2004, cited in World Bank 2005d; www.oecd.org/statistics.
Note: DAC = Development Assistance Committee; EU = European Union; ODA = official development assistance.

ported, particularly if these are not the same as the pet projects and programs of individual donors and recipient ministries. The transaction costs of aid transfers are also important in determining what portion of total aid flows is spent productively. When ministers have to spend their time hosting visiting dignitaries, and their officials are engaged in satisfying a wide range of donor reporting requirements, the administrative and other burdens imposed by the donors may not only undermine the benefits of the project but also distract officials and scarce skilled staff from more vital priorities. It is for this reason that the recent evolution of donor consultative forums, mobilized behind national strategies and reinforcing existing budget mechanisms and harmo-

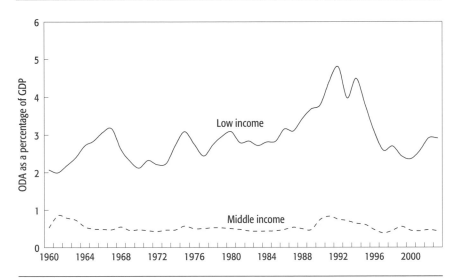

FIGURE 5.3 Foreign Aid Receipts as a Percentage of Low- and Middle-Income Country GDP, 1960–2003

Source: World Bank 2005b.

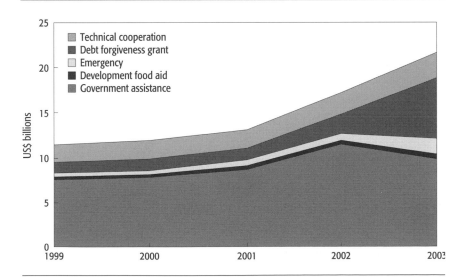

FIGURE 5.4 Breakdown of Aid Flows to Sub-Saharan Africa (excluding Nigeria)

Source: OECD Development Assistance Committee and World Bank and authors' calculations.

nized reporting standards, are so essential. Considerable progress has been made in recent years in harmonizing approaches. A growing number of national and multilateral agencies are reflected in the 2005 Paris Declaration on Aid Effectiveness, which emphasizes "ownership, harmonization, alignment, results and mutual accountability."[13]

One shortcoming of such donor consultative systems, however, is that, because they weaken the direct link between an individual donor and an individual project, they render attributions of individual ODA efforts with country or project outcomes more complex. While harmonization and common platforms almost invariably enhance the effectiveness of ODA, it may be more difficult to demonstrate to skeptical voters in rich countries where their tax payments have gone. For this reason, care may need to be taken in the design of such systems to ensure that donors can still point to concrete examples of where their funding has made a difference.

Modern Goals of Development Assistance

In recent years, the goals of development have come to embrace the elimination of poverty in all its dimensions—income poverty, illiteracy, poor health, insecurity of income, and powerlessness. A consensus is emerging around the view that development means increasing the control that poor people have over their lives—through education, health, and greater participation, as well as through income gains. This view comes not only from the testimony of poor people themselves, but also from advances in conceptual thinking about development.[14] It is clear that the various dimensions of poverty are related, and that income growth generally leads to strong progress in the non-income dimensions of poverty as well. It is also clear, however, that direct action taken to reduce poverty in these other dimensions can accelerate the reduction of both income and non-income poverty. Aid policy is beginning to reflect these new understandings.

Levels of development assistance are small compared with both other financial flows and the scale of the challenge at hand. Development aid totaled about US$54 billion in 2000, for example. This was only one-third as much as foreign direct investment (FDI) in developing countries (US$167 billion), which itself was only a small fraction of total investment (nearly US$1.5 trillion). Similarly, although the World Bank is the world's largest external provider of assistance in the education sector, it typically provides less than US$2 billion in direct assistance for education each year.[15] By comparison, annual public spending on education in the developing world totals more than US$250 billion. Given this discrepancy in scale, even if the World Bank were to greatly increase its lending in the sector from around 1 percent to 2 percent, its effectiveness would have to come primarily through catalyzing institutional development and policy change in education rather than through resource transfer alone.

Since, in comparison with domestic investment and government expenditures, aid flows are typically small and should not be viewed as a permanent source of finance, the key challenge is to ensure that they support systemic change, introducing ideas and improving practices that increase the overall size of the resources available for growth and poverty reduction. These indirect effects of aid are difficult to measure, however, and seeking attribution may undermine government leadership and harmonization with other donors. Measuring aid effectiveness is thus necessarily focused on its direct effects. However, because aid flows are relatively small, their direct effects in terms of income increases or reductions in mortality will often be swamped by other factors. For this and the reasons outlined in the next section, evaluating the impact of aid is extremely complex, although vital in order to enhance its effectiveness and create a virtuous cycle of greater willingness to provide aid.

The Multifaceted Impact of Aid

The complexity of social and economic change means that the impact of foreign aid cannot be easily separated from other factors. Countries themselves bear most of the burdens of development, and they rightly claim credit when development succeeds. Assistance works best and can be sustained only when the recipients are strongly committed to development and in charge of the process. In addition, successful projects that draw on foreign assistance in their early stages may later become self-sustaining and serve as sources for lessons that can be applied elsewhere without any foreign involvement at all. For these and other reasons, the positive impact of ODA can be very large. Nevertheless, identifying cause and effect and attributing outcomes to particular actions is often difficult.[16] Furthermore, any excessive attempt to claim credit for the successes of foreign aid can devalue the idea and practice of partnership and local leadership. Successful development strategies and actions generally depend on strong country ownership as well as good partnership among donors. This makes it difficult, even counterproductive, for any external actor to claim full credit for a reform or project.

When all aid is lumped together, some analyses have found no clear relationship between aid and growth or poverty reduction.[17] But not all aid is aimed directly at poverty reduction, nor has aid always been provided in ways that will maximize growth. Moreover, because aid is often provided to help countries cope with external shocks, even if aid is reasonably well designed and allocated—and thus effective in helping the poor—the positive impact of such aid may be obscured by the magnitude of the shocks.

Kinds of Aid: Disaster Relief and Transition

Disaster relief, for example, is not aimed directly at long-term poverty reduction and, thus, it is no surprise that such aid is not correlated with that result.[18] However, it does achieve its goal of helping to avert famine or assisting countries to recover from natural disasters. Similarly, large amounts of aid were directed at supporting the transition in Eastern Europe and Central Asia for both political and economic reasons. There, the mandate in the early 1990s was explicitly to help transform these countries into market economies, rather than to focus directly on reducing poverty.

In addition to these concerns with transition, donors initially placed too much emphasis on the role of what were often isolated projects, neglecting the quality of the overall country environment for growth—a mistake that adjustment (or policy-based) aid was intended to overcome. Finally, as mentioned above, aid was sometimes allocated for pure strategic reasons, with growth and poverty reduction in these cases being distinct secondary concerns, if indeed they were concerns at all. Given this diversity of motives, it is not surprising that aid did not always have the direct effects of spurring growth and reducing poverty.[19]

Kinds of Aid: Adjustment Programs

The ***adjustment programs*** that came into their own in part in response to the severe macroeconomic imbalances of the 1970s, including those that were the result of oil shocks, had their own problems. Donors incorrectly believed that conditionality on loans and grants could substitute for country ownership of reforms. Too often, governments receiving aid were not truly committed to reforms. Moreover, neither donors nor governments focused sufficiently on alleviating poverty in designing adjustment programs.[20] In the late 1970s and early 1980s, the pendulum in leading donor countries swung to the new policies of Ronald Reagan in the United States, Margaret Thatcher in the United Kingdom, and Helmut Kohl in the Federal Republic of Germany. This was reflected in the World Bank by a new emphasis on "getting the prices right" and the articulation of the ***Washington Consensus,*** and the aid community focused on macroeconomic reform in developing countries.[21] While it was necessary to achieve macroeconomic stability as a prerequisite for sustainable growth and poverty reduction, both donor and recipient countries underestimated the importance of governance, of institutional reforms, and of social investments as a complement to macroeconomic and trade reforms. Prescriptions for reform were too often formulaic, ignoring the central need for country specificity in the design, sequencing, and implementation of reforms.[22]

As a result, weak governance and institutions reduced the amount of productivity growth and poverty reduction that could result from the macroeconomic reforms. Many of these factors came together in Africa, contributing to the lack of progress in the region. There are many causes to slow development in Africa, including poor domestic policies and institutions and weak commitment to reform, but too often aid did little to improve the situation and in some cases even worsened it. The notable case of Zaire is discussed in box 5.1.

Rethinking Development Models and the Role of Aid

During the 1990s, a rethinking of development models and the role of aid began. This was facilitated by a combination of four developments.

- First, the end of the Cold War reduced the geopolitical pressures on aid agencies.
- Second, there was an increasing recognition of the successes of India, China, and other developing countries that had achieved macro balance

---

BOX 5.1   Aid in Zaire

If there is a worst case of geopolitical aims undermining the effectiveness of foreign aid, it may be Zaire (now the Democratic Republic of Congo) under President Mobutu Sese Seko, who ruled from 1965 to 1997. Mobutu was primarily motivated by amassing his own personal fortune, which peaked in the mid-1980s at US$4 billion, even as GNP per capita fell from US$460 in 1975 to US$100 in 1996. Domestic policies were either nonexistent or bad, and private sources of credit consequently disappeared by the mid-1980s. However, with its huge size and strategic location, Zaire was seen as a buffer against the spread of communism in southern and central Africa. Consequently, both bilateral and multilateral aid began to fill the gap as private credit dried up. Between 1960 and 2000, donors disbursed more than US$10 billion in aid to Zaire, with the bulk of this beginning in the 1980s.

Failure to pay adequate attention to corruption and wasteful use of funds severely undermined the effectiveness of this foreign aid. Indeed, total capital flight from the country has been estimated by Ndikumana and Boyce (1998) to be US$12 billion in real 1990 dollars, and Transparency International estimates that US$5 billion was stolen by Mobutu himself. It would be hard to argue much was achieved in Zaire, either in economic or social terms, as a result of the aid.

The result has been increasing skepticism in the donor countries that aid is effective. Well over half of respondents in successive polls believe that aid is wasted, as indeed it often was when it was not aimed at poverty reduction. For aid to lead to poverty reduction, three things are necessary:

- It must aim for poverty reduction rather than geopolitical or other objectives.
- It must go to countries where poor people live.
- It must go to countries whose governments are committed to the eradication of poverty.

Sources: Burns, Holman, and Huband 1997; Ndikumana and Boyce 1998; *Financial Times,* October 13, 2004; and Goldin, Rogers, and Stern 2002; Transparency International 2004.

and sustained growth while adopting their own particular development models.[23]

- Third, mounting evidence suggested an apparent failure of orthodox adjustment models adopted, albeit reluctantly, by African and other highly indebted countries, as seen by the lack of positive growth and poverty outcomes.
- Finally, as discussed in chapter 7, a growing body of analytic literature highlighted the importance of the need for a more comprehensive approach to development and wider understanding of poverty, focusing on human capital (education, health) and physical capital (infrastructure) as well as institutions, governance, and participation.[24]

As discussed in chapters 1 and 2, the understanding that poverty is about more than income leads to the recognition that growth is not the only determinant of poverty reduction. Social indicators—health and education—improved far faster in all developing countries during the 20th century than would have been expected, given the rate of income growth these countries experienced. Most countries have made major progress in increasing educational attainment and health outcomes by targeting these goals directly and by applying new knowledge and technologies to them specifically, rather than just waiting for the effects of income growth to improve these indicators. At every level of income, infant mortality fell sharply during the 20th century. For example, a typical country with per capita income of $8,000 in 1950 (measured in 1995 US dollars) would have had, on average, an infant mortality rate of 45 per 1,000 live births. By 1970, a country at the same real income level would typically have had an infant mortality rate of only 30 per 1,000, and by 1995, only 15 per 1,000. Similar reductions occurred all along the income spectrum, including in the poorest countries.

The improvements in social indicators have been remarkable by historical standards. Life expectancy in developing countries increased by 20 years over a period of only 40 years, as it increased from the mid-40s to the mid-60s. By comparison, it probably took millennia to improve life expectancy from the mid-20s to the mid-40s. Literacy improvements have also been remarkable: whereas in 1970 nearly two out of every four adults were illiterate, now it is only one out of every four.

These advances in education and health have greatly improved the welfare of individuals and families. Not only are education and health valuable in themselves, but they also increase income-earning capacity. Where macroeconomic analyses of the growth effects of education have been somewhat ambiguous, the microeconomic evidence of the returns to education is overwhelming and robust.[25] Research suggests that each additional year of education increases the average individual worker's wages by at least 5 to 10 percent.[26] Educating girls and women is a particularly effective way to raise the human development levels of children. Mothers who are more educated have healthier children, even at a given level of income. They are also more productive in the labor force, which raises household incomes and thereby increases child survival rates—in part because, compared with men, women tend to spend additional income in ways that benefit children more.[27]

The Importance of Public Policy

These trends make it clear that *public policy matters.* As we discuss in chapter 7, government has a role not only in ensuring delivery of good basic services in health and education, but also in ensuring that technology and knowledge is spread widely through the economy. The dramatic improvement in life expectancy at a given income level is attributable to environmental changes and is the result of public health actions. The control of diarrhea-related diseases, including the development of oral rehydration therapy to reduce child mortality, is one example; the education of women was an important component of these efforts. Smallpox eradication, made possible through a combination of advances in public health research and effective program management, is another example of a successful 20th century public health effort.[28]

The statistical evidence shows that large-scale financial aid can generally be used effectively to reduce poverty when reasonably good policies are in place.[29] In recent years, donors have increasingly acted on these findings by tailoring support to local needs and circumstances. Thus, the balance of support has moved toward providing large-scale aid to those who can use it well and focusing on knowledge and *capacity-building* support in other countries. This has been reflected in greater selectivity and coordination in lending on the part of aid agencies, shifting resources toward governance and institutions, emphasizing ownership, and making room for diverse responses to local needs. These new approaches and procedures have begun to pay off. However, it is clear that there is still much to learn: for example, more work is needed on the question of how best to catalyze and support reforms and institution-building in countries with very weak policies, institutions, and governance.

Collier, Deverajan, and Dollar (2001) and Collier and Dollar (2001) sought to quantify the extent to which policies matter for aid effectiveness. Their analysis claims that in 1990, countries with worse policies and institutions received US$44 per capita in ODA from all sources (multilateral and bilateral), while those with better policies received less: only US$39 per capita. By the late 1990s, the situation was reversed: better-policy countries received US$28 per capita, or almost twice as much as the worse-policy countries (US$16 per capita). As a result, the poverty-reduction effectiveness per dollar of overall ODA has grown rapidly. In 1990, a one-time aid increase of US$1 billion allocated across countries in proportion to existing ODA would have permanently lifted an estimated 105,000 people out of poverty; but by 1997–8, that number had improved to 284,000 people lifted out of poverty.[30] In other words, the estimated poverty-reduction productivity of ODA nearly tripled during the 1990s. Similar lines of inquiry (for example, Collier and Dollar 2002) suggest that reallocating existing levels of aid more effectively could double the numbers of people lifted out of poverty by these flows.

Why would the overall environment matter so much in determining the effectiveness of ODA? The first reason is very straightforward: policies and institutions affect project quality. For example, a major reason for the dramatic decline in measured World Bank project outcomes in the 1970s and 1980s was the deterioration in policy quality and governance in many borrowing countries. No matter how well designed, a project can easily be undermined by high levels of macroeconomic volatility or of government corruption.

The second reason is more subtle. Even if a project does seem to succeed—based on narrow measures of economic returns and successfully attaining project objectives—the actual marginal contribution of aid funneled through that project may be small or even negative. This is because government resources are often largely fungible: money can be moved relatively easily from one intended use to another. Thus if donors choose to finance a primary education project, displacing local money that would have been used for education, that local money could then be shifted to less productive purposes, such as military spending. In a country with poor public expenditure management, the displaced money could even be diverted to the personal uses of corrupt officials. In this case, the indirect but very real effect of aid could be to promote corruption.[31]

Should we then use only policy and institutional quality as measures in determining aid flows? Should countries with poor policy and poor institutional quality receive no aid at all? This would probably be too rash a conclusion. Recent research by Clemens, Radelet, and Bhavnani (2004) takes an entirely different approach. Instead of focusing on the different policy and institutional characteristics of recipient countries, they focus on the characteristics of different types of aid flows. Importantly, they consider only what they term "short-impact" aid, which includes budget and balance of payments support, infrastructure investments, and aid for productive sectors such as agriculture and industry. In contrast to previous studies, they find a strong impact of aid on growth (and thus on poverty reduction, at least to some extent) regardless of institutions and policies.[32] In light of such evidence, it is necessary to be cautious and avoid a new fadism or herd behavior in the reallocation of aid flows to a small group of countries that meet the criteria. Timely interventions to support reform efforts and to avert famines and other crises remain a vital function of aid.

The above considerations suggest that aid can indeed be very productive. Evidence also suggests that developing countries have never as a group been better able to absorb distributed aid. Additionally, aid agencies have never been better able to disburse aid more effectively. Remarkably, however, as discussed above, although there is virtual unanimity that aid effectiveness has improved, the amount of aid given by rich countries as a share of their income has declined. Since 2001, this trend has reversed, but even optimistic predictions indicate that aid will only account for 0.30 percent of OECD donors' income in 2006, down from 0.33 percent in 1992 but up from the trough of 0.22 percent.

Improving the Effectiveness of Aid

As we have seen, the development community's understanding of both development and poverty has evolved in some significant ways. Most importantly, it is now widely accepted that poverty reduction efforts should address poverty in all its dimensions—not only lack of income, but also the lack of health and education, vulnerability to shocks, and poor peoples' lack of control over their lives.[33] This conception of poverty can call for different approaches than those used in the past. Examples of these different approaches include an increased focus on public service delivery to vulnerable groups and greater attention to early disclosure of information that poor people can use.

As we discuss in chapter 7, experience has shown that neither the central planning approach followed by many countries in the 1950s and 1960s nor the minimal-government, free-market approach advocated by many aid agencies in the late 1970s and the 1980s will achieve these development and poverty alleviation goals. Most effective approaches to development will be led by the private sector, but they need to have effective government to provide the governance framework, to assist with or provide physical infrastructure, to invest in education and health, and to ensure the social cohesion necessary for growth and poverty reduction.[34] Institutional development has too often been neglected in past policy discussions, but it is now recognized to be essential to sustained poverty reduction. Although a number of key principles for effective development are clear, there is no single road to follow. Countries must devise their own strategies and approaches, appropriate for their own country circumstances and goals.

The most successful development assistance will have effects that reverberate far beyond the confines of the project itself, either because the ideas in the project are replicated elsewhere or because the intervention has helped institutionalize new approaches. As noted above, levels of aid are small relative to the private capital and public resources that it can leverage. Therefore, aid's largest impact will come through the effects of such demonstration and institution-building. These wider or deeper effects of aid are far harder to measure than its direct effects.

China, India, Mozambique, Poland, Uganda, and Vietnam are all examples of countries where, within the past two decades, policy and institutional reforms have sparked an acceleration of development. In each of these cases, the country and its government have been the prime movers for reform, and each country mapped out its own development strategy and approach. Their experiences do have some common features—most notably an increase in market orientation and macroeconomic stability—and all have seen their growth powered by private sectors (both farms and firms) that have begun to thrive. Although these countries did act along those broad guidelines on development, none of them closely followed any external blueprint for development offered by international institutions and foreign donors.

Yet in all of these cases, development assistance from many sources has supported the transformation. In some cases, advice was more important than lending. In China, for example, aid flows have been dwarfed by inflows of private capital. But development assistance helped pave the way for private sector growth and international integration. For example, external analysis and advice was provided to help China open its economy to investment, unify its exchange rate, and improve its ports early in its transition period.

The converse is also clearly true. There are many examples of countries that have received very large volumes of aid over time, with little result in terms of poverty reduction. A case in point, discussed in box 5.1, is the Democratic Republic of Congo (formerly Zaire). Also, donor-supported progress on human development indicators in a number of countries has been reversed by the AIDS epidemic or by conflict. In Botswana, which otherwise has a highly successful economy, AIDS reduced life expectancy from 57 years to 39 years in the 1990s. In Sierra Leone, conflict and its aftermath have kept life expectancy at around 35 years. We take up the issues of both HIV/AIDS and conflict in chapter 8 when we present our policy agenda.

Commitment of the leadership is one of the most critical conditions for ensuring the success of reforms, whether they are in the area of the macroeconomy or in combating epidemics such as HIV/AIDS. Evidence has shown that policy change is driven by the country's own initiative, capacity, and political readiness rather than by foreign assistance and associated loan condition-ality.[35] Relying heavily on conditionality is ineffective for several reasons:

- It can be difficult to monitor whether a government has in fact fulfilled the conditions, particularly when external shocks muddy the picture.
- Governments may revert to old practices as soon as the money has been disbursed.
- When assessments are subjective, donors may have an incentive to emphasize progress to keep programs moving.

Without country ownership, adjustment lending has not only failed to support reforms, but may have contributed to their delay. For example, case studies of Côte d'Ivoire, the Democratic Republic of Congo, Kenya, Nigeria, and Tanzania all concluded that the availability of aid money in the 1980s postponed much-needed reforms.[36]

In practice, country commitment has often proved difficult to assess. For example, a government may be seriously committed to a reform program but subsequently find it impossible to implement key measures, sometimes for reasons not fully under the government's control. In other cases, the government may be interested primarily in the funds, not in the reforms on which the funding is conditional. For this reason, the government's track record, as measured by the quality of the policies and institutions it has already put in place, is often a good indicator of its commitment to reform. That said, as discussed in the previous section, some types of aid might be effective even with a limited degree of reform. For example, the delivery of aid to eliminate school fees or through providing an incentive to attend school has the potential, already in progress, to educate millions more African children than are educated today.[37]

Assisting Weak States

If the conclusion of the past 50 years of aid is that aid (and debt relief) should be allocated to countries with a policy and institutional environment that is conducive to effective use, what should be done in countries where this does not exist? Or to put it another way, how can the international community assist countries where states can be characterized as "weak" or "failed?" Approaches that work in the typical low-income country may not be appropriate in post-conflict and weak states, as such states usually lack the governance, institutions, and necessary leadership for reform. In these circumstances, traditional lending conditionality has not worked well to induce and support reform.

Countries with weak or failed states vary widely in their problems and opportunities. As for the better-performing countries, no single strategy will be appropriate for all of them. Each has its specific challenges and must look for unique solutions. Nevertheless, it is useful to distinguish approaches in post-conflict and weak states from those that will work in countries with better policies, institutions, and governance.

Approaches for Post-Conflict and Weak States

Large-scale financial transfers are unlikely to work well in post-conflict and weak states because the absorptive capacity in these environments is quite limited. Instead, donors should focus on knowledge transfer and capacity-building to facilitate change. Because of constraints on government capacity, such efforts should concentrate on a limited reform agenda that is both sensible in economic terms (that is, mindful of sequencing issues—what is possible to achieve and what should be prioritized) and feasible from a socio-political standpoint. Only when they develop greater capacity will these countries generally be able to make good use of large-scale aid. There will often be a case for using aid to improve basic health and education services. To be effective, however, funding should probably be directed through channels other than the central government. This suggests wholesale-retail structures in which a donor-monitored wholesaling organization contracts with multiple channels of retail provision, such as the private sector, NGOs, and local governments. The role of the United Nations and its agencies in emergency relief and coordination with donors on refugees for funding and provision of basic services is important and not always sufficiently recognized. The very least that poor people in dire emergencies should be able to expect is that the international community demonstrates that it is able to coordinate and act effectively.

Experience of Sub-Saharan Africa

Improvements in policies and institutions in many Sub-Saharan African countries, combined with examples of successful poverty reduction in a few countries, now provide grounds for hope.[38] As policies in many Sub-Saharan African countries improved, so did economic performance: GDP growth rates rose to an average of 4.3 percent in 1994–8, or nearly 2 percentage points higher than it was in the 1980s. A few countries, such as Mozambique and Uganda, have seen especially strong returns to reform. These developments have important implications for aid allocation: although not every country in Africa could absorb an increase in large-scale aid (for reasons described in the previous section), as the effectiveness of aid rises, so too should the amount of aid allocated to the region. Instead, African countries with good policy saw a substantial decline in aid flows in the 1990s, with aid per capita falling by roughly a third, even as prices for export commodities also fell sharply. Annual per capita aid in Africa is currently well below the levels of 20 years ago, while policies are greatly improved, both in the recipient and in the donor countries. For these reasons, much more aid than is currently given to well-performing countries can be effectively utilized.

Aid for Post-Conflict Countries in Need of Reform

Although aid effectiveness requires that large-scale financial assistance be allocated to poor countries that have demonstrated the capacity to use aid well, the international community cannot simply abandon people who live in countries that lack the policies, institutions, and governance necessary for sustained growth and for effective use of aid. Poor people in these countries are among the poorest in the world and face the greatest hurdles in improving their lives. Experience suggests that current technical assistance for capacity-building efforts, as well as the promise of greater financial assistance if policies, institutions, and governance improve, is often insufficient to enable these countries to initiate and sustain reform.

Of the two or three dozen countries with the poorest institutions and policies, only a few have made major improvements in their environments for growth and poverty reduction over the past decade, in contrast to the broad improvements in policies in other developing countries. Ethiopia, Mozambique, and Uganda are unusual among former post-conflict countries in having achieved significant progress. Other post-conflict countries have seen little development progress, and the performance of the development agencies lending portfolio in this group has been relatively poor. Projects have failed there at double the rate for other countries.

Innovative Aid Programs

Despite huge advances in science and in the understanding of the aid and development processes, there is much that we still do not know. Perhaps most important, we do not understand fully how to help improve institutions and governance, especially in the poorest countries where the needs are greatest.[39] And we are still learning how best to deal with pressing cross-border issues—such as disease, environmental problems, and political instability—that threaten development.

Global development challenges such as conflict, loss of biodiversity, deforestation, climate change, and the spread of infectious diseases cannot be handled solely by individual countries acting at the national level. They require sustained, multilateral action. As the number and scope of global challenges have grown, so too have the number of actors involved, creating a need for new partnerships and networks among stakeholders. Private charities have become a force in the areas of environment and health. Pharmaceutical companies have become donors to global health initiatives. As discussed in chapter 4, private capital flows to developing countries (especially in the form of FDI) now dwarf official development assistance. The search for international common ground, together with a variety of formal and informal international agreements, have led to new alliances and revised roles for a range of institutions that include the Global Environment Facility, the World Trade Organization, and the various UN bodies. No single actor can speak to all of these challenges, but efforts to address them have been growing rapidly.

According to the UN Secretary General's office, hundreds of new programs to address issues of global scope are being created each year. Although multinational initiatives are required, they often must be linked to country actions. Many global initiatives address problems that have both important domestic effects and major cross-border spillovers, such as financial contagion, the spread of AIDS, ozone depletion, and toxic pollution. Other global problems call for increasing the efficiency of resources spent at the country level through the use of science and technology available only in the richer countries or globally supported research centers. In most cases, complementary national efforts in developing countries are central to either achieving objectives of the global programs (such as biodiversity conservation, which often builds on local programs) or ensuring developing countries' access to their benefits (such as agricultural productivity, where new crop varieties must be matched to locally adapted cultivation practices). Here, we take up just three examples of effective global programs, which highlight the benefits of global action on aid.

Onchocerciasis Control Program (OCP)

The first program addresses riverblindness or onchocerciasis, a disease widespread in Africa. It causes blindness, disfigurement, and unbearable itching in its victims, and has rendered large tracts of farmland in Africa uninhabitable. The Onchocerciasis Control Programme (OCP) was created in 1974 with two primary objectives. The first was to eliminate onchocerciasis as a public health problem and as an obstacle to socioeconomic development throughout an 11-country area of West Africa (Benin, Burkina Faso, Côte d'Ivoire, Ghana, Guinea, Guinea-Bissau, Mali, Niger, Senegal, Sierra Leone, and Togo). The second objective was to leave participating countries with the capacity to maintain this achievement. OCP was sponsored by four agencies: the United Nations Development Programme (UNDP), the Food and Agriculture Organization (FAO), the World Bank, and the World Health Organization (WHO).

OCP has now halted transmission and virtually eliminated prevalence of onchocerciasis throughout the 11-country subregion containing 35 million people. About 600,000 cases of blindness have been prevented, 5 million years of productive labor added to the economies of 11 countries, and 16 million children born within the OCP area have been spared any risk of contracting onchocerciasis. In addition, control operations have freed up an estimated 25 million hectares of arable land that is now experiencing spontaneous settlement. OCP has been hailed as one of the most successful partnerships in the history of development assistance.[40] As summarized by Benton and others (2002), "Through a combination of persistence, dedication, and happenstance, the Onchocerciasis Control Programme evolved from an ambitious plan to a sterling example of disease control" (pp. 8–9).

Given this success, the program has extended operations to what is now called the African Program for Onchocerciasis Control. This program, begun in 1995, extends the OCP to the remaining 19 infested African countries. This effort involves establishing networks of community-directed drug distributors (CDD) that can potentially be used to combat other health problems in the region. Again, as summarized by Benton and others (2002), "What began as a top-down, vertical, disease-control programme has evolved into a bottom-up, integrated approach that couples strong regional co-ordination with the empowerment of local communities to address not only onchocerciasis but, potentially, many other health problems" (p. 12). The potential of the CDD to help combat HIV/AIDS is particularly of interest here.

The Green Revolution

Sometimes building on success involves helping to diffuse ideas across countries and regions through partnership with other development actors.[41] The *Green Revolution,* which began in South Asia in the 1970s and spread to Africa and Latin America, has led to impressive gains in production of basic food crops across the developing world, as shown in table 5.5. Between 1970 and 1997, yields of cereals in developing countries rose more than 75 percent, coarse grains 73 percent, root crops 24 percent, and pulses nearly 11 percent. International aid agencies supported this sweeping change through its lending for irrigation, rural infrastructure, and agriculture, and by mobilizing support with other donors through the Consultative Group for International Agricultural Research, better known by its acronym, the CGIAR. This is a second example of an effective aid program.

TABLE 5.5 Yields of Major Food Crops [kg/ha] in Developing Nations, 1970–2004

Period	Cereals[a]	Coarse grain[b]	Root crops[c]	Pulses[d]
1970–4	1,522.1	1,112.8	9,393.7	586.7
1975–9	1,745.4	1,308.6	10,009.1	611.8
1980–4	2,055.5	1,500.1	10,539.7	620.6
1985–9	2,257.1	1,561.4	10,945.0	633.2
1990–4	2,488.7	1,756.8	11,228.4	638.6
1995–9	2,711.0	1,955.9	11,811.6	656.9
2000–4	2,798.6	2,040.7	12,135.9	684.8
Change[e]	**+83.86%**	**+83.38%**	**+29.19%**	**+16.72%**

a. Wheat, rice, other.
b. Corn, barley, rye, oats, millet, sorghum, other.
c. Potatoes, sweet potatoes, cassava, taro, yams.
d. Dry beans, broadbeans, dry peas, chickpeas, cowpeas, pigeon peas, lentils, other.
e. Percentage change from 1970-4 to 2000-4.
Source: FAO Statistics (http://www.fao.org).

The CGIAR, created in 1971, now includes 16 international agricultural research centers. The 8,500 CGIAR scientific staff members work to develop and produce in the following areas:

- higher-yield food crops
- more productive livestock, fish, and trees
- improved farming systems
- better policies
- enhanced scientific capacity in developing countries.[42]

The knowledge generated by CGIAR—and the public- and private-sector organizations that work with it as partners, researchers, and advisors—has paid poor consumers handsome dividends in terms of increased output and lower food prices. More than 300 varieties of wheat and rice and more than 200 varieties of maize developed through CGIAR-supported research are being grown by farmers in developing countries. Food production has doubled, improving health and nutrition for millions. New, more environment-friendly technologies developed by CGIAR have released between 230 and 340 million hectares of land for cultivation worldwide, helping to conserve land and water resources and biodiversity. CGIAR's efforts have helped to reduce pesticide use in developing countries. For example, control of cassava pests alone has increased the value of annual production in Sub-Saharan Africa by US$400 million.

Yet the CGIAR must now meet new challenges. Agriculture research technology has changed, giving prominence to molecular biology and genetic approaches. More robust intellectual property rights have produced an explosion in private investment for agricultural research. These changes pose new challenges to the CGIAR size, organization, and approach as does the urgent need to lift agricultural productivity in Africa. The Commission for Africa (2005) notes that US$340 million a year is required by the CGIAR to help offset Africa's agricultural productivity deficit.

African Economic Research Consortium (AERC)

A third example of a successful global program is the African Economic Research Consortium (AERC), which is less well known than the first two. Like the river blindness control program, the AERC is a regional program focused on addressing one of Africa's greatest needs: strong domestic capacity for policy analysis and formulation. Recent development experience shows clearly that development strategies must be "owned" by the countries that implement them, not dictated by outside donors. But the ability to participate in design and decision making that is necessary for ownership depends on local capacity for policy analysis. For this reason, capacity building is an essential element of development assistance.

The international nature of the AERC has made it stronger by supporting a critical mass of researchers and academic institutions, and by encouraging the sharing of experiences across countries. Its mission statement has as its principle objective "to strengthen local capacity for conducting independent, rigorous inquiry into problems pertinent to the management of economies in Sub-Saharan Africa." Established in 1988, this initiative now covers 22 countries.

Established by six international and bilateral agencies and private foundations, AERC is now funded by 15 donors, including foundations, governments, and multilateral organizations. It has a budget of approximately US$7 million a year. The AERC conducts research in-house and administers a small grants program for researchers in academia and policy-making institutions.[43] In addition to its research program, the AERC began in 1992 to administer a two-year collaborative Masters of Arts (MA) program in economics with students and faculty from 20 universities in 15 Sub-Saharan African countries. The program has produced about 800 MA graduates in economics to date, and 200 more students now participate in this program. Many graduates of the AERC have gone on to research and teaching posts throughout the region, and others to high-level positions in African central banks and finance ministries.

Easing the Burden of Debt

As we related in chapter 4, debt financing has been an important part of financing in developing countries for centuries and no reading of economic history is complete without reference to the debt crises of previous eras. The first recent major debt crisis to take place, and in which aid policies included significant debt components, occurred when an oil-price shock and global recession hit in the late 1970s and early 1980s. Commodity prices turned sharply against the non-oil commodity exporters, making it difficult for them to pay for both imports and debt service. While interest rates were rising, official lending increased to help cushion the effects of the shock, and to substitute for finance from commercial sources, which for most borrowing countries evaporated.

Components of Foreign Debt

For all countries, including developing countries, any deficit on the current account (such as through trade deficits) that is not made up for by net factor receipts, transfers such as foreign aid, FDI, or a reduction in foreign reserves necessarily translates into foreign debt as the country sells financial assets of various kinds to generate an offsetting surplus on the capital account.[44] It sometimes makes sense for developing countries to engage in short-term borrowing of this kind to cover short-term current account deficits.

Build Up of Unsustainable Debt in Highly Indebted Countries

Increasingly from the 1950s, developing countries had access to more long-term borrowing, which in most instances is better suited to their needs. However, where such borrowing is not used to make productive investments that increase output of the tradable sectors of the economy (which increase exports relative to imports), current accounts will persist indefinitely, and debt will build up to unsustainable levels.

In many of the highly-indebted countries, the expected improvements in policy performance did not materialize, whether because of insufficient commitment by borrowers or because the design of the adjustment had not paid enough attention to the political economy of reform, governance, and corruption or to social concerns. In other cases, reforms were implemented but did not lead to the expected supply and growth response. As a result, the GDP average growth rate between 1980 and 1987 of the 33 countries that were characterized in the mid-1990s as the most severely indebted low-income countries was just 1.9 percent—which translated into an income decline in per capita terms. The cumulative effect of the shock and economic decline was that a debt burden that had been reasonable became unsustainable. Between 1982 and 1992, the debt-to-export ratio of the 33 most highly indebted countries rose from 266 to 620 percent.[45]

FIGURE 5.5 External Debt of Developing Countries

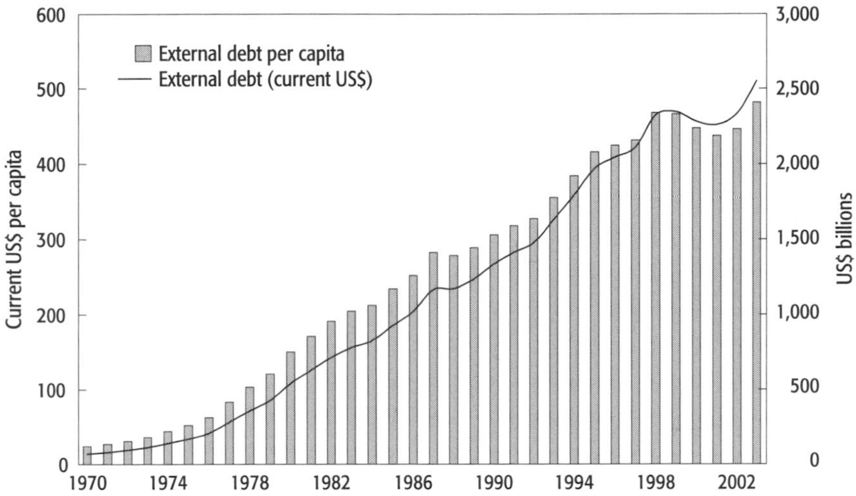

Source: World Bank, World Development Indicators 2005.

The Debt Crisis

The recent history of external debt is traced in figure 5.5, both in total terms (solid line and right-hand axis) and in per capita terms (vertical bars, left-hand axis). Significant increases in both measures began in the mid-1970s. As reported in Reinert (2005), "Beginning in 1976, the IMF began to sound warnings about the sustainability of developing-country borrowing from the commercial banking system. The banking system reacted with hostility to these warnings, arguing that the Fund had no place interfering with private transactions" (p. 259).

The IMF's warnings became clear when the "debt crisis" began in 1982. The initiating event was Mexico's announcement that it would stop servicing its foreign currency debt. Within months, the debt crisis had spread to Brazil and Argentina. In 1982, the total external debt of developing countries was approximately US$750 billion and per capita external debt was approximately US$200. As can be seen in figure 5.5, both total and per capita external debt continued to increase significantly through 1999 to approximately US$2.4 billion and US$470 per capita. Indeed, between 1990 and 2002, the total external debt for developing countries increased by approximately US$1 trillion, the bulk of which was for middle-income countries. These continued debt burdens in the developing world negatively affect both growth prospects and the financing of basic public services. Both of these, in turn, negatively affect poverty in all its dimensions.

International Debt Relief Efforts: HIPC Initiative

Since the late 1980s, the international development community has attempted to address the problem through a variety of debt-reduction mechanisms. In 1996 it went a step further, creating the Heavily Indebted Poor Countries (HIPC) debt relief initiative to deepen debt relief for poor countries suffering from unsustainable debt burdens. The initiative aims to *increase the effectiveness of aid* by helping poor countries achieve sustainable levels of debt while strengthening the link between debt relief and strong policy performance. Forty-two countries, primarily from the Sub-Saharan Africa region, are identified as potentially eligible to receive debt relief under this initiative. As of October 2004, 27 countries had met the required governance and other standards and are receiving debt relief that will amount to about US$54 billion over time.[46] ***Debt-service-to-export ratios*** have been reduced for this set of countries to an average of 10 percent.[47]

Not only does HIPC reduce ***debt overhang***, it also supports positive change toward better poverty reduction. Debt relief under the HIPC initiative is intended for countries that are pursuing effective poverty reduction strategies as ascertained by the World Bank and the IMF; both better public expenditure management and increased social expenditures are critical elements of this affirmation of effectiveness (www.worldbank.org/debt). For the countries that have received HIPC relief, the ratio of social expenditures to GDP is projected to increase significantly. The challenges are to ensure that these expenditures translate into better outcomes in the social sector; that vital infrastructure improvements also increase; and, more important, that the broader policy environment continues to improve and support growth and poverty reduction.

The HIPC experience has demonstrated that debt relief can work. It is clear, however, that the amounts allocated within HIPC—the debts that are written off—are insufficient to put all low-income countries on a sustainable debt repayment path and to ease the pressure on their debt servicing sufficiently to allow an accelerated reallocation of funds toward required investments in infrastructure, education, health, and other poverty reduction expenditures. A new framework for debt sustainability was therefore needed to match the need for funds in low-income countries with their ability to service debt. This requires substantial increases in the funds available. The July 2005 commitment at the Gleneagles, Scotland, summit of the Group of Eight leaders to allocate US$40 billion for additional debt relief is a significant step forward. The Group of Eight confirmed that these funds will be "additional" to previous commitments to increase aid (including to the International Development Association) and that finance that would go to the better performers who had paid their debts would not be cannibalized to write off the debts of the eligible HIPC countries.

While the accelerated cancellation of debt has been widely welcomed, there are concerns regarding the moral hazard and incentive effect of debt write-offs. For those countries that have diligently repaid their debts or carefully constrained their debt burden, the prospect of additional aid flows being given to reduce the obligations of those who have been less prudent may seem unfair. To add to this complexity is the question of the intertemporal nature of debt—the debts being repaid today typically were incurred by previous generations of leaders. Many individuals and some current governments in countries where dictators incurred debts argue that these debts are illegitimate. There are moves that do not necessarily have government support in a wide range of countries, including Indonesia, Nigeria, and South Africa to write off what may be termed illegitimate or "odious" debts, and this precedent has been established for Iraq.[48]

Without debating the virtues of this position, the key issue is the source of these additional funds. Global flows, like national flows, need to be sourced and paid for with additional commitments. In honoring their commitments to increasing aid, the rich countries need to ensure that funding to meet debt forgiveness is additional and does not represent a claim on existing or future commitments to other forms of aid. They also need to ensure that all countries that are able to use aid effectively benefit from additional flows, so that easing the burden of debt does not come at the expense of poor people in other countries.

The Millennium Development Goals and Donor Coordination

A key driver of the effectiveness of aid flows is that they become more predictable and that there is harmonization behind country-owned programs. Too many ministers and civil servants in poor countries spend their time servicing the needs of donors—from taking visiting dignitaries to visit their pet projects to meeting the unique audit and reporting needs of the different aid and donor agencies. In Tanzania, for example, it was estimated that well over a thousand quarterly reports need to be completed for donors. Aid agencies have a responsibility to ensure that their requirements are harmonized in a set of common standards and that their demands on countries are focused on ensuring that the money goes to projects and programs prioritized in national budgets, rather than to individual projects in localities favored by foreign or domestic politicians. In addition, donors have a responsibility to ensure that their flows are predictable, that they agree to multiyear commitments, and that they are not restricted to contracts or goods and services procured from the donor country. A visit to virtually any low-income country reveals the carcasses of projects and programs initiated through donor pressure and promises and that have failed through lack of follow-through in funding and maintenance.

The commitment in 2002 by heads of state of both rich and poor countries to achieving the Millennium Development Goals (MDGs) requires the following, as set out in more detail in box 5.2:

- halving poverty and hunger by 2015
- achieving universal primary education
- eliminating gender disparity in education
- reducing by three-quarters maternal mortality
- combating HIV/AIDS and other diseases
- halving the proportion of people without access to potable water
- a global partnership for development.

This agreement reflected a unique coming together in terms of defining the problem and the role of different actors. It has given clear common goals to the international community, and not least to donor agencies and the multi-lateral institutions, as well as a set of agreed measurable targets and results.

Unfortunately, it is now becoming clear that many or most of these goals will be missed. Indeed, there is a consensus developing that perhaps only one goal, that of halving income poverty, will be met at the aggregate global level. To help meet this and other goals, a set of high-income countries have committed themselves to increasing their aid donations to 0.7 percent of GDP. Nearly every rich country, however, has failed so far to meet this target,[49] although Sweden , Denmark, Luxembourg, Norway, and the Netherlands by 2004 had allocated over 0.7 percent of their income to aid. It is worth noting that the funds represented by this 0.7 percent of GDP target are approximately half of what the rich world spends on agricultural subsidies, so it is not a question of feasibility. It is, rather, a question of will.[50]

A New Way Forward

What does this analysis imply about aid flows and poverty? One lesson is that external resources alone will not be sufficient to ensure that poverty goals are met. The recipient country's level of commitment and the quality of its policies and institutions are the primary determinants of progress. Experience and analysis have taught us that outside aid cannot substitute effectively for these factors. It can, however, be an effective complement, supporting national efforts to reduce poverty. A second lesson is that, when a country is committed to reform and poverty reduction, external support has substantial payoffs. External support can take several forms including, but not limited to, aid.

BOX 5.2 Millennium Development Goals

The Millennium Development Goals are an ambitious agenda for reducing poverty and improving lives that world leaders agreed on at the Millennium Summit in September 2000. For each goal one or more targets have been set, most for 2015, using 1990 as a benchmark:

1. **Eradicate extreme poverty and hunger**
   Target for 2015: Halve the proportion of people living on less than a dollar a day and those who suffer from hunger.

2. **Achieve universal primary education**
   Target for 2015: Ensure that all boys and girls complete primary school.

3. **Promote gender equality and empower women**
   Targets for 2005 and 2015: Eliminate gender disparities in primary and secondary education preferably by 2005, and at all levels by 2015.

4. **Reduce child mortality**
   Target for 2015: Reduce by two-thirds the mortality rate among children under five.

5. **Improve maternal health**
   Target for 2015: Reduce by three-quarters the ratio of women dying in childbirth.

6. **Combat HIV/AIDS, malaria, and other diseases**
   Target for 2015: Halt and begin to reverse the spread of HIV/AIDS and the incidence of malaria and other major diseases.

7. **Ensure environmental sustainability**
   Targets:
   - Integrate the principles of sustainable development into country policies and programs and reverse the loss of environmental resources
   - By 2015, reduce by half the proportion of people without access to safe drinking water
   - By 2020 achieve significant improvement in the lives of at least 100 million slum dwellers.

8. **Develop a global partnership for development**
   Targets:
   - Develop further an open trading and financial system that includes a commitment to good governance, development, and poverty reduction—nationally and internationally
   - Address the least developed countries' special needs, and the special needs of landlocked and small island developing states
   - Deal comprehensively with developing countries' debt problems
   - Develop decent and productive work for youth
   - In cooperation with pharmaceutical companies, provide access to affordable essential drugs in developing countries
   - In cooperation with the private sector, make available the benefits of new technologies—especially information and communications technologies.

Source: United Nations Development Programme.

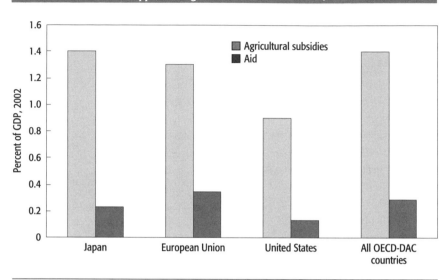

FIGURE 5.6 Aid and Support for Agriculture as a Share of GDP, 2002

Source: OECD-DAC 2004 and OECD 2003, cited in World Bank 2005c.

As we show elsewhere in this volume, an important area in which rich countries can provide support is through reforms of their own trade policies. The external environment has a strong influence on the returns to reform in developing countries. Robust global growth is important, but so is reform of the protectionist policies of rich countries, which target such areas as agriculture and textiles and are thus particularly damaging to poor countries. As we reported in chapter 3, estimates suggest that open market access for poor countries, combined with other trade reforms, would pull a minimum of 100 million people out of poverty, as measured by the US$2 per day standard.

Coherence between aid policies and other policies is vital to enhance aid effectiveness. For example, giving support to small farmers or entrepreneurs is undermined by shutting them out of the donors' markets or by applying tariffs that discriminate against processed goods. Similarly, aid donors' support for health and educational systems is undermined by the recruitment of teachers, doctors, and nurses to work in the rich countries. Donors' support for governance reforms and combating corruption is not always matched by donors' pursuit of their citizens or firms who are complicit in corruption or siphoning aid funds into donor country bank accounts. Ensuring greater coherence between aid and other potentially complementary government policies and actions is important to increase the quality of aid.

Many global development challenges—such as stopping the spread of infectious diseases; building an international trade and financial architecture that is fair to all countries; and halting deforestation, climate change, and loss of biodiversity—cannot be handled solely by individual countries. These challenges require multilateral action: unilateral aid flows and arrangements cannot deal with some of the most pressing global issues. Aid for multilateral institutions and objectives, be it aid targeted toward the environment, diseases, agricultural development or trade reform, is an essential complement to national bilateral aid efforts.

The decline in aid flows over the past decade has come precisely at a time when the returns on aid have increased sharply. We have summarized the evidence on returns—if countries are willing to take the steps necessary to reform, then assistance in the form of capacity building, financial assistance, and analytical support typically has large returns. With continued reform momentum and steady external support, past experience suggests strongly that developing countries can extend and deepen the progress of the last half century.

Despite the progress made in the past 50 years, an immense poverty challenge remains. Some 1.1 billion people still live on less than US$1 per day, and the challenge will grow as the population of the developing world increases by another 2 billion in the next 30 years. To address a challenge of these dimensions, aid will need to have effects far beyond the value of the money alone. This means that aid must support the frameworks for private economic activity and social improvements, ensuring that its effects go far beyond any individual project, and it must contribute to greater capacity and greater knowledge. Continued learning on the part of both developed countries and other parties in the development community is essential to these aims. Aid is a complement to the other flows we have identified—trade, capital, ideas, and migration—not a substitute.

Aid has never been more effective in supporting growth and poverty reduction. Much more aid and higher quality aid is needed. At a minimum, doubling the actual amount of aid—along with untying it to ensure it reflects real needs rather than disguised efforts to support domestic enterprises in rich countries—and coordinating its flows to ensure that predictable flows of highly concessional finance and other resources are mobilized in support of the many governments that can use it effectively are priorities for a more inclusive globalization.

Notes

1. This chapter draws on joint work with Halsey Rogers and Nicholas Stern. See Goldin, Rogers, and Stern (2002).
2. For example, in 2002, the leading recipients of ODA among high-income countries were Israel ($754 million), French Polynesia ($418 million), New Caledonia ($324 million), and Slovenia ($171 million). See World Bank (2004d).

3. For an accessible review, see chapter 14 of Szirmai (2005).
4. Recall that we discussed trade-related capacity building in chapter 3, for example.
5. The restriction of this early form of assistance was emphasized by Kanbur (forthcoming).
6. See, for example, Curtis (2001).
7. A comprehensive review of this era and subsequent decades is provided in Hjertholm and White (2000).
8. With regard to the ideology column of table 5.2, see also Lindaur and Pritchet (2002).
9. In the case of the IMF, it is worth noting that its resources were not sufficient to significantly support post-war reconstruction in Europe. Its Articles of Agreement set total drawing rights at $8.8 billion. By the time the IMF opened for business in 1947, post-war Europe's combined trade deficit was $7.5 billion. Given the size of this deficit in relationship to the IMF's resources, the United States had to step in to fill the gap. Through 1951, it provided $13 billion in Marshall Plan aid to Europe, thus significantly supplementing IMF resources. See Eichengreen (1996).
10. "Point Four" refers to the fourth point in Truman's inaugural address.
11. The Commonwealth members the United Kingdom, Australia, Canada, and New Zealand had signed the Colombo Plan for aid giving in 1950.
12. See Streeten (1979), for example.
13. OECD (2005), Paris Declaration on Aid Effectiveness, Paris, 2 March 2005.
14. See Sen (1999), for example.
15. The resources that organizations such as the World Bank can possibly provide in support of education are dwarfed by the needs of developing countries.
16. See Hansen and Tarp (2000).
17. See, for example, Boone (1996). Note, however, that Hansen and Tarp (2000 and 2001) find the contrary. For a recent review of the effectiveness of aid, see Clemens, Radelet, and Bhavnani (2004).
18. See Owens and Hoddinott (1998). As Clemens, Radelet, and Bhavnani (2004) note, "This kind of [disaster] assistance should have a negative simple correlation with growth, as the disaster simultaneously causes both low growth and large aid flows. While it is possible that aid might mitigate that fall in growth, any additional pathway of causation from humanitarian aid to growth is extremely difficult to detect" (p. 2).
19. Alesina and Dollar (2000) analyzed the pattern of aid flows from the 1970s through the early 1990s. They concluded that "Factors such as colonial past and voting patterns in the United Nations explain more of the distribution of aid than the political institutions or economic policy of recipients" (p. 55).
20. Stewart (1995) provides a useful overview of links between structural adjustment and poverty. For an introduction to structural adjustment itself, see chapter 23 of Reinert (2005).
21. Williamson (2000) provides a very useful overview and assessment of the Washington Consensus. For additional information, see also the discussion of ideas in chapter 7 of this book.
22. Taylor (1993) offered one forceful critique along these lines.
23. Some of these successes have been reviewed in the chapters contained in Rodrik (2003).
24. In the realm of foreign aid, some (but not all) of this new thinking was reflected in World Bank (1998).
25. See, for example, Psacharopoulos (1985, 1994) and Psacharopoulos and Patrinos (2004).
26. Krueger and Lindahl (1999) summarize the evidence.
27. See Schultz (2002) who notes, "The conclusion of many empirical studies of child development is that increased schooling of the mother is associated with larger improvements in child quality outcomes than is the increased schooling of the father. This has been studied with birth outcomes (e.g., birth weight), child survival, good nutrition, earlier entry into school, increases in school enrollment adjusted for age, and more years of schooling completed on reaching adulthood" (p. 212).
28. These significant health achievements do hide regional and country divergences. Like income growth, improvements in health status and life expectancy have not been equally distributed. The health status and life expectancy of the poorest nations lag behind the rest of the world, and within countries, the health of the poor is worse than that of the rest of the population. Poverty is the most important underlying cause of preventable death, disease, and disability; and there

is growing recognition that poor health, malnutrition, and large family size are key determinants of poverty.

29. See Burnside and Dollar (2000), as well as Collier and Dollar (2002). The Burnside and Dollar (2000) results have been recently questioned by Easterly, Levine, and Roodman (2004).

30. Poverty is defined here as living on less than US$1 per person per day, adjusted for cross-country differences in living costs. It must be emphasized that moving people above the poverty line represents just one effect of the aid, which also helped increase income and other dimensions of development throughout the economy.

31. The issue of fungibility is taken up in chapter 3 of World Bank (1998).

32. Clemens, Radelet, and Bhavnani note that "The result is robust over a wide variety of specifications. . . . It holds over various time periods, stands up whether we include or exclude influential observations, and remains robust when controlling for possible endogeneity of several independent variables" (p. 40).

33. This multidimensionality of poverty is embodied in the Millennium Development Goals (MDGs) adopted by heads of state at a United Nations summit in 2000.

34. Social cohesion or "social capital," as pointed out by Woolcock and Narayan (2000) and Fukuyama (2002), is an underappreciated element of development. It brings together the realms of culture, governance, and institutions.

35. See World Bank (1998) and International Monetary Fund (1998).

36. See Devarajan, Dollar, and Holmgren (2001).

37. See Dugger (2004) and chapter 1 of Oxfam (2005). Ethiopia, Kenya, Lesotho, Malawi, Tanzania, Uganda, and Zambia have all recorded large increases in enrollments with the reduction or abolition of school fees. In many cases, aid has supported these achievements.

38. Additionally, arguments that foreign aid given to weak African states tends to *exacerbate* problems appear to be untrue. For example, Goldsmith (2001), based on a statistical analysis, concluded, "Foreign aid provides the wherewithal for African states to pay for and carry out many basic public functions. Yet being reliant on aid does not necessarily mean that these states would have evolved in a dramatically more favorable direction had they received less aid. Something closer to the opposite seems more likely" (p. 144). See also Schwalbenberg (1998).

39. For a recent assessment, see Fukuyama (2004).

40. The OCP involved the pharmaceutical company Merck's drug ivermectin or Mectizan®. The partnership thus extended across public-private boundaries.

41. We take up the role of ideas in earnest in chapter 7.

42. One review was given by Greenland (1997).

43. A number of publications that are a result of this research are available at www.aercafrica.org.

44. See chapter 12 of Reinert (2005).

45. See World Bank (1994).

46. Cohen (2001) notes that, measured at market rather than at face value, the committed debt relief would be substantially smaller than this announced value. The IMF estimated the net present value of the debt relief involved to be US$37 billion.

47. As of April 2004, these countries were Benin, Bolivia, Burkina Faso, Cameroon, Chad, Democratic Republic of Congo, Ethiopia, The Gambia, Ghana, Guinea, Guinea-Bissau, Guyana, Honduras, Madagascar, Malawi, Mali, Mauritania, Mozambique, Nicaragua, Niger, Rwanda, São Tomé and Principe, Senegal, Sierra Leone, Tanzania, Uganda, and Zambia.

48. Interestingly, the government of South Africa does not support the writing off of apartheid-era debts. See www.worldbank.org/hipc.

49. See data from Oxfam (2005) based on information provided by the Development Assistance Committee.

50. Taking the combined GDP of the *entire* set of high-income countries, the 0.7 percent target translates into approximately US$180 billion in 2002, for example. This is about half the amount these high-income countries spend on agricultural protection in the same year. These aid volumes were around US$69 billion, less than one-quarter of that spent on agricultural protection.

6

Migration

with Andrew L. Beath

History shows that ***international migration*** flows can offer an effective way for poor people to escape poverty while promoting economic growth and enhancing technological progress.[1] The initial emigration of hunter-gatherers from Africa and later emigration of farming communities from the Fertile Crescent were among the most important events in the economic progress of humankind.[2] Throughout the 18th, 19th, and early 20th centuries, mass migrations from Europe to the Americas and Australasia enabled tens of millions of people to escape poverty and persecution and created what today rank as the world's most prosperous societies. In recent decades, migrant diasporas, such as India's "techies," have made manifest contributions to the state of technology while also promoting global integration, economic growth, and poverty alleviation in their home countries. Today more people wish to migrate than ever before. If the tremendous potential of migration as a force for reducing poverty is to be realized, however, greater attention must be paid to the impact of migration on sending communities and on the migrants themselves.

Although mere hours of flight today separate lands marred by extreme poverty from the promise of rich world metropolises, few legitimate avenues exist by which the world's poorest can migrate to high-income countries. The relatively meager supply of such opportunities relative to the desire of many citizens of less-developed countries to move to richer lands have given rise to a thriving black market in ***illegal migration***. The costs, both human and financial, imposed by this black market are large. Many thousands of illegal migrants have perished while attempting to evade border patrols and make it across the unforgiving deserts and treacherous stretches of water that form the natural borders of the United States and the European Union. Others have been left defrauded and stranded in impoverished third countries after entrusting their life savings to smugglers of people. In response to this illegal flow, high-income countries have allocated billions of dollars for border protection, yet in many cases this has forced illegal migrants to attempt even more remote—and risky—routes of entry.[3] While the taxpayers of high-income countries and aspiring migrants from low- and middle-income countries pay the cost, criminal syndicates that run people-smuggling operations benefit.

In the coming decades, the number of potential migrants is likely to swell, driven by a rising number of young adults living in low- and middle-income countries and increases in income that will allow more people than ever to afford the costs of migration.[4] If policies in recipient countries remain unchanged, rising migration pressures will place great strains on traditional methods of border protection. The result will be magnified demands on the taxpayers of destination countries, increased mortality among illegal migrants in transit, and the proliferation of human-smuggling syndicates. Yet in the great challenges posed by migration also lie opportunities that can potentially benefit both poor and rich countries. Researchers estimate that even a modest increase in migrant flows could boost global output by US$150 billion a year—around one-and-a-half times the predicted gains from the full liberalization of trade in goods and services.[5] The challenge is to use that potential to develop a global migration system that is able to improve the economic prospects of the greatest number of poor people worldwide, while also serving the interests of sources and destination countries and protecting the migrants themselves.

A Brief History of World Migration Flows

Migration has always been a central characteristic of the world's most dynamic and productive economies. Throughout medieval Europe, states at the forefront of economic progress hosted entrepreneurs and laborers from across the continent. When the Netherlands led the world economy during the 1600s, 10 percent of its population was of foreign birth. In Amsterdam, migrants totaled as much as a quarter of the population.[6] With the dawn of European colonialism, migration took on a transcontinental dimension, with labor chasing wealth across the globe. Initially, high costs and harsh conditions limited labor flows to intrepid aristocrats and those they exploited, either by contract or coercion.[7] Yet by the middle of the 19th century, the shift from sail to steam had dramatically lowered the cost of ocean-going transport and opened up the lucrative labor markets of the New World to a much wider segment of the European population. Thus began the age of mass migration.

KEY TERMS AND CONCEPTS

1951 Geneva Convention on Refugees	illegal migration
asylum seekers	international migration
brain drain	migration hump
guest workers	refugees
H-1B visa (United States)	

By the 1840s, trans-Atlantic flows of free European migrants were running at 300,000 every year.

Sources of Migrants in the Age of Mass Migration

Initially, Britain was the main source of migrants—a consequence of its colonial reach, its economic preeminence, and its surging demographic profile. Yet, as industrial revolutions spread across Europe, uprooting rural populations and fueling demographic booms, the continent's emigration flows diversified and grew significantly (table 6.1).[8] By the dawn of the 20th century, close to 1.4 million migrants were crossing the Atlantic annually, the majority from the poorer regions of Southern and Eastern Europe. In total, between 1850 and 1914 some 55 million Europeans migrated, mostly to the United States. The majority of migrants were unskilled young men lured abroad by the promise of higher wages.[9] Many others, though, left out of necessity. Ireland recorded massive levels of emigration in the wake of the disastrous famine that struck in the late 1840s, for instance, and eventually lost nearly half its labor force to emigration.

Asian Migration in the Colonial Era

With the demand for primary products booming throughout the 19th century, European colonies specializing in plantation agriculture and mining sought to import as much cheap labor as needed to keep production costs at minimal levels. With slavery rightfully precluded, colonial authorities increasingly turned to migrants from China, India, and Japan. In the hundred years after 1820, 3 million migrants from these countries fanned out across the globe, creating sizeable immigrant communities in East and South Africa and the Pacific Basin.[10] In California, the magnitude of inflows from Asia migrants incited a political backlash that eventually contributed to long-standing barriers to Asian immigration to the United States.[11] In most other cases, however, technological changes in agriculture and the slowdown in the growth in

TABLE 6.1 Historical Rates of Migration (per thousand persons)						
Country	1850s	1860s	1870s	1880s	1890s	1900s
Source Countries						
Norway	24.2	57.6	47.3	95.2	44.9	83.3
Denmark	–	–	20.6	39.4	22.3	28.2
Sweden	4.6	30.5	23.5	70.1	41.2	42.0
Finland	–	–	–	13.2	23.2	54.5
Ireland	–	–	66.1	141.7	88.5	69.8
British Isles	58.0	51.8	50.4	70.2	43.8	65.3
France	1.1	1.2	1.5	3.1	1.3	1.4
Netherlands	5.0	5.9	4.6	12.3	5.0	5.1
Belgium	–	–	–	8.6	3.5	6.1
Switzerland	–	–	13.0	32.0	14.1	13.9
Germany	–	–	14.7	28.7	10.1	4.5
Austria–Hungary	–	–	2.9	10.6	16.1	47.6
Portugal	–	19.0	28.9	38.0	50.8	56.9
Spain	–	–	–	36.2	43.8	56.6
Italy	–	–	10.5	33.6	50.2	107.7
Recipient Countries						
Canada	99.2	83.2	54.8	78.4	48.8	167.6
United States	92.8	64.9	54.6	85.8	53.0	102.0
Brazil	–	–	20.4	41.1	72.3	33.3
Argentina	38.5	99.1	117.0	221.7	163.9	291.8

Source: Hatton and Williamson 1998.
Note: – represents unavailable data.

demand for primary products gradually eliminated much of the need for further importation of low-skilled labor.

The Decline of the Age of Mass Migration

By the early 1900s, the wage gap between the New World and Europe's leading economies had been dramatically reduced, as migration swelled the New
World labor force by a third and reduced that of the Old World by an eighth.[12]
Where once demographic transitions had magnified the pool of young adults,
the bulk of the population had now moved beyond those ages from which the
vast majority of migrants are drawn. Yet, as Western Europe was reaching
the end of its migration cycle, other less-developed countries of Eastern Europe
were just getting started, giving rise to new sources of migration. These new

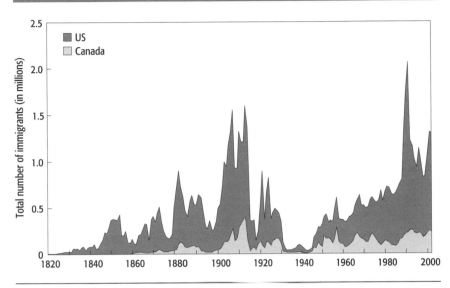

FIGURE 6.1 Inflow of Migrants to the United States and Canada, 1820–2000

Source: U.S. Department of Homeland Security 2003a; Citizenship and Immigration Canada 2003a.

migrants were generally less skilled, spoke new languages, and brought with them a culture that was unfamiliar to those who had come before. With rising levels of wage inequality, political focus was brought to bear on the new wave of immigrants. This resulted in intense political debate and a series of legislative measures aimed at stifling the inflow of immigrants from nontraditional sources. In 1917, the United States introduced a literacy test for migrants, intended to stifle further immigration of low-skilled workers. Later that year, the United States entered World War I, disrupting trans-Atlantic shipping routes and effectively bringing an end to the age of mass migration (figure 6.1).

The Fall and Rise of Migration Flows in the 20th Century

Starting in 1917 and continuing throughout the 1920s, waves of jingoism and economic isolationism swept through political systems across the Old and New Worlds. The onset of the Great Depression and the outbreak of World War II reinforced the trend, resulting in policies aimed to limit further migrant flows.[13] Transnational migration steadily slowed to a near halt.

In the aftermath of World War II, millions of refugees crossed the European continent, yet more traditional forms of migration remained hamstrung by a reluctance to roll back the isolationist policies of the Great Depression.

Interestingly, it was Western Europe—once a major source of migrants—that was first to attract immigrants. In France, Germany, the Netherlands, and the United Kingdom, rapid economic growth in the late 1940s and 1950s had generated a shortage of low-wage labor. Initially, this demand was met by migrants from southern European countries, though such sources quickly proved insufficient. By the 1960s, countries across Western Europe—Germany in particular—were importing millions of *guest workers* from Turkey and North Africa. While the 1973 oil crisis and the ensuing high unemployment brought an abrupt end to guest-worker programs in Western Europe, the oil-exporting countries in the Middle East later replicated and expanded upon the guest-worker model.

Perhaps the most defining change in modern immigration, however, came in the mid-1960s when Australia, Canada, and the United States overhauled their immigration policies. These reforms not only allowed for a much greater volume of flows, but also opened the door to migration from nontraditional sources in Africa, Asia, and Latin America. Together with the sharp decline in cost and increased speed of intercontinental transport and communication, the reform of migration restrictions has ensured a steady growth in both the volume and diversity of migrant flows over recent decades.

Legal Framework of Modern Migration

Throughout the 19th century, migration occurred mostly in a legal vacuum. The modern age of migration, on the other hand, has been defined by efforts to bring international migration under the aegis of a legal framework. The founding of the United Nations and the *1951 Geneva Convention on Refugees* established a process by which persecuted individuals could seek asylum free of fears of unjustified repatriation, while the 1948 Universal Declaration of Human Rights and the 1959 Declaration on the Rights of the Child affirmed the primacy of kinship in immigration law.[14]

Beyond such humanitarian principles, however, governments have generally enacted immigration policy to serve their national economic self-interests. For the great mass of countries, this has meant near zero immigration. Others, though, have sought to "cherry-pick" economically attractive immigrants. In 1965, Canada devised its archetypal points system, by which immigrant visas were awarded to those who possessed a desirable mix of education, experience, language skills, and investment capital.[15] Australia and New Zealand later copied the Canadian model, and the United States implemented a program to bring in immigrants specialized in targeted high-skill occupations. Although countries in Europe and the Middle East have resisted permanent immigration, many have found it necessary to establish systems of contract or seasonal migration to meet skill shortages.

TABLE 6.2 Stock of International Migrants, 1990 and 2000

| Geographical areas | Millions of persons | | Percent of population |
	1990	2000	2000
World	154	175	3
More-developed regions	81	104	9
Less-developed regions	73	71	2
Africa	16	16	2
Asia	50	50	1
Europe	48	56	8
Latin America and the Caribbean	7	6	1
Canada and the United States	28	41	13
Oceania	5	6	19

Source: United Nations Population Division 2002.
Note: Percent of Population refers to the number of migrants as a percentage of the total population of the host country

Structure of Migrant Flows

Currently around 175 million people—3 percent of the world's population—live outside their country of birth.[16] By historical standards, that figure is low, though in recent decades migration flows have grown rapidly. Since the late 1980s, in particular, European flows have surged, fueled by the end of communism in Eastern Europe and the conflict in the Balkans. Although Western Europe is proving to be an increasingly popular destination for migrants (table 6.2), the United States continues to accept more immigrants than any other country in the world. The Middle East has also emerged as a major host of migrants, particularly for low-skilled workers from South and Southeast Asia. Among countries of emigration, the middle-income countries tend to have the higher rates of outflow. Mexico and the Philippines, in particular, are major exporters of labor. The Philippines, for example, has over 7 million people overseas, equivalent to 10 percent of its population.

Since the age of mass migration, international flows of people have been thwarted by world war, global economic depressions, and populism, and then reorganized under a swathe of international treaties and national legislation. Nevertheless, the structure of immigration flows today broadly reflects those of the 19th century, which is a testament to the common human desires that underscore individual decisions to migrate and the common benefits that recipient societies reap from the contributions of migrants.

A Typology of Contemporary International Migration Flows

The legislative revolution that characterizes the modern age of migration has delineated a series of legal channels of migration. Some of these—such as flows of *refugees* and *asylum seekers*—have been defined by covenants of international law. Others—such as the flows of high-skill and low-skill expatriates and, to some extent, permanent settlers—are the result of stand-alone national policies drafted in observance of evolving norms of immigration law worldwide. Still others—primarily the flow of visa-free migrants—are the result of bilateral, sometimes multilateral, agreements among contiguous countries. Finally, a significant portion of migrant flows takes place outside the practical realm of international or national law. Table 6.3 identifies the major channels of modern international migration and provides summary data concerning the magnitude and composition of these flows. The paragraphs that follow examine one of these channels in further detail.

Permanent Settlers

Throughout the age of mass migration, flows of transnational migrants were composed overwhelming of permanent settlers who migrated with the intent to resettle permanently in another country. In the modern age, however, nation states have grown more resistant to conferring citizenship upon foreigners who lack a connection to the national cultural identity. In fact, from the 1960s until recently, only four countries have regularly granted permanent residence to nonrefugee foreigners devoid of familial, ethnic, or residential ties to the country. Perhaps unsurprisingly, these are the traditional countries of immigration—Australia, Canada, New Zealand, and the United States—whose cultural identities were forged by inflows of migrants.[17]

Economic Migrants

In contrast to those times in the 19th century when the people who crossed the Atlantic in search of a better life were virtually assured of entry, today the immigration regimes of the richer countries aggressively guard the national interest and seek out economic migrants who possess desirable socioeconomic characteristics. For Australia, Canada, and New Zealand, this is achieved through the points system, which grants permanent residence to applicants who offer the right mix of skills, capital, and adaptability.[18] The United States, on the other hand, assigns annual quotas to categories of persons eligible for permanent residence. Categories include "persons of extraordinary ability," religious workers, outstanding researchers, multinational executives, and investors.[19] A significant portion of these economic migrants originate from low- and

TABLE 6.3 Major Channels of Modern International Migration

Migrant category	Source countries (%)	Recipient countries (%)	Skill level	Duration of stay	Annual flow (millions)
Permanent settlers	Mexico (17) Turkey (9) China (7) Vietnam (6) India (5)	US (36) Canada (14) Germany (12) France (10) Australia (5)	Medium	Permanent	1.5
High-skill expatriates	India (26) US (9) China (4) Philippines (4) UK (3)	US (34) UK (14) Canada (14) Australia (7) Japan (4)	High	Temporary	0.6
Low-skill expatriates	Philippines (25) India (17) Poland (9) Indonesia (9) Bangladesh (9)	Saudi Arabia (43) UAE (11) Kuwait (10) Germany (9) Malaysia (7)	Low	Temporary	3.5
Asylum seekers	Iraq (6) Serbia (5) China (5) Congo, D.R. (4) Turkey (4)	UK (15) US (14) Germany (10) France (9) South Africa (6)	Medium	Permanent	0.9
Refugees	Afghanistan (45) Liberia (9) Gaza Strip (6) Congo, D.R. (4) Burundi (4)	Pakistan (45) Tanzania (7) Egypt, Arab Rep. of (5) US (4) Sierra Leone (4)	Low	Temporary	1.4
Undocumented migrants	Mexico (25) Morocco (6) Albania (6) Turkey (4) Romania (3)	US (30) Italy (8) UK (8) Germany (8) France (8)	Medium	Semi-permanent	1.2
Visa-free migrants	Italy (15) France (11) Germany (10) UK (10) Ireland (9)	Germany (37) UK (17) Spain (9) Belgium (8) Netherlands (6)	Medium	Semi-permanent	0.4
Students	China (8) Korea, Rep. of (4) India (4) Japan (3) Greece (3)	US (29) UK (14) Germany (12) France (9) Australia (7)	High	Temporary	1.6
Total	**Philippines (9)** **India (8)** **Mexico (5)** **China (5)** **Afghanistan (5)**	**US (17)** **Saudi Arabia (14)** **Germany (8)** **UK (6)** **Pakistan (5)**			**11.1**

Note: See the annex to this chapter for information on sources and methodology. Percentages represent proportion of the flows in respective categories accounted for by migrants to and from associated country.

middle-income countries, with China, India, and the Philippines being major contributors.

Family Migrants

In addition to the "economic channel" of permanent migration popularized by the traditional countries of immigration, a "family channel" also exists that allows resident nationals to sponsor non-national family members for permanent residence.[20] In some cases, this feature of immigration regimes has given rise to self-perpetuating chains of migration, by which an immigrant gains citizenship through economic, asylum, or other channels and then sponsors their extended family members, who in turn sponsor their extended family members, and so forth. Migrants from low-income countries, in particular, have taken advantage of this provision, resulting in immigrant flows unanticipated by policy makers and the public alike.[21]

The shift in the composition of immigrants and the seeming incapacity of governments to fully control inflows has generated predictable controversy. In response, policy makers have struggled with the challenge of balancing humanitarian obligations with public demands for limited immigration.[22] Constrained by constitutional obligations to treaties such as the Universal Declaration of Human Rights, many have erred on the side of humanitarianism. Accordingly, immigration as family reunification continues to represent the most significant channel of legal migration from low- and middle-income countries to high-income countries, with as many as a million people a year exchanging their citizenship.

Highly Skilled Expatriates

High-income countries use skilled migrant programs to fill occupational shortages that cannot be met by training resident nationals. Historically, such flows have been concentrated in education and health-related services. During the 1990s, however, booms in telecommunications and in information and communications technology (ICT) led to a shortage of related skills in many high-income countries, causing a renewed surge in flows of highly skilled migrants. As a result, developing countries with respected systems of higher education have emerged as major sources of particular skills for the developed world. India, for instance, has dominated the international market for computer-related skills, accounting for over 60 percent of migrants heading to the United States to work in the field.[23] The Philippines, to take another example, has been relied upon by many developed countries for its medical professionals.

Competition for Highly Skilled Expatriates

With the increased global demand for skilled labor, high-income countries have increasingly found themselves in competition with one another to secure talented expatriates. The result has been that high-income countries have introduced many new programs for skilled migrants and renovated existing programs to make these countries more attractive to potential highly skilled migrants and more responsive to the needs of domestic employers whose growth is constrained by a shortage of skilled people. Australia, Canada, France, Germany, Ireland, Japan, the Republic of Korea, and the United Kingdom have all recently instituted programs to grant temporary visas to workers in ICT or other industries. The biggest program for high-skill expatriates, however, remains the United States' *H-1B visa*, which is designed to meet shortages in specialty occupations such as accountancy, computer programming, education, engineering, and medicine.[24]

High-Skill Expatriate Visas as a Route to Permanent Residency

Although these programs provide migrants with explicitly temporary visas, many of them do offer migrants the possibility of eventually gaining the right of permanent residence. As such, the extended nature of many high-skill migration programs distinguishes them from low-skill programs, which ordinarily explicitly aim to prevent any adjustment by migrants to permanent status.

Low-Skilled Expatriates

In the modern age of migration, official programs to attract low-skilled expatriates have been implemented after rapid economic growth improved the wages and work conditions of the local workforce, leaving them less willing to work in low-wage but essential nontradable sectors such as construction or homecare. Initially, the main sources of labor for such programs have been poorer neighboring countries; when these prove insufficient, sources further abroad are tapped. Generally, these labor sources tend to be middle-income countries with comparatively good education systems.

Low-Skill Expatriates in Oil-Exporting Countries of the Middle East

In recent times, the largest beneficiaries of low-skilled migrant labor have been the oil-exporting countries of the Middle East, where the infusion of oil revenues generated low-skilled jobs that local workers were unwilling to occupy at the prevailing wages. Initially, migrant workers were drawn mainly from other Arab countries such as the Arab Republic of Egypt and the Republic of Yemen. When these sources proved inadequate, countries in South and Southeast Asia became increasingly important sources. Today, there are some 10 million expatriates working in the Middle East, 5 million of them in Saudi Arabia alone. Although most expatriate workers in the Gulf are employed either in the oil industry or in occupations supported by oil revenues, in recent years the United Arab Emirates (UAE) has used its large, low-wage migrant population not just as a response to labor shortages in specific nontradeable sectors, but also as a source of comparative advantage to be spread across a widening range of service industries. As a result, the UAE has experienced considerable success in attracting foreign investment and diversifying its economy.

Low-Skill Expatriates in East Asian Countries

Over recent decades, countries in East Asia have also undergone rapid economic growth and many have turned to migrant labor to fill low-skilled positions. Hong Kong (China), Japan, Malaysia, Singapore, Korea, and Thailand, for instance, are all major recipients of low-skilled expatriates from less-developed neighboring countries in Southeast Asia. Sometimes—as in Hong Kong (China), Malaysia, Singapore, and Thailand—these flows occur through official government-mandated programs. Other countries, such as Japan and Korea, have resisted instituting official programs to employ foreigners and instead fill low-skill jobs with foreign trainees and students, overstaying tourist visas. In a similar vein, Australia, Canada, the United Kingdom, and a number of Western European countries have developed "working-holiday schemes" for young people from other industrial countries. A number of high-income countries have also instituted low-skilled migrant programs to attract agricultural workers, although these programs tend to operate only on a strictly seasonal basis.[25] This use of low-skilled migrant workers not only ensures low prices for domestic consumers and low costs for producers, it also segments the labor market in a way that guards against the potentially damaging wage-price spirals that could result if domestic workers were employed.

Abuse and Exploitation of Low-Skilled Migrants

Unfortunately, for all the benefits that low-skilled migrant programs offer to the migrants themselves and their home and recipient countries, the migrants themselves often suffer greatly (see box 6.1). The market for low-skill expatriate workers suffers from abuse and exploitation. In source countries, recruitment agencies and brokers may demand large sums up front from prospective migrants. In Bangladesh and India, for instance, the average fee charged to those wishing to work in a major gulf destination has been estimated at between US$2,000 and US$2,500, about 80 percent of what low-skilled migrants can expect to earn in their first year.[26] Some migrants evidently consider this to be

BOX 6.1 Migrant Dreams Become Nightmares

In 2004, Human Rights Watch completed a thorough investigation into human rights abuses suffered by low-skilled migrant workers. The ensuing report paints a troubling picture of the extent to which vulnerable individuals are exploited by unscrupulous individuals in both source and destination countries and then ignored by the governments involved. Many victims, it seems, are doomed even before they leave home. Recruitment agencies demand substantial sums from prospective migrants for the promise of a job abroad. For this, migrants borrow heavily. Their confidence is ultimately belied, however, upon arrival in the destination country, when the contract they signed is replaced by a document promising far below the agreed wage. Unaware of their rights or fearful of being sent home without earning a cent, such exploitation is endured. This climate of fear—and the confined or isolated living quarters migrants often inhabit—also traps many female migrant workers in situations in which they are abused by employers. Such employers perhaps know that many migrants are afraid of the justice system, a fear that for some migrants may be well founded.

Source: Human Rights Watch 2004.

a price worth paying, although few are offered any reciprocal guarantees that the conditions of employment will be as promised. As noted by Barber (2004), it is all too common for employers "to force [migrants] to work long hours, to delay or withhold payment of wages altogether, to confiscate their passports or other identity documents, to dismiss them or blacklist them for joining workers' associations, . . . and to subject them to violence or sexual abuse" (p. 14).

Asylum Seekers

In the wake of horrors suffered by Jewish and Roma people during World War II, there existed great political will within the international community to create a durable system that protected refugees and bestowed upon them rights of resettlement. In 1951, the Geneva Convention on Refugees achieved this, establishing a process by which persons with a "well founded fear of persecution [by state agents] for reasons of race, religion, nationality, membership of a particular social group, or political opinion" could apply through the United Nations (UN) for resettlement in a signatory nation.[27] Although large numbers of refugees are resettled by the UN every year, it has over recent years been common for individuals seeking asylum to travel on their own accord to their desired country of resettlement before applying for refuge.[28] We distinguish here between these migrants—referred to as *asylum seekers* in the popular discourse—and conventional refugees who flee in desperation to neighboring countries and are often assisted by the UN agencies, but who are not necessarily entitled to resettlement under the 1951 Convention.

Changes to the Asylum System at the End of the Cold War

Prior to the late 1980s, annual applications for asylum rarely topped 200,000. As with many other aspects of political life, the Cold War dominated asylum outcomes; "defectors" from the Soviet Bloc won automatic asylum in the West, yet those fleeing allied countries received routine denials. Given the obstacles associated with leaving communist countries, the system was thereby inherently self-limiting. This changed irrevocably, however, with the collapse of the Eastern Bloc and the outbreak of civil war in the former Yugoslavia. Western European countries, in particular, received huge inflows of asylum seekers. Flows fell in the mid-1990s with the resolution of the Balkan conflict, but rose again toward the end of the decade. In 2002, over 900,000 people from 165 countries applied for asylum across 143 countries, though since then asylum claims have fallen considerably.[29]

Controversy of the Asylum System

Of the total number of asylum applicants, the vast majority are eventually found not to be in need of resettlement. Of the 967,097 asylum cases resolved in 2002, only 23 percent resulted in a grant of refugee status or other form of humanitarian status.[30] Few of those who fail in their bid to win asylum are returned home, however.[31] As a consequence, many politicians and commentators in major recipient countries have accused asylum seekers of being illegal immigrants out to "cheat the system"; a number of governments have enacted strict policies to prevent asylum seekers from making landfall and have meted out harsh treatment to those who do make it through.[32]

Remittances of Asylum Seekers

For source communities, however, those who have sought asylum abroad often serve as an invaluable source of income and support during precarious times. Because many who obtain asylum in high-income countries are among the most skilled and wealthiest in any refugee diaspora, they are often able to earn a significant income abroad, part of which is then remitted to support family and communities back home.[33] Remittances to Somalia were of such importance that when flows were disrupted in November 2001 by the closure of the al-Barakat *hawilad* network due to suspected ties with Al Qaeda, a food crisis ensued, severely affecting some 300,000 people.[34] In El Salvador, remittances sent by refugees living in the United States are estimated to sustain 15 percent of domestic households. To sustain these flows, the Salvadoran government went so far as to offer legal assistance to Salvadorans in the United States to pursue asylum claims.[35]

Refugees

Although asylum seekers typically attract substantial attention from the Western media, they are in fact greatly outnumbered by those refugees who have not opted to seek—and in most cases are not entitled to—resettlement by the United Nations under the 1951 convention. These are people who have fled to neighboring countries because of the onset of adverse civil, political, economic, or meteorological conditions, but who do not face any systematic or permanent form of persecution in their home country. In 1980 there were an estimated 8.8 million refugees. This figure peaked at 17.2 million in 1990 and stood at 10.4 million in 2003.[36]

Distinction between Refugees and Asylum Seekers

Usually refugees cross borders in extremely large groups, distinguishing them from asylum seekers who often travel more methodically, either as individuals or in small bands. As a consequence, camps are often established by international humanitarian agencies along the border of the affected country pending resolution of the disturbance that caused the outflow. The individual status of such refugees—and their entitlement to protections under the 1951 convention—are often not determined.[37] This is because of the logistical problems of doing so and also because resettlement is a relatively difficult and complex solution given the underlying assumption that the disturbance is temporary.[38] One of the most striking examples of how this system operates came during the Rwanda genocide in 1994. The border town of Goma, Zaïre,[39] was transformed overnight into a tent city hosting over a million Rwandan refugees, yet with the rapid victory of rebel forces and the stabilization of the situation, the population was repatriated relatively quickly.

Demands on the Refugee System

Most disturbances from which persons seek refuge, however, tend to be protracted and place demands on the refugee system for which it is ill designed and that it is ill prepared to handle.[40] As a consequence, large populations of refugees can become quasi-permanent, albeit technically illegal, residents in border towns of neighboring countries, generating resentment and persecution from local residents and governments who view them as unwelcome competitors for scarce local resources. Whole generations grow up in camps with makeshift schools, and entire villages are created to support refugee populations, as is the case for the Palestinean population of Gaza. Such was the case in certain border towns in Pakistan and Iran, for instance, from the early 1990s until recently, with each country hosting over 2 million Afghan refugees who had fled civil war in their home country.

Undocumented Migrants

Of all the different forms of migration, few seem to grip the public imagination and engender as much political consternation as flows of undocumented, or illegal, migrants. Undocumented migrants include both those who move voluntarily and those who are trafficked against their will. Due to its very nature, there is limited evidence on which to base estimates of how many people are involved; consequently, the estimates that do exist tend to vary wildly. Few commentators would disagree, however, that flows have increased markedly over the past decade, particularly to the European Union.

Voluntary Undocumented Migrants

Most people who cross borders illegally do so voluntarily. The United States receives large flows of such undocumented migrants from Mexico, with the common route being across arid, unforgiving deserts that stretch from California to Texas. In 2001, the journey claimed at least 500 lives, with over 1.2 million apprehensions made by U.S. authorities.[41] Comparable in danger are the attempts made by undocumented migrants to cross the Mediterranean or Adriatic Sea to reach the European Union. The journey across the Straits of Gibraltar, for instance, is composed of 19 kilometers of what at times becomes some of the most treacherous water to be found anywhere in the world. Many migrants pay up to US$750 to make this journey on fragile, flat-bottomed boats built for in-shore fishing but crammed with 20 or 30 migrants.[42]

Human Trafficking

Tragically, there also exist a significant number of persons whose undocumented migration takes place against their own wishes. According to the U.S. government, there are between 800,000 and 900,000 such victims of human trafficking every year.[43] Some are simply kidnapped, often with the complicity of relatives who profit from the transaction. More commonly, though, victims are duped with misleading information, such as an offer of a well-paid job in the service industry—upon arrival they are forced into jobs in the sex industry or other unattractive forms of employment.[44] In such cases, it is up to the traffickers' discretion whether they treat the victims as indentured servants, who must repay the costs of passage, or simply as slaves. In either case, the victim will be effectively imprisoned and denied access to authorities who would be able to assist.[45]

Visa-Free Migration

Prior to the advent of passports and immigration controls in the late 19th century, free cross-border movement was available to all with the means and

wherewithal to make the trip. In Europe, such movement was particularly significant. As noted earlier, it was quite sizeable in the case of inflows to such cities as Amsterdam and Antwerp, which attracted artisans and entrepreneurs from across the continent throughout the 17th century on account of their burgeoning wealth. Similarly, when famine blighted Ireland in the mid-19th century, many destitute persons set sail across the Irish Sea in search of better fortunes in the booming factory towns of northern England. The magnitude of this flow was also sizeable; by 1851, 25 percent of Liverpool's population was Irish.

Although most of these flows were disrupted in the first half of the 20th century by the two World Wars and the intervening depression, by the 1950s moves were afoot to liberalize intra-European migration. In part this was driven by economic concerns, with many of the booming northern European countries eager to draw upon the cheap labor offered by their southern counterparts. Today visa-free migration exists in the European Union, where the participating countries have formed a single labor market. Single labor markets also exist between New Zealand and Australia, granting citizens the unrestricted right to work in the other country for an unlimited term. A number of similar arrangements also exist between some European countries and their island colonies in the South Pacific and the Caribbean, as well as between the United States and territories such as Guam and Puerto Rico.

Students

Although individuals who travel to foreign countries for educational purposes are not ordinarily categorized as migrants, university study has emerged as a major avenue by which young people from developing countries can obtain the right to work and permanently reside in developed countries. This is particularly so in the United States, where it is common for foreign university graduates to use the one-year Optional Personal Training visa to build a rapport with a company that then, at the conclusion of the year, may sponsor them for the H-1B visa, which entitles them to work in the United States for three years and can be renewed for a further three years after that. At any point during this period, the employer may choose to sponsor the H-1B holder for permanent residency through the economic channel described previously. Many foreign students in the United States are eager to take advantage of this route, and it is estimated that only about half of foreign students return home at the conclusion of their studies.[46]

Understanding the Decision to Migrate

Economists explain human decisions, such as migration, using the concept of *utility maximization,* which assumes that the ultimate goal of all human beings is to maximize their personal utility or sense of happiness.[47] In the case of migration, for instance, potential migrants will consider how migration will affect their income, their friendships, and their relationships with family members, as well as other factors that affect their happiness, before deciding whether to migrate. Generally, people will opt to migrate only if they are reasonably confident that the sum total of all these changes will increase their overall level of satisfaction or personal, family, or community utility, to use the economic jargon, relative to their utility had they stayed home. Here we profile the conditions that stimulate and inhibit international migration.

What makes the migration decision especially complicated is that migration affects a very wide range of the many factors that constitute well-being, often in ways that are difficult to predict. Even in the presence of perfect information, migration is an activity fraught with personal risk, making it difficult for people to know with any degree of certainty whether migration will improve their overall level of happiness. Aversion to these risks tends to discourage people from leaving their home countries, even when doing so would increase their income. For instance, Puerto Ricans are free to migrate to the United States, which has over three times the average income and a quarter of the unemployment rate of Puerto Rico, yet only one in four people born on the island elect to migrate.[48] International migrants tend to be unusually willing to tolerate risk and, because of their typically young age, are often less constrained by domestic obligations to family members.

Costs of Migration

Although we may presume that a significant number of poor people would like to move to wealthier lands, migration to a high-income country, whether legal or illegal, may require risking large amounts of cash as well as life and limb. Given that the average per capita income in low-income countries stands at below US$500 a year, the cost of such journeys often exceeds the annual income of the vast majority of the world's poor.[49] In addition, because of historically low levels of migration, people from impoverished communities are much less likely to have family members who can sponsor their applications for migration through legal channels. They are also less likely to have access to social networks of migrants that can provide information prior to migration and provide assistance and aid acclimatization at the end of the journey. For all these reasons, long-distance migration is an especially risky endeavor for very poor people. Consequently, migrants from low-income countries generally come from the middle and upper reaches of the income distribution or otherwise journey only as far as neighboring low- and middle-income countries.

The Migration Hump

Impediments to migration are much less burdensome for persons migrating between high-income countries than for persons migrating from low- or middle-income countries to high-income countries. Nevertheless, even though large differences in income exist among high-income countries, only a small fraction of migrants to high-income countries come from other high-income countries. For example, citizens of member states of the European Union are free to live and work in the territory of other member states, yet non-EU migrants to EU countries outnumber EU migrants by a factor of four to one despite sizeable differences in per capita income within the European Union.[50] The difficulties facing people from low-income countries to migrate and the unwillingness of people from high-income countries to migrate gives rise to the **migration hump**.[51] Those with the highest inclination to migrate come from middle-income countries, where wages are high enough to provide the base level of wealth necessary to finance migration, but also low enough to generate significant financial incentives. Thus, as incomes in middle-income countries increase, migration rates tend to decline.[52] The migration hump for the United States is shown in figure 6.2. Here we see that emigration rises dramatically after per capita income reaches US$3,000 and falls sharply after per capita income exceeds US$10,000.

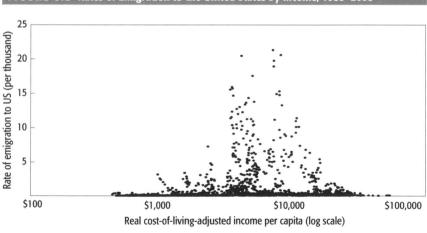

FIGURE 6.2 Rates of Emigration to the United States by Income, 1989–2000

Sources: Authors' calculations based on U.S. Department of Homeland Security 2003a and World Bank 2004d.
Note: "Real cost-of-living-adjusted income per capita" represents PPP-adjusted GDP per capita (in constant 1995 dollars). Each dot represents a country-year combination showing one country per year. The migration patterns observed between source countries and the United States may not necessarily represent those observed between source countries and other destination countries. PPP = purchasing power parity.

The Role of Information in Migration Decisions

The willingness of people to migrate will increase with the quantity and quality of information that is available. A common and relatively trusted source of information on the benefits and costs of migration are migrants who have returned to their home community or the friends and family of those who have migrated. Additional information may also be provided by recruiters or other agencies seeking to encourage persons to migrate abroad. Potential migrants are unlikely to have complete confidence in everything they are told, however, and may discount the purported benefits of migration based on their level of trust in the source of the information. If a large number of people from their community have migrated, potential migrants generally will have easy access to information and relatively high confidence in what they are told. Correspondingly, if potential migrants know of few who have gone before, they will view migration with much more trepidation.

Chain Migration

Immigrant enclaves—where members share a common source country or community of origin—can ease both the financial costs and the psychological adjustment associated with migrating to a new country. Immigrant communities also provide tangible services essential to new arrivals, such as accommodation, employment, and other forms of assistance, thereby lowering both the cost and risk of resettlement. Because of this, one person's decision to migrate will be affected by the migration decisions made by other members of that community in the phenomenon known as chain migration.[53]

For much the same reason that migrants are attracted to countries where other migrants from their home communities have settled, migrants also tend to cluster in particular industries and occupations. In some instances, industries become dependent on migrant labor to survive. Agriculture in developed countries has proved particularly susceptible. In the early 1990s, the U.S. Department of Labor found that around 85 percent of the 670,000 farm workers in the United States were immigrants, many of whom were undocumented.[54] European farmers have recruited Eastern Europeans who enter on tourist visas, but work as agricultural laborers.[55] Many developed countries have also come to depend on migrant labor to help meet shortfalls in various sectors, including medicine, a topic we discuss further below.

In some cases, particularly among lesser skilled expatriates, the decision to migrate may not belong to the individual, but rather to the family or community. Although migration may be risky for the individual, for a family with uncertain local income, sending offspring abroad may be a prudent way to diversify risks. Where there is collective decision making, the family or community may pool resources to pay the migrant's travel and adjustment costs, with the migrant then expected to remit a portion of his or her earnings once employed. In that way, if the local source of income should fail for some reason (such as through crop failure), the family or community will have an additional source of income to draw upon. It is thought that this phenomenon provides the explanation for increasing numbers of young Asian female expatriates, because daughters are usually regarded as a more reliable source of remittances than their male counterparts.[56]

Impact of Source Country Pressures on Emigration

Much of the discussion above has focused on "pull" factors of migration, yet it is also important to recognize that disturbances in the source country can be important in causing surges in migration flows. Civil strife and other forms of political turmoil can generate large outflows of refugees.[57] Less well recognized, though, are the longer-term flows that can arise from less dramatic changes in social or economic policy in source countries. For instance, with the cuts in once-generous farm subsidies by the Mexican government in the 1980s and the introduction of NAFTA in 1994, Mexican farmers have been forced to adapt to a more competitive trading environment. Some have succeeded, but those with the least fertile land struggled to make ends meet. The consequence of this has been an increase in the flow of undocumented Mexican migrants to the United States. It is estimated, for instance, that by 1996, around 750,000 subsistence farmers had migrated.[58] Financial crises, such as those discussed in chapter 4, can have similar effects.

Benefits and Costs for Source Countries

Because of the inherent risks of journeying abroad and the skill requirements imposed by the migration regimes of destination countries, emigrants are usually higher skilled, wealthier, and more economically productive than other members of their communities of origin. Therefore, the world's poorest residents are not—and are not ever likely to be—part of the international migration system. This is not to say, however, that migration does not affect them. Quite the contrary: emigration can impose sometimes unpredictable consequences on those left behind. Whole communities can be lifted out of poverty by a steady flow of remittances from a migrant diaspora. If migrants are successful in building business, trade, and investment networks and in facilitating the transfer of technology between destination and source countries, the economic payoffs to source countries can be even more profound.

Migration can also have harmful effects on those left behind. Some migrants may take with them skills in critical demand, such as medical knowledge. The loss of household heads, innovators, and leaders may also impose a broad range of social and political costs on families, communities, and even countries, undermining the social cohesion, dynamism, and growth potential of the economy. A recent study by the Organisation for Economic Co-operation and Development suggests that "emigration of highly skilled workers may adversely affect small countries by preventing them reaching a critical mass of human resources, which would be necessary to foster long-term economic development."[59] Emigration also deprives governments of tax revenues, depleting the quality of public services and preventing society from earning a return on money invested in the education of migrants. Whether migration positively or adversely affects those who do not migrate will depend upon which of the above factors are dominant.

The mass emigrations from Europe in the late 1800s and early 1900s are generally considered, in economic terms, to have had very beneficial effects on the source communities. Those leaving were generally not more skilled than those they left behind, and their departure had the effect of reducing the supply of labor in the source community, which led to a commensurate increase in the wage rate.[60] In this way, the dynamics of migration were inherently self-limiting, providing benefits to source communities. Today, though, the forces that govern the impact of emigration are more complicated and tend to yield results that are often difficult to predict and sometimes on aggregate not necessarily beneficial for the source community. One underlying difference is that today's skilled migrants are not typical of the communities they leave behind, as they often have been trained at substantial cost to the taxpayers of source countries with the expectation that they would serve their communities.

Brain Drain

Brain drain—the phenomenon of highly skilled workers leaving their home country and not returning, at least during their most productive years—has historically been viewed as one the most significant costs to source countries of international migration.[61] Since the 1960s, academics and policy practitioners have drawn attention to the potential damage to source countries caused by brain drain, yet it was not until recently that researchers attempted to empirically gauge its extent. Analysis of census and immigration data from destination countries indicates that, with a few exceptions, migration rates tend to be higher for highly educated individuals. Three-quarters of migrants entering the United States from Africa and India are highly educated, for example.[62] Given that highly educated migrants are more likely to have the resources to finance migration, and that migration policies in destination countries commonly favor those with verifiable skills and qualifications, this is perhaps not surprising.[63] What is more startling is just how many highly skilled workers low- and middle-income countries have lost. Meyer and Brown (1999) report that 400,000 scientists and engineers from developing countries are employed in research and development in high-income countries, compared with around 1.5 million who are working in their home countries.

Impact of Brain Drain on Capacity

Small countries with close transport and historical ties to developed regions and countries suffering from high levels of crime or civil unrest are those hardest hit by brain drain.[64] For example, Guyana has lost 70 percent of its university graduates to the United States, while the large diaspora of Jamaican migrants in the United Kingdom and the United States comprise over three-quarters of Jamaicans with tertiary education and a third of Jamaicans with secondary education.[65] Some African countries have suffered equally acutely, with 65 percent of Gambians, 51 percent of Somalis, 45 percent of Sierra Leoneans, and 44 percent of Ghanaians with university degrees estimated to be living abroad.[66] In total, about 70,000 professionals and university graduates are thought to leave Africa each year to take up work in Europe or North America.[67]

Impact of Brain Drain on Heavily Populated Countries

Heavily populated countries, even those with high emigration rates, generally suffer less from the brain drain simply because they have a larger base of highly skilled people. For instance, despite India being a major source of highly skilled migrants for developed countries, only 4 percent of Indians with university degrees have emigrated.[68] The Philippines has lost around 15 percent of its university graduates, as has Mexico.[69] For China, the figure is around 4 percent. The fact that it is the most talented among the highly skilled who elect to leave can make the loss of even a relatively small brain drain costly, however. For instance, a group of researchers estimated that the income earned by the relatively small number of Indians in the United States is equivalent to 10 percent of India's national income.[70]

Wealth Transfer from Brain Drain

There are around 3 million immigrants with university degrees residing in developed countries. With many of these degrees having been financed by source country governments, the total wealth transfer from poor to rich countries represented by the brain drain stands somewhere between US$45 and US$60 billion.[71] The fiscal losses of the brain drain do not stop there, however. Highly skilled workers in many countries generate the largest share of tax receipts. For instance, although India loses less than a third of its university graduates to emigration, researchers have estimated that it forgoes up to a third of individual income tax receipts through migration to the United States alone.[72] Many low- and middle-income governments would no doubt find such tax revenues to be of great benefit in the fight against poverty. On a number of occasions, source country governments have attempted to recoup some of their investment in emigrant's education through imposing taxes on remittances, but these have generally met with little success.[73] Numerous proposals have been advanced to share tax revenues of migrants between source and destination countries, but these have been met with predictable reticence by the destination countries, which benefit from immigrant flows. The effective transfer of billions of dollars from less developed to developed countries thus continues unabated.

Impact of Brain Drain on Training

A compensating benefit of the brain drain is that it does tend to increase the demand for training in the source country by raising the rate of return to education, thereby potentially increasing the domestic supply of skills. After the financial collapse in Russia in 1998, for instance, there was an increase in enrollments in science and technology. Interviews showed that, because well-paid domestic job opportunities were more limited, many students saw a science and technology education as the best road out of Russia. A survey in Bangladesh found that 72 percent of information technology specialists and 85 percent of information technology students planned to emigrate to take advantage of better opportunities abroad.[74] Even taking emigration into account, the increase in demand for education generated by the brain drain may actually increase the number of skilled workers in the population.

The impact of brain drain on a source country will obviously depend heavily on the specific skills of emigrants and the demand for those skills in the domestic economy. If emigrants are trained in skills that are wholly unemployed by domestic industry, then the remittances sent home by such emigrants may well be of more overall value to the source country than having the migrants at home, although the underlying rationale of the education system must be questioned—especially if public funds are devoted to educating people to leave. Unfortunately, though, a significant share of the skills sent from less developed to more developed countries are very much in demand in the countries that migrants leave behind. The case of medical services is considered in box 6.2.

Brain Drain and Foreign Direct Investment

When low-income communities permanently lose professionals such as teachers, engineers, accountants, and doctors, the effect can be severe. Yet the emi-

---

BOX 6.2 Musical Doctors

Health services are a common and growing source of demand for skilled migrants. Over a quarter of work permits issued by Britain go to people working in medicine. In Australia and the United States, a quarter of all physicians are foreign born. Competition for medical professionals is so fierce that many of these immigrant doctors are drawn from other high-income countries. To fill shortages that result, these countries recruit physicians from middle- and low-income countries. The resulting system of migration tends to resemble the game of "musical chairs," with countries competing to secure a limited and insufficient number of medical professionals. In this game, however, the losers lose their doctors—as many as 60 to 80 percent of them in the case of Ghana and Jamaica, for example.

In the Philippines, the education system has adjusted to meet the international demand for nurses and accordingly trains many more than are needed domestically. South Africa has partially covered its shortfalls by "borrowing" 450 doctors from Cuba. For other countries, however, the outflow of medical professionals has imperiled the public health system. Malawi, for instance, lost more than half its nursing staff to emigration over the past four years, leaving just 336 qualified nurses to serve a population of 12 million. Meanwhile, vacancy rates stand at 85 percent for surgeons and 92 percent for pediatricians. In the face of the HIV/AIDS pandemic, health services have been hard to come by in Malawi. Rates of prenatal mortality doubled from 1992 to 2000, a rise that is attributed to falling standards of medical care.

It is ironic that even as high-income countries invest millions of dollars to build up health systems in Africa, the same countries eviscerate those very systems by recruiting their personnel. Some destination country governments are beginning to appreciate this. In 2001, the British government stopped public sector recruitment of medical professionals from some developing countries. However, the lack of restrictions on private recruitment, along with the unwillingness of other countries to adopt similar self-restraint, has limited the measure's impact. The outflow of doctors and nurses from low- and middle-income countries is currently as large as it has ever been.

Sources: Anderson 1998; Clarke and Salt 2003; and Dugger 2004.

---

gration of skilled workers is not always so problematic. In particular, when a country's skill base is numerically large and relatively underutilized, as in some middle-income countries, emigration can play an instrumental role in alerting outside investors to the economic opportunities represented by the skill base in the source country. For instance, when the Indian diaspora established a record of success in the U.S. technology market, investors were prompted to inquire about whether there were others in India with similar skills, and if so, whether it would make economic sense to establish production facilities in India. The result was a large flow of foreign investment into India. This case demonstrates that when the conditions are right, skilled migrants are able to generate symbiotic networks of investment, trade, technology transfer, and skill acquisition that increase the productivity and demand for skills in the home country while extending the global technology frontier and lowering the cost of products used by billions of people worldwide. This is one key area where many of the dimensions of globalization considered in this book positively interact.

Remittances

The most common benefit of emigration to source countries is the flow of remittances sent by migrant workers to friends and family back home. In 2004, the value of these remittances to developing countries was estimated at US$160 billion, over five times the level in 1990.[75] A breakdown of remittances to major recipient nations is presented in table 6.4. As seen in this table, in some cases, remittances can be larger than both foreign direct investment (FDI) and official development assistance (ODA).

Figure 6.3 depicts the time trend of official remittance flows from 1975 to 2003 for the six regions of the developing world. Recorded remittance flows—particularly to countries in Latin America, South Asia, and East Asia and the Pacific—have risen dramatically in recent years. The extent to which in recent years this increase in recorded remittance flows is representative of an increase in actual remittances (that is, funds remitted through formal and informal channels) is unclear, however. Since the events of September 11, 2001, there has been an increased emphasis placed on monitoring and controlling international fund transfers, with many informal channels being closed completely. Accordingly, some of the increase in official remittance flows observed over the last two years of the sample may simply be a consequence of remitters switching from informal to formal channels. Nevertheless, the broader time series makes it clear that, over the past decade, flows of recorded remittances have risen significantly.

Remittances have been found to powerfully affect levels of poverty and consumption among recipients. They also tend to be stable or countercyclical to other capital flows, so they can help to stabilize local economies during times of recession or other crises. Because of this, there is little controversy among developing country governments about the aggregate benefits that remittances offer to their economies. The recent rise in recorded remittance flows, at a time when capital flows were undergoing great volatility, means that remittances sent through official channels are now second only to FDI as a source of hard currency for low- and middle-income countries.

Impact of Remittances on Small Countries

For small countries with large migrant populations, remittances are of particular significance to the health of the overall economy. For example, in

TABLE 6.4 Economic Importance of Remittances, 2003					
Geographic area	Total value (US$ million)	Per capita	Percent of GDP	Percent of FDI	Percent of ODA
Latin America and the Caribbean	**24,153**	**$63.84**	**1.97**	**93**	**634**
Mexico	14,595	$143	2	135	14,148
Jamaica	1,259	$477	16	175	36,599
Haiti	811	$96	30	10,397	406
South Asia	**15,959**	**$18.77**	**3.54**	**518**	**433**
India	17,406	$16	3	408	1,847
Bangladesh	3,191	$23	6	3,114	229
Sri Lanka	1,309	$68	7	572	195
East Asia and Pacific	**19,532**	**$10.53**	**0.95**	**33**	**285**
Philippines	7,880	$97	10	2,470	1,069
Tonga	66	$647	40	2,454	240
Vanuatu	53	$252	19	279	163
Middle East and North Africa	**14,400**	**$51.66**	**2.14**	**338**	**219**
Morocco	3,628	$120	8	159	694
Lebanon	2,700	$600	14	754	1,182
Jordan	2,201	$415	22	585	178
Sub-Saharan Africa	**4,901**	**$8.49**	**1.43**	**59**	**27**
Nigeria	1,676	$12	3	140	528
Lesotho	184	$103	16	439	232
Cape Verde	92	$196	11	622	64
Europe and Central Asia	**12,818**	**$27.12**	**0.92**	**36**	**135**
Poland	2,314	$61	1	56	194
Bosnia and Herzegovina	1,178	$285	17	309	219
Moldova	465	$110	24	796	399

Source: World Bank 2005b.

El Salvador, Eritrea, Jamaica, Jordan, Nicaragua, and the Republic of Yemen, remittances make up more than 10 percent of national income.[76] In Egypt, remittances have on some occasions provided as much foreign exchange as oil exports, tourism, and income from the Suez Canal combined; 15 percent of households in the Philippines receive income from abroad.[77] Such remittance flows can often make significant difference for families living in poverty. For example, families in Mali have been found to depend heavily on remit-

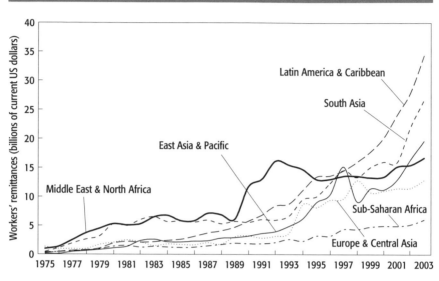

FIGURE 6.3   Flows of Official Remittances to Regions of the Developing World, 1975–2003

Source: World Bank 2005b.

tances from relatives in France to meet food consumption needs.[78] Similar research in the Dominican Republic found that 34 percent of residents received remittances, which made up 60 percent of family income on average.[79] The importance of remittances in alleviating poverty carries across much of the developing world. Research from the World Bank shows that among 74 low- and middle-income countries, poverty rates were significantly reduced by high emigration rates and large flows of remittances.[80]

Improving the Development Impact of Remittances

Historically, only a small portion of remittances have found their way to community development projects or local enterprises. However, with such investments, the impact of remittances might potentially be augmented. Recognizing this, a number of countries have implemented programs to attempt to extend the economic reach of remittances. Prompted by a government initiative, Mexican migrants working in the United States have helped to establish around 1,500 Home-Town Associations that support activities to enhance infrastructure and enterprise in the source communities.[81] States such as Jalisco have also established Economic Development Funds into which the associations can invest, with contributions matched by the Mexican government.[82] In the state of Guanajuanto, American-based migrants have invested some US$10 million in factories in their source communities.[83] Following the Mexican approach, Salvadoran migrants have established *Comités del Pueblo* to support activities back home. More research is needed to evaluate effectiveness of these types of schemes and the extent to which they assist migrants or their communities.

Improving Efficiency of Remittance Channels

Improving the development impact of remittance flows will also necessarily involve raising the efficiency of channels to remit money. Currently a few firms dominate the official global remittance market. Fees to send money internationally often exceed 10 percent, encouraging many migrants to use informal channels.[84] Estimates indicate that as much as half of total worldwide remittances are sent through these unofficial channels.[85] The fees imposed by money transfer organizations, and thereby the reluctance of migrants to use them, can be ameliorated by developing local banking sectors and working to link credit unions across countries.[86] For instance, the introduction of a network that brought together credit unions from the United States and six Central American and Caribbean countries in 2001 was able to reduce average fees for remittances down to 2.6 percent. Source country governments and local non-governmental organizations (NGOs) can also take a lead in this regard, by helping to inform migrants and remittance recipients on the most economical way to transfer funds.[87]

Benefits and Costs for Destination Countries

History shows that the world's most productive economies often require and benefit from the presence of migrant workers. Today, in spite of restrictions and controversies, the world's richest countries continue to import labor from abroad. In Singapore, Southeast Asia's richest state, migrants make up around one-quarter of the workforce. In Europe, those countries with the highest number of migrant workers—Switzerland and Luxembourg—are also the wealthiest. The Arab Emirate of Dubai, which is probably currently among the world's fastest expanding areas of economic activity, has nine times as many migrant workers as it has native workers. By lowering the costs of production and bringing in needed skills and expertise, migrants can indeed offer large positive benefits to growing economies.[88] Critics of immigration, however, are usually concerned with its impact on such things as social fabric, national culture, environment, and social welfare programs, or the wages of low-skilled workers. Correspondingly, in addition to their traditional focus on much-needed skills, advocates of increased immigration have turned their attention in recent years to the potential role further inflows could play in ensuring the sustainability of pension systems in the face of the aging of the population.

Fiscal Impact of Migration on Destination Countries

A common refrain of advocates of increased immigration restrictions is that immigrants, particularly those who are low skilled or undocumented, consume far more in public services than they contribute in tax revenue. For example, this argument has been made by Borjas (2004), who claimed that "illegal immigrants created a net burden for California's taxpayers of around $2 to $3 billion annually" (p. 26). However, there is a wide body of economic research that paints a very different picture of the fiscal impact of migration. Many European studies, for instance, conclude that immigrants—even those who are undocumented—contribute more in taxes and pension contributions than they consume in benefits or other public services.[89] In the United Kingdom, the contribution of immigration to public finances is so large that, in the words of the United Nations, "were it not for the immigrant population either public services would have to be cut or the government would need to increase the basic rate of income tax by one penny in the pound."[90] Even in the United States, immigrant families are less likely to claim social welfare benefits than native families once income levels are controlled for.[91]

Role of Migration in Sustaining Pension Systems

Contrary to the argument that migration undermines the sustainability of social welfare systems, it is increasingly recognized that migration may well have an integral role in helping to sustain these systems. As many residents of developed countries are now aware, the population of retirees is set to rise dramatically in coming years. Due to long-running declines in fertility rates to below replacement levels in high-income countries, the share of population that is working and thus paying taxes into those pension systems is also falling.[92] Thus, without large increases in taxes or public debt levels, retirees may be faced with the prospect of receiving less in pension benefits than they had been promised. Migration offers a way out of this dilemma. Many less-developed countries that currently send migrants overseas are at the opposite point in their demographic transition. By borrowing workers from low- and middle-income countries and using the tax receipts to support social security programs, high-income countries can slow the mushrooming liability of promised benefits to pensioners.

Effect of Immigration on the Labor Market

The contention that migrants take the jobs of native workers is probably the most ubiquitous and controversial argument advanced against immigration. For economists, it has proved to be a difficult debate to settle empirically. Basic theory suggests that increasing the size of the labor force will lower the wage level, all other things being equal. Yet in the real world all other things are not equal. When a city or region receives an influx of immigrant labor, native workers may opt to move to other regions, thereby masking and spreading out any changes in the aggregate wage. Firms also may decide to move into a region experiencing such an influx, causing local wages to go up. Migrants may also differ substantially from native workers in what they offer employers, and thus they may look for very different jobs.

Migrants who bring with them distinct skills or business contacts may also generate changes in technology, productivity, and trade patterns that can affect an economy in ways quite unforeseen before their presence. It does not thus follow that simply because a particular region experiences an inflow of migrant labor, the average wage of native workers will decline relative to what it would have been otherwise.

Impact of Migration on Wages

Much economic research has been devoted to attempting to discern the true relationship between immigration and wages, though controversies over the issue still abound. A common approach has been to examine how immigrant penetration of labor markets correlates with local wage levels. The general finding is that the average wage of native workers tends to be only slightly lower in labor markets with a large number of immigrants.[93] Although the sheer volume of evidence contributed by such studies may seem convincing, it does not necessarily tell us much about the true effect of immigration on wages. As outlined above, native workers are free to move to other regions when faced with an inflow of immigrants, and enterprising firms are free to move in. This will have the effect of equalizing wages across immigrant regions and nonimmigrant regions alike, though at a lower level than would have prevailed in the absence of immigrants. Thus, even though migrants may adversely affect the wages of native workers, this result may not be identifiable by any of the traditional methods outlined above.[94]

Skilled Migration and Innovation

Inflows of skilled migrants can stimulate innovation and lower the cost of producing high-tech goods and services in destination countries. The magnitude of these benefits is often sizeable, particularly in countries with long-established programs for attracting talent. In the United States, for instance, it has been estimated that a quarter of Silicon Valley firms are headed by immigrants from China and India.[95] Furthermore, entrepreneurial immigrants have frequently played a crucial role in establishing trade and investment links between destination and source countries. These links often prove equally crucial in raising the living standards of native citizens.[96] Immigrants can also help economies in much less tangible ways as well, such as by aiding in the adoption of foreign innovations and ideas.

Employment of Low-Skilled Migrants

There are many reasons why migrants—even low-skilled migrants—help destination economies and native workers. Often low-wage immigrant workers do not compete with low-wage native workers, but instead they are employed in sectors that traditionally have been dominated by migrants. Thus, one wave of migrants would displace another. Such sectors include child care, cooking, other household services, cleaning services, and menial farm jobs, all of which native workers have been unwilling to perform. Thus, without the presence of migrant workers to fill these jobs, society as a whole would be worse off.

Protecting the Vulnerable

In some respects, the current international migration regime is characterized by significant injustices. It costs thousands of lives each year, redirects hundreds of millions of dollars from poor people to the hands of criminal gangs, and deprives many needy communities of their most important members. History teaches us that migration can be a powerful force for world development, yet the current system, while making vital contributions, as is evident in remittance flows and diaspora networks, also contains elements that may actually exacerbate the world's inequalities. To spread the benefits of globalization, policy reform in migration should aim to enhance the development impact of migration and also protect the most vulnerable people involved.

Exploitation of Undocumented Migrants

While high-income countries are focusing on protecting their borders against inflows of undocumented migrants, they have paid relatively little attention to undocumented migrants who are already in the country. This has allowed the exploitation of undocumented migrants by unscrupulous employers, who can threaten to turn workers over to immigration authorities if they do not accept whatever conditions are presented to them.

Most of the countries that experience large inflows of undocumented workers rely heavily on the low-cost labor they provide. Political considerations, however, and perhaps past experiences, have prevented governments from instituting more official low-skilled "guest-worker" programs, except in particular industries such as agriculture. Unfortunately, the unintended consequence of such policies include unnecessary suffering among migrants attempting undocumented entry, and because they are often in a legal limbo, the potential for exploitation and abuse of undocumented workers who make it into the country. Implementing low-skilled migration programs, targeted at workers who would otherwise enter the country through undocumented means, can significantly prevent the most common forms of exploitation and abuse.

As noted in box 6.1, there is great variety in the scams and maltreatment that migrants can be subjected to, with perpetrators often spread between both source and destination countries. A common thread, though, is a lack of capacity among source and destination countries to deal with claims of migrant abuse, as well as a lack of knowledge among the migrants themselves of their rights throughout the migration process. Recently, the Philippines, which sends more low-skilled migrant workers abroad than any other country, has undertaken a concerted effort to protect its expatriates abroad. Some examples of this effort are detailed in box 6.3.

Effects of High-Skilled Migration on Source Countries

While high-skilled migration in sectors such as ICT seems to have played an integral role in helping spur economic development in a few source countries, high-skilled migration in other sectors—health and medicine, in particular—have done considerable damage to source countries. It may therefore be desirable to consider adopting and expanding measures by destination countries that limit the recruitment of doctors, nurses, educators, and other key professionals from countries facing a shortage in these sectors. The United Kingdom has already made steps in this direction, precluding recruitment by its National Heath Service of such personnel and encouraging members of the British Commonwealth to adopt similar rules. However, to be more effective, such measures must extend both to private operators and recruiters and to other countries that recruit health and other professionals. They should also be developed in partnership with the source countries that need to address the factors causing people to emigrate and improve the incentives for skilled people to remain at home.

Refugees and Asylum Seekers

The 1951 Geneva Convention, which provides the legal mainstay for refugee protection and resettlement programs, is severely tested by modern refugee

BOX 6.3   Migrant Labor Institutions of the Philippines

No country exports more labor annually than the Philippines. Given this importance of migration, the government of the Philippines has established a number of agencies to promote and protect the welfare of migrants. The Philippine Overseas Employment Agency (POEA) regulates, licenses, and monitors recruitment agencies. The Philippine Overseas Labor Office (POLO) maintains attachés in approximately 32 destination countries and provides such services as counseling, legal assistance, and liaison service to migrant nationals.

To ensure that employers and recruitment agencies do not seek to exploit workers, the government has also developed and disseminated "model employment contracts" with standards and requirements for a variety of different countries and occupations. The government of the Philippines requires all migrant workers leaving to register with POEA and undertake a day-long briefing, informing migrants of their rights and obligations, providing information on how to efficiently remit money to friends and relatives and on how to ensure that their health and occupational safety are protected. In addition, NGOs give seminars for migrants thought to be particularly vulnerable, such as female household workers.

The government of the Philippines has also entered into agreements with some 12 destination countries to protect and enhance migrants' welfare and has been known to place diplomatic pressure on a number of destination countries to sign and ratify the UN Convention on the Protection of the Rights of All Migrant Workers and Their Families. Although these efforts are not without shortcomings, they nevertheless represent a step forward in informing migrant nationals about their rights and how to protect those rights, and also provide something of a model for other source countries.

Source: Barber 2004.

flows. The traditional system of processing asylum seekers, in particular, is under great pressure, generating a level of controversy in leading destination countries that threatens many other forms of migration as well. Meanwhile, many large-scale regional refugee flows struggle to attract sufficient funding and attention. Although there are 10 times as many refugees in the world as asylum seekers, the UN agency charged with assisting those refugees receives less than one-tenth the resources that are expended on processing claims for asylum.

It seems appropriate to begin to think about ways in which the current arrangement could be improved. Means must be developed, for instance, to dissuade asylum seekers from undertaking dangerous and expensive illicit journeys to reach their choice country for resettlement. It has been suggested that a desirable option may be to establish UNHCR-operated "reception centers" in each region, to which asylum seekers would be forced to apply. Such proposals may have merit, but it is important that they be more fully studied to ensure that any alternative system does not dissuade asylum seekers from fleeing persecution in their home country or subject them to further persecution in neighboring countries as they await decisions on their cases. Once persons are granted asylum in a foreign country, it is also important that they are given the opportunity to contribute to their source and host countries.

Summary

Migration is a central and underappreciated feature of economic globalization. It has the potential to help poor people, but it also can hurt them in a variety of ways. Migrants send tens of billions of dollars worth of remittances to their home countries, and the remittances can directly contribute to alleviating poverty. However, many migrants, including refugees and undocumented workers, remain vulnerable to discrimination and abuse. Additionally, skill poaching, especially in the area of medical professionals, can undermine health systems in source countries, even while these systems are trying to combat public health crises such as AIDS, tuberculosis, and malaria.

Although migration holds great potential as an aspect of globalization that could significantly assist poor people, in part, the present system is open to abuse, is inefficient, and may at times even exacerbate inequalities. History shows that migration can be a powerful force for world development. To spread the benefits of globalization, migration reforms, as the Global Commission on International Migration (2005) identifies, should seek to enhance the benefits and mitigate the negative dimensions of current flows. Migration in the past has been a powerful driver of poverty reduction. Migration has enormous potential to interact positively with networks of trade, investment, and technology transfer between rich countries and the world's poorest societies to spur growth and development. In chapter 8, we draw a number of policy implications from our analysis of migration.

Annex: Sources and Methodology for Table 6.3

This annex documents data sources and procedures used in constructing table 6.3. Countries and flow volumes cited represent values for annual inflows and outflows, but not necessarily net flows.

Permanent Settlers: Here we are concerned only with those who cross borders with the right to settle permanently in the destination country. For the United States at least, most migrants who gain the right of permanent residence or citizenship do not fall into this category. In 2002, for instance, 9.6 percent of new permanent residents in the United States adjusted from temporary worker status, 9.5 percent from refugee status, 1.8 percent from student status, and 31.3 percent from undocumented, unknown, or unreported status. Accordingly, large differences may exist between the annual cross-border flow of permanent migrants and the total number of persons granted permanent residency.

For the United States, according to U.S. Department of Homeland Security (2003a), a total of 1,063,732 immigrants were admitted to the United States in 2002, of whom 384,427 were new arrivals and 679,305 were previously present in the United States and adjusted from temporary visa status. In assessing the magnitude of inflows of permanent settlers, we are specifically interested in those who initially enter the United States with the intent of settling permanently. Our assessment of the total inflows of permanent settlers thus included those who had previously been living abroad, persons adjusted to permanent resident status from business or pleasure visitor visas, fiancé or "other" status, plus persons with immigrant visas pending granted temporary admission under the Legal Immigration Family Equity (LIFE) Act. We concluded that 569,938 such persons immigrated to the United States in 2002.

For Canada, the figures in table 6.3 are "actual landings" in 2002 as listed in Citizenship and Immigration Canada (2003a). For Germany, they are "naturalizations of foreign nationals" in 2000, as listed in Table IV.11 of OECD (2004), p. 200. For France, they are inflows of permanent workers, persons entering under family reunification, and persons entering under additional permits relating to family reunification from non-EU countries in 2001, as listed in Table A1.1 of OECD (2004), p. 308. For Australia, they are settler arrivals in financial year 2002–3 as provided by Australian Government (2004a). To determine the volume of total annual flows and the leading countries of origin, we consulted the above sources and the tables supplied on the OECD Web site.

High-Skill Expatriates: For the United States, a total of 201,079 petitions for initial employment under the H-1B visa scheme were approved in 2001, according to U.S. Immigration and Naturalization Service (2002), which also provided data on the countries of origin of beneficiaries. For the United Kingdom, data on the UK Work Permit scheme and the countries of origin of beneficiaries were provided by Clarke and Salt (2003). For Canada, data on foreign workers entering Canada were provided by Citizenship and Immigration Canada (2003b). For Australia, data on skilled temporary residents were provided by Australian Government, Department of Immigration and Multicultural and Indigenous Affairs (2004a). For Japan, OECD (2004) provided lists of "residents with restricted permission to work" by occupation in table IV.16 on p. 221. Contrary to the OECD, we did not count "entertainers" as high-skilled migrants. Information on migrant worker flows to other OECD countries is provided in table 1.1 of OECD (2004), p. 28.

Low-Skill Expatriates: Data on the stock volumes of migrant workers in Saudi Arabia, Kuwait, the U.A.E., and other Gulf countries were provided by Human Rights Watch (2003). To assess flow volumes, we obtained estimates of the volume of Filipino workers in the respective countries from various sources, including Human Rights Watch (2004) and Philippine government documents. We then utilized these estimates with data on outflows of Filipino workers by destination, as provided by the Philippine Overseas Employment Administration (2004), to calculate a ratio of inflows to stocks for each destination country. Under the assumption that the ratio of inflows to stocks for migrant workers from other source countries did not differ substantially from those of Filipinos, we were able to determine inflow volumes for each destination country. The equation is as follows:

$$Inflow_{Destination}^{Total} = \frac{Outflow_{Philippines}^{Filipinos}}{Stock_{Destination}^{Filipinos}} \times Stock_{Destination}^{Total}$$

Data on inflows of contract and seasonal workers to Germany, with source country breakdowns, were provided in table IV.11 of OECD (2004), p. 200. Information on migrant worker inflows to Malaysia was provided by Scalabrini Migration Center (2000). Further information on outflows from leading source countries was provided by the Scalabrini Migration Center (2000) and the Philippine Overseas Employment Administration (2004).

Asylum Seekers and Refugees: The United Nations High Commissioner for Refugees (UNHCR) collects and disseminates detailed statistics on annual stocks and flows of refugees and asylum seekers. The data listed represent flows of *new* refugees and asylum seekers in 2002 and are sourced exclusively from UNHCR (2003). Table 5 lists the number of asylum applications filed since January 1, 2002, as 926,086 and provides a breakdown by country of asylum. Table 8 provides complementary information on the countries of origin of asylum seekers. Table 2 lists the number of new refugees in 2002 as 1,411,605 and provides a breakdown by country of asylum. Table 4 provides complementary information on the countries of origin of refugees. Note that although there were 632,340 *new* refugees from Afghanistan in 2002, a total of 1,997,474 Afghans were repatriated in 2002. Across the world, a total of 2,827,123 refugees were repatriated, so the total number of refugees in the world actually declined by 1,415,518 in 2002. At year end, there was a total stock of 10,389,582 refugees outside of their home countries. The total stock of asylum seekers was about a tenth of this: 1,014,300.

Undocumented Migrants: Data on the volume of inflows of undocumented migrants to the European Union countries were provided by Jandl (2003). Estimates of the origin of undocumented immigrants were extrapolated from nationality of undocumented immigrants regularized under amnesty programs, as provided in table I.14 of OECD (2004), p. 71. An estimate of undocumented inflows to the United States is provided by U.S. Department of Homeland Security (2003a), p. 213, "Average annual [unauthorized] population growth in the 1990s was estimated to be 350,000." Information on the composition of such flows is provided by the same source. No data on illegal flows in Asia or Africa are available; therefore, numbers represent an extreme lower bound.

Visa-Free Migrants: Estimates of intra-EU migrant flows are derived from tables B.1.1 of OECD (2003b). In the event that flow data between particular source and destination country pairs were unavailable, they were extrapolated from data on the stocks of EU foreigners in EU-15 member states, as provided in table 11 of Recchi and others (2003). When these data were unavailable (as in the case of non-British migrants residing in Ireland), flow data was extrapolated from aggregate intra-EU migration rates.

Students: Data represented stock of foreign students enrolled in tertiary education in 2001 and were sourced from table C3.5 of OECD (2003c).

Notes

1. Here we consider only international migration—that is, flows of persons across national borders. It should be noted, though, that many developing countries experience sizeable flows of internal migration (particularly from rural to urban areas), which can have powerful independent effects on levels of poverty and economic development.
2. See Diamond (1997)
3. See Cornelius (2001).
4. See Hatton and Williamson (2002).
5. See, for example, Walmsley and Winters (2003).
6. See Schrover (2004).
7. Of the 8 million people that crossed the Atlantic by the end of the 18th century, 7 million were enslaved Africans, and at least half of European migrant flows were composed of indentured servants (Chiswick and Hatton 2002, p. 2).
8. Massey (2003, p.2) finds a "significant positive association between the onset of industrialization and the initiation of large-scale international movement."
9. According to Hatton and Williamson (1998, p. 40), "a 10 percent rise in the real wage ratio [between the sending and receiving countries] reduced the emigration rate by 1.27 per thousand."
10. See Massey (2003).
11. The Chinese Exclusion Act of 1882 barred Chinese laborers from the United States; the 1908 gentlemen's agreement ended Japanese migration to the United States; and in 1917, legislation created the "Asiatic Barred Zone," which prohibited migration from Asia (Massey 2003, p. 8).
12. Hatton and Williamson (1998) report that "mass migration accounted for 208 percent of the real wage convergence observed in the Atlantic economy between 1870 and 1910."
13. The United States imposed literacy tests on immigrants in 1917 and, in the 1920s, country-based quotas limited inflows from Southern and Eastern Europe. Literacy tests were introduced in South Africa in 1897, Australia in 1901, New Zealand in 1907, and Canada in 1910. By the early 1930s, all these countries had adopted stringent migration restrictions (Chiswick and Hatton, 2002, p. 33).

14. In many countries, it took years for the principles of these conventions to be fully adopted. It was not until 1980 that the United States accepted the UN definition of refugees and began taking in refugees from non-Communist countries (Chiswick and Hatton 2002, p. 35).

15. See Chiswick and Hatton (2002), p. 36.

16. See United Nations Population Division (2002).

17. In 2000, foreign-born persons comprised 24 percent of the population in Australia, 19 percent in New Zealand, 16 percent in Canada, and 11 percent in the United States (International Organization for Migration 2003b, p. 157).

18. Characteristics rewarded by the points-based system include education, job experience, financial resources, linguistic skills, age, job offers, and relatives residing in the country.

19. The United States also accepts around 50,000 permanent residents through the annual "diversity lottery" from countries with comparatively low rates of emigration.

20. The existence of a family channel is arguably required by the Universal Declaration of Human Rights.

21. Vietnam, for instance, ranked third as a source of family migrants to Australia in 2002, through a chain that was initiated over a generation ago with a relatively small inflow of refugees (authors' calculations based on Australian Department of Immigration and Multicultural and Indigenous Affairs 2004b).

22. The United States has adopted the solution of imposing annual quotas on grants of permanent residence to extended relatives, with "subquotas" then limiting the number of those visas that can be issued to any one country. For some extended relatives of U.S. citizens living in countries with a high demand for visas, this has meant as much as a 20-plus year wait for a visa decision (U.S. Department of State 2004).

23. Authors' calculations based on U.S. Department of Homeland Security (2003b), Table 33.

24. With the economic growth of the 1990s, the annual quota on H-1B issuances was raised from 65,000 in 1998 to 195,000 in 2001; in 2004 the quota was reduced to 65,000 again.

25. Germany has the highest number of such workers, attracting 278,000 migrants in 2001, an overwhelming number of whom came from Poland. Other European countries, such as Austria, France, Italy, Switzerland, and the United Kingdom, attract between 10,000 and 50,000 seasonal agricultural workers annually (OECD 2003a).

26. See Human Rights Watch (2004, pp. 12–13).

27. The Convention does not oblige signatories to protect people who have fled their country due to war, famine, environmental collapse, or persecution by nonstate agents.

28. Studies of asylum seekers have found that the choice of destination is often influenced by transport costs, location of family and friends, perceptions of justice, or colonial, linguistic, or cultural affinities (Robinson and Segrott 2002). Asylum seekers at times pay human smuggling networks thousands of dollars to facilitate such journeys, which are often fraught with personal risk of death, injury, or exploitation.

29. Sources and destinations of asylum seekers are concentrated. Only 24 countries produced over 10,000 asylum seekers (authors' calculations based on UNHCR 2003, tables 5 and 8).

30. Among the 16 countries that received over 10,000 asylum seekers in 2002, that figure fell to 19 percent (authors' calculations based on UNHCR 2003, table 5).

31. According to the International Organization for Migration, across six countries that received large inflows of asylum seekers, only one out of every five people with rejected claims was returned home (IOM 2003b, p. 102).

32. In 1993, the German government adopted legislation that automatically rejected asylum claims filed by those who entered Germany via third countries considered "safe." In 1994, the United States shipped refugees fleeing civil disturbances in Haiti to Guantanamo Bay, Cuba. In 2001, the Australian government sent a boatload of Afghan asylum seekers to the desert island of Nauru, while accommodating others in an isolated location in the South Australian outback.

33. Research by the British Home Office found that one-third of all those accepted as refugees had university degrees, or post-graduate or professional qualifications (Stalker 2001).

34. See Koser and Van Hear (2003), p. 10.
35. See Koser and Van Hear (2003), p. 16.
36. See UNHCR (2003).
37. In the aftermath of the Rwandan genocide in 1994, the absence of any mechanism to determine the individual status of refugees had the unfortunate consequence of allowing *génocidaires* to organize and commit further crimes against humanity under the aegis of humanitarian protection provided by the international community.
38. During the Kosovo crisis in 1999, Western European countries granted blanket protection against return to all refugees. This precluded access to individual refugee status determination until the crisis was resolved and the overwhelming majority of people could return in safety.
39. Zaire is now the Democratic Republic of Congo.
40. It is noteworthy that the annual budget of the UNHCR is less than $1 billion, yet developed countries spend approximately $10 billion each year processing and hosting one-tenth the number of asylum seekers.
41. Note that the U.S. Department of Homeland Security does not track the number of people apprehended, only the number of apprehensions. Because of repeat arrests, it is highly plausible that the number of apprehensions greatly exceeds the actual number of individual people apprehended.
42. Stalker (2001).
43. See U.S. Department of State (2003).
44. The International Organization for Migration (1999) estimates that 300,000 women and children are trapped in "slavery-like" conditions in the Mekong Delta.
45. In a significant number of countries, trafficking victims can expect little assistance from legal authorities even if they do manage to escape from their captors.
46. See Szelényi (2003).
47. Note that many people have interdependent personal utility, which means that their happiness depends on the welfare of their close relatives or friends.
48. See Ramos (1992).
49. Migrants from poor countries often attempt to circumvent this "liquidity constraint" on migration by entering into contracts of indentured servitude with smuggling groups to finance the cost of illicit passage.
50. Authors' calculations based on data from Eurostat (2002).
51. For further discussion, see Martin and Taylor (1996).
52. Borjas (1999) reports that a US$5,000 increase in per capita GDP reduces the emigration rate by one percentage point
53. In economics, this is known as a *network externality*.
54. See Gabbard, Mines, and Boccalandro (1994).
55. See Stalker (2001).
56. For further discussion, see Stark (1991).
57. We briefly discuss civil conflict in chapter 8, where we propose a multilateral agreement on arms trade.
58. *Migration News* (1996) Vol. 3, No. 10, cited in Stalker (2001).
59. *Financial Times,* March 23, 2005 citing OECD (2005).
60. Hatton and Williamson (1998) report that "A CGE [computable general equilibrium] model estimated that the real wage in Sweden was 9.4 percent higher in 1890 than it would have been in the absence of twenty years of emigration after 1870" (p. 27) and that "Post-famine Irish emigration accounted for as much as a half of the growth in real wages at home and for as much as a third of the growth of income per head" (p. 189).
61. With the globalization of the tertiary education market over recent decades, a new dimension of brain drain has opened up whereby talented students head abroad to earn qualifications and elect to stay there. *The Economist* (2002) reports that half of all foreign students who earn doctorates in the United States are still there five years later.
62. See Carrington and Detragiache (1999).

63. *The Economist* (2002) reports that 21 percent of new legal immigrants to the United States had at least 17 years of education—a level reached by only 8 percent of native-born Americans.
64. See Adams (2003); and Özden and Schiff (2005).
65. See Carrington and Detragiache (1999).
66. See Docquier and Rapoport (2004).
67. See Weiss (2001).
68. See Docquier and Rapoport (2004).
69. See Docquier and Marfouk (2004).
70. See Desai, Kapur, and McHale (2001).
71. Authors' calculations.
72. See Desai, Kapur, and McHale (2001).
73. Mandatory earmarking of remittances failed in Bangladesh, Pakistan, the Philippines, and Thailand, but the Republic of Korea did experience some success in the taxation of temporary workers sent to the Middle East (Lowell 2001).
74. *United News of Bangladesh* (2000), cited in Stalker (2001).
75. World Bank 2005b. World Bank (2005F) provides an analyses of remittance data and its distribution and impact. It is thought that at least some of the large rise in recorded remittances over recent years reflects a switch to formal financial channels following the imposition of restrictions and higher levels of scrutiny on informal transfer agents in the wake of the events of September 11, 2001. These and other underlying questions on the remittance data mean that considerable caution should be exercised in interpreting these numbers—part of the rise in remittances may be accounted for by a switching from informal to formally recorded channels rather than an actual rise in the total amount of transfers. As is the case with other dimensions of migration, the net impact on the donor country or community cannot be assessed without reference to the full costs and benefits, including the potential negative impact of the loss of skills and social fabric, as well as factoring in the amount that the migrant could have contributed if he or she had stayed at home.
76. See United Nations Population Division (2002).
77. See Stalker (2001).
78. See Hatton and Williamson (2001).
79. See Waller Meyers (1998).
80. For further discussion, see Adams and Page (2003) and Maimbo and Ratha (2005).
81. See Stalker (2001).
82. See Stalker (2001).
83. See Martin and Teitelbaum (2000).
84. See Orozco (2003) and United Kingdom (2005).
85. See Stalker (2001).
86. See Orozco (2003).
87. One example of an attempt to reduce remittance costs through increased transparency is that of the United Kingdom Department for International Development (2005), which has conducted research on the alternative methods open to migrants in the United Kingdom. The Web site www.sendmoneyhome.org aims to provide information on the different options and rates.
88. In the case of the United States, for example, these positive effects have been estimated to be as large as US$10 billion dollars a year. See U.S. Commission on Immigration Reform (1997).
89. For further discussion, see Simon (1989), Glover and others (2001), and United Nations Population Division (2000).
90. United Nations Population Division (2000).
91. See Fix and Passel (1999), cited in Stalker (2001). The fact that migrants come to high-income countries seeking work not welfare is borne out by a recent study that finds that migrants in fact avoid destinations with generous social welfare programs and the attendant high tax rates. See Pederson, Pytlikova, and Smith (2004).
92. Fertility rates must be 2.2 children in order for the population to be stable. The average for high-income countries is now well below that, at approximately 1.7. Projections are that by 2050, 33 per-

cent of the population of developed countries will be over 65 as opposed to 19 percent in 2000. See United Nations Population Division (2000).

93. Pischke and Velling (1994) perform spatial correlations for Germany and find a weak negative correlation between the native wage and proportion of immigrants in the work force. Hunt (1992) reports that following the 900,000 persons who migrated to France from Algeria during the year after that country's 1962 independence, there was little change in the wage levels of affected localities. Glover and others (2001) report that a 1 percent increase in immigrant labor has only a very small effect on the wages of British-born workers. According to Borjas (1999), "A typical study finds that if one city has 10 percent more immigrants than another, the native wage in the city with more immigrants is only about 0.2 percent lower." The OECD (1997) has found no relationship between immigration and rates of unemployment in destination countries. Finally, Card (1990), who examined the influx of 125,000 Cuban immigrants to Miami in 1980, found that wage and employment trends among Miami's workers were barely altered by the inflow.

94. Borjas (2003) argues that ". . . despite all of the confusion in the literature, the available evidence teaches [that] the study of the geographic dispersion in native employment opportunities is not an effective way for measuring the economic impact of immigration; the local labor market can adjust in far too many ways to provide a reasonable analogue to the 'closed market' economy that underlies the textbook supply-and-demand framework" (p. 1339).

95. OECD (2002), p. 4.

96. Florida (2002) explores some of these issues for the case of the United States, drawing attention to what he calls the "three T's": technology, talent, and tolerance.

7

Ideas

In previous chapters, we examined trade, capital flows, aid, and migration and the interaction of these global flows with development. In each case, these dimensions of economic globalization had the ability to contribute to development *under certain conditions*. This chapter focuses on ideas, an often-neglected dimension of globalization, despite often being the most important. Ideas involve generating and transmitting distinctive intellectual constructs in any field that can affect production systems, organizational and management practices, governance practices, legal norms, and technological trends. Our scope here is thus very wide. Nevertheless, as with the other dimensions of economic globalization, there are distinct if subtle connections between the realm of global idea generation and dissemination and the realm of poverty and development. We attempt to convey some of these connections here.[1]

The Power of Ideas

Ideas are the most powerful influence on history. Globalization is above all about the flow and intermingling of ideas among the countries of the world. Ideas inform the evolution of politics and economics. The ways in which ideas flow and are absorbed shapes globalization and its impact on poor people. This has been true since the first migrations of "primitive" peoples across Africa, the Americas, Asia, and Europe. That the global spread of ideas is not a new phenomenon is evident in the rise of the earliest civilizations and the development and adoption of language, early implements, and agricultural technologies.[2] The spread of languages and cultures, of religion, and of specialization and trade reflect the forces of globalization. Although the expansion and then contraction of the influence of the ancient African, Chinese, Greek, Mayan, and other civilizations may be interpreted as the rise and decline of their military power, this power reflected an underlying set of ideas and technologies that shaped and informed the waxing and waning of the empires.

Development may be characterized as the application of better and smarter ways of dealing with key challenges. As a leading growth economist Paul Romer (1993a) has written, "Nations are poor because their citizens do not have access to the ideas that are used in industrial nations to generate economic value" (p. 543). Development marks the evolution of newer and more effective ideas that replace those that no longer reflect the opportunities and policy choices available to individuals and societies. The acceleration of growth and poverty reduction requires a more rapid evolution and dissemination of ideas. The challenge is the identification and assimilation of what works (and what does not work) in the fight against poverty, with local ideas addressing the uniqueness of local problems drawing on the full richness of global knowledge.[3]

Bad Ideas

Not all ideas are good. Indeed, some of the most negative effects of globalization can be attributed to the adoption of inappropriate ideas. One extreme case of this—the idea of *mercantilism*—is considered in box 7.1. However, creating barriers against the flow of ideas is not an appropriate response to the risk of adopting bad ideas. Insulating society from these flows, through intellectual autarky (intellectual self-sufficiency), is perhaps best illustrated by the Democratic People's Republic of Korea, which—after adopting and adapting the big, far-reaching idea of Marxist-Leninism—has virtually cut itself off from the world, with disastrous consequences for its population. We might imagine that if the Democratic People's Republic of Korea were to end its isolation and benefit from its proximity to its neighbors, the Republic of Korea and China, the dynamic effects of the new ideas flowing in would dwarf the development impact of foreign aid and even foreign investment flows.[4]

Identifying and Adapting Useful Ideas

The challenge for countries and individuals is to create the capacity to identify, from the myriad idea flows, those that are most interesting and that offer the most potential—and to then evaluate, reject, and adapt those ideas in a process that leads to local innovation and progress.

This is no small challenge. The evaluation and adaptation of ideas requires local capacity in the form of both skills and institutions.[5] It also requires a culture of learning and adaptation, of openness to ideas and to challenging past practices. In development projects, it requires the explicit recognition of the

KEY TERMS AND CONCEPTS

civil society organizations (CSOs)   mercantilism
global economy   nonexcludable nature of public good
Green Revolution   nonrival nature of public good
import-substitution model of trade   patent ladders
information gaps   public goods
intellectual property rights   Washington Consensus
knowledge gaps
market system

need for independent assessments based on accurate data, followed by frank discussions of what works and what does not, what can be improved and how.

Global Economy and the Market System

The fall of the Berlin Wall and the integration of China into the *global economy*, together with technological change—not least in telecommunications and transport—has been associated with an acceleration in the integration of the global economy and the reach of the particularly ubiquitous idea of the *market system*. As defined by Lindblom (2001), the market system "is a system of society wide coordination of human activities not by central command but by mutual interactions in the form of transactions" (p. 4). This system now informs economic governance virtually everywhere. This is not to say, however, that the system of market-based coordination is in any way monolithic, as China's strong central management of the market economy illustrates. Economic activity exists in many forms, shaped by the interface of global ideas with local ideas and preferences. The global economy is consequently in constant evolution, as well as in coevolution with systems of governance.

Flow of Ideas

The post–World War II period has been associated with an unprecedented increase and reach of the cross-border flow of ideas. It is no accident that this period also has been associated with unprecedented leaps in life expectancy and literacy, benefits brought by the spread and adoption of new policies and technologies. The combination of global knowledge and local innovation and adaptation and implementation has been particularly powerful. This is

BOX 7.1 Mercantilism

Mercantilism was one the most misguided development ideas of all time. In its myriad forms, mercantilism influenced development patterns from the mid-15th century through the end of the 19th century. This influence ranged from mild to catastrophic among the various regions of what we now call the developing world. The basic notion of mercantilism was that wealth was to be found in precious metals, primarily gold. As an admiral of Christopher Columbus stated, "of gold is treasure made, and with it he who has it does as he wills in the world and it even sends souls to Paradise." Where gold was not to be acquired directly, through mining, it was to be acquired indirectly, by generating a trade surplus. As stated by Thomas Mun in an early mercantilist treatise, "The ordinary means . . . to increase our wealth and treasure is by Foreign Trade, wherein we must ever observe this rule; to sell more to strangers than we consume of theirs in value." Gold was seen as important in part for its role in paying armies. Indeed, trade and war were closely related in much mercantilist thinking and practice, perhaps most famously in the case of the Dutch East India Company, which at its height maintained a force of 30,000 soldiers. As one of its employees wrote, "We can't trade without war, nor make war without trade."

It was mercantilism that provided the intellectual structure of Spain's brutal colonial conquests and set the stage for the famous inflows of gold into the capital of its empire, Sevilla. The barren nature of mercantilist ideas became apparent with Iberian inflation and, ultimately, the collapse of the empire by the end of the 17th century. Spain itself gained few long-term benefits from its empire, no less its brutalized colonial subjects. As Adam Smith noted in his anti-mercantilist *Wealth of Nations*, "Wealth does not consist in gold and silver; but in what money purchases."

In the late 1700s, Spain locked up the documents of its colonial history in the Old Exchange Building in Sevilla. In 1862, the young King Leopold of Belgium spent a month in these archives, carefully studying Spain's application of mercantilist practice to its colonies. These he applied to his own colony in the Congo after the Berlin Conference of 1885. Again, the effect was brutal, resulting in the deaths of approximately 10 million Congolese from 1885 through 1920. Thus, the mercantilist idea extended its devastating reach across more than four centuries, with each imperial power seeking to run a trade surplus by locking its colonies into patterns of trade that prevented the colonies trading with other imperial powers or their colonies, choking what now is known as South-South trade.

Sources: The Economist 1998, 1999; Galeano 1997; Hochschild 1999; Mun 1924, orig. 1664; Smith 1937, orig. 1776.

evident, for example, in the way that global knowledge about the relations between germs and diseases has been applied in local campaigns to encourage people to wash hands, and in how the biological advances in understanding HIV/AIDS have been combined with local knowledge to develop public health strategies that have saved hundreds of millions of lives. Similarly, the combination of global knowledge and local innovation provided the engine for the ***Green Revolution***, which benefited hundreds of millions of poor people through dramatically raising agricultural productivity, particularly in Asia.

Implications of Ideologies

Although the rapid spread and adoption of new ideas is behind the greatest leaps in development, ignorance and the failure to learn rapidly enough is behind some of the greatest development setbacks. For example, the failure to act earlier and more decisively against HIV/AIDS in a number of countries, such as Botswana and South Africa, has already reversed the gains of the life expectancy of the past 30 years.[6] However, the significance of ideas is not largely confined to health and technology. The implications of ideologies, including ideas about religion and economics, have an even more powerful influence.

Ideas of Destiny

Ideas of destiny, right, and might, enacted in the crusades, colonial conquest, and communism, have massive and continuing implications for development. Globalization does not appear to have diluted such ideas. Although in some senses there has been what Bell (2001, originally 1960) and Fukuyama (1992) heralded as "the end of ideology" and "the end of history," respectively, the tenacity of ideologies remains evident. Examples range from the growth of religious fundamentalism in many parts of the world to the dogged adherence in the richest countries to protectionist policies. As discussed in chapter 3, protectionism in rich countries has a devastating impact on millions of poor people whose struggle to escape poverty is frustrated by the barriers that rich countries place on their exports.[7] Protectionism in rich country agriculture is an idea that Sir Nicholas Stern (2004), the former Chief Economist of the World Bank, has characterized as "politically antiquated, economically illiterate, environmentally destructive and ethically indefensible."[8] Yet it persists.

Context of Ideas about Human Rights

Ideas on development cannot be divorced from the broader context of ideas of humanity, freedom, culture, and religious belief. These shape and inform economic development and globalization and, in turn, they evolve in response to the changes in their operating environment. The spread of ideas about human rights, for instance, has driven development progress.[9] Important phases of this spread have included the movement for the abolition of slavery, the struggle for suffrage for woman, the anticolonial movements, and the development of trade unionism. Today, thousands of international conventions and the development of hundreds of international organizations, not least the United Nations and Bretton Woods systems to which the great majority of the world's nations belong, have given institutional form to the globalization of ideas about rights and the broadening of our understanding of development

Global Governance System

The rise of this global governance system developed to spread ideas about human rights, poses numerous challenges, as is evidenced in the rich and complex debate about the management, reform, and evolution of global institutions. As the outcome of past compromises, it is not surprising that global institutions are neither ideally equipped to deal with current and future global challenges nor easy to reform. Indeed, it is not difficult to identify a raft of reforms that would better equip the international community to meet the challenges of the 21st century.[10] In practice, however, major structural reforms require new agreements, which are not easily reached by the relevant global constituents. More practical, therefore, is the evolutionary reform of the system and its component parts.[11]

Civil Society Organizations (CSOs)

In this area, *civil society organizations (CSOs)* and other global lobbying groups, often aided by the Internet, have demonstrated the new power of virtual networks in the international communities of ideas. Through pressure on governments and international organizations, global networks of lobbying groups can exercise a powerful influence on the evolution of policies at both the national and global level. The international networks have been associated with many reforms that have benefited poor people. Global campaigns, such as the Jubilee Campaign to Drop the Debt or the Live Aid event on famine in Africa, have proved particularly effective in contributing to increasing awareness about poverty reduction. However, the rising power of distant lobbyists is not without its dangers, as their interests and objectives and those of the local communities who are directly affected may not always coincide. For example, the activities of San Francisco–based activists against the construction of the Bujagali dam in Uganda was apparently largely uninformed by the preferences of the local communities who stood to benefit from the dam.[12]

Contagion and Unpredictability of Ideas

Ideas can be contagious and their flow unpredictable. Recent examples include the collapse of the seemingly deeply-entrenched communist regimes in Eastern Europe, the collapse of the apartheid regime in South Africa, and the rise of religious fundamentalism. The advent of mass communication technologies, particularly global television channels and the Internet, has lifted the globalization of ideas to new heights. In addition to transferring ideas that weaken government and other national monopolies over information, mass communication has profound implications for patterns of production and consumption. This is one of the defining features of the latest wave of globalization. As John Stuart Mill in the mid-19th century observed,

> *It is hardly possible to overrate the value . . . of placing human beings in contact with persons dissimilar to themselves, and with modes of thought and action unlike those with which they are familiar. . . . Such communication has always been and is peculiarly in the present age, one of the primary sources of progress.* (Mill 1846, volume 2, book 3, chapter 7, section 5, cited in Meier 2001, p. 5)

Ideas and Development

As we noted in the introductory chapter, perhaps the most fundamental change in ideas about development relates to our understanding of development itself. For example, our understanding of the goals of development has changed substantially even in the last 20 years. We now look beyond incomes to health, education, and human development. We now see the objectives of development as ensuring that all people have the ability to shape their own lives ("development as freedom" in the words of Sen 1999). Overcoming poverty means giving poor people opportunity, empowerment, and security. We have learned that empowerment is both an end and a means of development.[13]

The Power of Ideas

The focus of a growing number of economists on the challenges of development has been associated with a widening recognition of the power of ideas. For example, Meier (2001) has noted that "ideas are fundamental to the future progress of development" (p. 1). The examination by Paul Romer and others of the sources of economic growth has also been responsible for a growing understanding and emphasis on the role of ideas. In Romer's (1993b) view,

> *Ideas should be our central concern. . . . Ideas are extremely important economic goods, far more important than the objects emphasized in most*

economic models. In a world with physical limits, it is discoveries of big ideas, together with the discovery of millions of little ideas, that make persistent economic growth possible. Ideas are the instructions that let us combine limited physical resources in arrangements that are ever more valuable. (p. 64)

Innovations in Growth Theory

Building on Schumpeter (1949), recent innovations in growth theory emphasize the role of the evolution of ideas at the micro level in processes of firm innovation. For development to occur, ideas have to produce innovations in productive methods, including organization, sources of supply, and quality. The Schumpeterian vision is that of development being accelerated through an increase in the supply of ideas and their translation into innovations. For this to happen, the transmission and acceptance of ideas must be in a form that can be translated into capabilities. Increases in rates of growth and poverty reduction thus require both an acceleration of idea transmission *and* the adoption of ideas through innovations that contribute to technical and societal change.

Some time ago, Summers (1991) indicated that "To put it bluntly, since there will not be much development money over the next decade, there had better be a lot of good ideas" (p. 2). However, as Meier (2001) notes, "Although the creation of ideas is a necessary condition for development, it is not a sufficient condition. The absorptive capacity of the developing countries is crucial. . . . [I]f ideas on policy reforms require political conditions . . . and these do not exist, or if the absorptive capacity depends on institutional change that is not forthcoming [the ideas cannot be activated upon] . . . the preconditions must be in place for the acceptance and implementation of ideas" (p. 5). In fact, these preconditions often do not exist, especially in low-income countries.

Capacity to Absorb, Evaluate, and Adapt Ideas

Although it is vital to stress the importance of the capacity to absorb ideas, at least as important is the capacity to evaluate and either adapt or reject ideas. For too long, developing countries have suffered the burden of the imposition of inappropriate ideas. Although this characterized the colonial period, it is not confined to it. Tied aid and inappropriate conditions associated with financial flows have for many countries reflected the imbalance in their bargaining strength in the realm of ideas, an imbalance similar to the one they have in trade and in other dimensions of global interchange. The solution cannot be isolation, but rather judicious engagement on all key dimensions. As we discuss elsewhere with respect to trade, capital markets, migration, and aid, the question is not whether to engage, but how. In the realm of ideas and innovation, the key question for governments revolves around how they handle knowledge management.

Managing Knowledge

As suggested above, the deficiency of knowledge can be a more pervasive handicap to development than the scarcity of any other factor. Knowledge, however, is in many respects a ***public good***. Once something is known, that knowledge can be used by anyone, and its use by any one person does not preclude its use by others. This characteristic of knowledge is precisely the hallmark of a public good, and suggests that knowledge, like other public goods, will be underprovided by market systems. The challenge, then, is the effective development and management of knowledge, recognizing its public good nature.[14]

Characteristics of Knowledge

The *World Development Report* (World Bank 1999) noted that "Knowledge is like light. Weightless and intangible, it can easily travel the world, enlightening the lives of billions of people everywhere. Yet billions of people live in the darkness of poverty—unnecessarily" (p. 1). The World Bank went on further to distinguished between ***knowledge gaps*** in know-how or technical knowledge (such as birth control, software engineering, and accountancy) and ***information gaps*** in areas such as product quality, creditworthiness, and other types of incomplete information that lead to market failures.

Addressing Knowledge Gaps

For developing countries to address the problem of knowledge gaps, the authors of the *World Development Report* recommended three key actions:

- *Acquiring knowledge* by tapping into and adapting knowledge available elsewhere in the world—for example through trade, foreign investment, and licensing—as well as by creating knowledge locally through research and development and building on indigenous knowledge.
- *Absorbing knowledge* by ensuring universal basic education, creating opportunities for lifelong learning, and supporting tertiary education.
- *Communicating knowledge* by taking advantage of new information and communications technology. This requires that poor people have access and that information flows be promoted, using vibrant media and modern technologies, among other methods.

Addressing Information Gaps

To address information gaps, the World Bank report recommended that priority be given to ensuring transparency and accountability in financial flows, reducing the risk of capture and corruption, and increasing knowledge of opportunities. It also highlighted the need to overcome information deficits that discriminate against poor people and isolate them from markets, as well as those that lead to failing to account for the environment.

Disseminating Knowledge

A vibrant media can play a vital role in disseminating knowledge. Higher literacy rates, lower printing costs, and new broadcast technologies (including the Internet) can promote the potential of the media to inform citizens and create global constituencies and commerce. At the global level, media can move currency markets and influence international trade. At the other end of the spectrum, however, are the local, vernacular media. These can help develop market opportunities for poor farmers through daily radio broadcasts of prices, for example. They can also increase awareness of local threats and opportunities, considerably improving local health and knowledge.

Information and Institutional Reform

As emphasized by the World Bank (2002d), open information flows can promote institutional reform by affecting peoples' incentives and by promoting the sharing of ideas and knowledge. New information can change people and culture and create demand for new institutions as well as facilitate debate and collective action. The combination of providing information and voice (the ability to access views and express them effectively) can and does facilitate social change.

Effect of the Media

The extent to which the media improve governance and support markets depends to a large extent on their ability to provide relevant information and reflect diverse ideas and social views. Too often, the capture of the media by narrow political or financial interests, coupled with weak capacity and heavy constraints on journalism, lead to the media not rising to their potential. Diversity of perspective, as well as financial and editorial independence, is vital for both state and private media. This is a major regulatory challenge, which, in the age of increasing global concentration, needs ongoing and increased attention. This challenge is not simply confined to the poorest societies, where lack of capital and capacity and the constraints placed on markets by the poverty and illiteracy of readerships and advertisers undermine the potential for the use of media in addressing knowledge deficits. In the most advanced societies, a plethora of choice and availability, as is evidenced in the more than 600 channels available on satellite TV and the unprecedented access offered by broadband Internet, is coupled with a homogenization of content. Consumers typically choose among a widening range of similar products owned and operated by a narrowing set of major multinational corporations.

Although the potential to learn about the world and develop a global citizenry has never been greater than it is now, the irony is that global and national polls do not appear to reflect a rising knowledge among consumers who spend hours a day watching television, "surfing" the Internet, or reading newspapers and journals. Clearly, content is at least as important as capacity.

Effect of Education and Training

Education and training in all its form is about exposure to ideas. The education of children and adults is a vital starting point for development. In particular, literacy, numeracy, and the ability to absorb and evaluate information are central. In the important phrase of development economics, education and training are all about "learning to learn." Without this capacity, ideas have no vitality.[15]

Intellectual Property

Trade in goods and services and flows of capital are often packaged with ideas and innovations, and there is an extensive literature on the role of technology transfer in foreign direct investment.[16] Here we go beyond the arguments of chapter 3 to discuss the particular questions of trade in knowledge products.

Public Good Characteristics of Knowledge

As stated above, knowledge has strong public good characteristics. Because of this, it tends to be underprovided by a market-based system. For example, "The innovator's inability to obtain adequate compensation for his effort would, under a competitive system, cause too few resources to be allocated to research" (Leach 2004, p. 174). This problem is typically addressed in the coevolution between markets and governance systems through various types of intellectual property protection, a key form of knowledge management.[17]

Intellectual Property Rights Controversy

The area of ***intellectual property rights*** is among the most controversial in economics. One area of intense debate concerns the role of intellectual property rights in growth. The common argument is that the presence of strong intellectual property rights spurs innovation, which leads to higher rates of economic growth and increasing benefits for all. The kernel of the argument is that, if strong property rights provide good incentives for the production of things, they must also provide appropriate incentives for the production of ideas. Boldrin and Levine (2002, 2004a, 2004b) question this, arguing that intellectual property has come to mean not only the right to own and sell ideas, but also the right to regulate their use, which can create a socially inefficient monopoly.[18] They agree that for efficiency reasons ideas should be protected and available for sale, just like any other commodity. They object, however, to the idea of an intellectual monopoly, arguing that monopoly is neither needed for, nor a necessary consequence of, innovation and that intellectual property is not necessary for innovation and growth—that in fact it may hurt more than help. They suggest that, although the producers of a new product or service should have the right to benefit from its sale, they should not be able to appropriate the right of others to learn from the ideas embodied in that product, just as the producers of potatoes or French fries cannot monopolize the ideas embodied in their production.[19]

The Role of Intellectual Property Rights

Intellectual property rights are designed to increase innovation by offering incentives to those who develop new techniques. As Wolf (2004) has noted, "given the role of innovation, intellectual property is not a marginal feature of the property-rights regime of a modern market economy, but its core. It is the most important example of property that only a powerful state can protect. The reason that such action is needed is because ideas are public goods" (p. 51). The problem for developing countries is that intellectual property rights are a legally sanctioned restraint of trade. They can lead to the monopolization of ideas and innovation by first-comers and those with the most well-endowed research and legal systems. Not surprisingly, their application requires careful analysis of both benefits and costs on the part of the development community if they are not to lead to further inequities, and to ensure both growth and more equitable development, benefiting poor people and poor countries.

How this can best be done is a question to which answers greatly diverge. As noted by the International Centre for Trade and Sustainable Development (2003), "since the early 1990s, Intellectual Property (IP) policy has become one of the most economically and politically contentious issues in the international arena, whether in discussions on public health, food security, education, trade, industrial policy, traditional knowledge, biodiversity, biotechnology, the Internet, or the entertainment and media industries" (p. 1). In each of these areas, consensus of the development community members on correct policy is often elusive.

Reach of Intellectual Property Protection

As the above list of issue areas suggests, the range over which intellectual property protection can help or harm poor people is large. A summary of some of these areas, including potential costs and benefits, is presented in table 7.1.

TABLE 7.1 Potential Effects of Intellectual Property Protection on Poor People

Area of concern	Potential costs	Potential benefits
Health	Increased prices of essential drugs.	Greater innovation of drugs of importance to developing countries.
Food and agriculture	Loss of self reliance for poor farmers. Increased privatization of genetic materials and biological resources.	Increased use of geographical indications to promote commercialization of products.
Traditional knowledge, folklore, and culture	Piracy of traditional knowledge in the form of medicinal plants, agricultural products, and forest products.	Increased protection of and royalties for music industries. Provision of intellectual property registration systems to indigenous peoples.
Access to knowledge and innovation	Restrictions of fair use of digital information. Increased licensing costs.	Support of knowledge generation and diffusion. Promotion of inflows of private capital, especially FDI. Increased protection of textile designs and emergent software industries.
Education	Increased prices of educational materials.	Development of new educational resources of relevance to developing countries.

Source: International Centre for Trade and Sustainable Development 2003.

Patents

Patents are a central concern with regard to the impact of intellectual property protection on poor people, affecting three areas of table 7.1: health, food and agriculture, and access to knowledge and innovation. As stated by Leach (2004), "The essential tradeoff in choosing the patent life is that a longer patent life raises the rate at which discoveries occur, but reduces the social benefits of each discovery" (p. 175). The proponents of stronger patent protection in developing countries argue that this protection will promote domestic innovation as well as the flow of ideas through increased FDI and exports. There is not complete agreement on this matter, however. In addition to the arguments of Boldrin and Levine (2004a, 2004b) cited above, Kash and Kingston (2001), for example, argue that, in the case of complex technologies, patent protection can actually inhibit innovation. To some extent, then, the ability of increased patent protection to deliver access to knowledge and innovation is uncertain.[20]

Pharmaceuticals and Patent Rights

One key area regarding patent protection and the poor is in the field of pharmaceuticals and the extension of patent rights to developing countries as required by WTO membership. Although some argue that the extension of intellectual property rights may lead to more research on drugs to address developing country needs, the evidence on the short experience since this extension remains hotly contested.[21] For many commentators, the relatively small size of the purchasing power in developing countries and the apparent lack of commercial interest by the pharmaceutical companies rather than patent issues explain the tiny portion of research devoted to diseases prevalent in tropical and other low-income developing countries. Whereas the average health care budget per person per year in the United States is approximately US$4,000, in Sub-Saharan Africa it averages less than US$20 per person per year; in the poorest rural areas it is even lower. With the average cost of bringing a new drug to market currently running at about US$800 million, and the annual sales from the three leading therapy classes—cholesterol reducers, anti-ulcerants, and antidepressants—exceeding US$70 billion per year, the incentives for the major drug companies are overwhelmingly skewed in favor of the primary problems facing rich countries.[22]

Boosting Investment in Research

Recent years have seen a number of highly significant efforts to boost investment in research and its application in developing countries. The Measles

Initiative, started in 2000 with significant support from the World Health Organization (WHO), the Red Cross, and media entrepreneur Ted Turner has contributed to reductions of 60 percent in mortality rates from measles in children in Sub-Saharan Africa. Vaccination campaigns over the past five years are estimated to have saved one million lives in this region. Despite these remarkable gains, the ongoing limited access of many people to the vaccine, which costs under $1 per dose and has been available since 1963, results in over 400,000 deaths among children a year, half of them in Africa. The Global Alliance for Vaccines and Immunizations (GAVI) is an impressive example of a new type of public-private partnership, bringing together donor and developing country governments, established and emerging vaccine manufacturers, nongovernmental organizations (NGOs), research institutes, UNICEF, the World Health Organization, the World Bank, and the Bill & Melinda Gates Foundation.[23] The devastating impact of malaria is receiving increasing attention from this widening coalition of partners, whose efforts aim to reverse the more than 3 million deaths per year, including 1 million child deaths per year in Africa alone, in the Roll Back Malaria Partnership. Malaria alone is estimated to cost Africa over US$12 billion per year in lost productivity and is closely correlated with poverty. This is both because it is most rampant where the associated drugs, bednets, and public health systems are least affordable, and because malaria itself undermines productivity, clogs public health systems, and undermines the economic and technical capacity of countries to cope with it as well as with other diseases such as HIV/AIDS.

Meeting the Challenge of HIV/AIDS

With over 5 million people becoming infected each year, and with 15 million children orphaned by AIDS, the global community is belatedly organizing itself to meet the devastating challenge of HIV/AIDS.[24] Since 1990, the number of people living with HIV/AIDS has quadrupled to around 40 million worldwide, and in 2004, 3.1 million people died from this disease, more than from any other infectious disease. Sub-Saharan Africa remains the worst affected region, with two-thirds of all cases. In nine African countries life expectancy has fallen below 40 years, and already 11 million African children have been orphaned because of the disease.

The key to combating HIV/AIDS is forthright national leadership, widespread public awareness campaigns, and intensive prevention efforts, including the availability of affordable drugs. The debate on intellectual property and incentives for innovation is being severely tested in this area. Work continues on vaccine development, and the number of people with access to antiretrovirals has doubled in two years—to 700,000 in 2004. Given the scale of the problem, this remains grossly inadequate. With increased advocacy and coordination around UNAIDS, financing commitments for HIV/AIDS prevention and treatment jumped from less than US$400 million in the late 1990s to around US$6 billion in 2005. Research and its application remains a critical stumbling block, with questions of affordability and availability of drugs and the timing of their development, as well as the availability of skilled professionals and health care systems for their application, posing key constraints.

The recent example of the governments of Brazil, India, and South Africa challenging U.S. patents on HIV/AIDS drugs, which raised the costs of these drugs to AIDS patients in these countries, received widespread attention. In 2001, WTO members gathered in Doha Qatar for the fourth Ministerial Conference of the WTO. At this meeting, pressure over the HIV/AIDS issue was intense. As a result, the members issued a special declaration allowing for measures "to protect public health." More specifically, the declaration reaffirmed certain "flexibilities," including the following statement: "Each member has the right to determine what constitutes a national emergency or other circumstances of extreme urgency, it being understood that public health crises, including those related to HIV/AIDS, tuberculosis, malaria and other epidemics, can represent a national emergency or other circumstances of extreme urgency." This was a victory for those in developing countries with a concern for AIDS and other public health issues. However, for countries with no domestic productive capacity in pharmaceuticals, the right to import cheaper, nonpatent drugs remains a contested issue.

Intellectual Property Protection for Traditional Knowledge

To enhance development, it is important that intellectual property protection be extended to what table 7.1 calls "traditional knowledge, folklore, and culture," or what Finger (2004) calls "poor people's knowledge." It is not only vital that intellectual property regimes allow developing countries to benefit from ideas developed in rich countries, but also that their own indigenous ideas are suitably protected. The key issue here, as expressed by Finger, is that of "enhancing the commercial value of poor people's knowledge in which there are no worries about this use being culturally offensive to members of the community or about this use undermining the traditional culture of the community" (p. 3). Examples include the protection of the craft designs of the nearly 10 million artisans in India, Congolese wire toy designs, the recordings of the Senegal Musicians' Association, *Kente* designs in Ghana, and many, many others. By enhancing the returns on these types of knowledge, intellectual property protection could help poor communities.

Reform of Intellectual Property Arrangement

One suggested reform of current intellectual property arrangements is to modify rules governing patents under the Agreement on Trade Related Aspects of Intellectual Property Rights (TRIPS) of the WTO to allow for *patent ladders*, in which the minimum extent of patent protection varies according to level of per capita income. Although designing such a system is not straightforward, this is a way to avoid what, in the case of environmental or labor standards, is called a "one-size-fits-all" approach to standardization of governance systems.

Global Brands

The crowding out of local ideas and culture by global brands—such as McDonalds, Nike, and Coke—is of particular concern to many who worry that this undermines local cultures and products. The appeal of many global products transcends national borders and ideologies. To the extent that they crowd out consumption of traditional or local products or are seen as a symbol of U.S. or "Western" economic and cultural domination, they have become rallying points for antiglobalization protests.[25] This presents some cause for concern. As expressed by Sen (1999), "Equity in cultural as well as economic opportunities can be profoundly important in a globalizing world" (p. 241). However, Sen concludes that "The one solution that is *not* available is that of stopping globalization" (p. 240, emphasis added). Rather, what is required is that people, including poor people, be empowered enough to take part in social decisions about cultural issues. In the case of poor people, deprivations of access, information, participation, and education make this very difficult. Sen casts this issue in terms of "human rights in the broadest sense" (p. 242).

Ideas About the Roles of States, Markets, and Institutions

How governments and societies organize themselves and how they absorb ideas and allow their citizens and firms to operate is a key determinant of growth and poverty reduction. Much of the intellectual property debate is about the private appropriation of ideas, and hence is vital in considering the role of ideas embodied in technologies and processes that are developed and adopted by private firms and individuals. Until recently, for many countries and firms, the very idea of a private or market-based economic system was foreign. Through the absorption and adaptation of ideas, new economic systems have evolved, which in turn, over time, fundamentally change the way in which ideas are generated, transmitted, and absorbed.

Evolution of the Development Community's Ideas on Economic Management

The development community's understanding of the most effective way to achieve development objectives has evolved over time with the accumulation of evidence and experience. Approaches that once appeared to be both correct and obvious have been shown not to work by experience and closer analysis. In the same way, our current ideas will no doubt give way to others as experience accumulates and thinking evolves. This surely reminds us to beware of simplistic solutions or "silver bullets" in development thinking. Perhaps the most important questions on which our understanding has deepened over the past decades are: What are the respective roles of governments and markets in spurring development? How do institutions fit into the picture? At the risk of oversimplification, we can identify at least three major phases in the evolution of our answers to these questions.

In practice, we recognize that there is a continuum of approaches, both in developed and in developing countries, and that the phases described here do not match precisely the evolution of thinking in any particular region. Instead, the discussion of these phases is intended to capture the broad shifts in the thinking of the development community and development practitioners. It is also the case that successful countries throughout this post-World War II period have seen both state and market play positive roles. With those caveats, this broad-brush picture can nevertheless provide a useful context for a discussion of development assistance by suggesting where that assistance is most likely to be effective.

Phase One: Confidence in Government

The 1950s and 1960s were a period of great confidence on the part of the development community. Development practitioners and thinkers trusted government both for its intentions and for its ability to make economic progress happen, in both the richer and the poorer countries. Development thinking focused on market failures, which were especially prevalent in developing countries and seemed to provide a strong rationale for state intervention. The private sector was thought to be too uncoordinated, too poorly developed, and too focused on private interests to allow it to serve as the locomotive for growth. In Africa, newly independent countries searched for a postcolonial model of development and a strengthened leadership role for the national state. In many countries around the world, the confidence in government was reflected in the heavy role of central planning and in the relatively closed (import substitution) trade policy.[26]

This state-led approach had some initial development successes. Leading economies of Latin America, where state economic management did not completely crowd out the private sector, grew rapidly for decades under the ***import-substitution model***. And even in some "tiger economies" of East Asia, industry managed to grow and become more productive behind high trade barriers, thanks to otherwise good economic management. Nevertheless, the costs of state economic control became clearer over time. State planners were not omniscient: they could not possibly acquire all the information needed to make decisions that reflected both efficiency considerations and people's differing preferences.

Worse, governments revealed themselves to be collections of interests rather than disinterested and benevolent "social planners." Even had they been effective in their role as social planners, government officials would not have been able to create the entrepreneurial dynamism essential for sustained development and change. Behind protective barriers, firms in many countries (India and Mexico, to name just two) became less efficient as they focused on obtaining government favors rather than improving productivity. Finally, fiscal and macro instability rose with the oil price shocks of the 1970s and early 1980s, contributing to the debt crisis and revealing the weaknesses in the statist model.

Phase Two: Primacy of Markets

As a result of the disappointing results of the state-led approach, the 1980s and early 1990s saw a strong reaction that stressed the primacy of markets in development.[27] This reaction was a necessary corrective in many ways: it refocused attention on production efficiency and market signals, and it inspired the move to lower trade barriers as a way to spur productivity. Macro stability and balanced fiscal accounts were seen as fundamental building blocks for development and became early priorities for reform. This period saw substantial improvements in both macroeconomic stability and openness to trade and financial and other flows through much of the developing world. This important change in development thinking was summarized by Lindauer and Pritchett (2002) along the dimensions of table 7.2. These include the role of government, encouragement of savings, trade and integration, foreign capital, and development assistance. Development policy changed in each of these dimensions to reflect new thinking.

Phase Three: Importance of Institutions

By the mid 1990s, it became increasingly widely recognized that this purely "pro-market" school of development thinking failed to address some key points. Once countries began to achieve macro stability and greater openness to trade, it became clear that these elements were *necessary* but *not sufficient* for growth and poverty reduction. In particular, the free-market view tended to neglect the institutional foundations of effective private markets. The impor-

TABLE 7.2 Idea Changes in Development Thinking		
Dimension	**State-led approach**	**Pro-market approach**
Government	Plays a central role; acts as the driving force behind development.	Plays a central role, but acts as the main obstacle to development.
Accumulation	Is central to development process; coordination and scale problems require government involvement.	Is central to development process; private sector investment is the key.
Trade and integration	Has no particular advantage beyond the import of capital goods and the purchase of necessary inputs.	Exports bring dynamic advantages; import competition is necessary for disciplining domestic producers.
Foreign capital	FDI is to be avoided, but government borrowing is acceptable, preferably from foreign sources.	Government borrowing is to be avoided, but FDI is encouraged.
Development assistance	Provide project-based lending of foreign exchange and resources to governments.	Quick disbursing; policy-based lending to establish conditions for FDI and domestic investment.

Source: Lindauer and Pritchett 2002.

tance of institutions was underscored by major shifts: the economic decline in the countries of the former Soviet Union; the continued growth in China, a country that moved forward with market-oriented reforms without excessive disruption of institutional foundations; and, later in the 1990s, the financial crisis in East Asia, to which institutional weaknesses contributed heavily. Furthermore, even as it performed a useful service by spotlighting government failure, the free-market reaction had minimized very real problems of market failure that are prevalent in the developing world. As a result, growth performance fell short of expectations in many parts of the developing world.

Current Thinking: Complementarities Between Markets and Governments

Recent years have seen a greater recognition in the policy debate of the complementarities between markets and governments. Clearly, experience shows that the private market economy must be the engine of growth; but it shows also that a vibrant private sector depends on properly functioning state institutions to build a good investment climate and deliver basic services competently.

This view of complementarities pursued in the remainder of this chapter draws heavily on what we have learned in the past two to three decades in the more successful cases of income growth, such as East Asia and Chile. It also draws on learning from the transition process in the former Soviet Union, where a lack of institutional development combined with excessively optimistic expectations led to disappointing development outcomes and demonstrated clearly the importance of a sound state in providing the environment for growth. The role of institutions has come through more strongly than it did in earlier views of development, and particularly than it did in the policy debate in the 1980s and early 1990s. Countries that have combined institutional improvements with market-oriented policy reforms and greater engagement with the world economy saw their per capita incomes grow in the 1990s at the historically very rapid pace of 5 percent per year.[28]

No Single Model for Development

We have also learned more about the diversity of approaches among countries that have been effective in accelerating growth and reducing poverty.

- Evidence from past successes and failures suggests strongly that neither the more statist approach of the 1950s and 1960s nor the more minimal-government, free-market approach that dominated policy debate in the 1980s and early 1990s will achieve these goals.
- Effective approaches will be led by the private sector, but with effective government to provide the governance framework as well as the physical infrastructure and human capital investments necessary for growth and poverty reduction. In fact, to set state and market against each other is to miss the central question: how can they best complement each other to promote growth and reduce poverty?
- A public-private development partnership is essential, especially in the area of health and education. Institutional development has too often been neglected in the development policy debate, but strong institutions are now recognized to be essential to sustained poverty reduction.

We now apply this broad perspective of complementarities to the important subjects of economic growth and development learning.

Ideas about Economic Growth

Ideas about development are constantly in flux, evolving over time and flowing from one country to another. It is therefore misleading to talk about a universal model of development. Development is about change. It is about the contesting and evolution of ideas. It involves learning about what works and what does not in particular circumstances. It is informed by historical circumstances and is intensely local. It cannot be replicated. There is little to be gained from seeking to define a universal economic model, which would suggest that we can collapse all our learning into a summary formula.[29] The challenge for policy makers is to draw on a wide range of experience and to be informed by both the past and others' experiences to identify those common factors that are associated with progress in development. In part, these factors associated with progress confirm the widely appreciated key dimensions of macroeconomic stability; trade reform; and an emphasis on health, education, and infrastructure. However, it is also a confirmation of the inherently idiosyncratic nature of development processes.

Economic Growth as Force for Reducing Poverty

A distillation of the lessons of experience suggests that the most powerful force for reducing income poverty is economic growth. Countries that have reduced income poverty most effectively are those that have grown the fastest over a sustained period, and poverty has expanded most in countries that have stagnated or fallen back economically. As stated by the United Nations Development Programme (1991), "Although growth is not the end of development, the absence of growth often is" (p. 13). There has been no example of development without sustained and prolonged periods of high per capita growth of output that, in turn, depends upon a stable macroeconomic and institutional environment. Unstable macroeconomic conditions—often resulting from unsustainable fiscal positions—undermine the confidence of individuals and firms in making decisions to invest in their own or their firm's future.

Market Model as Organizing Principle

In the realm of economics, with the end of the Cold War and the decline of communism, there has arisen a growing acceptance of the market model as a fundamental organizing principle for economic activity. The model is far from homogeneous, however, and no two countries interpret the framework in the same way. Even within countries, and especially in large federal countries such as India, variation abounds. China is evolving on a path that in critical respects cannot be characterized as "market based." Although far from universal, greater acceptance of the market model has opened space to explore economic options and new possibilities. This is particularly true in the formerly communist countries, but is also the case in the market economies whose policies to differing extents were shaped in opposition to communism.

The past decade has consequently been characterized by perhaps unprecedented experimentation and learning based on the absorption and adaptation of ideas from elsewhere. To the extent that leaders have been freed from ideological straightjackets and have been able to draw on, without simply replicating or copying, ideas tried by others, and to seize opportunities to find new and better ways of organizing, they have been rewarded.[30] A strong contesting of the balance between market and state has become part of the norm in Europe and in a wide range of democratic developing countries, including Brazil, India, and South Africa. So, too, has been the search for new ways of doing things and the rejection by sizeable minorities of what is seen as the dominant "idea of capitalism." This idea has not yet become common currency in many countries or is reflected in the strength of recent anti-globalization protests in Latin America and parts of Western Europe. For Friedman (2000), as for Max Weber and the economic historian Richard Tawney, this clash between the modern and traditional has a considerable distance to travel. It helps to explain the constant struggling for new ways to self-identify and new ways to confront the fears embodied in the association of globalization with integration and being molded by foreign ideas and products.

Interplay of States and Markets

The most rapidly growing economies, and those where poverty is being reduced most rapidly, have benefited from an increasingly nuanced understanding of the relationship between states and markets. In no two countries has this interplay taken the same form. The adjustment costs of going from communism to capitalism, as well as of other major transitions, have been high. Consequently, for politicians, the challenge is to ensure that the benefits of these policy transitions are felt in the short term. The political economy of policy reform is a central challenge in the implementation of ideas. This, together with the associated institutional dimensions, remains one of the least researched and least understood dimensions of the social sciences. Clearly, however, the form of transition and the particular adjustment paths followed have a powerful impact on the outcomes and the sustainability of reform. A comparison of the Russian Federation and many other parts of the former Soviet Union, where poverty has increased over the past decade, with China, where opening the economy has been associated with unprecedented increases in income, highlights the crucial role of leadership and choices about transition paths.

Development as Learning

If there is a new consensus, it is around the need for a more nuanced and broader approach to development.[31] The intermingling of ideas evidenced over the past decade has meant that even the more orthodox economic leaders are seeking to go beyond the standard ideas, such as what came to be known as the *Washington Consensus*.[32] In certain dimensions, such as capital account liberalization and privatization, there is a widening appreciation of the need for a differentiated approach—one that takes account of vulnerabilities, not least in institutional development.[33] The importance of institutions and governance, as we emphasize below, is also increasingly seen as a vital element in development. So, too, is the need to examine the sequencing of reforms, and a recognition that their simultaneous implementation can be disruptive and even counterproductive. For example, depending on the tax structure, measures toward privatization, trade liberalization, or deregulation can, in the short term, conflict with maintaining fiscal discipline and with objectives of social peace and equity.

Elements of the Political Economy of Reforms

Some interpretations of the Washington Consensus principles pushed too rapidly for a liberalization of markets and did not pay sufficient attention to four issues that are closely related to the political economy of reforms:

- governance and institutions
- the role of empowerment and democratic representation
- the importance of country ownership
- the social costs and pace of transformation.

Other issues related to the political economy of reforms have long been part of the discourse on reform and poverty reduction.

Governance and Institutions

For example, the setbacks of the structural adjustment programs in developing countries of the 1980s, as well as the transition of the 1990s in Eastern Europe and the former Soviet Union, showed that these elements are at the heart of the development challenge. In retrospect, it was naive to think that demand for institutions and state capacity would create its own supply and that markets would "work" by themselves.[34]

The State as a Complement to the Market

The state is not a substitute for the market, but a critical complement. We have learned that markets need government and government needs markets. We have also learned that government action is crucial to the ability of people to participate in economic opportunities. These lessons point to the need for an active state that fosters an environment where contracts are enforced and markets can function, basic infrastructure works, there is provision for adequate health, education, and social protection, and people are able to participate in decisions that affect their lives.

The Role of the Private Sector

Notwithstanding the importance of an active and effective state, the strongest force—indeed the driving force—for sustained economic growth is the private sector. Within the private sector, small and medium-size enterprises play a particularly important role in generating employment opportunities for poor people. The most important small enterprises in poor economies, and often the most neglected, are farms.[35]

Problems for Investment Climate

Bureaucratic harassment, corruption, and organized crime are all profoundly damaging to the investment climate, imposing barriers to entry, adding to operating costs, and creating uncertainty once the firm is established. This applies to both large and small firms, but it is especially important for smaller firms and farms, with their weaker capacity to finance the costs of dealing with regulation and to use "political contacts" and other means to resist harassment. The World Bank's *Doing Business Report* (World Bank 2005) highlights the extent of the burdens that frustrate private initiative and the progress made by policy makers in improving the climate for investment. Clear and predictable rules of the game are necessary, with contract enforcement evenly applied and regulations designed to facilitate, not frustrate, legitimate individual enterprise and the establishment of competitive firms.

The Role of Empowerment

Development activities function much more effectively if poor people are empowered—that is, if they have the ability to shape their own lives. This implies a focus on education and health but also on effective participation that, in turn, depends on information, accountability, and the quality of local organizations. Effective participation and social inclusion enhance growth and the sustainability of economic reforms. "The recent *World Development Report* on equity and development makes a significant contribution by highlighting through its analysis and numerous examples the ways in which equity in opportunity should be a central concern of policy makers (World Bank 2005d). It shows how improving access to education, health, and finance and broader civil participation enhances both the level and quality of growth and development.

Ownership of the Development Agenda

Reform programs forced from outside, with weak societal commitment, are likely to fail. Ownership of the development agenda by a country and society is a vital ingredient for its effective implementation. Understanding the political economy of reforms in the particular country is crucial. However, there are areas where our knowledge of the development process, of what works and what does not, of the right sequencing of policies and of the responses from different groups is still weak. Under the same set of macroeconomic fundamentals, the development process can generate different results, reflecting the specific circumstances and political economy.

Infrastructure

The quality, quantity, and affordability of physical and financial infrastructure, such as clean water, power, transport, telecommunications, and finance, strongly influence the ability of individuals to escape poverty and participate in economic activity. Infrastructure enables individuals, firms, and countries to extend their opportunities. Entrepreneurship in developing and transition countries is often smothered by failures in basic communications, inadequate and unreliable supplies of water and electricity, and inadequate telecommunications and transport. These failures undermine trade opportunities at the local levels, as well as at the regional and global levels. Infrastructure should be a priority area for policy makers. As infrastructure investments often require large, lumpy, long-term claims on budget resources, have intergenerational consequence, and have significant social and environmental impacts, they are among the most complex decisions for governments, which may particularly lend themselves to analyses and multidisciplinary support from multilateral and regional development finance institutions.

Education and Health

An educated and healthy workforce contributes to development and growth, with widespread basic education (primary and secondary) being especially important.[36] Not all empirical analyses find such an effect. One reason that the effects of education have been hard to pin down empirically is that the quality of education matters as much as the quantity, and yet we are much better at measuring quantity than quality. Another reason is that, like physical capital, human capital in inhospitable environments may be relatively unproductive from a societal standpoint. In an environment of weak institutions, corruption, or crime, the return to illegal activities may provide the logical option, in terms of returns on education and getting employment. Although the case is not fully established empirically, strong basic education and reasonable levels of health have been a precursor to many development successes, and recent analyses suggest strongly that additional education does indeed spur development. The evidence on the substantial benefits derived from education at the microeconomic level is less ambiguous: education lifts people out of poverty, raising their earnings by some 5 to 10 percent per year of schooling.[37]

Education and health are key factors, but just as important is fostering mechanisms for participating in the decisions that affect individuals' lives and those of their families. Human rights that protect security and health, for example, and contractual rights that protect livelihoods and assets are essential. All these elements allow poor people to shape their own lives, invest in their future, build assets, and be included in the society in which they live.

Good Governance

Stable and effective government institutions, respect for property rights, equal treatment under the law, the absence of bureaucratic harassment, a lack of corruption, and protection from organized crime all matter for growth. Investment and productivity depend on predictability, which in turn hinges on confidence that government will not act opportunistically or capriciously. The "soft infrastructure" of an effective legal and judicial system is critical for achieving economic growth, empowering poor people, and security. Good governance and controlling corruption also reduces the costs faced by producers. Sound supervision and regulation of financial institutions decreases the costs of capital to businesses and contributes greatly to macroeconomic stability. Indeed, it has been argued by Rodrik (2003) that institutional quality and governance are the underlying variables that drive all of the other growth-enhancing factors.

Gender Equality

Recent research provides evidence that gender equality—not only in health and education, but also in voice and rights—is an important element in development (World Bank 2001; World Bank 2005d). Aside from the obvious direct benefits for women, equality in these dimensions also has instrumental benefits in terms of growth and poverty reduction. Cross-country research suggests that low investment in female education has been a barrier to growth in the Middle East and North Africa, South Asia, and Sub-Saharan Africa. East Asia closed the gender gap more rapidly. Even after controlling for income and other factors, greater participation by women in public life is associated with cleaner business and government and better governance, which in turn promotes growth. Inequalities along other dimensions—such as race, ethnicity, or religion—can also retard development.

Geography

Geography seriously impedes growth for some countries, making development much more difficult. As Gallup, Sachs, and Mellinger (1999) have argued, if a country is landlocked, mountainous, and surrounded by poor neighbors, or if its population centers are in remote areas, it may encounter additional difficulties in developing domestic markets of efficient size, engaging in international trade, or acquiring technology from abroad. In such cases, it will be especially important to build effective infrastructure links and to improve transportation and communications both domestically and internationally. Regional integration and customs unions that facilitate trade may also be important in overcoming geographic barriers. Ecological fragility is another geography-linked barrier to development: ecological stresses may most directly affect poor people, and these stresses, too, require specific policy and institutional responses.

The Challenge of Reform for Growth

Putting these factors together to spur sustained growth is a challenge: it requires proper sequencing and selection of reforms, as well as consistency over time, neither of which is easy to achieve.

Where to Focus Efforts

Although our understanding of the importance of all these factors has grown during recent years, to put them together in a way that yields sustained growth remains a daunting task. One major challenge for governments is to decide where to focus their efforts as they strive to make the conditions for growth as favorable as possible. Strategies have to be determined in each country context, but it is clear that administrative capacities of low-income governments are typically so limited that an assessment of where they should be focused is essential: these governments simply cannot push ahead effectively on all fronts at once. At the same time, sequencing is necessary. It is by now widely recognized that the East Asian financial crisis of 1997–8, which exacted a substantial toll in poverty and lost output, stemmed in no small measure from financial and capital-market liberalization that proceeded before the appropriate regulatory safeguards were in place.[38] Although some sequencing problems are easy to identify, finding the best sequence of steps in the context of a particular country is a great challenge, and it remains an area where our knowledge needs to expand.

Sustained Growth, Not Spurts

The challenge is sustaining robust growth. Rapid growth episodes of a few years or a decade are not uncommon. For example, countries that successfully emerge from civil war often experience relatively rapid economic rebounds for several years.[39] What has been much less common is sustained rapid growth over a period of decades, which is what is necessary to eliminate absolute poverty.[40] The need for consistency underlines the importance of attaining sustained productivity growth. Only a portion of growth is driven by increases in physical and human-capital intensity of production, which can be difficult to sustain over long periods. Countries also need rapid growth in productivity.

Adaptation and Customization

We need to be modest about how much we understand about economic growth and eschew formulaic solutions in favor of supporting the adaptation and customization of global lessons for national and local conditions and objectives. Successful economies have demonstrated the importance of learning by doing and of an active partnership between governments and the private sector to create an investment climate that supports job creation and growth. Understanding economic growth has proved to be intractable and has preoccupied generations of economists, with the renowned economist Elhanan Helpman going so far as to refer to the "mystery of economic growth."

Elements of Successful Empowerment

We also still have a lot to learn about empowerment. However, successful efforts to empower poor people and increase their freedom of choice typically share four elements:

- access to information
- participation
- accountability
- local organizational capacity.

These four elements are closely related. Access to information is crucial for effective action, but without institutional mechanisms and accountability, citizens may not have the means to take such action. Examples of empowerment at work include community involvement in running schools, water users associations, and local health groups. According to the World Bank (2004d; 2005e), mechanisms such as these can play a powerful role in tailoring services to the needs of poor people.

Evolution of Development Thinking

Development thinking evolves continually, and this evolution has accelerated over the past 50 years. In response to the lessons of experience and analysis, development practitioners have adapted their approaches to promoting development, and even the goals of development work. We have learned that strategies that seemed obvious to many at some point—for example, both the heavily statist and minimal-government free-market approaches—have had to be reconsidered and changed as part of a continuous learning process. This is one reason why a careful and measured look at experience is so important and why the extent of openness to the flow of ideas is vital for growth.

Global Public Goods

Global action is a vital complement to national and local level policies. One important area of action is in the provision of global public goods. Public goods have benefits that are *nonexcludable* and consumption that is *nonrival.* These types of goods (for example, traffic safety) may be underprovided by market systems. Global public goods have benefits that extend across all countries.[41]

Demand and Supply of Global Public Goods

Demand for global public goods has grown rapidly with globalization, but supply is constrained by the difficulty of putting in place coordinating mechanisms to pay for the benefits or recoup costs. At the International Conference on Financing for Development held in Monterrey, Mexico, in 2002, global leaders established firm poverty reduction targets and highlighted the need for a clear strategy to strengthen the provision of global public goods.

Action that Can Yield Large Global Benefits

In five areas of particular interest, concerted international action can yield very large benefits across borders and contribute to individual country poverty reduction.

Fighting Infectious and Communicable Diseases

As indicated above, infectious diseases in developing countries kill millions of people, exacerbating poverty and severely disrupting economic life. The benefits to individuals of advances in this area are vast and go beyond any attempt at measurement. These benefits, in terms of enhancing the quality of life, reducing lost workdays, and raising productivity are widely shared, even in countries or communities where other interventions or investments are ineffective. Infectious diseases are carried more and more frequently across borders through trade and travel, so fighting them is increasingly becoming a direct need for all countries.

Improving the Global Environment

Our water, our land, our forests, and our biodiversity are vital assets, with potentially catastrophic losses if international protective action is inadequate. Tropical countries in particular are vulnerable to projected climate change and environmental degradation, including loss in food production resulting from global warming, and an expanding range of tropical diseases. Global action must be complemented by environmental policies on national and local levels. Rich countries have a special contribution to make here because they dominate energy use and because they are the largest consumers for most natural resources and they generate the most pollutants. The demographic and growing economic weight of developing countries—together with their share of environmental resources and challenges—means that their participation in global compacts on the environment is essential (see Goldin and Winters 1995).

Promoting Orderly Cross-Border Movement of Goods and Services

The fall in international transportation and communication costs has led to a rapid growth in cross-border trade in goods and services. International markets provide tremendous opportunity to developing countries to expand trade flows, provided they have market access. The WTO is dedicated to removing barriers to trade but it faces an uphill battle against protectionist interests in both developed and developing countries.

Encouraging Global Financial Stability

As discussed in chapter 4, the integration of global capital markets greatly increased the volume of international private capital flows. This has helped support a rapid expansion of economic activity in developing countries, but it has also brought heightened vulnerability to financial shocks and market contagion, the social burden of which often falls most sharply on the urban poor. A new framework for harmonizing supervisory practices, relying more on internal risk management, is being developed by the international institutions, including the International Monetary Fund, the World Bank, and others.

Creating and Disseminating Knowledge on Development Issues

Multilateral development agencies must play a lead role in research on development and in disseminating the lessons of development experience. Initiatives such as the Development Gateway, which provides local to global connectivity, have the ability to empower local communities, build knowledge networks, and serve citizenry more effectively through enhanced and low-cost information.[42] Such gains through disseminating knowledge are most effective when knowledge is a public good accessible to all.

The Challenge of Cooperation

The challenge to all of the above pressing priorities is one of cooperation.[43] As noted by Kaul, Grunberg, and Stern (1999), "billions of people do not negotiate directly with each other. In many instances their governments do it on their behalf, reducing the number of negotiating partners to about 185—still an unwieldy group for creating cooperative arrangements" (p. 15). Unwieldy though this process may be, fulfilling the important promise of the global public goods idea requires the international community to forge ahead with these efforts.

Summary

To ignore the development and flow of ideas as a component of economic globalization is to miss a central feature of the globalization process, a feature that has important implications for poverty alleviation. Poverty responds to effective development, and effective development is, in large measure, the deployment of appropriate ideas in appropriate ways. As we have repeatedly emphasized here, there is no single model of how this can be done. Rather, effective development from the point of view of ideas is largely about tailoring existing, global knowledge to evolving local circumstances in ways that directly and indirectly benefit poor people.

Connection of Flows of Ideas and Other Elements of Globalization

Important connections exist among the global flows of ideas and the other globalization elements considered in this book: trade, capital flows especially in the form of foreign investment, aid, and migration. Trade, as we have shown in Chapter 3, embodies ideas reflected in technologies and processes. The benefits of foreign investment involve both basic and deep learning. These, in turn, require threshold levels of skills and education. In the case of migration, international movements of labor and experts facilitate the less formal processes of knowledge transfer. The effective deployment of ideas is therefore facilitated by the global movements of goods, services, capital, and people.

Importance of Knowledge Management

One important theme to emerge from this chapter is the theme of knowledge management. There is a fundamental tension here that remains largely unresolved from a policy perspective. As we emphasized, knowledge is a global public good that has great potential to help the poor. However, there has been a growing tendency, supported by WTO agreements, to advance the privatization of knowledge. In some respects, this can help the poor. In other respects, this is cause for alarm. In the realms of environmental and labor standards, international economists have resisted a "one-size-fits-all" approach to forming policy.[44] Ensuring that this is also the case with intellectual property, so that it supports development, requires attention.

Ideas about Growth and Development

With regard to ideas concerning growth and development, the pendulum has swung back and forth between the poles of government-led and market-led policy regimes. This has clarified the features of government and markets in the processes of growth, development, and poverty alleviation. An emerging consensus in the realm of development ideas, reflected in a coevolution between market and state, offers effective institutional frameworks and accounts for local conditions.

Central Role of Learning

This chapter has sought to highlight the central role of learning and ideas in development. Policy makers and practitioners require opportunities to understand what works and what does not, based on evidence and on analysis that draws on the widest possible data, experience and skills. By reducing the constraints posed by information, education, language, and access, policy makers at the global, national, and local levels can make a significant contribution to improving the chances that globalization will offer more opportunities for growth and poverty reduction.

Notes

1. Some of the elements considered in this chapter have been previously identified by Meier (2001).
2. These processes have been effectively described by Diamond (1997), who emphasizes the role of continental East-West axes in facilitating the early diffusion of agricultural technologies.
3. In international economics, the importance of local knowledge was first emphasized by Pack and Westphal (1986). The concept of local knowledge is well developed throughout the social sciences as well. See, for example, de Walt (1994).
4. The authors are grateful to F. Halsey Rogers, who contributed this scenario in the course of our discussions on the role of ideas.
5. Rodrik (2000) emphasizes that "large-scale institutional development by and large requires a process of discovery about local needs and capabilities" (p. 14).
6. Interestingly, the commitment of Bill Gates to provide unprecedented private support to combat HIV/AIDS and other preventable diseases also reflects the power of ideas. Gates, at the United Nations on May 9, 2003, stated "My personal commitment to improving global health started when I learned about health inequities . . . in the 1993 (World Bank) World Development Report . . . my wife Melinda and I were stunned to learn that 11 million children die each year from preventable diseases. That is when we decided to make improving health the focus of our philanthropy."
7. Recall from chapter 3 that estimates of the number of people kept in poverty by rich country protectionism is at least 100 million.
8. Efforts to argue for agricultural protection in terms of the "multifunctionality" of agricultural production in the rich (but apparently not the poor) world (for example, Jules 2003) is no less an exercise of right and might than previous ideologies have exercised.
9. See, for example, chapter 10 of Sen (1999).
10. See, for example, Rischard (2002) and Nowotny (2004).
11. For an example of such evolutionary reform, see the United Nations' recent proposals to reform to keep pace with evolving peacekeeping and security demands (United Nations 2005).
12. See Mallaby (2004) pp. 7–8.
13. A key original contribution in this area was Sen (1989).
14. In the terminology of microeconomics, the benefits of knowledge are "nonexcludable," and its consumption is "nonrival." As pointed out by Stiglitz (1999), knowledge is actually a *global* public good. We consider global public goods later in this chapter.
15. See, for example, Stiglitz (1987).
16. See Hoekman, Maskus, and Saggi (2004) as well as chapter 4.
17. The economics of intellectual property protection is a rich area of research. See, for example, the debate on optimal patent length and breadth in Gilbert and Shapiro (1990).

18. See Boldrin and Levine (2002, 2004a, 2004b) and also Shapiro (2004), who argues that excessive issuing of patents in the United States restricts competition and harms innovation.
19. The authors are grateful to Jean-Jacques Dethier for highlighting a number of the points in this paragraph.
20. See Goldin, Stern, and Dethier (2003).
21. See Cockburn and Lanjouw (2001) for examples of the hotly contested debate or evidence.
22. *New Scientist* 2005.
23. See www.vaccinealliance.org for an explanation of what GAVI does.
24. *New Scientist* 2005.
25. On concerns over cultural homogenization, see Barber (1996). For a flavor of the ideas of the antiglobalization networks, see the Web site antiglobalization.com. Klein (2000) has become core reading for those opposing globalization, and Wolf (2004) marshals many of the economic arguments for the proponents of globalization. Chua (2003) raises concerns about globalization in the context of what she terms "market-dominant minorities." See also, for example, Mander and Goldsmith (1996) and Helleiner and Pickel (2005) on more "market-dominant minorities."
26. The import substitution idea is skillfully reviewed by Bruton (1998).
27. Wolf (2004) is a modern advocate of this point of view.
28. We consider institutional issues further in the following section.
29. This point has been made by Adelman (2001). See also Stern (2002) and Ranis (2004).
30. We are thus in disagreement with Friedman's (2000) notion of a "golden straightjacket" limiting policy options. Policy spaces do exist and far from being constrained, these are expanding and are an important part of the explanation for the acceleration in economic growth and poverty reduction in recent decades.
31. This section and those that follow draw extensively on Goldin, Stern, and Dethier (2003). See also Stern, Dethier, and Rogers (2004).
32. See Williamson (1990, 1994), often cited as the author of the Washington Consensus.
33. See, for example, Stiglitz (2000).
34. A theoretical explanation of why these outcomes are not likely was given by North (1990).
35. The emphasis on family farms and on bureaucratic harassment here is attributable to Nick Stern, who focused on these neglected areas in Stern (2002).
36. See Hanushek and Kim (1995) and Krueger and Lindahl (1999) on the role of education and Gupta and Mitra (2004) on the role of health.
37. See chapter 7 of World Bank (2003b).
38. See our discussion in Chapter 4.
39. See Collier and Gunning (1995).
40. See Pritchett (2000) and Easterly (2001) for a discussion of why this is difficult to achieve.
41. See Kaul, Grunberg, and Stern (1999) and Kaul and others (2003). The latter authors advocate a very general definition of global public goods: "Global public goods are goods with benefits that extend to all countries, people, and generations" (p. 23).
42. See www.developmentgateway.org.
43. The problem of cooperation is discussed by Martin (1999).
44. See, for example, chapter 13 of Hoekman and Kostecki (2001).

8

Toward a Policy Agenda

Globalization is currently held out by competing groups as both the only means by which global poverty can be reduced and as the cause of poverty. Neither of these contrasting claims is helpful. First, they fail to adequately distinguish among the many aspects of globalization. Second, they fail to recognize that most dimensions of globalization have both positive and negative potential for eliminating poverty. Third, they fail to adequately address the role of policy in influencing outcomes.

In this book, we have focused primarily on the economic aspects of globalization. We bring together, perhaps for the first time, the key flows that underpin globalization. In examining the links between poverty reduction and flows in trade, finance, aid, migration, and ideas, we have sought to clarify whether and how economic globalization can work for poor people.

Globalization for Poor People?

To the question "Can globalization work for poor people?" our answer is "Yes." We have shown that it can, but also that it is far from automatic. Whether globalization can work for poor people depends crucially on the policies that accompany it. In our view, it is these policies that are of utmost importance. Ultimately, the policies determine whether globalization helps or hurts poor people. This last chapter seeks to develop a policy agenda that aims to enhance the positive impact of globalization on poor people.

Policy Recommendations

No measure considered and recommended here is a panacea. First, our book does not cover such vital dimensions of globalization as peace and security, human rights, culture and the environment. Second, without forceful policy interventions in the areas of education, health, and empowerment, many millions of people will continue to perish each year because of poverty in all its dimensions. However, the struggle to overcome poverty requires advances on many fronts, and the policies recommended here can contribute to these gains and an accumulation of "small wins."[1]

We do not claim that our policy suggestions are original. They draw on the sources referenced and are "in the air" at conferences or in conversations among development practitioners and international economists. Our value added is in prioritizing and bringing together a broad range of policy suggestions in one place and linking them to the dimensions of globalization and poverty reduction considered in this book.

Levels of Policy Enactment

Policies can be enacted at four levels: global, regional, national, and local or community. Policies should not be considered as simply part of a global or national agenda that ordinary people in both developing and developed countries in their everyday lives cannot affect. The broad range of policies in favor of a pro-poor globalization is presented in table 8.1, which illustrates the multiple levels at which policies are made. For example, if developed countries commit to reducing their subsidies for agricultural goods as part of multilateral trade negotiations under the WTO, they engage in a global policy change. If members of a regional trade agreement issue temporary visas to guest workers among member countries, they effect a regional policy change. If a country engages in an effort to ensure universal primary education, it exercises national policy making. Finally, if a firm or individuals in a local community seek to reduce their pollution, or to increase the incentives for children to attend school, they are making local policies that over time will contribute to investment and growth. All of these policy levels are potentially important in influencing globalization processes in ways that might be beneficial for poor people. The room for action, therefore, is larger than is often appreciated.

Interaction of Levels in Policy Making

Policy making at the global, regional, national, and local or community levels interacts in significant ways. For example, developing an effective banking regulatory system at the national level could support increased liberalization of trade in financial services at the multilateral or global level. National educational advancements can support learning from foreign direct investment, which in turn can be supported by regional investment agreements. And when certain rich countries refuse to make concessions on global trade talks, saying that farmers at the local level will protest, they are undermining the opportunities for poor people in local communities of poor countries. Because the

KEY TERMS AND CONCEPTS

brain waste	multifunctionality
capital accounts	plurilateral (WTO terminology)
Doha Development Round	Tobin Tax
Equator Principles of good governance	virtuous circles
Mode 4 (WTO terminology)	

various levels of policy making interact, it is often important to pay attention to the timing and sequence of policy changes. In some cases, such as universal primary education and the fight against infectious diseases, however, "timing" comes down to making dramatic changes as quickly as possible.

Globalization and Policy Formation

Many people believe that globalization has significantly eroded the abilities of countries and citizens to form national and local policies. We believe this is an unhelpful characterization of globalization. Although it is true that globalization does place some new and significant restrictions on policy, it also creates new opportunities and spaces for policy engagement. Globalization changes the ways policies at various levels can be deployed. In many respects, it widens rather than narrows the range of policy options. The claim made by Friedman (2000) that globalization puts countries' policy-making abilities inside "golden straightjackets" misses these points. Globalization does pose constraints, but it also presents opportunities. Policy still matters for poverty alleviation, and it matters a great deal. For example, governments can still tax and then spend revenues; the effectiveness with which they do so matters a great deal to the poor people of the world.[2] Indeed, some international economists view effective government expenditures as a *prerequisite* for global integration.[3]

The diversity of experience for both countries and individuals in dealing with the same broad external globalization constraints and opportunities points to the need to focus on the specific questions of how globalization can be made to work for poor people. The fact that the experiences of both countries and individual poor people in dealing with the same broad external globalization constraints and opportunities are sometimes good but sometimes very bad shows that we need to focus on how to make globalization work better, especially for poor people and cultures that are currently marginalized.

We believe that policies about the flows outlined in this book determine the ways in which globalization processes affect poor people. In the remainder of

TABLE 8.1 Examples of Policies Affecting Globalization Processes and Outcomes

Globalization dimension	Policy Levels			
	Global	Regional	National	Local or community
Trade	Multilateral trade agreements	Regional trade agreements	Trade-related capacity building	Business best practice centers
Finance	A plurilateral investment agreement[a]	Regional investment agreements	Sequenced liberalization of various components of the capital account and focus on building investment climate	Development of effective banking systems and other forms of financial intermediation, addressing priority issues from investment climate surveys
Aid	Increased multilateral and bilateral aid and higher quality aid	Regional capacity building programs	Ensuring policies benefit poor people, donors are coordinated, and corruption eliminated	Improved needs assessment, impact evaluation, and service delivery
Migration	A multilateral agreement on migration A GATS "Mode-4" visa program[b]	Mobility of labor provisions in common markets	Changes in national visa and citizenship requirements, fair treatment of foreigners	Refugee support Improve remittance security and savings options
Ideas	Increased technology transfer to developing countries	Increasing the research capacity of regional development institutions	Increased government funding of basic research, openness to ideas	Inventories of traditional knowledge
Other examples of activities at different levels	Multilateral efforts to fight the spread of infectious diseases	Regional infrastructure investment coordination	Universal primary and secondary education	Municipal water supply and sewerage upgrades

Source: Authors.
a. Plurilateral in the terminology of the WTO implies that members are free not to take on the negotiated commitments. In the case of investment, see Graham (1996).
b. Mode-4 in the terminology of the WTO refers to the provision of services through the temporary movement of natural persons.

this chapter, we will be primarily focused at the global level. However, we want to emphasize that, because poor people live in countries, regions, and localities, policies at all these levels can have a significant impact. The role of national policies are particularly vital. How governments tax and spend; what they do about corruption; and how they encourage private investment and provide opportunities for individuals to get educated, be healthy, lead safe lives, and participate in the choices affecting their lives make an enormous difference to poor people.

We will proceed by taking up each of our economic globalization dimensions and identifying policy changes associated with them. These policy recommendations are summarized at the end of the chapter in the form of a global policy checklist in table 8.2.

Trade: Proposed Policy Changes

The first dimension of globalization considered in this book is international trade—the exchange of goods and services among the countries of the world economy. The policy changes we propose for international trade fall into the following areas:

- market access
- trade-related capacity building
- arms trade
- forced labor.

We consider each in turn.[4]

Market Access

An urgent policy change that would make the international trade dimension of economic globalization friendlier to poor people is the *substantial* increase in market access for goods and services from the developing countries. This is particularly, but not exclusively, important for labor-intensive manufactured goods, including processed food products and agricultural products.

Agricultural Subsidies

In particular, there needs to be a *significant* reduction in the agricultural subsidies of the developed countries. As we noted in chapter 3, these subsidies have been in the US$300–$370 billion range, exceeding the entire GDP of Sub-Saharan Africa. In recent decades, they have hovered at over five times the value of all foreign aid.

Agricultural subsidies are often justified in terms of various external benefits to agricultural production.[5] Such arguments are unhelpful for at least two reasons. First, nearly all economic activity has external benefits of one kind or another. Second, to the degree that agriculture does have these external benefits, they are present in all countries, not just the rich countries. Subsidies to support agriculture in the rich world undermine the most important external benefit of agriculture in developing countries: poverty alleviation.

Recommendations

What do we mean by "substantial" and "significant?" Any improvement in market access and reduction in agricultural subsidies is a step in the right direction. Given the scale of existing distortions and their devastating impact on poor people, however, bold actions are needed. We make three recommendations:

- First, there should be immediate and full market access for the low-income countries.
- Second, there should be the elimination of all tariff peaks and tariff escalation for the developing countries as a whole within five years.[6]
- Third, the total agricultural protection of the high-income countries should be reduced to the level of their total foreign aid contributions within five years (currently this is around US$65 billion, or 20 percent of the costs of agricultural protection).

All of these changes would go a long way in allowing the trade dimension of globalization to better help poor people. In rich countries, agricultural protection costs the average consumer around US$1,000 per year through increased prices and taxes. As lower-income people spend a higher share of their income on food, these policies are highly regressive. In poor countries, it is because the policies penalize rural producers and communities, who tend to be the lowest income groups, that the current policies are also highly regressive, negatively affecting poor people the most.

Increased Market Access: Consequences

In chapter 3, we discussed the problem of the long-term decline in primary product prices and the problems associated with their volatility. Increases in market access will reduce the negative impact of these problems:

- First, reductions of agricultural subsidies will raise world prices for these goods. This is because production will decline in those countries where it is now highly subsidized. In these areas (Europe, Japan, and the United States) prices for products such as sugar, cotton, dairy, and meat are many times world prices—as prices are lowered to world levels, demand will increase and the use of substitutes (such as synthetic sweeteners and synthetic textiles) will decrease.

- Second, removing tariff escalation (by which more processed products face higher tariff levels) will make it easier for developing counties to escape their dependence on exporting raw materials and to vertically diversify their exports toward processed commodities that have more value.

- Third, reducing protection levels for nontraditional agricultural goods (such as flowers and fruit) and for manufactured goods will reduce the pressure on developing countries to concentrate production in primary commodities, such as coffee and cotton, where they have market access. By making it easier for developing countries to diversify horizontally into a wider variety of goods, and also to diversify along the value chain into processed goods (coffee powder rather than beans, or chocolate rather than cacao and sugar), the risks associated with fluctuations in the primary production of prices and markets will be reduced.

- Finally, increases in market access according to legally binding multilateral rules will reduce the uncertainty that all developing countries face about potential future protection and indiscriminate actions that can close access to markets. This uncertainty undermines investor confidence and raises the barriers to many potential investments, both in primary commodities and in nontraditional exports in developing countries.

For all of these reasons, increased market access will help to mitigate the problem that many developing countries face in being dependent on primary products.

Trade-Related Capacity Building

Substantial increases in market access must be combined with efforts to promote export *capacity* in low- and middle-income countries. Capacity constraints are multidimensional and include infrastructure, market information, skills, and credit.

Capacity Building: Consequences

Capacity building in all these areas can also help developing countries to implement WTO commitments, to be properly represented at the WTO, to overcome trade barriers in the form of standards, to effectively negotiate regional commitments, and to overcome supply-side constraints. They are also vital to compensate for the losses that may be incurred in certain developing countries (such as Malawi and Mauritius) through loss of preferential access to the markets, such as those of the European Union, which currently offer preferential access.

Capacity Building Efforts Underway

The two major efforts in this regard already underway should be supported. The first is the Integrated Framework, discussed in some detail in chapter 3. The second is a cooperative effort between the OECD and the WTO focused on developing the Doha Development Agenda Trade Capacity Building Database. These worthwhile activities provide much needed support for the development agenda of the **Doha Development Round**. To take advantage of increased opportunities, substantial improvements in market access have to be linked to significant investments in capacity building. The sequencing of the two is vital. Market access without capacity to benefit undermines the growth and poverty potential of trade reform. And, conversely, if countries have the capacity to compete but are prevented from doing so by unfair trading rules, they, too, cannot realize their potential.

Capacity Building: Infrastructure and Software

Countries should be supported in building the "behind the border" hardware, such as infrastructure (including ports, roads, airports, equipment, and transport), and software, such as customs and marketing and market intelligence capacity. Translating these improvements in trade capacity into widespread employment and growth opportunities requires addressing broader countrywide constraints. In particular, improvements in the investment climate, including in the legal and judicial system, in the regulatory environment, and in the overall levels of education and health of the population may be necessary. Firms also require reliable electricity, water supply, and other infrastructure. This is particularly the case for small firms and family enterprises, which cannot afford their own generators or other basic infrastructure to take advantage of new opportunities. Trade opportunities are a necessary but not sufficient condition for countries to take advantage of economic integration.

Capacity Building: Negotiation

Although often overlooked, the capacity to engage and negotiate in bilateral, regional, and multilateral trade is a key requirement for a more equitable globalization. The negotiating playing field is highly uneven. Further effort should be made to improve the capacity of developing countries, particularly the smaller and poorer countries, to enter into negotiations on an informed and equitable basis. Too often, whether in bilateral trade agreements or in Geneva at the WTO, teams of highly qualified and seasoned trade civil servants and expert consultants from one of the richest countries confront a handful of junior, relatively unqualified civil servants from one of the poorer countries.

In the WTO, the increasing complexity and breadth of the negotiations—many of which take place simultaneously, especially during the crucial final days of negotiations—make it all but impossible for the majority of developing countries to even attend all the sessions, let alone negotiate on a fully informed and capable basis. To help developing countries engage more effectively in trade negotiations, efforts need to be made both to prevent the overload of the negotiations across an ever-widening span of issues and to support developing country trade-policy staff in data gathering, understanding complex texts, analyzing the implications of different options, and negotiating with other WTO members.

Arms Trade

The notion of gains from trade and the benefits trade expansion can bring to poverty reduction do not apply to trade in arms or illicit trade.[7] Of the approximately US$25 billion in global arms sales in 2002, about US$17 billion was in sales to developing countries.[8] It is estimated that these trade flows contribute to the deaths of more than 300,000 persons each year and fuel civil conflicts that set back development processes for up to decades at a time.[9] This is particularly true for human development, because expenditures on arms rival expenditures on health or education in many developing countries.[10] One proposal, recently endorsed by the Foreign Secretary of the United Kingdom, and the Commission for Africa (2005), is an international Arms Trade Treaty that would tightly control weapons exports to countries with significant records of human rights abuses, to criminal organizations, and to conflict zones. Efforts of this nature, which provide a multilateral, legal framework to international arms trade, are not a panacea, but could have substantial positive effects by reducing mortality rates from armed conflict in the developing world. For this reason, control of the global arms trade is a politically sensitive but important area for global cooperation.

Forced Labor

The benefits of any market transaction, including international trade, presume that the participants in the transaction are engaged as a result of choice, not coercion.[11] If coercion is present, the market transaction is unlikely to be beneficial. This is most certainly the case with forced labor. Workers in many poor countries are pressured by circumstances to find jobs that may pay very poorly, but choose to remain employed in this type of employment because it is superior to the poverty they fled, often in rural areas. Forced labor, however, is entirely different because freedom of choice has been infringed upon through a violation of human rights. The WTO has a general exception for the case of prison labor (Article XXe). This general exception, however, could be extended to all forms of forced labor to expand the global commitment to human rights as part of the globalization process. Trade should not be permitted with employers who produce goods made by individuals who are coerced into employment.

The issue of child labor has become important in discussions of globalization and development. On this issue, we want to note that, as emphasized by Sen (1999), "The worst violations of the norm against child labor come typically from the virtual slavery of children in disadvantaged families and from their being forced into exploitative employment" (p. 30). Our suggestions on forced labor address these worst violations. We do not, however, call for an outright ban on all forms child labor as part of the multilateral trade system because this has real risks of making the situation worse for the children involved. For example, it is entirely plausible that children removed from more conventional forms of child labor will end up poorer and that, as they and their families become increasingly desperate, they could end up working in sectors that are not part of international trade, such as prostitution. Non–forced child labor is much better dealt with by providing food programs and health services within school systems, subsidies for school attendance, and other means to increase the incentives and means to attend school,[12] as well as by addressing the underlying economic and other factors that lead to child labor.

Finance: Proposed Policy Changes

The second dimension of globalization considered in this book is finance in the form of capital flows. This includes foreign direct investment (FDI), equity portfolio investment, bond finance, and commercial bank lending.

In chapter 4, we compared these flows and demonstrated the extent to which private flows to developing countries have grown relative to other flows, currently accounting for the lion's share of capital flows to middle-income developing countries. Although a handful of the resource-rich low-income countries have had substantial private inflows, the majority of low-income countries are more dependent on remittance flows and aid flows than private investment. Attracting equity flows—investments in firms and productive capacity that creates jobs—and reducing the share of their budgets that go to debt repayment can greatly assist countries to benefit from globalization. The policy changes we propose for capital flows fall into the following two areas: a heterodox approach to capital account reform and requirements for multinational enterprises.

A Heterodox Approach to Capital Account Reform

Global capital flows take place on countries' *capital accounts*, which record their transactions with the rest of the world involving productive and financial assets of various kinds. The policy of international financial institutions on capital accounts has evolved in recent years. In late 1997, the International Monetary Fund (IMF) considered making capital account liberalization an explicit policy goal to be part of its articles of agreement. However, there is a distinct lack of consensus on this matter among prominent international economists and among governments.[13] Two of the economies that have been most effective in avoiding crises in their capital accounts and that have seen the most stable and high levels of growth over the past decades have been China and India, and both maintain controls on their capital accounts. With both practical experience and theory indicating that the case for capital account liberalization is not proven for developing countries, the global policy community needs to maintain a tolerant and heterodox posture toward the issue.

Why does this matter to poor people? As we discussed in chapter 4, and as has been seen in cases such as the Asian and Argentina crises, mistakes made in this area can have devastating consequences for poverty levels, education, and health. The identification, adoption, and diffusion of best practice here can play an important role in preventing future crises of this kind and can help reduce levels of flight capital. However, in the absence of best practice, it does not make sense to force countries into a one-size-fits-all mold. For capital account and accompanying financial sector liberalization, it makes sense to err on the side of caution to prevent costly crises. This would allow countries to adopt a carefully sequenced and prepared set of steps toward fully integrating their capital markets and capital accounts with the world markets.

Corporate Social Responsibility, Standards, and Transparency for MNEs

The polarization of policy discussions about globalization and poverty appears with some intensity in the case of foreign investment and the role of multinational enterprises (MNEs). This is perhaps most apparent in the ongoing debate over sweatshops and minimum standards. As for the other dimensions of globalization, the actual relationship between FDI and poverty is more subtle and complex.[14] FDI typically provides jobs and offers new products and opportunities. However, the extent to which poor people benefit varies greatly by country, sector, and firm. It also changes over time.

Extractive Industries

For example, whereas in South Africa the mining industries at the outset colluded with the government to force vibrant rural communities off their land and introduce the world's most systematic migrant labor system, the descendants of these same companies today in some areas are among the standard setters for foreign investors in developing countries. The South African case highlights the particular problems associated with mining and other extractive industries.

In line with a recent major review of extractive industries, we recommend adopting widespread safeguards and revenue review and transparency mechanisms to ensure that decent employment conditions are guaranteed and that the taxes and other public revenues derived from the investments are properly managed. The World Bank recently has made such undertakings and its private sector arm, the International Finance Corporation, has, in a similar vein, encouraged the adoption of the *Equator Principles of good governance.* The Extractive Industries Transparency Initiative (supported by the British government) and the civil society initiative Publish What You Pay are indicative of the new attention focused on providing transparent means of accounting for revenues, with a view to enhancing the poverty reduction impact of the underlying investments.[15] These initiatives and a growing range of corporate responsibility charters are examples of new standards of behavior for investors. In our view, these should be adopted more widely, with the support of source and destination governments and international agencies.

Guidelines for Behavior of MNEs

There have been many proposed guidelines about the behavior of MNEs.[16] Currently, these include (but are not limited to) the United Nations Human Rights Commission's Norms on the Responsibilities of Transnational Corporations and Other Business Enterprises, the United Nations' Global Compact, and the Organisation for Economic Co-operation and Development's Guidelines for Multinational Enterprises.[17]

These existing schemes have two limitations. First, none of them is binding. Second, they are not all *de minimis.* Debate continues as to whether it is advisable and practical to establish a small set of binding requirements that limits the range of acceptable MNE behavior in a few key dimensions. These requirements would be multilateral in character. Key areas that could be addressed are forced labor, corruption, transfer pricing, and health and safety.

It will always be difficult to develop and maintain a consensus for global economic integration in the face of well-publicized exploitation of host countries by MNEs, no matter how rare these are alleged to be. However, there appears to be little appetite on the part of either source or destination countries, the international agencies, or the companies themselves for *de minimis* requirements on investment and MNEs. In branded consumer products, concerns of the brand being contaminated have led global firms (such as Nike) to club together to support independent inspections of their production facilities. A growing number of global firms that are concerned about reputational risk are, for this and other reasons, adopting their own or more credibly, collectively or independently validated standards. Such voluntary arrangements are not a substitute for global and national standards, but they should, through scrutiny and example, be actively supported, as they contribute to improvements in practice.

Foreign Aid: Proposed Policy Changes

The third dimension of globalization considered in this book is foreign aid, which includes the transfer of funds in the form of concessional loans and grants and the provision of technical assistance and capacity building. The policy changes we advocate for aid are

- doubling the amount of aid
- untying aid and its allocation to country-driven poverty reduction strategies,
- harmonizing donors' activities to reduce the heavy management burden on recipient countries
- the widespread use of evidence-based evaluation and learning processes to increase aid effectiveness and knowledge sharing
- debt relief funded out of additional commitments.

Increasing International Aid

Reaching the Millennium Development Goals (see box 5.2) requires that aid flows be *doubled* to around US$100 billion per year. We have noted that aid alone cannot bring development. Making aid effective requires further improvements in national policies, as well as supportive trade and other policies at the global level to provide the greatest benefit. In chapter 5, we showed that foreign aid commitments have stagnated. For example, both the years 1972 and 2000 saw per capita aid to the low-income countries below 1995 US$10 per capita. For most low-income countries, aid is more important than total portfolio investment, FDI, and remittances. It is vital both to increase and to make more predictable commitments of aid to low-income countries. What sort of difference would such a doubling make in current dollar terms? In 2002, the per capita U.S. dollar value of foreign aid to the low-income countries was US$12. This needs to rise to at least US$24, roughly equivalent to an incremental cost to U.S. citizens of six cappuccinos per year.

Untying International Aid

The decline in aid flows in recent decades has come at precisely the time when the impact of benefits derived from it has increased sharply. If countries are willing to take the steps necessary to reform, then assistance in the form of capacity building, financial assistance, and analytical support yields strong results. A critical lesson of past decades is that the countries themselves must be responsible and be fully behind their actions, that is, the commitment of the recipient countries is essential. This requires not only that aid be allocated without conditions that require that the donor's firms, consultants, or equipment be used, but also that it is aligned and accounted for in the recipient countries' budget process and national growth and poverty reduction strategies. Aid flows should be uncoupled from requirements that the recipient countries purchase items from donor countries, whatever these items might be.

Harmonization, Alignment, and Predictability

Alignment behind country-driven programs reduces the cost to recipients of creating new projects and programs for the donors and spending their very scarce resources and time to support individual donors' requirements. This management burden imposed on recipients is considerable, with ministers and other key staff often spending too much of their time meeting donors' needs rather than their domestic constituents' needs. The harmonization agenda needs to be pursued vigorously to ensure that, instead of each donor requiring very burdensome reporting and chaperoning, these administrative requirements are done collectively. Wherever possible, this should be through reinforcing and building the recipient countries' own existing systems, rather than creating additional systems to satisfy donor requirements. The reinforcement of country systems should cover not only the accounting and fiduciary reports required by donors, but should also extend to the governance and environmental, social, and other safeguards that increasingly dominate the discussions between aid donors and recipients.

A vision that ensures that the recipients share a concern to embrace these safeguards—and that part of the aid program is concerned with transforming these safeguards from externally imposed to internally built processes— means that external agencies are helping low-income countries to develop a sustainable approach that will allow them over time to reduce transactions costs, build domestic capacity, and eventually withdraw. Improving the quality of aid behind government programs also requires that aid be made more timely, predictable, and support multiyear programs. For example, support for investment in rural infrastructure such as roads and water, or for recurrent expenditures in education and health such as salaries for teachers and nurses, cannot be turned on and off year by year, with leads and lags that reflect donor-driven processes and priorities rather than recipients' needs.

Increased Evaluation and Knowledge Sharing

The often neglected and perhaps the most important element in aid is the role that it plays in learning and the evolution of policy. This role has many dimensions. It has also, as we illustrated in chapter 5, been associated with some of the most controversial aspects of aid, as donors in past decades sought to use aid to promote their own ideologies and geopolitical agendas. Although this risk remains, chapter 7 on ideas showed that there is a convergence around development ideas and an increasing recognition of the need for country specificity. Policy makers and citizens are more effectively able to engage in policy discussions and make policy if they are informed by the wealth of experience of other countries. By providing access to these lessons of experience—both the successes and the failures—donors can support the introduction of new perspectives and ideas. Equally vital, and similarly too often neglected, is assistance in establishing statistics and data, designing projects that can be assessed against their objectives, and then incorporating the result of a rigorous examination of the lessons of these evaluations into future program and project design. Data that help inform policy makers, such as those contained in national household surveys and in surveys of the obstacles facing small business, provide vital information for policy makers and help prioritize overcrowded reform agendas.

We recommend that building evaluation and learning into aid programs be an explicit objective rather than an afterthought. For policy makers and for the public at large in developing countries, the key questions are what works, what does not, and how scarce resources—time and money—can be better mobilized to achieve growth and poverty reduction. Long menus of required steps, which are beyond the reach of even the wealthy countries, are not helpful. Rigorous analysis of what works and what does not and how things may be improved, based on lessons of the countries' own experiences as well as on comparative data and the lessons of others, are vital tools. Globalization offers great potential in terms of drawing on the lessons of others and not repeating their mistakes. For this potential to be realized requires a determined effort on the part of developing countries, and also of aid agencies and other international players.

Debt Relief

Many poor countries continue to spend more of their budget on debt service than on water supply, rural roads, health and education, or other productive investments. This situation has real costs for the world's poor people and undermines these highly indebted countries' abilities to grow and reduce poverty. Although it is not difficult to pin blame on both the countries themselves and the public and private lenders for creating excessive debts, it is also the case that the current problems for many are the legacy of past regimes that today's leadership are trying to put behind them. The Heavily Indebted Poor Country (HIPC) initiative described in chapter 5 offers the most comprehensive approach yet to support the poorest and most indebted countries that are prepared to make a fresh start. The July 2005 G-8 agreement to cancel the approximately US$40 billion debt of HIPC countries to the international agencies and to make up the lost earnings to the World Bank and the African Development Bank marks a major step forward.

Determinants of Countries Eligible for Increased Debt Relief

Following the agreement in November 2004 to cancel up to 80 percent of Iraq's official (Paris Club) debt of almost $40 billion, the G-8 leaders in mid 2005 agreed to cancel a similar amount of debt owed by 18 highly indebted poor countries. Increased debt relief for countries that have crushing debt burdens and that have demonstrated that they can use it effectively is vital. This should extend *beyond* the poorest 30 countries, to the many other low-income countries whose repayments of debts from previous eras undermines their abilities to make a fresh start in poverty reduction. The important determinant should be the effective use of the savings. The programs should be designed to minimize moral hazard but also to provide funds for those that assiduously have made sacrifices to repay past debts. To ensure that countries that have not taken excessive debt or have already repaid debt do not suffer, it is vital that debt relief be financed out of additional money being made available by the rich countries. This means it should be in addition to any increased aid already committed and now allocated to debt relief. Various proposals to finance additional aid, including the United Kingdom's International Finance Facility (IFF), a tax on airline tickets, and the Tobin Tax have been investigated, and pilot programs for the IFF and the airline tax are being implemented.[18] Together with a commitment of the rich countries to raise their aid level to the 0.7 percent goal agreed to over 30 years ago, these financing mechanisms reflect a welcome new commitment to increasing the quantity and quality of aid that must be delivered.

Migration: Proposed Policy Changes

The fourth dimension of globalization considered in this book is migration, which we define as the temporary or permanent movement of persons between countries. Migration is an ancient globalization flow, and over the ages its form and impetus have changed significantly. With increased restrictions on movements, the global community is at a policy crossroads. Research and policy debate has been dominated by concerns of the rich countries. The challenge is to ensure that policies are developed to meet these concerns, but also to enhance the impact of migration when seen from a developing-country perspective. The policy changes we propose for migration fall into the following areas:

- multilateral coordination for migration policy
- temporary movement of natural persons for service delivery
- management of outflows of skilled people
- management of remittances
- reduction of brain waste and enhancement of diaspora networks
- research agenda.

Multilateral Coordination of Migration Policy

One in 35 persons in our world society is a migrant, falling into one of the categories of migration we presented in chapter 6. However, as noted by Klein, Solomon, and Bartsch (2003), "there is no comprehensive and harmonized system regulating international migration through which the movement of people can be managed in an orderly and cooperative way" (p. 2). As we noted in chapter 6, international migration can offer substantial benefits to poor people, but it can also involve heavy costs, especially to vulnerable populations. Further, migration is attracting the participation of international criminal organizations in both smuggling and trafficking activities. Moves to reform and harmonize the global migration system on a multilateral basis can reduce the injustices and improve the efficiency of current, piecemeal arrangements. Particular areas of concern here include dual citizenship, low-skill migration programs, managing remittances, and enforcing human rights for migrants.

Multilateral Coordination Avenues

As the Global Commission on International Migration (2005) has concluded, greater multilateral coordination of migration policy could proceed through a number of avenues. The Berne Initiative, launched in 2001, has engaged in extensive consultation with a view to developing nonbinding guidelines for best practice to manage the international movement of people "in a humane and orderly way." As such, this initiative is worth supporting. The Global Commission on International Migration was established in December 2003 by the UN Secretary-General, who identified "migration as a priority issue for the international community" and sought to "provide a framework for the formulation of coherent, comprehensive and global response to migration issues."[19] Although this international commission is supported by an ad hoc alliance of countries rather than the UN as a whole, and although it excludes some key countries, it nevertheless reflects a growing recognition of the importance of migration as a neglected dimension of international politics and development policy. Clearly there will be no quick fixes, but every effort should be made to build on this momentum to improve the multilateral system for migration.

Strengthening the Voice of Migrants

One of the reasons why migration policy at the national and global level, despite its importance, has lagged behind the evolution of other key dimensions of globalization is the fact that migrants are relatively disenfranchised. Once they have left, they typically are unable to vote and have less influence on the politics of their home country than those who remain behind. Meanwhile, as new arrivals in their host country, they are usually excluded from the domestic politics of their host. Strengthening the voice of migrants is a key challenge.

Temporary Movement of Workers

Under the auspices of the WTO, liberalization of trade in services has occurred in a number of areas of interest to developed countries. However, as recognized some time ago by Streeten (1995), "A consistent policy of free trade in goods and services would remove all restrictions on migration of people who can provide services, at least on temporary immigration while the service is provided" (p. 187). Under the WTO's General Agreement on Trade in Services (GATS), this temporary movement of persons composes *Mode 4* of service delivery. Although there is a protocol under the GATS for Mode 4 service delivery, this "refers almost exclusively to higher-level personnel, especially to intra-corporate transferees, whose mobility is basically an adjunct to foreign direct investment" (Winters and others 2002a, b). In other words, it is designed to benefit developed rather than developing countries, which have a key interest in the mobility of medium and less-skilled service providers, as well as some skilled service providers.[20]

What needs to be done in this area is to immediately pursue a multilateral system of identifying individuals seeking temporary movement, provide them with national security clearance, and grant them *multi-entry* GATS visas.[21]

This is a necessary step to harness temporary migration for poverty alleviation; no doubt it will require a new GATS protocol dedicated to the issue. As Walmsley and Winters (2003) have shown, the gains for developing countries from an increase of only 3 percent in their temporary labor quotas would exceed the value of total aid flows and be similar to the expected benefits from the Doha Round of trade negotiations, with most of the benefits to developing countries coming from increased access of unskilled workers to jobs in developed countries.

Managing the Brain Drain

As we discussed in chapter 6, the widespread recognition that capacity constraints are a critical obstacle to development is reflected in growing attention to the need for education and training facilities and opportunities for developing country nationals. At the same time, high-income countries increasingly reach out globally in their search for much needed professional skills, offering new opportunities to precisely those who could provide leadership and scarce skills in their home countries. At the top end of the labor market, and in an evolving range of specialized areas—such as information technology and medicine—the restrictions imposed on migration are significantly reduced or even waived in favor of programs that seek to recruit foreign nationals. A range of financial and other incentives also provide magnets to skilled graduates. This "brain drain" has assumed a centrality in policy discussions and research on migration, which reflects the importance that high-income countries attach to attracting skilled labor.

Impact on Donor and Host Countries

Highly skilled people have better access to politicians, lawyers, the media, academics, and others who make policy. Indeed, a growing number of these influential groups are first- or second-generation migrants. The selective admission of skilled people offers great benefits to the host countries. Its impact on the donor countries is less clear and, as we discussed in chapter 6, involves the direct costs of the loss of skills. From a government perspective, education and other wide-ranging costs are neither compensated for by the service of professionals, nor by their tax revenues and pensions. Donor counties also do not benefit directly from the impact of these skilled people on the dynamics of growth.[22] As the reverse flows of ideas, money, and skilled people into the Indian high-tech sector show, these are not necessarily one-way losses. Governments can also influence the decisions of skilled people not to leave and to keep their capital in the country to some degree by shaping the overall environment for skilled people, by providing a safe and secure working environment, by reaching out to their skilled people and seeking their involvement in decision making, and through other incentives. However, given the gaps in earning power and the attractions of cosmopolitan environments, this holding power is limited, particularly for the small and poor countries.

Policies of Restricting Recruitment

A recent British parliamentary investigation into migration and development concluded that "it is unfair, inefficient and incoherent for developed countries to provide aid to help developing countries to make progress . . . on health and education, whilst helping themselves to the nurses, doctors and teachers who have been trained in, and at the expense of, developing countries."[23] The British government, to increase the coherence between its aid and skilled migration policies, has committed itself to restricting its recruitment of essential skilled health professionals. Our recommendation is that such policies be extended in the light of careful analysis to be undertaken of the costs and benefits of such skilled migration for the sending country. Where the extent of recruitment and the resulting critical shortages are shown to have a serious impact on development objectives, such restrictions on government recruitment could go beyond doctors and nurses. It is important also to include teachers, engineers, accountants, and others whose services are vital if developing countries are to achieve essential education, governance, and infrastructure improvements and create the *virtuous circles* that will encourage skilled people to stay at home.

Incentives that Capture Costs and Benefits

For human liberty, economic, and enforceability reasons we do not believe that it is practical to include recruitment agencies or private firms in binding commitments, although for many skilled people they provide the bridge for migration. Consideration, however, should be given to developing tax and other incentives that serve to better capture the costs to the source country and the benefits to the destination country of recruitment of skilled people. In particular, the often extensive public investment in education and training could be calculated and reimbursed, at least in part, through additional aid or other transfers. For example, every surgeon recruited from abroad implies a saving of over US$1 million in education investments and a cost to the donor country of this amount. For developing countries, in addition to the direct impact of the loss of skills, migration represents a reverse flow to the rich countries of public investments that for many exceeds the flows derived from aid.

Greater coherence between migration and aid policies is urgently required. This would include further investment in education and training in poor countries to raise the supply and competence levels of skilled people. Attention should also be given to raising the incentive to stay, as there is some evidence that certain students see higher education as a stepping stone to migration.

Reducing Brain Waste

Although much needed attention has recently focused on the brain drain, a neglected dimension of this problem is the underutilization of the skills of migrants in rich countries, or ***brain waste***. This is particularly the problem for migrants who are escaping persecution and refugees, as they have not been directly recruited by head hunters due to their skills, but the problem extends well beyond refugees. In the United States, for example, the anecdotes from conversations with taxi drivers who are engineers or accountants are borne out by the data: a minority (typically a third to a half) of migrants who entered the United States with a bachelor's degree undertake work requiring such a degree, and examining the relatively well educated among some categories of migrants, such as the Mexicans and Poles, the probability is only around 20 percent that they will enter a skilled job that matches their qualifications.[24] This reflects the issues of brain drain, including the need to keep and utilize skilled people in the source countries and create an investment climate where potential migrants can prosper. It also reflects the coherence of aid and migration policies in rich countries and their ability to absorb migrants into the labor market and society.

Enhancing Diaspora Benefits

Migrants can and sometimes do play a vital role in investing, transferring technology, and serving as informal and even formal marketing agents for their home countries. The scant evidence on this suggests that although there is much spontaneous generation of such flows, policies in the host and home countries, at the local and the national levels, can make a significant difference to the beneficial impact of diasporas. The role of the Indian technology diaspora was discussed in chapter 6. Initial research suggests that countries that give more migrants tend to benefit most from return investment flows from the host countries.[25] In Western Europe, there are determined efforts to encourage diasporas from the Balkans to invest and even to return home to offer training and share the skills and technologies they have learned abroad. Policies to support such formal and informal networks as well as to encourage such investment and technology flows are to be encouraged.

Managing Remittances

Migrants' remittances are increasingly recognized as a highly significant financial flow, with officially recorded flows well over double aid flows, and second only to foreign investment as a source of external financing for developing countries.

Remittance Flows

Although remittance flows, like other capital flows, are highly unevenly distributed among developing countries, they tend to be more evenly distributed than other flows and also more stable. To the extent that the supply of migrants increases in bad times and these migrants send back more money, remittance flows are also countercyclical. Officially recorded global flows of remittances rose sharply to US$225 billion in 2004, of which developing countries received an estimated US$160 billion. Growth in remittances was particularly strong in low-income countries, notably India.[26] Remittances are expected to continue to grow, and in 2004 already are estimated to have exceeded US$20 billion in India, US$16 billion in Mexico and US$8 billion in the Philippines. In part, the surge in recent years in reported remittances may be attributed to the growing scrutiny of flows and the restrictions placed on informal channels, due to security concerns. The reduction in the costs of remittance flows through regulated channels is also thought to have contributed to the switch from informal to formal channels.

Financial Infrastructure Support for Remittances

Improving the benefits of migration includes strengthening the financial infrastructure supporting remittances. With average fees estimated at 13 percent (and often much higher), increased competition and the provision of lower-cost remittance services would greatly benefit both the sender and the beneficiary of the transfer. Increased competition can be fostered in a variety of ways, including through a facilitative regulatory and compliance framework. The preclusion of exclusive bilateral monopolies between official remittance agents and the licensing of a wider variety of certified competitors is to be encouraged. New e-commerce technologies, including in foreign exchange markets and in electronic cards, offer great potential to reduce the overall transactions costs. Similarly, increased competition and scrutiny may be expected to reduce the highly regressive structure of the markets; the smaller the transaction, the greater the cost relative to the amount transferred, which discriminates against lower-income migrants and those who wish to make smaller but more frequent transfers. The availability of accessible remittance services near the workplace or residence of migrants and near the destination of the people to whom the funds are to be transferred, which offer simple processes in languages understood by the migrants, will also greatly facilitate remittance flows. Such services will also encourage the movement of remittances from unofficial unregulated networks into regulated flows, which is important for addressing security as well as developmental concerns.

Policies to Enhance Impact of Remittances

In addition to reducing costs and facilitating remittance flows in other ways, a range of possible policy measures may be expected to enhance the development impact of remittance flows. Before recommending tax measures, official savings associations, and other government-led mechanisms to increase the beneficial impact of remittances, care must be taken to ensure that these measures will be welcomed by the migrants themselves. If such measures are not welcome, migrants will reduce their remittances or revert to unofficial channels or other strategies. Remittances are private, person-to-person flows, and coordination and policy interventions should be formulated with this in mind.

Need for Research

More empirical research is needed before we can with certainty identify the extent to which remittances have grown or whether the net impact of migration on the donor countries is positive. The net impacts should not be measured in terms of remittances alone, but rather the overall context. This point is perhaps most starkly illustrated by the flow of remittances during the apartheid period in South Africa, when higher levels of remittances reflected the increasingly destructive impact of apartheid on the lives of families that were forcibly separated

Research and Data

As the British Parliamentary Investigation into Migration has recently noted, "Policy should not be designed on the basis of hunches and anecdotes . . . the evidence-base urgently needs improving."[27] The absence of reliable data and the paucity of research on migration are striking. This fundamentally frustrates any attempt to examine the issue with a development perspective. Whereas there are literally thousands of researchers and research papers and a wide range of data sets focused on trade, capital flows, aid, and development, the number of researchers residing in developing countries dedicated to international migration issues can be counted on two hands. This may be contrasted with the rapid growth of academic work examining migration issues from the perspective of the rich countries. For example, in the United Kingdom alone, a number of research institutes have been created in the past few of years to address European migration issues, with an investment that we estimate exceeds all the work being conducted in developing countries on cross-border migration issues.

Developing a development perspective on migration is urgently needed. Recent efforts in the World Bank and in a number of developing countries to create capacity to analyze these issues require support if the necessary data and analysis are to be provided to inform much-needed policy reforms at the national and global level. With such research will also come a better understanding of the interrelationship of flows, and the extent and manner in which trade, capital flows, and aid are a substitute or complement to flows of migrants.

Research on remittances has grown most rapidly, with the scale of these flows finally attracting deserved attention by both researchers and officials. However, much more work is needed to address the questions of who migrates and why; what the short- and long-term costs and benefits are to the home community and country; and how temporary migration, brain drain, brain waste, and the links between diasporas and trade and investment can be enhanced to the benefit of poor people. Migration can again become one of the most powerful forces for poverty reduction, and migration policies offer great potential for enhancing the beneficial effects of globalization for the world's poor. Research to inform better policies is urgently required to realize this development potential.

Ideas: Proposed Policy Changes

Ideas are potentially the most powerful influence on development. Globalization and technical progress have meant that ideas are transmitted and exchanged as never before. The key question is how this potential may be harnessed to accelerate poverty reduction. What policies should countries adopt to facilitate the evolution of ideas and their generation, transmission, adaptation, and adoption? Knowledge management is often seen as a particularly difficult challenge for firms; for countries it is even more daunting. However, ignoring or giving only passing attention to knowledge management and the transmission of ideas is not a solution. The policy changes we propose for ideas fall into the following areas:

- increasing the voice of developing countries
- knowledge management
- intellectual property harmonization
- rights to key pharmaceuticals
- technology transfer.

Increasing the Voice of Developing Countries

An essential ingredient for ensuring a more inclusive globalization is that the ideas generated by developing countries must be given greater weight than they are given now. This is especially important in global consultation and decision-making forums where decisions that have direct consequences for the citizens of developing countries are made.[28] Without adequate representation and voice, decisions reached are less informed, less legitimate, and less effective.

Effectiveness of Global Institutions

In addition to ensuring that global institutions more adequately represent the different participants, it is also vital to ensure that those institutions that are representative, such as the United Nations, are effective and strengthened. The importance of leveling the playing field in the negotiations at the WTO was stressed above. The governance of the World Bank and the IMF reflects agreements and the balance of power of 60 years ago. There is widespread recognition of the need for enhancing the participation of developing countries, in light of their increased significance globally and their role as the primary recipients of Bank and IMF programs. Although progress has been made in increasing the participation of developing countries in formulating programs— as, for example, with the Poverty Reduction Strategy Paper approach— and in enhancing the capacity of the multistakeholder boards, the structural issues of voting rights and board representation remain intractable. While improvements in the effectiveness of the UN system and the Bretton Woods Institutions will contribute to more effective global management, the issue of more effective global governance goes well beyond these institutions and is a key challenge of our time.

Country Voice on the Global Level

Much of the discussion on global governance has centered on the Bretton Woods Institutions, but the question of developing country voice is much wider. At the global level, the 2005 Report of the Secretary General of the United Nations, *In Larger Freedom,* identifies the need for fundamental reform of global governance to ensure the following freedoms:

- freedom from fear (through security council reform and the establishment of a peacebuilding commission)
- freedom from indignity (through human rights commission reform and the establishment of a human rights council)
- freedom from want (through the implementation of the Monterrey Consensus to reduce poverty by half by 2015 and achieve other UN Millennium Development targets).

In the realm of economic governance, the extent of participation of developing countries has varied from universal or almost full participation in standard-setting bodies, to much more limited participation in the Bank for International Settlements (BIS), which has 55 member central banks, the G-10, and the Financial Stability Forum which brings together 25 high-income goverments and international institutions.

Need for Inclusive Solutions

Over the past decade, the economic and political muscle of the developing countries has increased both because of their rapid economic growth and because of rising awareness of global fragility and interdependence. The need for inclusive solutions has been highlighted first by the economic crises of the late 1990s and then by the security crisis associated with terrorism following September 2001. The expansion of the G-7 to include Russia and now also frequently China, and the creation of new forums such as the G-20 and G-24, has given more voice to large developing countries. These and other outreach efforts are useful, but as Bhattacharya and Griffith-Jones (2004, p. 205) point out, "it is important to go beyond consultation to full representation of developing countries in bodies that deliberate and set international norms and action plans" that affect the global community. Similarly, the current arrangements by which the richest countries agree among themselves the leadership appointments for key global institutions disenfranchises developing countries. The principles of transparency and good governance that governments are applying with increasing frequency to themselves and at the corporate level should also apply in global governance, thereby reinforcing the legitimacy and effectiveness of the global institutions.

Knowledge Management

Knowledge management embraces a wide range of activities designed to enhance countries' abilities to acquire, absorb, and take advantage of new information and ideas. The range of activities includes acquiring knowledge in the following ways:

- by establishing links
- by being open to ideas available elsewhere (for example, through trade, foreign investment, and licensing)
- by creating knowledge locally through research and development
- by building on indigenous knowledge.

Policies for Enhancing Knowledge Acquisition

The policies suggested under our discussion of trade and capital flows apply equally here: greater openness to trade and investment, and ensuring that trade and investment are associated with the transfer of technologies and expertise, are all policies that contribute to deepening knowledge acquisition. So, too, does closing the digital divide and the combination of open access to the Internet and developing a regulatory environment that allows competitive entry into the telecommunications sector, reducing high-speed connectivity charges. Creating and adapting knowledge locally—by investing in public sector research and creating incentives for private sector research and collaboration—is vital. It can be encouraged by establishing a facilitative intellectual property environment, as we discuss below.

Absorbing information builds on the fundamentals of literacy and numeracy, but to generate adaptation and innovation also requires the development of an inquisitive spirit and the ability to evaluate ideas and information. Exposure to the experiences of others provides helpful insights to development practitioners. Equally important is the careful evaluation of the impact of those experiences. By diligently examining the extent to which policy initiatives and interventions reach or fall short of their objectives, and by promoting a culture of critical analysis and open admission of weaknesses and strengths, governments can set the standards for the acceleration of learning. Equally, international partners and global and regional institutions have a major responsibility to engage in research and make available the benefits of their global and long-term experience in development.

Including Poor Communities in Knowledge Sharing

As we discussed in chapter 7, knowledge management requires the acquisition of ideas and information (as a spillover from trade and investment and also directly through research and data collection), absorbing information (through educated analysis and increasing the learning from own and others' experience), and communicating knowledge to ensure that it is widely shared. In addition to investments in education and research, governments can facilitate the sharing of knowledge and make special efforts to overcome the exclusion of poor people and poor communities from information. Global institutions and partners have a responsibility to assist with the distillation and dissemination of the wide-ranging lessons of experience and research. A particular challenge is to make this available to developing countries in ways and languages that can be understood not only by a small leadership group who read English but also by wider audiences, ranging from school children to development practitioners such as those who design and implement policies in provincial and local governments.

Communication, Knowledge, and Risk Management

In recent years, the role of communication and knowledge in risk management has become better understood. Timely and effective information flows on issues important to poor people can help them to manage their risks and maximize their opportunities. Such practical efforts include providing market prices to poor farmers through village mobile phones, broadcasting weather information and disaster warnings on local radios, and highlighting the risks of HIV/AIDS and the benefits of public health measures in community information campaigns. In these and other respects, knowledge really does provide power to poor people to improve their lives.

The Knowledge Assessment Methodology

The Knowledge Assessment Methodology helps countries understand their strengths and weaknesses in transitioning to knowledge economies.[29] It is now available for 128 countries and provides useful means for countries to identify their performance and potential in terms of their needs and capabilities along a wide variety of dimensions. Although still under development, this and other initiatives, such as those that focus on the development of African science and math capacity and the African Virtual University, provide the basis for a rapid scaling up of knowledge in support of the acquisition, adoption, and communication of ideas to support poverty reduction and growth.

Further Intellectual Property Harmonization

As we discussed in chapter 7, knowledge is typically a global public good. However, there is an ongoing process of knowledge privatization in the form of increased intellectual property protection.[30] This is taking place at the WTO under the Agreement on Trade-Related Aspects of Intellectual Property Rights (TRIPS), at the World Intellectual Property Organization (WIPO), and in regional trade agreement negotiations in "TRIPS-plus" formats. From a development perspective, the TRIPS Agreement is controversial.[31] International economists and lawyers have significant disagreements on the long-run benefits of restricting knowledge transfer to developing countries.[32] The majority of developing countries, supported by many leading scientists and academics, have argued that intellectual property protection needs to be applied in a manner that allows developing countries greater access to research and new technologies. Given this lack of consensus on the benefits and the costs to developing countries of meeting TRIPS implementation requirements,[33] an intensive examination of the issues by an independent panel accompanied by a temporary moratorium of further commitments demanded of developing countries has been suggested.[34] Correa (2003) notes this should include regional and bilateral agreements where "TRIPS-plus" obligations are being negotiated that go beyond the existing commitments made by developing countries. The argument is that demands for harmonization are now ahead both of intellectual capacity in many countries and of demonstrated benefits. A moratorium for a predetermined fixed period of time may therefore be worth considering to allow expert evaluation to enable policy decisions to be made on a more credible basis of considered research into the issues.

Establishing Rights to Key Pharmaceuticals

As we mentioned in chapter 7, patents are a central concern for the impact of intellectual property protection on poor people, particularly in the case of pharmaceuticals for HIV/AIDS, tuberculosis, and malaria.[35] In 2001, WTO members reaffirmed certain "flexibilities" with regard to access to pharmaceuticals needed to address public health crises. This included the production of generic drugs under compulsory licensing arrangements under Article 31 of TRIPS. Article 31(f) limits the use of these generic drugs to the domestic markets of the producing countries. Matthews (2004) notes the problem here:

> *This has the practical effect of preventing exports of generic drugs to countries that do not have significant pharmaceutical industries themselves. Only about a dozen developing countries, among them China, India, Brazil, Argentina and South Africa, have the level of manufacturing capacity capable of producing significant quantities of off-patent generic drugs. For countries with insufficient manufacturing capacity, the only realistic sourcing mechanism is importation.* (p. 78)

Unfortunately, importation of this kind is restricted under TRIPS Article 31(f). A WTO "decision" on this issue was adopted in August 2003 that allows least-developed WTO members (and other members that notify the TRIPS Council) to import off-patent, generic drugs. It is not yet clear that these provisions ensure that existing knowledge is effectively deployed to confront some of the most serious health crises of modern times. There are several concerns with this decision:

- First, the August 2003 decision is procedurally demanding.[36]
- Second, deliberations at the TRIPS Council regarding the application of the decision could be lengthy.
- Third is the concern that developed countries with pharmaceutical industries will take unilateral action against developing countries making use of the decision.
- Fourth is evidence of bilateral, TRIPS-plus activity that might be extended to rights under the decision.[37]

Given these concerns, the August 2003 decision could be revisited to ensure a fast-track procedure for national health emergencies.

Increased Technology Transfer to Developing Countries

The global transfer of ideas in the form of technology is one of the most important development processes. For decades, the apparently growing gulf between developed and developing countries has raised concerns regarding a "technology divide." In recent years, leading developing countries such as Brazil, China, India, and South Africa have demonstrated that certain countries cannot only overcome but even leap ahead in selected areas. Partly as a result of these advances, developing countries increasingly are looking to each other for ideas and collaboration.

Although learning from the deliberate policies put in place by those countries that have increasingly developed and adapted technologies, the overwhelming majority of developing countries will remain dependent on technology transfer. Article 66.2 of the WTO TRIPS Agreement commits developed countries to providing "incentives to enterprises and institutions in their territories for the purpose of promoting and encouraging technology transfer" to the least-developed countries. This commitment needs to be implemented *in practice* and applied to a wider set of countries. As outlined by Maskus (2003) and Hoekman, Maskus, and Saggi (2004), this can occur through a variety of measures. These measures include the following:

- incentives for corporations and nongovernmental organizations to transfer mature patent rights or to provide technical assistance
- public support for research into the specific technology needs of developing countries
- university training for students from the low-income countries in science and technology

- finance to enable the participation of developing country representatives in standard-setting bodies
- public purchase of patents on certain technologies for free use in developing countries.

In addition, we would suggest that the rich countries consider the possibility of creating incentives—for example, through negotiating patent extensions on technologies primarily destined for high-income groups in return for lowering or waiving patent fees and restrictions on technologies destined for low-income markets. These and other steps can better ensure that international technological development is more likely to help poor people.

A Global Policy Checklist

Having described our policy agenda in some detail, it is useful to present its elements in a more concise format. We do so in table 8.2. Without significant progress toward the changes described by the entries in table 8.2, it will be much less likely that we can count on the globalization dimensions discussed in this book bringing positive benefits to poor people.

Summary and Assessment

The post–World War II period of accelerated global integration has been associated with unprecedented progress on key dimensions of development. This is mainly because of countries adopting better national policies and directing cross-border flows of ideas, people, capital, and goods to meet the challenges faced by their citizens. Some examples of these leaps in development include[38]

- ***Health.*** Over the past 40 years, life expectancy at birth in developing countries increased by 20 years. It is likely that the previous 20-year increase in longevity took millennia. The improvement resulted partly from higher incomes and better education, particularly of women and girls, but also in large measure from improved knowledge and understanding about the prevention and treatment of disease, and new programs to share this knowledge and put it into practice. The pandemic of HIV/AIDS has reduced life expectancy by 20 years in some countries of the world. However, with our improved knowledge of the prevention and treatment of disease, the combination of effective actions at the country and global levels holds the hope of reinstating that surge in longevity to all countries.

- *Education.* Over the past 30 years, illiteracy in the developing world has been cut nearly in half, from 47 percent to 25 percent of all adults. Steady expansion of school enrollments worldwide and increases in education quality made key contributions to this improvement, as did better infrastructure and nutrition. These commitments need to be renewed and sustained.
- *Income poverty.* The number of people subsisting on less than US$1 per day rose steadily for nearly two centuries, but in the past 20 years it has begun to fall. As a result of better and more market-oriented economic policies through much of the developing world—but most importantly in China and India—the number of poor people worldwide has fallen by over 300 million, even as the world's population has risen by about 1.8 billion since 1980. The challenge is to widen these achievements, to read the poor people in Africa and elsewhere.

Engines of Progress

Driving much (though not all) of this progress in income poverty has been an acceleration in economic growth rates in the developing world. Since 1965, the per capita gross domestic product (GDP) of the developing world as a whole has increased by an average of over 2 percent per year, more than doubling the income of the average developing-country resident. Since 1990, developing countries' economies have on average grown faster in per capita terms than those of OECD countries. Again, this is a huge change by historical standards and substantially higher than growth rates achieved by the developed countries in the 19th century and most of the 20th century.

This progress in health, education, and income is not accidental. Governments, with the support of the development community and civil society organizations (CSOs), have accelerated growth and poverty reduction by improving their policies, institutions, and governance, and through well-designed projects and programs. The challenge is to extend the progress that has already improved the well-being of so many people to all regions and countries. To do so, the development community must learn from past failures, and must understand the origins of the successes. Like aid recipients, who have often followed weak policies or allowed institutions to deteriorate, donors also have made mistakes that slowed development. We must design policies at the global, regional, national, and local or community levels that ensure that the benefits of globalization reach the billion and more people who are currently marginalized and who have not benefited from the fruits of globalization. The policies discussed in this chapter will make this outcome more likely.

Peace and Security

As we stated in the introduction to this book, our purpose has been to assess the links between the dimensions of economic globalization and global poverty. Necessarily, then, we have chosen to ignore some important issues that deserve, and sometimes are receiving, full treatment elsewhere. The most important of these issues is that of peace and security. The relationship between increased economic interdependence and conflict is complex, and there is conflicting evidence on the nature of this relationship.[39] However, it is clear that aspects of globalization more broadly conceived can indeed exacerbate conflict. This is the case, for example, in global criminal and warlord networks.[40] Naim (2005) has highlighted the extent to which illegal trade has accompanied globalization. Illicit trade of commodities for arms fuels conflicts and leads to development in reverse. Focusing attention on illegal flows that undermine development requires placing this in the context of managing globalizations benefits, rather than engaging in protectionism. These are issues that require attention.[41]

Addressing these problems involves a concept we have touched upon at various points in this book: global public goods. As noted by Hamburg and Holl (1999) and Mendez (1999), the prevention of deadly conflict as part of efforts to provide peace and security inherently involves benefits that are nonexcludable. Because they are nonexcludable, there are no direct specific incentives for countries that are not part of the conflict, so these efforts tend to be underprovided. Ensuring the benefits of globalization for the poorest, then, will require substantially more efforts to provide this and other global public goods.

Coherence

Coherence across the dimensions outlines in this book is a vital for globalization to work more effectively for development. The flows of trade, finance, aid, migration, and ideas can converge, providing a powerful force for poverty reduction, or they can flow in opposing directions, causing turbulence and diluting their potential benefits. Development is multidimensional, as are the ways in which the global economic flows can support development.

Hope and Tasks for the Future

Our recommendations are not novel. Nor do we consider them to be a panacea. However, through our analysis and prioritization of practical actions, we hope to contribute to ongoing discussions of globalization and poverty. Globalization can work for poor people if we pursue the right policies. Let us all act to ensure that the huge opportunities globalization offers lead to a better life for all.

TABLE 8.2 A Global Policy Checklist

Globalization dimension	Policy area	Description
Trade	Market access	A sharp increase in market access for labor-intensive goods and services from developing countries, including the commitment to a rapid reduction in tariff escalation and agricultural subsides in the rich countries of the world.
Trade	Trade-related capacity building	The substantial and sustained increase in trade-related capacity building for low-income countries that is explicitly linked to increases in market access. This capacity building needs to address meeting WTO commitments, full WTO representation, the effective negotiation of regional agreements, and supply-side constraints.
Trade	Arms trade	The adoption of a multilateral agreement to create legally binding arms controls and to ensure that all governments control the arms trade according to the same international standards, which restrict exports to countries with significant records of human rights abuses, to criminal organizations, and to conflict zones.
Trade	Forced labor	The extension of the World Trade Organization's general exception to commitments in the case of prison labor (Article XXe) to all forms of forced labor.
Finance	Heterodox capital account reform	The maintenance of a heterodox approach to capital account reform in the absence of consensus on best practice. There should not be a one-size-fits-all approach to capital account liberalization.
Finance	Corporate social responsibility and standards.	The development of norms for corporate social responsibility and the application of standards and policies that encourage best practice by foreign and domestic public sector investors.
Aid	Increasing volume and stability of aid flows	The rapid doubling of aid flows, with a commitment to continued increases to achieve the agreed target of 0.7 per-cent of GDP, as well as the transfer of a higher share of these increased resources to developing countries.
Aid	Untying aid	The decoupling of aid commitments from requirements to purchase consultancy or other services or goods from the donor country.

Category	Topic	Description
Aid	Harmonization and alignment	The coordination and harmonization of aid flows with those of other donors, and the alignment of these with recipient governments' own priorities.
Aid	Evaluation and knowledge sharing	The inclusion of impact evaluation in projects and transparency in sharing results to ensure that lessons of development are widely shared.
Aid	Debt relief	The acceleration of debt relief to ensure that all developing countries that have the necessary commitments to sustainable policies benefit, with this debt relief funded by additional financial commitments from the rich countries.
Migration	Multilateral migration policy	Reform and harmonization of the global migration system on a multilateral basis to protect migrants' rights and improve efficiency and security. Particular areas of concern include dual citizenship and voting rights, low-skill migration programs, managing remittances, and the enforcement of human rights for migrants.
Migration	Regularization of the temporary movement of persons for service delivery	The establishment of a multilateral system of identifying individuals seeking temporary movement, providing national security clearance to them, and granting multi-entry visas to them under the General Agreement on Trade in Services.
Migration	Brain drain	The adoption and expansion of measures by destination countries to limit the recruitment of highly skilled professionals from countries facing shortages in these areas, particularly those facing public health emergencies; and the ensuring of greater coherence between aid and migration policies, through investing in capacity building and incentives to retain vital skills.
Migration	Brain waste and diaspora	An increase of the matching of skilled personnel with opportunities by increasing the rights of employment. The promotion of diaspora networks and encouragement of return investment and technology transfer.
Migration	Remittance services	An increase of competition in remittance services, the end of monopolies, and the encouragement of entry into money transfer systems that facilitate migrants' use of officially recorded channels, including through electronic smart cards and other technologies.

(Continued)

TABLE 8.2 A Global Policy Checklist *(Continued)*

Globalization dimension	Policy area	Description
Migration	Data and research	Increased funding for research and data collection, with view to understanding costs and benefits of migration and enhancing development impacts.
Ideas	Increase voice of developing countries	More adequate representation of the ideas coming from developing countries in bilateral, regional, and global discussions, negotiations, and institutions to ensure that decisions that affect the developing countries better reflect their views and interests.
Ideas	Support of the knowledge economy	Support of countries' efforts to develop coherent knowledge strategies focused on acquisition, absorption, and communication of ideas and information. Use of knowledge assessment methodologies can help identify weaknesses across key dimensions, including hardware (telecommunications, infrastructure) and software (education, Web access, media access, and so on).
Ideas	Intellectual property harmonization	Evaluation of the costs and benefits to developing countries of the current intellectual property negotiations in TRIPS, and to build common agreement to ensure that intellectual property rules support access for developing countries to key health and other technologies.
Ideas	Establishing rights to key pharmaceuticals	The swift and permanent establishment of the right of countries without pharmaceutical manufacturing capacity to access generic pharmaceuticals to fight AIDS, tuberculosis, and malaria. This would include a fast-track procedure for national health emergencies.
Ideas	Increased technology transfer to developing countries	The extension of developed-country TRIPS commitments on technology transfer to a larger number of developing countries and an honoring of this commitment through a variety of specific means.

Notes

1. On small wins in the social sciences, see Weick (1984). Weick notes that "it seems useful to consider the possibility that social problems seldom get solved because people define these problems in ways that overwhelm their ability to do anything about them. Changing the scale of a problem can change the quality of resources that are directed at it. Calling a situation a mere problem that necessitates a small win moderates arousal, improves diagnosis, preserves gains, and encourages innovation. Calling a situation a serious problem that necessitates a larger win may be when the problem starts" (p. 48).

2. For the case of the OECD countries, for example, see chapter 12 of Wolf (2004).

3. This point is made by Rodrik (1998b), for example. Rodrik states that "The scope of government has been larger, not smaller, in economies taking greater advantage of world markets" and suggests that "the reasons have to do with the provision of social insurance" (p. 1028).

4. We take up policy proposals in the area of trade-related intellectual property under the ideas dimension of globalization later in the chapter.

5. The term generally employed to describe the external benefits of agricultural production is ***multi-functionality***. See, for example, Jules (2003).

6. Wolf (2004) has referred to tariff escalation as a "long-standing scandal" (p. 206). It is time to end this scandal.

7. This point has been made by Wolfensohn (2002) and Reinert (2005).

8. See Grimmett (2003). The five largest exporters of arms to the developing world were, in order of importance, the United States, the United Kingdom, Russia, France, and China.

9. In its first *World Report on Violence and Health,* the World Health Organization (2002) estimates that there were 320,000 deaths due to civil conflict in 2000. See Collier and Sambanis (2003) and Naim (2005).

10. See Oxfam (2004b).

11. The importance of freedom in market transactions has been emphasized in chapter 1 of Sen (1999). He notes that "a denial of opportunities of transaction, through arbitrary controls, can be a source of unfreedom in itself" (p. 25).

12. One model of this approach is Brazil's Bolsa Escuela program.

13. Former IMF Managing Director Stanley Fischer (1998) argued in favor of capital account liberalization. However, Jagdish Bhagwati (1998), Dani Rodrik (1998a), Paul Krugman (1999), Barry Eichengreen (1999), Kaplan and Rodrik (2001), and Joseph Stiglitz (2000, 2002a) all strongly questioned the goal of capital account liberalization and called for capital controls of one kind or another. These range from market-friendly taxes on short-term capital inflows (Eichengreen 1999) to more stringent controls on capital outflows (Kaplan and Rodrik 2001). For a recent discussion in the context of poverty reduction, see Cobham (2002).

14. For a recent review of the debate from a pro-market or liberal perspective, see chapter 11 of Wolf (2004).

15. The view that extractive industry investments mainly have a negative impact in resource-rich countries may be found in the report of the *Extractive Industries Review* (2004) external review conducted for the World Bank; the World Bank's response argues that strengthened policies can mitigate the risks and enhance the benefits. See www.ifc.org/ifcext/eir.nsf. See Extractive Industries Transparency Initiative at www.eitransparency.org and Publish What You Pay at www.publishwhatyoupay.org.

16. For an early review, see chapter 21 of Dunning (1993).

17. On the last of these, see OECD (2003a).

18. A Tobin Tax is a small tax on foreign exchange transactions proposed by Tobin (1978). The original purpose is to reduce the volatility of flexible exchange rates by throwing "sand in the wheels of international finance," but it has been identified as a means of raising funds for a variety of global goods.

19. United Nations (2003) and speech of UN Secretary-General on December 9, 2003, in Geneva.

20. As pointed out by Puri (2004), there is an important gender element here: "For the majority of women, Mode 4 provides the only opportunity to obtain remunerative employment with temporary movement to provide services abroad. It has been found to have a net positive effect on the economy and poverty reduction in the home country. There are dramatic examples of how remittances from female domestic service suppliers from Bangladesh, Ethiopia, and Sri Lanka; nurses from Jamaica, Malawi, and the Philippines; nurses and doctors from India and South Africa; agricultural service suppliers from Honduras and Mexico; and personal care providers from Caribbean and Latin American countries have substantially improved women's status in their home country and augmented their command over resources" (p. 8).

21. Similar (and other) proposals are considered in Walmsley and Winters (2003). Although this proposal might strike the average citizen as extreme, we need to emphasize that the developing countries have negotiated to their advantage the liberalization of trade in services through FDI. It stands to reason that, if Citibank can provide financial services in the Philippines, then Philippine nurses should be able to provide nursing services in the United States.

22. Economists increasingly recognize the role of skilled people and their contribution to innovation as essential to endogenous growth.

23. United Kingdom, 2004, House of Commons, Migration and Development, Paragraph 7.

24. See Mattoo, Neagu, and Ozden (2005); and Ozden and Schiff (2005).

25. See Özden and Schiff (2005).

26. This section on remittances draws on Ratha (2004) and World Bank (2004d). See World Bank (2005f) for analysis of remittances.

27. House of Commons, International Development Committee, 2004.

28. This section draws extensively on conversations with Amar Bhattacharya and on Bhattacharya and Griffith-Jones (2004).

29. See http://www.worldbank.org/kam.

30. This trend has been widely noted. See, for example, Maskus and Reichman (2004).

31. Even Keith Maskus, perhaps the most prominent proponent of the potential benefits of TRIPS for developing countries, confines his claim to "middle-income and large developing countries." See, for example, Maskus (2003).

32. McCalman (2001) estimates the annual transfers from the developing world to the developed world (primarily the United States) to be on the order of billions of U.S. dollars. For some developing countries, these transfers offset entirely the static "gains from trade" due to standard trade liberalization in the Uruguay Round.

33. See, for example, Finger and Schuler (2000).

34. This section benefits from discussion with Bernard Hoekman. Recently, a group of NGOs issued a "Geneva Declaration" calling for a moratorium on new patent treaties. See International Centre for Trade and Sustainable Development (2004).

35. For a review of the issues, see Correa (2002).

36. As described by Matthews (2004), "The new arrangements will require that the importing country first attempt to obtain a voluntary license from the patent holder on reasonable commercial terms for a reasonable period. If this is not possible, the importing country must then assess its generic industry's capacity to produce the medicine locally and, if capacity is deemed insufficient, then notify the WTO with a detailed justification of its decision. The importing country must then notify a potential importer, which must in turn seek a voluntary license from its own government on a single-country basis, with compensation payable on standards of reasonableness in the importing country" (p. 97).

37. Bilateral activity in the area of intellectual property in general is discussed by Drahos (2001).

38. This list is drawn from Goldin, Rogers, and Stern (2002), to which readers are referred for a fuller discussion of the achievements in development in recent decades.

39. For reviews and analysis, see Barbieri and Schneider (1999); Gartzke, Quan, and Boehmer (2001); and Collier and Sambanis (2003).

40. See, for example, Cooper (2002) on the role of conflict trade.

41. See Hick (2001), and Naim (2005).

References

Abella, M. 1995. "Policies and Institutions for the Orderly Movement of Labour Abroad." *International Migration Papers No. 5.* Geneva: International Labour Organisation.

Adams, R. H. 2003. "International Migration, Remittances and the Brain Drain: A Study of 24 Labor-Exporting Countries." Policy Research Working Paper 3069, World Bank, Washington, DC.

Adams, R. H., and J. Page. 2003. "International Migration, Remittances and Poverty in Developing Countries." Policy Research Working Paper 3179, World Bank, Washington, DC.

Adelman, I. 2001. "Fallacies in Development Theory and Their Implications for Policy." In *Frontiers of Development Economics: The Future in Perspective,* ed. G. M. Meier and J. E. Stiglitz, 103–34. Oxford: Oxford University Press.

Aitken, B. J., and A. E. Harrison. 1999. "Do Domestic Firms Benefit from Direct Foreign Investment? Evidence from Venezuela." *American Economic Review* 89 (3): 605–18.

Alesina, A., and D. Dollar. 2000. "Who Gives Foreign Aid to Whom and Why?" *Journal of Economic Growth* 5 (1): 33.

Anderson, P. 1998. "Manpower Losses and Employment Adequacy Among Skilled Workers in Jamaica, 1976–85." *When Borders Don't Divide.* New York: Center for Migration Studies.

Australian Government-Department of Immigration and Multicultural and Indigenous Affairs. 2004a. *Population Flows: Immigration Aspects 2002–03 Edition.* Canberra: Department of Immigration and Multicultural and Indigenous Affairs.

———. 2004b. *Australian Immigration Statistics.* Canberra. http://www.immi.gov.au/statistics/index.htm

Axworthy, L. 2001. "Human Security and Global Governance: Putting People First." *Global Governance* 7 (1): 19–23.

Balls, A. 2005. "Emerging Markets Record Boom 2004." *Financial Times,* January 20.

Barber, B. 1996. *Jihad vs. McWorld.* New York: Ballentine.

Barber, C. 2004. "South-South Migration: A Synthesis Report." Unpublished, Department for International Development, London.

Barbieri, K., and G. Schneider. 1999. "Globalization and Peace: Assessing New Directions in the Study of Trade and Conflict." *Journal of Peace Research* 36 (4): 387–404.

Barnes, W. 2004. "Food Safety Fears Used As Excuse to Ban Imports." *Financial Times,* April 6, p. 7.

Battat, J., I. Frank, and X. Shen. 1996. *Suppliers to Multinationals: Linkage Programs to Strengthen Local Companies in Developing Countries.* Washington, DC: Foreign Investment Advisory Service, World Bank.

Bayes, A., J. von Braun, and R. Akhter. 1999. "Village Pay Phones and Poverty Reduction: Insights from a Grameen Bank Initiative in Bangladesh." ZEF Bonn-Zentrum für Entwicklungsforschung (Center for Development Research) Discussion Papers on Development Policy, Bonn.

Beck, T., R. Levine, and N. Loayza. 2000. "Finance and the Sources of Growth." *Journal of Financial Economics* 58 (1–2): 261–300.

Behrman, J. R., H. Alderman, and J. Hoddinott. 2004. "Hunger and Malnutrition." Copenhagen: Copenhagen Consensus.

Bell, D. 2000 (orig. 1960). *The End of Ideology.* Cambridge, Massachusetts: Harvard University Press.

Benton, B., J. Bump, A. Sékétéli, and B. Liese. 2002. "Partnership and Promise: Evolution of the African River-Blindness Campaigns." *Annals of Tropical Medicine and Parasitilogy,* 96 (S1): S5–S14.

Berkowitz D., K. Pistor, and J.-F. Richard. 2003. "Economic Development, Legality, and the Transplant Effect." *European Economic Review* 47 (1): 165–95.

Beynon, J. 2003. "Poverty Efficient Aid Allocations–Collier/Dollar Revisited." Economic and Statistics Analysis Unit Working Paper 2. Overseas Development Institute, London.

Bhagwati, J. 1998. "The Capital Myth." *Foreign Affairs,* 77(3) (May/June): 7–12.

———. 2004. *In Defense of Globalization.* New York: Oxford University Press.

Bhattacharya, A., and S. Griffith-Jones. 2004. "The Search for a Stable and Equitable Global Financial System." In *Diversity in Development: Reconsidering the Washington Consensus* eds. Jan Joost Teunissen and Age Akkerman. The Hague: FONDAD. http://www.fondad.org/publications/diversity/Fondad-Diversity-Chapter15.pdf.

Bhattacharya, A., and M. Miller. 1999. "Coping with Crises: Is There a 'Silver Bullet?'" In *The Asian Financial Crisis: Causes, Contagion and Consequences,* eds. R. Agenor, M. Miller, D. Vines, and A. Weber, 357–85. Cambridge: Cambridge University Press.

Bhinda, N., S. Griffith-Jones, J. Leape, and M. Martin. 1999. *Private Capital Flows to Africa.* The Hague: Fondad.

Bigelow, B., and B. Peterson. 2002. *Rethinking Globalization: Teaching for Justice in an Unjust World.* Milwaukee: Rethinking Schools Press.

Blomström, M., and A. Kokko. 2003. "The Economics of Foreign Direct Investment Incentives." NBER Working Paper 9489, National Bureau of Economic Research, Cambridge, MA.

Blomström, M., and F. Sjöholm. 1999. "Technology Transfer and Spillovers: Does Local Participation with Multinationals Matter?" *European Economic Review* 43 (4–6): 915–23.

Boldrin, M. and D. K. Levine. 2002. "The Case Against Intellectual Property." *The American Economic Review* 92 (2): 209–12.

———. 2004a. "The Case Against Intellectual Monopoly." *International Economic Review* 45 (2): 327–360.

———. 2004b. "Rent-Seeking and Innovation." *Journal of Monetary Economics* 51 (1): 127–160.

Boone, P. 1996. "Politics and the Effectiveness of Foreign Aid." *European Economic Review* 40 (2): 289–329.

Borensztein, E., J. De Gregorio, and J.-W. Lee. 1998. "How Does Foreign Direct Investment Affect Economic Growth?" *Journal of International Economics* 45 (1): 115–35.

Borjas, G. J. 1999. *Heaven's Door: Immigration Policy and the American Economy.* Princeton: Princeton University Press.

———. 2003. "The Labor Demand Curve *Is* Downward Sloping: Reexamining the Impact of Immigration on the Labor Market." *Quarterly Journal of Economics* 118 (4): 1335–74.

———. 2004. "Making It Worse: President Bush Has Tackled the Immigration Problem Wrongly." *National Review* 56 (2): 24–6.

Bourguignon, F., and C. Morrisson. 2002. "Inequality Among World Citizens: 1820–1992." *American Economic Review* 92 (4): 727–44.

Brown, M., and I. Goldin. 1992. *The Future of Agriculture in Developing Countries.* Paris: OECD Development Centre.

Bruton, H. J. 1998. "A Reconsideration of Import Substitution." *Journal of Economic Literature* 36 (2): 903–36.

Bruton, H. J., and D. Fairris. 1999. "Work and Development." *International Labour Review* 138 (1): 5–30.

Buitelaar, R. M., and R. Padilla Pérez. 2000. "Maquila, Economic Reform and Corporate Strategies." *World Development* 28 (9): 1627–42.

Burns, J., M. Holman, and M. Huband. 1997. "How Mobutu Built Up His $4 Billion Fortune: Zaire's Dictator Plundered IMF Loans." *Financial Times,* May 1.

Burnside, C., and D. Dollar. 2000. "Aid, Policies, and Growth." *American Economic Review* 90 (4): 847–68.

Calvo, G. A., L. Leiderman, and C. M. Reinhart. 1996. "Inflows of Capital to Developing Countries in the 1990s." *Journal of Economic Perspectives* 10 (2): 123–39.

Card, D. 1990. "The Impact of the Mariel Boatlift on the Miami Labor Market." *Industrial and Labor Relations Review* 43 (2): 245–57.

Carrington, W. J., and E. Detragiache. 1999. "How Extensive Is the Brain Drain?" *Finance and Development* 36 (2): 46–50.

Caves, R. E. 1974. "Multinational Firms, Competition, and Productivity in Host-Country Markets." *Economica* 41 (162): 176–93.

———. 1996. *Multinational Enterprise and Economic Analysis.* Cambridge: Cambridge University Press.

Charitonenko, S., and A. Campion. Undated. "Expanding Commercial Microfinance in Rural Areas: Constraints and Opportunities." Chemonics International. http://www.microfinancegateway.org/files/19863_19863.pdf.

Chen, S., and M. Ravallion. 2001. "How Did the World's Poorest Fare in the 1990s?" *Review of Income and Wealth* 47 (3): 283–300.

———. 2004. "How Have the World's Poorest Fared Since the Early 1980s?" *World Bank Researcher Observer* 19 (2): 141–70.

Chiswick, B. R., and T. J. Hatton. 2002. "International Migration and the Integration of Labor Markets." IZA Discussion Paper 1119. (August). Forschungsinstitut zur Zukunft der Arbeit—Institute for the Study of Labor, Bonn.

Choe, H., B.-C. Kho, and R. M. Stulz. 1999. "Do Foreign Investors Destabilize Stock Markets: The Korean Experience." *Journal of Financial Economics* 54(2): 227–64.

Chua, A. 2003. *World on Fire.* New York: Random House.

Chuhan, P., S. Claessens, and N. Mamingi. 1998. "Equity and Bond Flows to Latin America and Asia: The Role of Global and Country Factors." *Journal of Development Economics* 55 (2): 439.

Citizenship and Immigration Canada. 2003a. *Facts and Figures 2002: Immigration Overview.* Ottawa: Communications Branch, Citizenship and Immigration. http://www.cic.gc.ca/english/pdf/pub/facts2002.pdf.

———. 2003b. *Facts and Figures 2002: Statistical Overview of the Temporary Resident and Refugee Claimant Population.* Ottawa: Communications Branch, Citizenship and Immigration.

Claessens, S., D. Klingebiel, and S. L. Schmukler. 2002. "The Future of Stock Exchanges in Emerging Economies: Evolution and Prospects." Brookings-Wharton Papers on Financial Services, 167–202.

Clarke, J., and J. Salt. 2003. "Wage Permits and Foreign Labour in the UK: A Statistical Review." *Labour Market Trends* 111 (11): 563–74.

Clemens, M., S. Radelet, and R. Bhavnani. 2004. *Counting Chickens When They Hatch: The Short-Term Effect of Aid on Growth.* Working Paper 44, Center for Global Development, Washington, DC.

Cobham, A. 2002. "Capital Account Liberalization and Poverty." *Global Social Policy* 2 (2): 163–88.

Cockburn, I. M., and J. O. Lanjouw. 2001. "New Pills for Poor People? Empirical Evidence After GATT." *World Development* 29 (2): 265.

Cohen, D. 2001. "The HIPC Initiative: True and False Promises." *International Finance* 4 (3): 363–80.

Collier, P., and D. Dollar. 2001. "Development Effectiveness: What Have We Learnt?" Development Research Group, World Bank, Washington, DC.

———. 2002. "Aid Allocation and Poverty Reduction." *European Economic Review* 46 (8): 1475–500.

Collier, P., and J. W. Gunning. 1995. "War, Peace and Private Portfolios." *World Development* 23 (2): 233–41.

Collier, P., S. Devarajan, and D. Dollar. 2001. "Measuring IDA's Effectiveness." Unpublished. World Bank, Washington, DC.

Collier, P., A. Hoeffler, and C. Pattillo. 2001. "Flight Capital as a Portfolio Choice." *World Bank Economic Review* 15(1): 55–80.

Collier, P., and N. Sambanis. 2003. *Understanding Civil War.* Washington, DC: World Bank.

Commission for Africa. 2005. "Our Common Interest." London: Commission for Africa.

Cooper, N. 2002. "State Collapse as Business: The Role of Conflict Trade and the Emerging Control Agenda." *Development and Change* 33 (5): 935–55.

Cordon, W. M. 2002. *Too Sensational: On the Choice of Exchange Rate Regimes.* Cambridge, Massachusetts: MIT Press.

Cornelius, W. A. 2001. "Death at the Border: The Efficacy and 'Unintended' Consequences of U.S. Immigration Control Policy, 1993–2000." Working Paper 27, Center for Comparative Immigration Studies, University of California, San Diego: La Jolla, California.

Correa, C. M. 2002. "Public Health and Intellectual Property Rights." *Global Social Policy* 2 (3): 261–78.

———. 2003. "Formulating Effective Pro-Development National Intellectual Property Policies." In *Trading in Knowledge: Development Perspectives on TRIPS, Trade and Sustainability,* ed. C. Bellmann, G. Dutfield, and R. Meléndez-Ortiz, 209–17. Geneva: International Centre for Trade and Sustainable Development.

Crafts, N. 2001. "Historical Perspectives on Development." In *Frontiers of Development Economics: The Future in Perspective,* ed. G. M. Meier and J. E. Stiglitz, 301–34. Oxford: Oxford University Press.

Cragg, M. I., and M. Epelbaum. 1996. "Why Has Wage Dispersion Grown in Mexico? Is It the Incidence of Reforms or the Growing Demand for Skills?" *Journal of Development Economics* 51(1): 99–116.

Crook, C. 2003. "A Cruel Sea of Capital: A Survey of Global Finance." *The Economist,* May 3, pp. 1–2. http://www.economist.com/displaystory.cfm?story_id=1730317.

Curtis, M. 2001. *Trade for Life: Making Trade Work for Poor People.* London: Christian Aid.

de Ferranti, D., G. E. Perry, D. Lederman, and W. F. Maloney. 2002. *From Natural Resources to the Knowledge Economy: Trade and Job Quality.* Washington, DC: World Bank.

de la Torre, A., and S. Schmukler. 2004. *Whither Latin American Capital Markets?* Washington, DC: World Bank.

Desai, M. A., D. Kapur, and J. McHale. 2001. "The Fiscal Impact of the Brain Drain: Indian Emigration to the U.S." Paper prepared for the third annual NBER-NCAER Conference, Harvard University and National Bureau for Economic Research: Cambridge, Massachusetts, December 17–18, 2001.

Dethier, J.-J., and F. H. Rogers. 2005. *Growth and Empowerment: Making Development Happen.* Cambridge, Massachusetts: MIT Press.

Devarajan, S., D. Dollar, and T. Holmgren, eds. 2001. *Aid and Reform in Africa.* Washington, DC: World Bank.

de Walt, B. R. 1994. "Using Indigenous Knowledge to Improve Agricultural and Natural Resource Management." *Human Organization* 53 (2): 123–31.

Diamond, J. 1997. *Guns, Germs, and Steel.* New York: Norton.

Dicken, P. 1998. *Global Shift: Transforming the World Economy.* New York: Guilford.

Dobson, W., and G. C. Hufbauer. 2001. *World Capital Markets: Challenge to the G-10.* Washington, DC: Institute for International Economics.

Docquier, F., and A. Marfouk. 2004. "Measuring the International Mobility of Skilled Workers, 1990–2000 (Release 1.0)." World Bank Policy Research Working Paper No 3381, World Bank, Washington, DC.

Docquier, F., and H. Rapoport. 2004. "Skilled Migration and Human Capital Formation in Developing Countries—A Survey." Unpublished, Stanford Center for International Development, Stanford.

Dollar, D., and A. Kraay. 2004. "Trade, Growth, and Poverty." *Economic Journal* 114 (493): 22–49.

Drahos, P. 2001. "Bilateralism in Intellectual Property." Oxford: Oxfam.

Dugger, C. W. 2004. "Where Doctors Are Scarce, Africa Deploys Substitutes." *New York Times,* Nov. 23: Section A, Page 4, Column 3.

Dunning, J. H. 1993. *Multinational Enterprises and the Global Economy.* Workingham: Addison-Wesley.

Easterly, W. 2001. *The Elusive Quest for Growth.* Cambridge, Massachusetts: MIT Press.

Easterly, W., R. Levine, and D. Roodman. 2004. "Aid, Policies, and Growth: Comment." *American Economic Review* 94(3): 774.

The Economist. 1998. "A Taste of Adventure." December 17. www.economist.com.

———. 1999. "The East India Companies." December 23. www.economist.com.

———. 2002. "Outward Bound." September 26. www.economist.com.

———. 2004a. "The Economist's Commodity Price Index." February 12. www.economist.com.

———. 2004b. "Innovative India." April 3. www.economist.com.

———. 2004c. "A Remedy for Financial Turbulence?" April 17.

———. 2005a. "Argentina's Debt: Grinding Them Down." January 15. www.economist.com.

———. 2005b. "Argentina's Debt Restructuring." March 3. www.economist.com.

Edmonds, E., and N. Pavcnik. 2002. "Does Globalization Increase Child Labor? Evidence from Vietnam." National Bureau of Economic Research Working Paper 8760, National Bureau of Economic Research, Cambridge, Massachusetts.

Edwards, L. 2004. "A Firm Level Analysis of Trade, Technology and Employment in South Africa." *Journal of International Development* 16 (1): 45–61.

Eichengreen, B. 1996. *Globalizing Capital: A History of the International Monetary System.* Princeton: Princeton University Press.

———. 1999. *Towards a New International Financial Architecture: A Practical Post-Asia Agenda.* Washington, DC: Institute for International Economics.

———. 2004. "Financial Instability." University of California, Berkeley. Accessible at http://emlab.berkeley.edu/users/eichengr/

Eichengreen, B., R. Hausmann, and U. Panizza. 2003. "Currency Mismatches, Debt Intolerance and Original Sin: Why They Are Not the Same and Why It Matters." NBER Working Paper 10036, National Bureau of Economic Research, Cambridge, Massachusetts.

Ellerman, D. 2003. "Policy Research on Migration and Development." Policy Research Working Paper 3117, World Bank Group, Washington, DC. http://econ.worldbank.org/files/29100_wps_3117.pdf

European Commission. 2005. *Attitudes Towards Development Aid.* Brussels: Directorate-General Development.

Eurostat. 2002. *European Social Statistics–Migration, 2002 Edition.* Luxembourg: Office for Official Publications of the European Communities.

Extractive Industries Review. 2003. http://www.eireview.org.

Feenstra, R. C. 1998. "Integration of Trade and Disintegration of Production in the Global Economy." *Journal of Economic Perspectives* 12 (4): 31–50.

Fernandez-Arias, E., and P. J. Montiel. 1996. "The Surge in Capital Inflows to Developing Countries: An Analytical Overview." *World Bank Economic Review* 10 (1): 51–77.

Fields, G. 2001. *Distribution and Development: A New Look at the Developing World.* Cambridge, Massachusetts: MIT Press.

Financial Times. 2004. [Need article title for box 5.1]. Oct 13.

Financial Times. 2005. [Need article title for endnote 59 in Chapter 6]. March 23.

Finger, J. M. 2004. "Introduction and Overview." In *Poor People's Knowledge: Promoting Intellectual Property in Developing Countries,* ed. J. M. Finger and P. Schuler, 1–36. Washington, DC: World Bank.

Finger, J. M., and P. Schuler. 2000. "Implementation of Uruguay Round Commitments: The Development Challenge." *World Economy* 23 (4): 511–25.

Fischer, S. 1998. "Capital-Account Liberalization and the Role of the IMF." In *Should the IMF Pursue Capital-Account Convertibility?* ed. S. Fischer, R. N. Cooper, Rudiger Dornbusch, Peter M. Garber, C. Massad, J. J. Polak, Dani Rodrik, and S. S. Tarapore, 1–10. Princeton Essays in International Finance series 207, May 1998.

Fiszbein, A., P. Giovagnoli, and N. Thurston. 2003. "Household Behavior in the Presence of Crisis: Evidence from Argentina, 2002." Washington, DC: World Bank.

Fix, M., and J. Passel. 1999. *Trends in Non-Citizens' and Citizens' Use of Public Benefits Following Welfare Reform: 1994–97.* Washington, DC: Urban Institute.

Florida, R. 2002. *The Rise of the Creative Class.* New York: Basic Books.

Francois, J. F. 2000. "The International Economy and Economic Development," Erasmus University, Rotterdam. http://www.intereconomics.com/francois.

Francois, J. F., and W. Martin. 2002. "Binding Tariffs: Why Do It?" In *Development, Trade, and the WTO*, ed. B. Hoekman, A. Mattoo, and P. English, 540–7. Washington, DC: World Bank.

Francois, J., and K. A. Reinert. 1996. "The Role of Services in the Structure of Production and Trade: Stylized Facts from a Cross-Country Analysis." *Asia-Pacific Economic Review* 2 (1): 35–43.

Frankel, J. 2000. "Globalization and the Economy," NBER Working Paper 7858, National Bureau of Economic Research, Cambridge, Massachusetts.

Frenkel, M., and L. Menkhoff. 2004. "Are Foreign Institutional Investors Good for Emerging Markets?" *The World Economy* 27 (8): 1275–93.

Friedman, M. 1958. "Foreign Economic Aid: Means and Objectives." *The Yale Review* 47(4), 500–16.

Friedman, T. L. 2000. *The Lexus and the Olive Tree: Understanding Globalization.* New York: Random House.

Friedman, T. L. 2005. *The World Is Flat.* New York: Farrar, Straus and Giroux.

Fukuyama, F. 1992. *The End of History and the Last Man.* New York: Free Press.

———. 2002. "Social Capital and Development: The Coming Agenda." *SAIS Review* 22 (2): 23–37.

———. 2004. *State-Building: Governance and World Order in the 21st Century.* Ithaca: Cornell University Press.

Gabbard, S., R. Mines, and B. Boccalandro. 1994. *Migrant Farmworkers: Pursuing Security in Unstable Markets.* ASP Research Report 5. U.S. Department of Labor. Washington, DC.

Galeano, E. 1997. *Open Veins of Latin America.* New York: Monthly Review Press.

Gallini, N. T., and B. D. Wright. "Technology Transfer under Asymmetric Information." *The Rand Journal of Economics* 21(1):147–60.

Gallup, J. L., J. D. Sachs, and A. D. Mellinger. 1999. "Geography and Economic Development." *International Regional Science Review* 22 (2): 179–232.

Gartzke, E., L. Quan, and C. Boehmer. 2001. Investing in the Peace: Economic Interdependence and International Conflict." *International Organization* 55 (2): 391–438.

Ghatak, M., and T. W. Guinnane. 1999. "The Economics of Lending with Joint Liability: Theory and Practice." *Journal of Development Economics* 60 (1): 195–228.

Gilbert, R. J. 2000. "Antitrust Policy for the Licensing of Intellectual Property: An International Comparison." *International Journal of Technology Management* 19 (1,2): 206.

Gilbert, R., and C. Shapiro. 1990. "Optimal Patent Length and Breadth." *The Rand Journal of Economics* 21(1):113–30.

Gilbert, R., C. Shapiro, L. Kaplow, and R. Gertner. 1997. "Antitrust Issues in the Licensing of Intellectual Property: The Nine No-No's Meet the Nineties," *Brookings Papers on Economic Activity,* 283.

Gilpin, R. 2000. *The Challenge of Global Capitalism: The World Economy in the 21st Century.* Princeton: Princeton University Press.

Gindling, T. H., and D. Robbins. 2001. "Patterns and Sources of Changing Wage Inequality in Chile and Costa Rica During Structural Adjustment." *World Development* 29 (4): 725–45.

GCIM (Global Commission on International Migration). 2005. *Migration in an Interconnected World: New Directions for Action.* Geneva: GCIM.

Glover, S., C. Gott, A. Loizillon, R. Portes, R. Price, S. Spence, V. Srinivasan, and C. Willis. 2001. "Migration: An Economic and Social Analysis." RDS Occasional Paper 67. Home Office, London.

Goldin, I., ed. 1994. *Economic Reform, Trade and Agricultural Development.* London: MacMillan.

Goldin, I., and O. Knudsen, eds. 1990. *Agricultural Trade Liberalization: Implications for Developing Countries.* Paris and Washington, DC: OECD and World Bank.

Goldin, I., and D. van der Mensbrugghe. 1993. *Trade Liberalization: What's at Stake.* Paris: OECD.

Goldin, I., and L. A. Winters, eds. 1992. *Open Economies.* Cambridge: Cambridge University Press.

———. 1995. *The Economics of Sustainable Development.* Cambridge: Cambridge University Press.

Goldin, I., O. Knudsen, and D. van der Mensbrugghe. 1993. *Trade Liberalization: Global Economic Implications.* Paris and Washington, DC: OECD and World Bank.

Goldin, I., H. Rogers, and N. Stern. 2002. "The Role and Effectiveness of Development Assistance: Lessons from World Bank Experience." In *A Case for Aid: Building a Consensus for Development Assistance,* 25–183. Washington, DC: World Bank.

Goldin, I., N. Stern, and J.-J. Dethier. 2003. "Development as Learning." Unpublished, World Bank, Washington, DC.

Goldsmith, A. 2001. "Foreign Aid and Statehood in Africa." *International Organization* 55 (1): 123–48.

Goldstein, M., and P. Turner. 2004. *Controlling Currency Mismatches in Emerging Markets.* Washington, DC: Institute for International Economics.

Goldstein, M., G. L. Kaminsky, and C. M. Reinhart. 2000. *Assessing Financial Vulnerability: An Early Warning System for Emerging Markets.* Washington, DC: Institute for International Economics.

Graham, E. M. 1996. *Global Corporations and National Governments.* Washington, DC: Institute for International Economics.

Greenland, D. J. 1997. "International Agricultural Research and the CGIAR System: Past, Present and Future." *Journal of International Development* 9 (4): 459.

Grimmett, R. F. 2003. *Conventional Arms Transfers to Developing Nations, 1995–2002.* Washington, DC: Congressional Research Service, U.S. Library of Congress.

Gupta, I., and A. Mitra. 2004. "Economic Growth, Health and Poverty: An Exploratory Study for India." *Development Policy Review* 22(2): 193–206.

Haddad, M., and A. Harrison. 1993. "Are There Positive Spillovers from Direct Foreign Investment? Evidence from Panel Data for Morocco." *Journal of Development Economics* 42(1): 51–74.

Hamburg, D. A., and J. E. Holl. 1999. "Preventing Deadly Conflict: From Global Housekeeping to Neighbourhood Watch." In *Global Public Goods,* ed. I. Kaul, I. Grunberg, and M. A. Stern, 366–81. Oxford: Oxford University Press.

Hansen, H., and F. Tarp. 2000. "Aid Effectiveness Disputed." *Journal of International Development* 12 (3): 375–98.

———. 2001. "Aid and Growth Regressions." *Journal of Development Economics* 64 (2): 547–70.

Hanson, J. A., P. Honohan, and G. Majnoni. 2003. "Globalization and National Financial Systems: Issues of Integration and Size." In *Globalization and National Financial Systems,* ed. J. A. Hanson, P. Honohan, and G. Majnoni, 1–32. Washington, DC: World Bank.

Hanushek, E., and D. Kim. 1995. "Schooling, Labor Force Quality and Economic Growth." NBER Working Paper 5399, National Bureau of Economic Research, Cambridge, Massachusetts.

Hardy, D. C., P. Holden, and V. Prokopenko. 2003. "Microfinance Institutions and Public Policy." *Journal of Policy Reform* 6 (3): 147–58.

Harrison, G. W., T. F. Rutherford, and D. G. Tarr. 2003. "Trade Liberalization, Poverty and Efficient Equity." *Journal of Development Economics* 71 (1): 97–128.

Haskel, J. E., S. C. Pereira, and M. J. Slaughter. 2002. "Does Inward Foreign Direct Investment Boost the Productivity of Domestic Firms?" NBER Working Paper 8724, National Bureau of Economic Research, Cambridge, Massachusetts.

———. 1998. *The Age of Mass Migration: Causes and Economic Impact.* Oxford: Oxford University Press.

———. 2001. "Demographic and Economic Pressure on Emigration Out of Africa." NBER Working Paper 8124, National Bureau of Economic Research, Cambridge, Massachusetts.

———. 2002. "Out of Africa? Using the Past to Project African Migration Pressure in the Future." *Review of International Economics* 10 (3): 556–73.

Hawkins, E. K. 1970. *The Principles of Development Aid.* Harmondsworth: Penguin.

Hayter, T. 1971. *Aid as Imperialism.* Harmondsworth: Penguin.

Hejazi, W. H., and A. E. Safarian. 1999. "Trade, Foreign Direct Investment, and R&D Spillovers." *Journal of International Business Studies* 30 (3): 491–511.

Helleiner, E., and A. Pickel, eds. 2005. *Economic Nationalism in a Globalizing World.* Ithaca: Cornell University Press.

Hertz, N. 2003. *The Silent Takeover: Global Capitalism and the Death of Democracy.* New York: Harper-Business.

Hick, S. 2001. "The Political Economy of War-Affected Children." *Annals of the American Academy of Political and Social Science* 575: 106–21.

Hjertholm, P., and H. White. 2000. "Foreign Aid in Historical Perspective." In *Foreign Aid and Development,* ed. F. Tarp, 80–102. London: Routledge.

Hochschild, A. 1999. *King Leopold's Ghost.* Boston: Houghton Mifflin.

Hoekman, B. M., and M. M. Kostecki. 2001. *The Political Economy of the World Trading System.* Oxford: Oxford University Press.

Hoekman, B. M., K. E. Maskus, and K. Saggi. 2004. "Transfer of Technology to Developing Countries: Unilateral and Multilateral Policy Options." World Bank Policy Research Paper 3332, Washington, DC.

Hoff, K., and J. E. Stiglitz. 2001. "Modern Economic Theory and Development." In *Frontiers of Development Economics: The Future in Perspective,* ed. G. M. Meier and J. E. Stiglitz, 389–459. Oxford: Oxford University Press.

Hossain, A., and A. Chowdhury. 1998. *Open-Economic Macroeconomics for Developing Countries.* Cheltenham: Edward Elgar.

House of Commons International Development Committee. 2004. *Migration and Development: How to Make Migration Work for Poverty Reduction, Sixth Report of Session 2003–04, Volume 1* (July). The Stationary Office Limited: London.

Human Rights Watch. 2003. Population Statistics: Gulf Cooperation Council States [Electronic Resource]. http://www.hrw.org/press/2003/04/gccstats.htm.

———. 2004. "Bad Dreams: Exploitation and Abuse of Migrant Workers in Saudi Arabia." *Human Rights Watch* 16: 5(E), New York.

Hunt, J. 1992. "The Impact of the 1962 Repatriates from Algeria on the French Labor Market." *Industrial and Labor Relations Review* 43 (3): 556–72.

Hymer, S. 1976. *The International Operation of National Firms.* Cambridge, Massachusetts: MIT Press.

Ianchovichina, E., A. Nicita, and I. Soloaga. 2002. "Trade Reform and Poverty: The Case of Mexico." *World Economy* 25 (7): 945–72.

IMF (International Monetary Fund). 1993. IMF's *Balance of Payments Manual.* Washington, DC: International Monetary Fund.

———. 1998. *External Evaluation of ESAF: Report by a Group of Independent Experts.* Washington, DC: International Monetary Fund.

Inama, S. 2002. "Market Access for LDCs: Issues to Be Addressed." *Journal of World Trade* 36 (1): 85–116.

Institute of International Finance. 2005. "Capital Flows to Emerging Market Economies." January 19. http://www.iif.com/verify/data/report_docs/cf_0305.pdf

International Bank for Reconstruction and Development. 2003. *A Guide to the World Bank.* Washington, DC: IBRD.

International Centre for Trade and Sustainable Development. 2003. *Intellectual Property Rights: Implications for Development.* Geneva: International Centre for Trade and Sustainable Development.

———. 2004. "Winds of Change Blow on WIPO." *Bridges* 8 (8): 1–2.

International Forum on Globalization. http://www.ifg.org.

IITA (International Institute of Tropical Agriculture). 2002. *Child Labor in the Cacao Sector of West Africa.* Ibadan, Nigeria: IITA.

IOM (International Organization for Migration). 1999. *Turner Fund Trafficking Project in Trafficking in Migrants,* No. 20, Geneva.

———. 2003a. *Labour Migration in Asia: Trends, Challenges and Policy Responses in Countries of Origin.* Geneva: International Organization for Migration.

———. 2003b. *World Migration 2003: Managing Migration—Challenges and Responses for People on the Move.* Geneva: International Organization for Migration.

James, H. 1996. *International Monetary Cooperation Since Bretton Woods.* Oxford: Oxford University Press.

Jandl, M. 2003. "Estimates of the Number of Illegal and Smuggled Immigrants in Europe." Presentation at Workshop 1.6, 8th International Metropolis Conference. Vienna, Austria. September 18.

Jayanthakumaran, K. 2003. "Benefit-Cost Appraisals of Export Processing Zones: A Survey of the Literature." *Development Policy Review* 21 (1): 51–65.

Jayne, T. S., L. Rubey, D. Tschirley, M. Mukumbu, M. Chisvo, A. Santos, M. Weber, and P. Diskin. 1995. "Effects of Market Reform on Access to Food by Low-Income Households: Evidence from Four Countries in Eastern and Southern Africa." Policy Synthesis 5 for USAID-Bureau for Africa Office of Sustainable Development.

Jeanne, O. 2000. "Foreign Currency Debt and the Global Financial Architecture." *European Economic Review* 44: 719–27.

Jenkins, R. 2004. "Vietnam in the Global Economy: Trade, Employment and Poverty." *Journal of International Development* 16 (1): 13–28.

Johansson, H., and L. Nilsson. 1997. "Export Processing Zones as Catalysts." *World Development* 25 (12): 2115–28.

John, R., G. Ietto-Gillies, H. Cox, and N. Grimwade. 1997. *Global Business Strategy.* London: International Thompson Business Press.

Jules, P. 2003. "The Externalities and Multifunctionality of Agriculture." *EuroChoices* 2 (3): 40–5.

Kabeer, N. 2004. "Globalization, Labor Standards, and Women's Rights: Dilemmas of Collective (In) Action in An Interdependent World." *Feminist Economics* 10 (1): 3–35.

Kabeer, N., and S. Mahmud. 2004. "Globalization, Gender, and Poverty: Bangladeshi Women Workers in Export and Local Markets." *Journal of International Development* 16 (1): 93–109.

Kanbur, R. (Forthcoming). "The Economics of International Aid." *Handbook on the Economics of Giving, Reciprocity and Altruism,* ed. L.-A. Gérard-Varet, S.-C. Kolm, and J. Mercier Ythier. Amsterdam: North-Holland.

Kaplan, E., and D. Rodrik. 2001. "Did the Malaysian Capital Controls Work?" NBER Working Paper 8142, National Bureau of Economic Research, Cambridge, Massachusetts.

Kapur, D., and R. Ramamurti. 2001. "India's Emerging Competitive Advantage in Services." *Academy of Management Executive* 15 (2): 20–31.

Kash, D. E., and W. Kingston. 2001. "Patents in a World of Complex Technologies." *Science and Public Policy* 28 (1): 11–22.

Kassouf, A. L., and B. Senauer. 1996. "Direct and Indirect Effects of Parental Education on Malnutrition Among Children in Brazil: A Full Income Approach." *Economic Development and Cultural Change* 44 (4): 817–38.

Kaul, I., I. Grunberg, and M. A. Stern. 1999. "Defining Global Public Goods." In *Global Public Goods: International Cooperation in the 21st Century,* ed. I. Kaul, I. Grundberg, and M. A. Stern, 2–19. Oxford: Oxford University Press.

Kaul, I., P. Conceição, K. Le Goulven, and R. U. Mendoza. 2003. "How to Improve the Provision of Global Public Goods." In *Providing Global Public Goods: Managing Globalization,* ed. I. Kaul, P. Conceição, K. Le Goulven, and R. U. Mendoza, 21–58. New York: Oxford University Press.

Keynes, J. M. 1920. *The Economic Consequences of the Peace.* New York: Harcourt, Brace, and Howe.

Kim, S. J., K. A. Reinert, and G. C. Rodrigo. 2002. "The Agreement on Textiles and Clothing: Safeguard Actions from 1995 to 2001." *Journal of International Economic Law* 5(2): 445–68.

Kim, W., and S.-J. Wei. 2002. "Foreign Portfolio Investors Before and During a Crisis." *Journal of International Economics* 56 (1): 77–96.

King, R. G., and R. Levine. 1993. "Finance and Growth: Schumpeter Might Be Right." *Quarterly Journal of Economics* 108(3): 717–37.

Klein, N. 2000. *No Logo: Taking Aim at the Brand Bullie.* New York: Picador.

———. 2001. *No Logo.* London: Flamingo.

Klein Solomon, M., and K. Bartsch. 2003. "The Berne Initiative: Toward the Development of an International Policy Framework on Migration." Geneva: International Organization for Migration.

Koeberle, S. G. 2003. "Should Policy-Based Lending Still Involve Conditionality?" *World Bank Research Observer* 18 (2): 249–73.

Kokko, A. 1994. "Technology, Market Characteristics, and Spillovers." *Journal of Development Economics* 43 (2): 279–93.

Kokko, A., and M. Blomström. 1995. "Policies to Encourage Inflows of Technology Through Foreign Multinationals." *World Development* 23 (3): 459–68.

Kokko, A., R. Tansini, and M. C. Zejan. 1996. "Local Technological Capability and Productivity Spillovers from FDI in the Uruguayan Manufacturing Sector." *Journal of Development Studies* 32 (4): 602–11.

Kose, M. A., E. S. Prasad, and M. E. Terrones. 2003. "Financial Integration and Macroeconomic Volatility." *IMF Staff Papers* 50: 119–42.

Koser, K., and N. Van Hear. 2003. "Asylum Migration and Implications for Countries of Origin." World Institute for Development Economics Research (WIDER) Discussion Paper No. 2003/20. (March). United Nations University: Helsinki.

Kostecki, M. 2001. *Technical Assistance Services in Trade-Policy: A Contribution to the Discussion on Capacity-Building in the WTO*, ICTSD Resource Paper No. 2, International Centre for Trade and Sustainable Development, Geneva.

Kovacic, W. E., and C. Shapiro. 2000. "Antitrust Policy: A Century of Economic and Legal Thinking." *The Journal of Economic Perspectives* 14 (1): 43–60.

Kreuger, A. B., and M. Lindahl. 1999. "Education for Growth in Sweden and the World." *Swedish Economic Policy Review* 6 (2): 289–339.

Krueger, A. O., M. Schiff, and A. Valdes. 1988. "Agricultural Incentives in Developing Countries: Measuring the Effect of Sectoral and Economywide Policies." *World Bank Economic Review* 2 (3): 255–71.

Krueger, J. 2001. "The Basel Convention and the International Trade in Hazardous Wastes." *Yearbook of International Co-operation on Environment and Development 2001/02*, Earthscan, London, 43–52.

Krugman, P. 1999. *The Return of Depression Economics*. New York: Norton.

Kwok, Y. 2000. "On Hire to the Cruelest Bidder," *South China Morning Post*, June 7.

Laird, S. 2002. "Market Access Issues and the WTO: An Overview." In *Development, Trade, and the WTO*, ed. B. Hoekman, A. Mattoo, and P. English, 97–104. Washington, DC: World Bank.

Lall, S. 1998. "Exports of Manufactures by Developing Countries: Emerging Patterns of Trade and Location." *Oxford Review of Economic Policy* 14 (2): 54–73.

———. 2000. "The Technological Structure and Performance of Developing Country Manufactured Exports, 1985–98." *Oxford Development Studies* 28 (3): 337–69.

Lall, S., and M. Teubal. 1998. " 'Market-Stimulating' Technology Policies in Developing Countries: A Framework with Examples from East Asia." *World Development* 26 (8): 1369–85.

Landes, D. S. 1998. *The Wealth and Poverty of Nations: Why Some Are So Rich and Others So Poor*. New York: Norton.

Lanjouw, J. O., and M. Schankerman. 2004a. "Patent Quality and Research Productivity: Measuring Innovation with Multiple Indicators." *The Economic Journal* 114 (495): 441–65.

———. 2004b. "Protecting Intellectual Property Rights: Are Small Firms Handicapped?" *Journal of Law and Economics* 47 (1): 45.

Lapper, R. 2004. "More Latin American Migrants Sending More Money Home." *Financial Times*, May 17.

Leach, J. 2004. *A Course in Public Economics*. Cambridge: Cambridge University Press.

Levine, R., and S. Zervos. 1998. "Stock Markets, Banks, and Economic Growth." *American Economic Review* 88 (3): 537–58.

Lindauer, D. L., and L. Pritchett. 2002. "What's the Big Idea? The Third Generation of Policies for Economic Growth." *Economia: Journal of the Latin American and Caribbean Economic Association* 3 (1): 1–28.

Lindblom, C. E. 2001. *The Market System*. New Haven: Yale University Press.

Lipton, M. 2005. "Interview: Michael Lipton." In K. A. Reinert. *Windows on the World Economy: An Introduction to International Economics*, pp. 399–402. Mason, Ohio: South-Western Thomson.

Little, I. M. D., and J. M. Clifford. 1965. *International Aid.* London: George Allen and Unwin Ltd.

Lowell, B. L. 2001. *Policy Responses to the International Mobility of Skilled Labor.* Geneva: International Labor Office, International Migration Branch.

Lucas, R. 1990. "Why Doesn't Capital Flow from Rich to Poor Countries?" *American Economic Review* 80 (2): 92–6.

Maddison, A. 2001. *The World Economy: A Millennial Perspective.* Paris: OECD.

Maimbo, S. M., and D. Ratha, eds. 2005. *Remittances: Development Impact and Future Prospects.* Washington, DC: World Bank.

Mallaby, S. 2004. *The World's Banker: Failed States, Financial Crises and the Wealth and Poverty of Nations.* New York: Penguin.

Mander, J., and E. Goldsmith, eds. 1996. *The Case Against the Global Economy.* San Francisco: Sierra Club.

Markusen, J. R. 1981. "Trade and the Gains from Trade with Imperfect Competition." *Journal of International Economics* 11 (4): 531–51.

Martin, L. L. 1999. "The Political Economy of International Cooperation." In *Global Public Goods: International Cooperation in the 21st Century,* ed. I. Kaul, I. Grundberg, and M. A. Stern, 51–64. Oxford: Oxford University Press.

Martin, W., and D. Mitra. 2001. "Productivity Growth and Convergence in Agriculture versus Manufacturing." *Economic Development and Cultural Change* 49(2): 403–22.

Martin, P., and J. E. Taylor. 1996. "The Anatomy of a Migration Hump." In *Development Strategy, Employment and Migration: Insights from Models,* ed. J. Edward Taylor, pp. 43–62. Paris: OECD.

Martin, P., and M. Teitelbaum. 2000. *Emigration and Development: Focus on West-Central Mexico.* Report of the Eighth Migration Dialogue Seminar. Guadalajara, Mexico.

Maskus, K. E. 2000. *Intellectual Property Rights in the Global Economy.* Washington, DC: Institute for International Economics.

———. 2003. "Transfer of Technology and Technological Capacity Building," ICTSD-UNCTAD Dialogue, 2nd Bellagio Series on Development and Intellectual Property.

Maskus, K., and J. H. Reichman. 2004. "The Globalization of Private Knowledge Goods and the Privatization of Global Public Goods." *Journal of International Economic Law* 7 (2): 279–320.

Massey, D. S. 2003. *Patterns and Processes of International Migration in the 21st Century.* Paper prepared for Conference on African Migration in Comparative Perspective, Johannesburg, South Africa, June 4–7.

Matthews, D. 2004. "WTO Decision on Implementation of Paragraph 6 of the Doha Declaration on the TRIPS Agreement and Public Health: A Solution to the Access to Essential Medicines Problem?" *Journal of International Economic Law* 7 (1): 73–107.

Mattoo, A., I. Neagu, and C. Özden. 2005. "Brain Waste? Educated Immigrants in the US Labor Market." World Bank Policy Research Working Paper 3581, Washington, DC.

McCalman, P. 2001. "Reaping What You Sow: An Empirical Analysis of International Patent Harmonization." *Journal of International Economics* 55 (1): 161–86.

McCulloch, N., A. Winters, and X. Cirera. 2001. *Trade Liberalization and Poverty: A Handbook.* London: Centre for Economic Policy Research.

McKinnon, R. I., and H. Pill. 1997. "Credible Economic Liberalization and Overborrowing." *American Economic Review* 87 (2): 189–93.

Meier, G. M. 2001. "Introduction: Ideas for Development." In *Frontiers of Development Economics: The Future in Perspective,* ed. G. M. Meier and J. E. Stiglitz, 1–12. Oxford: Oxford University Press.

Mendez, R. P. 1999. "Peace as a Global Public Good." In *Global Public Goods,* ed. I. Kaul, I. Grunberg, and M. A. Stern, 382–416. Oxford: Oxford University Press.

Messerlin, P. A. 2001. *Measuring the Costs of Protection in Europe: European Commercial Policy in the 2000s.* Washington, DC: Institute for International Economics.

Meyer, B., and M. Brown. 1999. "Scientific Diasporas: A New Approach to the Brain Drain. Management of Social Transformations." *UNESCO Discussion Paper No. 41.* United Nations Educational, Social, and Cultural Organization: Paris.

Migration News. 1996. 3 (10). October.

Mihir, D., D. Kapur, and J. McHale. 2004. "Sharing the Spoils: Taxing International Human Capital Flows." *International Tax and Public Finance,* 11:5, 663–693.

Minot, N., and F. Goletti. 1998. "Export Liberalization and Household Welfare: The Case of Rice in Vietnam." *American Journal of Agricultural Economics* 80 (4): 738–49.

———. 2000. "Rice Market Liberalization and Poverty in Vietnam." Research Report 114, International Food Policy Research Institute, Washington, DC.

Mody, A. 2004. "Is FDI Integrating the World Economy?" *The World Economy* 27 (8): 1195–222.

Moran, T. H. 1998. *Foreign Direct Investment and Development.* Washington, DC: Institute for International Economics.

———. 2001. *Parental Supervision: The New Paradigm for Foreign Direct Investment and Development.* Washington, DC: Institute for International Economics.

Morduch, J. 1999. "The Microfinance Promise." *Journal of Economic Literature* 37 (4): 1569–614.

Mun, T. 1924 (orig. 1669). "England's Treasure by Foreign Trade." In *Early Economic Thought,* ed. A. E. Monroe, 171–97. Cambridge, Massachusetts: Harvard University Press.

Naim, M. 2005. *Illicit: How Smugglers, Traffickers, and Copycats Are Hijacking the Global Economy.* New York: Doubleday.

Ndikumana, L., and J. K Boyce. 1998. "Congo's Odious Debt: External Borrowing and Capital Flight in Zaire." *Development and Change* 29 (2): 195–217.

Newland, K. 2003. "Migration as a Factor in Development and Poverty Reduction: The Impact of Rich Countries' Immigration Policies on the Prospects of the Poor." Paper presented at the Global Development Workshop, Cairo, Egypt, January.

New Scientist, 2005. "Curing Diseases Modern Medicine Has Left Behind." January 15. pp. 40–41.

New York Times. 2004. "Ending the Cycle of Debt," October 1.

Ngugi, R., V. Murinde, and C. J. Green. 2002. "Does the Revitalisation Process Really Enhance Stock Market Microstructure? Evidence from the Nairobi Stock Exchange." *African Finance Journal* 4 (1): 32–61.

Nordas, H. K. 2003. "The Impact of Trade Liberalization on Women's Job Opportunities and Earnings in Developing Countries." *World Trade Review* 2 (2): 221–31.

North, D. C. 1990. *Institutions, Institutional Change and Economic Performance.* Cambridge: Cambridge University Press.

Nowotny, T. 2004. *Strawberries in Winter: On Global Trends and Global Governance.* Frankfurt: Peter Lang.

Nussbaum, M. C. 2000. *Women and Human Development: The Capabilities Approach.* Cambridge: Cambridge University Press.

Obstfeld, M. 1998. "The Global Capital Market: Benefactor or Menace?" *Journal of Economic Perspectives* 12 (4): 9–30.

Ocampo, J. A., and J. Martin. 2003. *Globalization and Development: A Latin American and Caribbean Perspective.* Stanford: Stanford University Press.

Ocampo, J. A., and M. A. Parra. 2003. "The Terms of Trade for Commodities in the Twentieth Century," *CEPAL Review* 79: 7–35.

Odell, M. 2004. "Airbus Signs $1bn Military Deal with South Africa." *Financial Times,* December 16. www.ft.com.

OECD (Organisation for Economic Co-Operation and Development). 1997. *Trends in International Migration–Annual Report 1996 Edition.* Paris: OECD.

———. 2002. "International Mobility of the Highly Skilled." *OECD Policy Brief* (July). OECD, Paris. www.oecd.org/dataoecd/9/20/1950028.pdf.

———. 2003a. "The OECD Guidelines for Multinational Enterprises: A Key Corporate Responsibility Instrument." *OECD Economic Observer,* June. www.oecd.org/dataoecd/52/38/2958609.pdf

———. 2003b. *Trends in International Migration–Annual Report 2004 Edition.* Paris: OECD.

———. 2003c. *Education at a Glance 2003–Tables* [Electronic Resource]. OECD, Paris. http://www.oecd.org/document/34/0,2340,en_2649_34515_14152482_1_1_1_1,00.html

———. 2003d. *Agricultural Policies in OECD Countries: Monitoring and Evaluation 2003.* Paris: OECD. www.oecd.org/dataoecd/25/63/2956135.pdf.

———. 2004. *Trends in International Migration–Annual Report 2003 Edition.* Paris: OECD.

———. 2005. *Trends in International Migration–Annual Report 2004 Edition.* Paris: OECD.

OECD-DAC (Organisation for Economic Co-Operation and Development–Development Assistance Committee). 2004. *Final Official Development Assistance (ODA) Data for 2003.* Paris: OECD.

O'Rourke, K. H. 2002. "Globalization and Inequality: Historical Trends." *Aussenwirtschaft* 57 (1): 65–101.

O'Rourke, K. H., and J. G. Williamson. 1999. *Globalization and History: The Evolution of a Nineteenth-Century Atlantic Economy.* Cambridge, Massachusetts: MIT Press.

Orozco, M. 2003. "Worker Remittances: An International Comparison," Working Paper: Inter-American Development Bank, Multilateral Investment Fund. Inter-American Development Bank: Washington, DC.

Osei, R., O. Morrissey, and R. Lensink. 2002. "The Volatility of Capital Inflows: Measures and Trends for Developing Countries," CREDIT Research Paper 02/20, University of Nottingham.

Otsuki, T., J. S. Wilson, and M. Sewadeh. 2001. "Saving Two in a Billion: Quantifying the Trade Effect of European Food Safety Standards on African Exports." *Food Policy* 26 (5): 495–514.

Owens, T., and J. Hoddinott. 1998. "Investing in Development or Investing in Relief: Quantifying the Poverty Tradeoffs Using Zimbabwe Household Panel Data." Working Paper WPS/99–4, Centre for the Study of African Economies, Harare.

Oxfam. 2002a. *Rigged Rules and Double Standards: Trade, Globalization, and the Fight Against Poverty.* Oxford: Oxfam.

———. 2002b. *Mugged: Poverty in Your Coffee Cup.* Oxford: Oxfam.

———. 2004a. "Dumping on the World: How EU Sugar Policies Hurt Poor Countries." Oxfam Briefing Paper 61. Oxford.

———. 2004b. *Guns or Growth? Assessing the Impact of Arms Sales on Sustainable Development.* Oxford: Oxfam.

———. 2004c. "Stitched Up: How Rich-Country Protectionism in Textiles and Clothing Trade Prevents Poverty Alleviation." Oxfam Briefing Paper 60, Oxfam.

———. 2005. *Paying the Price: Why Rich Countries Must Invest Now in a War on Poverty.* Oxford: Oxfam.

Özden, C., and M. Schiff, eds. 2005. *International Migration, Remittances, and the Brain Drain.* Washington, DC: World Bank.

Pack, H., and L. E. Westphal. 1986. "Industrial Strategy and Technological Change: Theory versus Reality." *Journal of Development Economics* 22 (1): 87–128.

Pagano, M. 1993. "Financial Markets and Growth: An Overview." *European Economic Review* 37 (2–3): 613–22.

Park, A., and B. Johnston. 1995. "Rural Development and Dynamic Externalities in Taiwan's Structural Transformation." *Economic Development and Cultural Change* 44 (1): 181–208.

Pederson, P. J., M. Pytlikova, and N. Smith. 2004. "Selection or Network Effects? Migration Flows into 27 OECD Countries, 1990–2000." IZA Discussion Paper 1104. (April). Forschungsinstitut zur Zukunft der Arbeit—Institute for the Study of Labor, Bonn, Germany.

Perlez, J., and E. Rusli. 2004. "Spurred by Illness, Indonesians Lash Out at U.S. Mining Giant." *New York Times,* September 8. www.nytimes.com.

POEA (Philippine Overseas Employment Administration). 2004. *Overseas Employment Statistics,* Manila. [Electronic Resource]. http://www.poea.gov.ph/html/statistics.html.

Pischke, J., and J. Velling. 1994. "Wage and Employment Effects of Immigration to Germany: An Analysis Based on Local Labor Markets." Unpublished, Massachusetts Institute of Technology, Cambridge, Massachusetts.

Plender, J. 2004. "A Big Squeeze for Governments: How Transfer Pricing Threatens Global Tax Revenues." *Financial Times,* July 22. www.ft.com.

Pogge, T. W. 1999. "Human Flourishing and Universal Justice." *Social Philosophy and Policy* 16 (1): 333–61.

Pomerantz, P. R. 2004. *Aid Effectiveness in Africa: Developing Trust Between Donors and Governments.* New York: Lexington Books.

Poulton, C., P. Gibbon, B. Hanyani-Mlambo, J. Kydd, W. Maro, M. Larsen, Marianne Nylandsted, A. Osorio, D. Tschirley, and B. Zulu. 2004. "Competition and Coordination in Liberalized African Cotton Market Systems." In *World Development* 32(3), 519–36.

Prahalad, C. K. 2005. *The Fortune at the Bottom of the Pyramid: Eradicating Poverty Through Profits.* Philadelphia: Wharton School Publishing.

Prasad, E., K. Rogoff, S.-J. Wei, and M. A. Kose. 2003. "Effects of Financial Globalization on Developing Countries: Some Empirical Evidence." International Monetary Fund, Washington, DC. http://www.imf.org/external/np/res/docs/2003/031703.pdf.

Preston, S. H. 1975. "The Changing Relation Between Mortality and Level of Economic Development." *Population Studies* 29 (2): 231–48.

Pritchett, L. 2000. "Understanding Patterns of Economic Growth: Searching for Hills Among Plateaus, Mountains, and Plains." *World Bank Economic Review* 14 (2): 221–50.

Psacharopoulos, G. 1985. "Returns to Education: A Further International Update and Implications." *Journal of Human Resources* 20 (4): 583–97.

———. 1994. "Returns to Investment in Education: A Global Update." *World Development* 22 (9): 1325–43.

Psacharopoloulos, G. and H. A. Patrinos. 2004. "Returns to Investment in Education: A Further Update." *Education Economics,* 12(2): 111–34.

Puri, L. 2004. "The Engendering of Trade for Development: An Overview of the Main Issues." In *Trade and Gender: Opportunities and Challenges for Developing Countries,* Tran-Nguyen, A.-N. and A. Beviglia Zampetti (eds.). United Nations Conference on Trade and Development, Geneva.

Rajan, R. G., and L. Zingales. 1998. "Financial Dependence and Growth." *American Economic Review* 88 (3): 559–86.

Ramos, F. 1992. "Out-Migration and Return Migration of Puerto Ricans." In *Immigration and the Work Force: Economic Consequences for the United States and the Source Areas,* ed. G. J. Borjas and R. B. Freeman, 49–66. Chicago: University of Chicago Press.

Ramos, J. 1998. "A Development Strategy Founded on Natural Resource-Based Production Clusters." *CEPAL Review* 66: 105–27.

Randel, J., T. German, and D. Ewing, eds. 2004. *The Reality of Aid: An Independent Review of Poverty Reduction and Development Assistance.* London: Zed Books.

Ranis, G. 2004. "The Evolution of Development Thinking: Theory and Policy." Discussion Paper 886, Yale University Economic Growth Center, New Haven.=

Ratha, D. 2003. "Workers' Remittances: An Important and Stable Source of External Development Finance." In *Global Development Finance 2003,* 157–75. Washington, DC: World Bank.

Ratha, D. 2004. "Recent Trends in International Remittance Flows." Note presented to the Technology of Remittances Workshop, San Francisco, December 11.

Ratha, D. and K. M. Vijayalakshmi. 2004. "Recent Trends in International Remittance Flows." Note presented to the Technology of Remittances Workshop convened by the Inter-American Development Bank and the World Resource Institute, San Francisco, December 11.

Ravallion, M. 2004a. "Pessimistic on Poverty?" *The Economist,* April 10. www.economist.com.

Ravallion, M. 2004b. "Competing Concepts of Inequality in the Globalization Debate." *Brookings Trade Forum: 2004,* 1–38. Brookings Institution, Washington, DC.

Raynolds, L. T. 2000. "Re-Embedding Global Agriculture: The International Organic and Fair Trade Movements." *Agriculture and Human Values* 17 (3): 297–309.

Recchi, E., D. Tambini, E. Baldoni, D. Williams, K. Surak, and A. Favell. 2003. "Intra-EU Migration: A Socio-demographic Overview." PIONEUR Working Paper 3, Centro Interuniversitario di Sociologia Politica (CIUSPO), Università di Firenze.

Reinert, K. A. 1998. "Rural Non-Farm Development: A Trade-Theoretic View." *Journal of International Trade and Economic Development* 7 (4): 425–37.

————. 2000. "Give Us Virtue, But Not Yet: Safeguard Actions Under the Agreement on Textiles and Clothing." *The World Economy* 23 (1): 25–55.

————. 2004. "Outcomes Assessment in Trade Policy Analysis: A Note on the Welfare Propositions of the 'Gains from Trade.' " *Journal of Economic Issues* 38 (4): 1067–73.

————. 2005. *Windows on the World Economy: An Introduction to International Economics.* Mason, Ohio: South-Western Thomson.

Reisen, H., and M. Soto. 2001. "Which Types of Capital Inflows Foster Developing-Country Growth?" *International Finance* 4 (1): 1–14.

Rischard, J.-F. 2002. *High Noon: 20 Global Problems, 20 Years to Solve Them.* New York: Basic Books.

Robbins, D., and T. H. Gindling. 1999. "Trade Liberalization and the Relative Wages for More-Skilled Workers in Costa Rica." *Review of Development Economics* 3 (2): 140–54.

Robinson, V., and J. Segrott. 2002. "Understanding the Decision-Making of Asylum Seekers." (July). Home Office Research Study 243. Home Office Research, Development and Statistics Directorate: London.

Rodrigo, G. C. 2001. *Technology, Economic Growth and Crises in East Asia.* Cheltenham: Edward Elgar.

Rodríguez, F., and D. Rodrik. 2001. "Trade Policy and Economic Growth: A Skeptic's Guide to the Cross-National Evidence." In *Macroeconomics Annual 2000,* ed. B. Bernanke and K. S. Rogoff, 261–325. Cambridge, Massachusetts: MIT Press.

Rodrik, D. 1998a. "Who Needs Capital-Account Convertibility?" In *Should the IMF Pursue Capital-Account Convertibility?* ed. S. Fischer, R. N. Cooper, Rudiger Dornbusch, Peter M. Garber, C. Massad, J. J. Polak, Dani Rodrik, and S. S. Tarapore. Princeton Essays in International Finance 207, May 1998, 55 65.

————. 1998b. "Why Do More Open Economies Have Bigger Governments?" *Journal of Political Economy* 106 (5): 997–1032.

————. 1999. *The New Global Economy and Developing Countries: Making Openness Work.* Washington, DC: Overseas Development Council.

————. 2000. "Institutions for High-Quality Growth: What They Are and How to Acquire Them." *Studies in Comparative International Development* 35 (3): 3–31.

————. 2003. "Introduction: What Do We Learn from Country Narratives?" In *In Search of Prosperity: Analytic Narratives on Economic Growth,* ed. D. Rodrik, 1–19. Princeton: Princeton University Press.

Romer, P. 1993a. "Idea Gaps and Object Gaps in Economic Development." *Journal of Monetary Economics* 32 (3): 543.

————. 1993b. "Two Strategies for Economic Development: Using Ideas and Producing Ideas," *Proceedings of the World Bank Annual Conference on Development Economics 1992,* 63–91.

Rousseau, P. L., and P. Wachtel. 2000. "Equity Markets and Growth: Cross-Country Evidence on Timing and Outcomes, 1980–1995." *Journal of Banking and Finance* 24 (12): 1933–57.

Sarno, L., and M. P. Taylor. 1999. "Hot Money, Accounting Labels and the Permanence of Capital Flows to Developing Countries: An Empirical Investigation." *Journal of Development Economics* 59 (2): 337–64.

Scalabrini Migration Center. 2000. *Asian Migration Atlas 2000* [Electronic Resource]. http://www.scalabrini.asn.au/atlas/amatlas.htm.

Schiff, M., and A. Valdes. 1995. "The Plundering of Agriculture in Developing Countries." *Finance and Development* 32 (1): 44–7.

Schrank, A. 2001. "Export Processing Zones: Free Market Islands or Bridges to Structural Transformation?" *Development Policy Review* 19 (2): 223–42.

Schrover, M. 2004. "Migration: A Historical Perspective." *BBC News Online.* March 23. http://news.bbc.co.uk/1/hi/world/3557163.stm

Schultz, T. P. 2002. "Why Governments Should Invest More to Educate Girls." *World Development* 30 (2): 207–25.

Schumpeter, J. 1934. *The Theory of Economic Development.* Cambridge, Massachusetts: Harvard University Press.

————. 1949. *The Theory of Economic Development.* Cambridge, Massachusetts: Harvard University Press.

Schwalbenberg, H. M. 1998. "Does Foreign Aid Cause the Adoption of Harmful Economic Policies?" *Journal of Policy Modeling* 20 (5): 669–75.

Sen, A. 1989. "Development as Capability Expansion." *Journal of Development Planning* 19: 41–58.

————. 1999. *Development as Freedom.* New York: Knopf.

————. 2002. "How to Judge Globalism." *The American Prospect* (Winter): 13(1): A2–A6 (supplement).

Shapiro, C. 2004. "Patent System Reform: Economic Analysis and Critique." *Berkeley Technology Law Journal* 19 (3): 1017–47.

Simon, J. 1989. *The Economic Consequences of Immigration.* London: Blackwell Publishing.

Smith, A. 1937 (orig. 1776). *The Wealth of Nations.* New York: Modern Library.

Stalker, P. 2001. *The No-Nonsense Guide to International Migration.* Oxford: New Internationalist Publications Ltd.

Stark, O. 1991. *The Migration of Labor.* London: Blackwell Publishing.

Steil, B. 2001. "Creating Securities Markets in Developing Countries: A New Approach for the Age of Automated Trading." *International Finance* 4 (2): 257–78.

Stern, N. 2002. *A Strategy for Development.* Washington, DC: World Bank.

————. 2004. "Scaling Up Poverty Reduction." Paper presented at the Scaling Up Poverty Reduction: A Global Learning Process Conference, Shanghai, May 25–27.

Stern, N., J.-J. Dethier, and H. Rogers. 2004. *Growth and Empowerment: Making Development Happen.* Cambridge, Massachusetts: MIT Press.

Stewart, F. 1995. *Adjustment and Poverty: Options and Choices.* London: Routledge.

Stiglitz, J. E. 1987. "Learning to Learn, Localized Learning and Technological Progress." In *Economic Policy and Technological Performance,* ed. P. Dasgupta and P. Stoneman, 125–153. New York: Cambridge University Press.

————. 1999. "Knowledge as a Global Public Good." In *Global Public Goods: International Cooperation in the 21st Century,* ed. I. Kaul, I. Grunberg, and M. A. Stern, 308–25. Oxford: Oxford University Press.

————. 2000. "Capital Market Liberalization, Economic Growth, and Instability." *World Development* 28 (6): 1075–86.

————. 2002a. *Globalization and Its Discontents.* New York: Norton.

————. 2002b. "Globalism's Discontents." *The American Prospect* 13(1): A16–A21 (supplement).

Stiglitz, J. E., and A. Bhattacharya. 2000. "The Underpinnings of a Stable and Equitable Global Financial System: From Old Debates to a New Pragmatism." In *Annual World Bank Conference on Development Economics 1999,* ed. B. Pleskovic and J. E. Stiglitz, 91–130. Washington, DC: World Bank.

Stiglitz, J. E., and A. Weiss. 1981. "Credit Rationing in Markets with Imperfect Information." *American Economic Review* 71 (3): 393–410.

Streeten, P. P. 1979. "From Growth to Basic Needs." *Finance and Development* 16 (3): 28–31.

————. 1995. *Thinking About Development.* Cambridge: Cambridge University Press.

Suárez-Orozco, C., and M. M. Suárez-Orozco. 2001. *Children of Immigration.* Cambridge, Massachusetts: Harvard University Press.

Subramanian, A., and D. Roy. 2003. "Who Can Explain the Mauritian Miracle? Meade, Romer, Sachs, or Rodrik?" In *In Search of Prosperity: Analytical Narratives on Economic Growth,* ed. D. Rodrik, 205–43. Princeton: Princeton University Press.

Summers, L. 1991. "Research Challenges for Development Economics." *Finance and Development* 23 (3): 2–5.

Suryahadi, A., S. Sumarto, and L. Pritchett. 2003. "Evolution of Poverty During the Crisis in Indonesia." *Asian Economic Journal* 17 (3): 221–41.

Szelényi, K. 2003. "Explaining the Migration and Settlement of Foreign Graduate Students: Global Integration Theory and the Theory of Cumulative Causation." Unpublished, UCLA Ronald W. Burkle Center for International Relations.

Szirmai, A. 1997. *Economic and Social Development: Trends, Problems and Policies.* London: Prentice Hall.

———. 2005. *The Dynamics of Socio-Economic Development.* Cambridge: Cambridge University Press.

Tan, H. W., and G. Batra. 1995. *Enterprise Training in Developing Countries: Incidence, Productivity Effects and Policy Implications.* Washington, DC: World Bank.

Tarp, F., ed. 2002. *Foreign Aid and Development.* London: Routledge.

Taylor, A. M., and J. G. Williamson. 1994. "Capital Flows to the New World as An Intergenerational Transfer." *Journal of Political Economy* 102 (2): 348–71.

Taylor, L. 1993. "Stabilization, Adjustment, and Reform." In *The Rocky Road to Reform,* ed. L. Taylor, 39–94. Cambridge, Massachusetts: MIT Press.

TeleCommons Development Group. 2000. *Grameen Telecom's Village Phone Programme in Rural Bangladesh: Multimedia Case Study,* Ontario, Canada. http://www.telecommons.com/villagephone/finalreport.pdf.

te Velde, D. W. 2001. *Government Policies Toward Inward Foreign Direct Investment in Developing Countries.* Paris: OECD Development Center.

te Velde, D. W., and O. Morrissey. 2003. "Do Workers in Africa Get a Wage Premium If Employed in Firms Owned by Foreigners?" *Journal of African Economies* 12 (1): 41–73.

Thomson, G. 2003. "Behind Roses' Beauty, Poor and Ill Workers." *New York Times* February 13. www.nytimes.com.

Timmer, A. S., and J. G. Williams. 1998. "Immigration Policy Prior to the 1930s: Labor Markets, Policy Interactions, and Globalization Backlash." *Population and Development Review* 24 (4): 739–71.

Tobin, James. 1978. "A Proposal for International Monetary Reform." *Eastern Economic Journal* (4):153–59.

Transparency International. [Need source for data in box 5.1]

Tsang, E. W. K., D. T. Nguyen, and M. K. Erramilli. 2004. "Knowledge Acquisition and Performance of International Joint Ventures in the Transition Economy of Vietnam." *Journal of International Marketing* 12 (2): 82–103.

United Kingdom, Department for International Development. 2005. *Sending Money Home: A Survey of Remittance Products and Services in the United Kingdom.* London: Profile Business Intelligence.

UN (United Nations). 2000. *General Assembly Document A/55/383.* Retrieved from http://www.undcp.org/palermo/convmain.html

UN. 2003. "Strengthening of the United Nations: An Agenda for Further Change." Document A/57/387. New York: UN.

———. 2004. *World Economic and Social Survey 2004: International Migration.* New York: UN Department of Economic and Social Affairs.

———. 2005. In *Larger Freedom: Toward Development, Security, and Human Rights for All."* Report of the Secretary-General. New York: UN.

UNCTAD (United Nations Conference on Trade and Development). 2000. *The Post-Uruguay Round Tariff Environment for Developing Country Exports: Tariff Peaks and Tariff Escalation,* TD/B/COM.1/14/Rev.1, Geneva.

———. 2001. *World Investment Report.* Geneva: UNCTAD.

———. 2003. *Economic Development in Africa: Trade Performance and Commodity Dependence.* Geneva: UNCTAD.

———. 2004. *The Least Developed Country Report 2004.* Geneva: UNCTAD.

UNDP (United Nations Development Programme). 1991. *Human Development Report.* New York: Oxford University Press.

———. 2003. *Making Global Trade Work for People.* London: Earthscan.

———. 2004. *Human Development Report 2004.* Oxford: Oxford University Press.

UNHCR (United Nations High Commissioner for Refugees). 2001. *Asylum Applications in Industrialized Countries: 1980–1999.* Geneva: United Nations High Commissioner for Refugees.

———. 2003. *Statistical Yearbook 2002: Trends in Protection, Displacement and Solutions.* Geneva: United Nations High Commissioner for Refugees.

United Nations Population Division. 2000. *World Population Prospects: The 2000 Revision.* New York: United Nations Department of Economic and Social Affairs.

———. 2002. *International Migration 2002.* New York: United Nations Department of Economic and Social Affairs.

United News of Bangladesh. 2000. "85% of Students Studying IT Want to Leave the Country." United News of Bangladesh.

U.S. Commission on Immigration Reform. 1997. *Becoming an American: Immigration and Immigrant Policy.* Washington, DC: U.S. Government Printing Office.

U.S. Department of Commerce. 2001. *An Aging World: 2001.* Washington, DC: U.S. Department of Commerce.

U.S. Department of Homeland Security. 2003a. *Yearbook of Immigration Statistics, 2002.* Washington, DC: U.S. Government Printing Office.

———. 2003b. "Fiscal Year 2002 Yearbook of Immigration Statistics." Office of Immigration Statistics. [Electronic Resource] http://uscis.gov/graphics/shared/aboutus/statistics/ybpage.htm

U.S. Department of State. 2003. *Trafficking in Persons Report-June 2003.* Washington, DC: U.S. Government Printing Office.

———. 2004. *Visa Bulletin–Immigrant Numbers for September 2004.* Washington, DC: U.S. Government Printing Office.

U.S. Foreign Agricultural Service. 2003. "European Union Trade Policy Monitoring: Tariff Escalation 2003." Brussels.

U.S. Immigration and Naturalization Service. 2002. *Report on Characteristics of Specialty Occupation Workers (H-1B): Fiscal Year 2001.* Report Mandated by Public Law 105-277, Division C, American Competitiveness and Workforce Improvement Act of 1998: Washington, DC (July).

Vos, R., and N. de Jong. 2003. "Trade Liberalization and Poverty in Ecuador: A CGE Macro-Microsimulation Analysis." *Economic Systems Research* 15 (2): 211–32.

Wallace, W. 2004. "African Farmers Dig in to Comply with EU Food Rules." *Financial Times* April 7, p. 16.

Waller Meyers, D. 1998. *Migrant Remittances to Latin America: Reviewing the Literature.* Unpublished. Inter-American Dialogue and Tomas Rivera Policy Institute, Washington, DC.

Walmsley, T. L., and L. A. Winters. 2003. "Relaxing the Restrictions on the Temporary Movement of National Persons: A Simulation Analysis." Centre for Economic Policy Research Discussion Paper No. 3719 (January).

Wei, S.-J. 2000. "Local Corruption and Global Capital Inflows." *Brookings Papers on Economic Activity,* 2000:2, 303–354.

Weick, K. E. 1984. "Small Wins: Redefining the Scale of Social Problems." *American Psychologist,* 39(1): 40–49.

Weiss, T. L. 2001. "L'Afrique à la Poursuite de Ses Cerveaux." *Jeune Afrique/ L'Intelligent* 2104: 8–14.

Williamson, J. 1990. *Latin American Adjustment: How Much Has Happened?* Washington, DC: Institute for International Economics.

———. ed. 1994. *The Political Economy of Policy Reform.* Washington, DC: Institute of International Economics.

———. 2000. "What Should the World Bank Think About the Washington Consensus?" *World Bank Research Observer* 15 (2): 251–64.

———. 2003. "Migration and Development: Policy Issues." Paper presented at IBRD/IDD Paris Workshop on "Migration and Development: Policy Issues," May 19.

Williamson, S. D. 1987. "Costly Monitoring, Loan Contracts, and Equilibrium Credit Rationing." *Quarterly Journal of Economics* 102 (1): 135–45.

Wilson, J. S. 2002. "Standards, Regulation, and Trade." In *Development, Trade, and the WTO,* ed. B. Hoekman, A. Mattoo, and P. English, 428–38. Washington, DC: World Bank.

Winters, L. A. 2000. *Trade and Poverty: Is There a Connection?* Special Studies 5, World Trade Organization, Geneva.

Winters, L. A., N. McCulloch, and A. McKay. 2004. "Trade Liberalization and Poverty: The Evidence So Far." *Journal of Economic Literature* 42 (1): 72–115.

Winters, L.A., T. L. Walmsley, Z. Kun Wang, and R. Grynberg. 2002b. "Negotiating the Liberalisation of the Temporary Movement of Natural Persons." Discussion Papers in Economics No. 87, October. University of Sussex, Brighton.

Winters, L. A., T. L. Walmsley, Z. Kun Wang, and R. Grynberg. 2002a. "Liberalizing Labour Mobility Under the GATS." Commonwealth Secretariat, Economic Paper No. 53. London.

Winters, L. A., T. L. Walmsley, Z. K. Wang, and R. Grynberg. 2003. "Liberalizing the Temporary Movement of Natural Persons: An Agenda for the Development Round." *The World Economy* 26 (8): 1137–61.

Wolf, M. 2004. *Why Globalization Works*. New Haven: Yale University Press.

Wolfensohn, J. D. 1998. *The Other Crisis*. Washington, DC: World Bank.

———. 2002. "A Partnership for Development and Peace." In *A Case for Aid: Building a Consensus for Development Assistance*, 3–14. Washington, DC: World Bank.

Woolcock, M., and D. Narayan. 2000. "Social Capital: Implications for Development Theory, Research, and Policy." *World Bank Research Observer* 15 (2): 225–49.

World Bank. 1994. *Reducing the Debt Burden of Poor Countries: A Framework for Action*, Development in Practice Series, World Bank, Washington, DC.

———. 1998. *Assessing Aid: What Works, What Doesn't, and Why*. Washington, DC: World Bank.

———. 1999. *World Development Report 1998/99: Knowledge for Development*. New York: Oxford University Press.

———. 2001. *Engendering Development: Through Gender Equality in Rights, Resources, and Voice*. New York: Oxford University Press.

———. 2002a. *A Case for Aid: Building a Consensus for Development Assistance*. Washington, DC: World Bank.

———. 2002b. *Global Economic Prospects 2002: Making Trade Work for the World's Poor*. Washington, DC: World Bank.

———. 2002c. *Globalization, Growth, and Poverty: Building an Inclusive World Economy*. Washington, DC: World Bank.

———. 2002d. *World Development Report 2002: Building Institutions for Markets*. New York: Oxford University Press.

———. 2003a. *Global Economic Prospects 2004: Realizing the Development Promise of the Doha Agenda*. Washington, DC: World Bank.

———. 2003b. *World Development Report 2003: Sustainable Development in a Dynamic World*. New York: Oxford University Press.

———. 2004a. "Aid Agency Competition." Public Policy for the Private Sector. No. 277 (October). Private Sector Development Vice Presidency, World Bank, Washington, DC: http://rru.worldbank.org/Documents/277-harford-hadjimichael.pdf.

———. 2004b. *Global Development Finance: Harnessing Cyclical Gains for Development*. Washington, DC: World Bank.

———. 2004c. *Global Economic Prospects 2004*. Washington, DC: World Bank.

———. 2004d. *World Development Indicators*. Washington, DC: World Bank.

———. 2004e. *World Development Report: Making Services Work for Poor People*. New York: Oxford University Press.

———. 2005a. *Global Development Finance: Mobilizing Finance and Managing Vulnerability*. Washington, DC: World Bank.

———. 2005b. *World Development Indicators*. Washington, DC: World Bank.

———. 2005c. *Global Monitoring Report*. Washington, DC: World Bank.

———. 2005d. *World Development Report 2006–Equity and Development*. Washington, DC: World Bank.

———. 2005e. *Doing Business in 2006: Creating Jobs*. Washington, DC: World Bank.

————. 2005f. *Global Economic Prospects 2006*. Washington, DC: World Bank.

World Commission on the Social Dimension of Globalization. 2004. *A Fair Globalization: Creating Opportunities for All*. Geneva: International Labour Organization.

WHO (World Health Organization). 2001a. "FAO/WHO: Amount of Poor-Quality Pesticides Sold in Developing Countries Alarmingly High," Press Release WHO/04, February.

————. 2001b. *Macroeconomics and Health: Investing in Health for Economic Development*. Geneva: World Health Organization.

————. 2002. *World Report on Violence and Health*. WHO: Geneva.

Zohir, S. C. 2001. "Social Impact of the Growth of Garment Industry in Bangladesh." *Bangladesh Development Studies* 27 (4): 41–80.

Index

China (*continued*)
  migration
    Chinese Exclusion Act, 188n111
    economic migrants, 158, 160
    impact of brain drain on, 173
    to Silicon Valley, 182
    and poverty reduction, 111n49
Chinese Exclusion Act, 188n11
Chuhan, P., 109n7
Citibank, 263n21
citizenship, 160
civil society organizations (CSOs), 198, 258
Claessens, S., 102, 109n7
Clemens, M., 130, 148n18, 149n32
Clifford, J. M., 114
coffee prices, 68
Cohen, D., 149n46
Cold War, 115, 117, 119–24, 164, 189n29
Collier, P., 129
Colombia, 73, 113
Colombo Plan, 148n11
Colonial Development Act, 113, 114
Colonial Development Corporation, 114
colonial systems, 6, 114–15, 152–53
Columbus, Christopher, 196b7.1
commercial bank lending, 12, 20n19, 81, 99, 103f4.6, 104–5
  as primary source of capital to low-income countries, 82
  as source of capital flows, 85, 86
  as source of foreign capital, 84
commercial banks, 90b4.2, 91, 109–10nn23–24
commercialization, of MFIs, 90b4.2
commercial service exports, 35f2.12, 36, 45–46n16, 51
Commission for Africa, 78n42, 139
commodities, 66–67, 259
commodity price index, 68, 78n35
commodity prices, 67–68, 68
  in 20th century, 67f3.5
  declines in, 68, 75
  impact of foreign aid on, 69
community development, 178–79
community-directed drug distributors, 137

comparative advantage, 10
competition
  impact on poverty alleviation, 48, 53–55, 76n4, 77n15, 77n18
  and remittances, 248–49
computer sector, 94
conflicts, 235, 259, 263n9
Consultative Group for International Agricultural Research (CGIAR), 137–39
consumer products, 239
consumption, 4, 110n27, 176
contagion behaviors, 91, 99, 102, 198–99
corporate social responsibility, 237–38
Correa, C. M., 255
corruption, 108, 111n51
Costa Rica, 56
Costa Rican Investment Board, 95b4.3
cotton industry, Zimbabwe, 54–55, 77n18
counterfeiting, 74
Crafts, N., 22, 45n8
credit rating agencies, 89
Crook, C., 109–10n23
cross-border movements, 159t6.3, 166, 223
CSOs. *See* civil society organizations (CSOs)
Cuba, 192n93
culture
  homogenization of, 209
  impact on host-country, 80, 109n5
currencies, 104, 105, 110n28, 111n45
cut flower export industries, 73

D
Dailami, M., 218
debt, 140
  debt flows compared with equity flows, 106
  debt swaps, 111n44
  external debt, 111n44, 141, 141f5.5
  international relief efforts, 142–43, 149nn46–47
  See also bond finance; commercial bank lending
debt issuance. *See* bond finance

literacy test for migrants, 155,
188*n*13
make up of workforce, 182
quotas on, 189*n*22
student visas, 167
visa-free, 167
protectionism in, 64
textile and clothing sectors, 65*b*3.2
Universal Declaration of Human Rights,
42, 156, 160, 189*n*14, 189*n*20
UN Millennium Declaration, 39
Uruguay, 32, 96
utility maximization, 167–68, 190*n*47

V

vaccination campaigns, 207
value added, 62
value chains, 50, 76*n*7
values, globalization of, 42
Velling, J., 192*n*93
Venezuela, 96
Vietnam, 51–52, 77*nn*11–12, 93–94, 97,
132, 189*n*21
virtuous circles, 246
visas
competition for highly-skilled workers,
161
H-1B visas, 161, 167, 189*n*24
visa-free migration, 159*t*6.3, 166–67,
188

W

Wachtel, P., 99
wages, 97
avoiding low-income low-skills trap, 97
export sector workers, 47–48
gaps in, 154, 188*n*12
impact of migration on, 172, 181,
190*n*60, 192*nn*93–94
Wallace, W., 65
Wallich, C., 218
Walmsley, T. L., 245, 264*n*21
Washington Consensus, 126, 216
weak states
allocation of aid to, 133–34

approaches for post-conflict in, 134,
135
experience of Sub-Saharan Africa,
134–35, 149*n*38
wealth transfer, 173–74, 191*n*73
Weick, K. E., 263*n*1
welfare gains, 66, 78*n*34
West Africa, 19*n*8, 136–37, 149*n*40
Western Europe, 22, 190*n*38
WHO. *See* World Health Organization
(WHO)
widgets, 38, 38*b*2.2
Williamson, J. G., 188*n*9, 188*n*12, 190*n*60
Winters, L. A., 78*n*47, 245, 264*n*21
Wolf, M., 1, 204
Wolfensohn, James, 78*n*41
women
status of, 263–64*n*20
See also females
Woolcock, M., 149*n*34
workforce, 179, 182–83, 184*b*6.3
abuse and exploitation of, 162–63,
182–83, 184*b*6.3
agricultural laborers, 48, 170
banana workers, 73
education and health of, 218
effect of immigration on destination
countries, 181–82, 192*nn*93–94
export sector workers, 47–48
forced labor, 235–36, 263*nn*11–12
garment industry, 52–53, 76*n*13
highly-skilled workers migration to
high-income countries, 159*t*6.3,
160–61, 189*n*24
low-skilled workers, 159*t*6.3, 162–63
migrants from Asia, 153–54, 188*n*11
policies to restrict recruitment, 246
skilled vs. unskilled workers, 49, 76*n*6
telecommunications industry, 54
temporary movement of workers,
14–15, 20*n*25, 244–45,
263–64*nn*20–21
undocumented migrants, 182–83,
184*b*6.3
Vietnam's rice sector, 51–52
virtuous circles, 246
and visa-free migration, 166–67